THE MEANING OF RIGHT AND WRONG

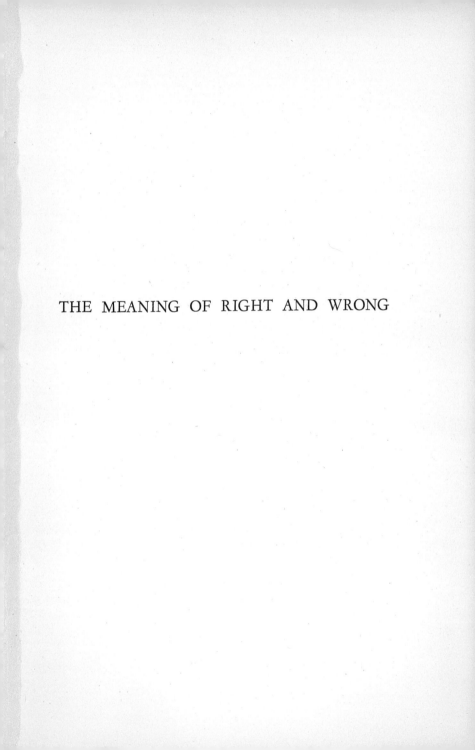

THE MACMILLAN COMPANY
NEW YORK · BOSTON · CHICAGO · DALLAS
ATLANTA · SAN FRANCISCO

MACMILLAN & CO., Limited
LONDON · BOMBAY · CALCUTTA
MELBOURNE

THE MACMILLAN COMPANY
OF CANADA, Limited
TORONTO

THE MEANING OF
RIGHT AND WRONG

BY

RICHARD C. CABOT, M.D.

PROFESSOR OF SOCIAL ETHICS
PROFESSOR OF CLINICAL MEDICINE
HARVARD UNIVERSITY

NEW YORK

THE MACMILLAN COMPANY

1933

Set up and electrotyped.   Published May, 1933.

SET UP AND ELECTROTYPED BY T. MOREY & SON

·PRINTED IN THE UNITED STATES OF AMERICA·

To

WILLIAM ERNEST HOCKING

Finder, Transmitter, and
Lover of Wisdom,
Steadfast and Illuminating Friend

PREFACE

I dare say that a good many of those who have written on ethics have cherished, as I do, the idea of constructing a framework of right and wrong out of materials gathered directly from life and not from books.

It may be an illusion, but such is what I suppose to be the origin of this book. The great help that Kant, Sidgwick, Spencer, Green, James, Royce, and many others have given me serves chiefly, I believe, to make me contemplate more intelligently and more persistently the behavior of ordinary men and women when they try to do what they believe is right, or slide along pathways which they know are wrong.

Writers on ethics disagree sharply. But, as I see it, the theories behind the feelings and actions of fact-facing and of fact-dodging people lead them right or wrong in essentially the same way. It is quite possible to hear the tune to which they move, and to recognize in it phrases from most of the classical as well as the more modern theories of ethics.

Since I began writing this book I have been steered away from several stupid errors by the criticism of two friends and colleagues, William Ernest Hocking and Ralph Barton Perry, who have kindly and serviceably passed judgment on portions of it. Another and still more helpful critic prefers to remain unnamed, but will, I hope, permit me to thank him here.

My wife has added many essential suggestions and modifications, as she has to each of my non-medical books.

My thanks are due to Messrs. Dodd, Mead & Company,

Henry Holt and Company, Houghton Mifflin Company, and The Macmillan Company, for permission to quote in this book from works published by them.

R. C. C.

CAMBRIDGE, MASSACHUSETTS,
April, 1933

TABLE OF CONTENTS

D. SUPERMORALS

APPENDICES

THE MEANING OF RIGHT AND WRONG

THE MEANING OF RIGHT
AND WRONG

INTRODUCTION

Why write another book on ethics? Because our generation faces new events and new ideas bound to support, destroy, or modify the current beliefs about right and wrong. The World War and the Peace of Versailles; the economic consequences and the international adventures to which this war led us; the career and the writings of Gandhi; Freud's widely diffused ideas; the Russian dictatorship with its huge experiments in planned production; the present economic world-crisis, and the resulting doubts about capitalistic economy,—these have set men thinking afresh about economics and about politics. They may well stir any one who is interested in a reasonable plan of life to think again about the meaning of right and wrong.

Here are some ethical problems raised by the challenge of our time:—

1. Are treaties sacred? We have often said so, because if there is anything solid in ethics it is the principle that broken promises destroy self-respect. But we are spurred to reconsider this belief when China, a nation that is not a nation, makes a treaty under a threat of force from Japan. How can a nation that has no national unity bind itself (when it has no self) to keep an agreement which most of its people do not agree to? How sacred is an impossible

and self-contradictory treaty? Can the representatives of a people whom they do not represent promise that the nation will carry out its contracts when it cannot even control its limbs?

When the nations that won the World War solemnly assert in the treaty of peace that Germany and her allies were alone responsible for the damage of that war,[1] and force her to promise reparations which she obviously can never pay, is that a holy and binding agreement? In the teeth of fact this treaty flings the challenge of the conquerors' power. It is barbarous and absurd. But what then? Does it follow that Germany has a moral right to break this treaty or secretly to undermine it, because it was forced upon her and because it is impossible to perform? In view of the stubborn resistance of realities, may a nation rightly laugh at the nonsense to which it has plighted its word? We need to think out more clearly what we mean by the binding force of such promises.

2. Fresh thought is needed on another aspect of our human need to tie ourselves together, not only with words but with the bonds of international trade. We seem to have accepted the principle that we are so far members one of another that we need each other's goods. We have planned large-scale production so that our nation turns out vastly more food, steel, automobiles, and petroleum than it can use. Other nations want these goods and (so far as tariffs permit) we exchange them for whatever foreigners can make better and cheaper than we. We take pride in this international solidarity, as we do in the

---

[1] *Treaty of Peace between the Allied and Associated Powers and Germany, Part VIII: Reparation, Art. 231:* "The Allied and Associated Governments affirm and Germany accepts the responsibility of Germany and her allies, for causing all the loss and damage to which the Allied and Associated Governments and their nationals have been subjected as a consequence of the war imposed upon them by the aggression of Germany and her allies."—(Official British edition, H. M. Stationery Office, London, 1919), p. 203.

spread of science, technology, art, literature, preventive medicine, and the postal union.

But lately we have begun to doubt the blessings of world-wide interdependence. A change of habits in one country throws thousands out of work in another. The political stupidities, the economic superstitions, the new inventions, the freakish fashions of one country upset the industries of another and bring many workmen close to starvation. Switzerland and France, where large-scale production and world-trade have been less developed than in England, Germany, and the United States, seem to enjoy today the advantage of their relative economic independence.

It has been the fashion to exalt the virtues of free trade, free competition, world markets. We are pleased to see a division of labor among nations so that each serves and depends on the rest. But today the service is a question and the dependence an obvious clog. The solidarity of nations is like that of people trying to get out of a burning theater.

3. Nature has found out by massive experimentation that animals much bigger than elephants cannot keep themselves warm, cannot move swiftly, and so tend to disappear when pressed in the race for subsistence. At the other end of the scale, insects below a certain size cannot find room in their bodies for all the machinery that they need, and are too light to manage themselves in wet or windy weather. Hence anything very small has to be a simple vegetable like the bacteria. The advantages of being the right size [1] have been worked out and remembered in the animal kingdom. Experiments in animals as big as houses or as small as bacteria are discouraged. Manageable units of life are found and adhered to.

[1] J. B. S. Haldane, "On Being the Right Size," *Harper's Magazine*, March, 1926.

Civilized man, on the contrary, has thus far taken little pains to work out manageable units in government, family life, trade organization. It is an ethical duty not to fall over our own feet, not to get in our own way, not to be any stupider than we need to be in arranging our civilization. We vitally need, we morally ought to find out by experiment how big and how small a unit is most manageable for a committee, for a family group, for a college class or a college " house," for a trade organization, for a chorus, a hospital, or a city. Gladstone said, I believe, that the manageable number for a committee is seven or less. His long experience had convinced him of this, and I suppose he was right. Teachers and pupils seem to be approaching agreement that they accomplish most in groups of from fifteen to twenty-five. Colleges are beginning to limit the size of the class taken in each year. A hospital unit of more than 500 beds is seldom managed for the patients' best welfare, though it may be cheaper to care for them in larger groups.

In these instances we know something about the most manageable unit. But who knows how large a congress, a city, a nation, a scout troop, a trade union, can be without losing the power to control itself and to fulfill its special purpose? Once we cheerfully assumed that the larger any such group became the better. No intelligent person thinks so today. But we seem content to pause in this ignorance, or to muddle through in spite of it. When the best interests of civilization wait for the decision of a question which well-planned experiments can decide, it seems to me criminal to postpone them. The one thing that seems to be clear in this matter is that the best size for each unit is that which best suits the development of its particular purpose and so has to be settled by a separate course of investigation in each case. There is no good reason to assume that the number found best for a college class is best for a glee club or football team. More than nine men would clutter up a baseball diamond, but that number is lost in a university lecture room. Assuming that lectures are sometimes useful, an audience of ninety draws better results from the lecturer than an audience of nine. The ninety auditors need not coöperate with each other. The nine ball players must. There is no general rule to settle the right size of any group, but I have tried in this book to show what the yardsticks should be.

4. We face a need for ethical reorientation about the worth of ethics itself. It is attacked by the psychological-medical group which today dominates public opinion almost as the medieval church did. Is the attack justified? Partially, I think. There is a sense in which ethics and moralizing are as dead as last week's newspaper. The effort to manage people by ordering them to do this, by forbidding them to do that, by exhorting them, by scolding them, by lamenting their sins, by begging them to exert their will-power, by telling them what they ought to do,—such effort is almost fruitless. A moment's mechanical obedience, a flash of emotional fervor or shame, is the only result we can expect. To use such psychical tools as ordering, forbidding, and scolding, is as absurd as it would be to reproach a crooked poker or to flatter the sea. We are newly aware today that the fiber of human character is too tough to be re-formed, except temporarily, by such soft and easy methods. Good teachers, skillful parents, have long known this. Yet the *New Republic* continues to scold and the stupider sort of parent to order and forbid, with all the energy of the savage who berates his stone idol because his crops are failing.

The leaders of the mental hygiene movement have done good service by pointing this out. Unfortunately they

have emptied out the baby with the bath-water. Because
ethics has been stupidly conceived they try to do without
it altogether and to put psychology in its place. Freud and
his followers have tried to abolish not only the theological
ideas of sin, eternal punishment, and eternal reward, but
the familiar ideas of right and wrong. I go with them a
certain distance. I grant that blaming and punishing people
for unsatisfactory behavior generally does them harm.
On the other hand, is it not an insult (as G. K. Chesterton
says) to assume that any one is incapable of blameworthy
conduct? A dog and an idiot are not held morally responsible for their inconvenient behavior, because they know
no better. But does any man want to be managed, as we
manage a dog or an imbecile, without any appeal to his
power to control himself, to criticize himself, to blame
himself (though *we* need not assume the right to blame
him), and to redirect himself, as a dog and an idiot cannot, toward his own ideals?

Freudian doubts about the validity of ethics are relatively
new. Adolescent doubts are perennial or recurrent. At
adolescence we move into a new psychological climate and
soon after we often migrate into a college. There we find
standards widely different from those which we have
grown up with. We study history or anthropology and
learn that people have held every sort of belief about marriage and sex relations, about dress, about bargaining and
commerce, about the keeping of Sunday, about the treatment of women, children, and old people. Then we begin
to wonder whether ethics is anything more than the fashion of the time. Tolstoi doubted it:—

Louis XVI was beheaded because he was convicted as a criminal;
but within a year those who had beheaded him were also put to death
for something or other.
What is wrong? What is right? What should one love? What is hate-

ful? What is the object of life and what am I? I have a hundred rubles which I don't know what to do with. This peasant peddler in her ragged sheepskin stands there and looks at me timidly. But what good would my money do her? Would it add the value of a single hair to her happiness or to her peace of mind? [1]

G. Bernard Shaw doubted it:—

Undershaft: Is there anything you know or care for?
Stephen: I know the difference between right and wrong.
Undershaft: You don't say so! What, no capacity for business, no knowledge of law, no sympathy with art, no pretension to philosophy; only a simple knowledge of the secret that has puzzled all the philosophers, baffled all the lawyers, muddled all the men of business, and ruined most of the artists: the secret of right and wrong. Why, man, you're a genius, a master of masters, a god! [2]

5. Ethical discriminations seem to be in a flux. Yet in this fluidity there are certain fixed points. Always and everywhere people hate treachery to a friend. Wherever money is used we agree that counterfeiting is intolerable. There are few who think it right to steal from a blind beggar. To get women into trouble, as Goethe did, and then desert them, is just as mean in a successful writer of the late eighteenth century as it was centuries earlier and will be centuries hence. To buy your wife expensive clothes and ocean voyages out of the money deposited in your bank by domestic servants and small tradesmen, is not a matter of taste and fashion. Everybody knows that it is scoundrelly, has known it, and will know it as long as banks last.

It would be easy to multiply examples proving that though customs vary almost without limit in different times and places, certain principles of ethics remain as fixed as man's need for security amid the chances of his life. Moreover, men have always needed and always will

---

[1] Leo Tolstoi, *War and Peace* (New York: Thomas Y. Crowell, 1889), p. 67.
[2] G. B. Shaw, *Major Barbara* (New York: Brentano's, 1907), Act III, p. 126.

need to learn; yet the inertia of accumulated habits will always tend to block their growth. The duty to learn and the temptation to stagnate will collide again and again through the centuries, and the choices we make in such crises will always steer us right or wrong. Perhaps men will get over deceiving themselves. But until that distant heaven arrives on earth, self-deceit will continue the favorite dodge of civilized man when he faces what he knows is his duty but wishes to avoid.

These three facts,—the need of security, the need to learn, and the tendency to self-deceit, do not change much in civilized man. Ethics is just as solidly planted in him. These beliefs are among the factors which have led me to write this book.

6. Freud's enormous influence, not only in psychology and medicine, but in novels, in education, and in ethics, has, I think, one clear benefit to balance the harm of its exaggerations. By dramatizing the " censor " who represses within us our obstreperous impulses, by popularizing the barbarous but useful term " rationalization," he has focussed the attention of our time on one of man's most comfortable but suicidal habits, the timeworn trick of self-deception.[1] It is 150 years since Jane Austen began packing her novels with proof that we forever fool ourselves in our attempts to fool others. George Meredith, Tolstoi, Dostoievsky, and other great novelists have followed her in showing us how man tricks himself, hides from himself, confuses himself, excuses himself, dresses up his shady impulses in the bright colors of the rainbow. William James put into his *Psychology* some brilliant illustrations of these tricks. Yet writers on ethics and teachers of morals have not yet made us realize that self-deceit is

---

[1] Freud and his followers usually assume that self-deceit is unconscious. But the facts seem to me against him.

ubiquitous, that it destroys character, and that it is therefore essential for us to be familiar with its classic forms if
we are to have a chance of conquering it. One of my chief
interests in writing this book is to put self-deceit on the
ethical map, and to show that it covers an area as huge as
all the sins of man.

7. I believe that the ethics of discussion has taken on a
new phase in our time. We have begun to realize that
though civilized people no longer accost each other as
" Thou Fool " when they meet in drawing-rooms, they
frequently write about each other in terms equivalent to
that insult. Literary manners still permit us to say things
about our opponent's views which assume him to be a
blockhead. Writers set out not to understand other writers
but to refute them, that is to prove that they are fools. In
ethics, for instance, we still refute Kant, the Hedonists,
the Utilitarians or the Evolutionists. Until very recently
it has been hardly respectable in academic circles not to
refute somebody. Scholarship and the virile energy of independent thought are supposed to demand that we should
" show up " some one's foolish errors, with a pitying
smile, perhaps, but with remorseless inflexibility. Today
we see the emergence of a humbler and more sensible school
of controversy in which the integration of opposing views,
not the demolition of any, is the goal. Miss Follett [1] and
Professor A. D. Sheffield [2] have made a place for this trend
in American political and sociological thought; but in
ethical writings we still pursue for the most part the old
violent and contemptuous methods.

I believe that the Kantians, the Hedonists, the Intuition-
ists, the Evolutionists, and the Utilitarians have each

[1] Mary P. Follett, *Creative Experience* (New York: Harper & Brothers, 1928).
[2] A. D. Sheffield, *Joining in Public Discussion* (New York: G. H. Doran Co.,
1922), and, *Training for Group Experience* (New York: The Inquiry, 1929).

something essential to contribute to ethical theory. They are like different climates of the mind or different seasons of the year. When we are very cold it is hard to remember that we ever were thoroughly warm. In the vigor of Kantian logic we nearly forget the ardent desire which sets that logic in motion. Yet the ordinary respectable citizen is both a Kantian and a Utilitarian. He uses evolutionary ethics and intuitionist ethics, not alternately but at once. Without compromise or eclecticism, but without believing that every writer on ethics has meant every word of his text where it contradicts other writers who face the same facts, we can let them all play into each other's hands in good teamwork. Logic, politics, and biology,—Kant, Bentham, and Spencer—, paint very different scenery on the backdrop of one's mind. But their pictures contradict each other as little as a full face picture contradicts a profile.

I see no sense in refuting anybody. If a writer is worth considering at all it is for the help we can get from him. The ideas worked out in this book owe essential elements to each of the ethical schools just listed. I am grateful to each for emphasizing, even for overemphasizing, his pet aspect of ethical truth. Without this overemphasis I might have failed to see his point at all.

8. Ethics and science need to shake hands. They are too isolated and too suspicious of each other. College students who try their luck in history, economics, physics, or languages are offered a diet of facts. They are asked to recognize and to grasp what exists. They are rightly warned not to warp historical sequences and economic generalizations by any wishes of their own, because truthful thinking, not wishful thinking, is their goal. Ideals have no place in physics nor in German grammar.

Facts, then, are for science; wishes, hopes, sentiments, and ideals for ethics. So the material is divided. Any hard-headed, realistic American knows which to choose. He is proud to be tough-minded; he scorns to be tender-minded; and apparently all the toughness is with science and all the tenderness with ethics. In contrast with this way of dividing our knowledge I want to show that fact and desire, observing and choosing, are inseparable. The scientist is set at work by certain deep desires; the moralist depends continually on facts. There is as much divergence and as little contradiction as there is between bacteriology and logic.

9. Gandhi's ethics seems as far from Freud's psychology as one can well conceive. Yet I think they have in common the peculiar and relatively novel path by which they are led to revere the ancient concept of Truth. Both Freud and Gandhi tell us that wrongdoing is due to self-deceit. Freud accents the " rationalizations " by which we confuse ourselves until we are cleared up by psychoanalysis. Gandhi hopes to open our blind eyes not by talk but by self-sacrifice. Why should we treat men as brothers? Because in fact and in truth, he says, they are so. How are we to realize and to make our " enemies " realize this? By passive resistance tied up with humble self-abnegation. Selfishness, he says, is an illusion, and hate a blunder. The actual fact is that we need each other. When we wake up to this fact our hate will die out. But by what stimulus can we be aroused to see the fact that we are members one of another? Not by argument or by psychoanalysis. Only by serving the man we oppose. The man whom we serve begins to like us. His liking rouses ours, especially if there is shown on each side readiness to suffer not only for other people but for one's own principles, readiness to suffer though not to use violence.

Gandhi has staked a good part of his life to prove that under certain conditions a man can be waked from the illusions of hate and even, I take it, from the self-illusion of selfishness. He can be enlightened by any friend who will suffer for his own principles and will prove that his own eyes are open because he does favors for his enemies. This is the Christian principle of turning away wrath by serving your wrathful enemy. It is a new application of our basic need to see facts as they are. Here Gandhi supports Freud, and I find myself carried along like a chip on the creedal stream which runs through these two lives. They convince me that the quest of duty is the quest of truth about our needs and about the promises by which we secure ourselves from day to day on the path of that quest.

10. The need of "psychical brakes and psychical tractors" in morals has not been sufficiently advertised. My central interest in ethics is to make it work. To remain aloof from the practical applications of ethical principles seems to me like being "for the law but agin the enforcement." Therefore the "implementation of ethical ideas" occupies three chapters in this book. Any one who takes the trouble to decide what he ought to do in a given situation needs, I think, all the suggestions that any one can give him about how to make himself do it. Ethical insight without ethical technique seems to me futile. Most of us have picked up some rough and ready ethical skill, but not from books on ethics. To fill this lack I have tried to assemble a group of devices familiar enough as handy tricks, but not ordinarily united to the main principles of ethics. Mental hygiene exploits one such group. The management of personnel in industry is skillful with another. Ethics is weakened by ignoring such applications. I hope to give them due scope.

11. We need tools to pry open ethical problems. The attempt to bring ethics down to earth does not imply the belief that one can hand out standard solutions of imagi-

nary problems after the manner of the casuists. Most of us are meeting new ethical situations almost every day, and no rules can tell us in advance how to meet all their novelty. But this is just as true of the problems which confront a carpenter or a plumber. Each of his jobs is a little different; yet he begins each with essentially the same kit of tools, which is sufficient to make a start with. So in ethics we can offer each other a group of well-tried tools of analysis, which usually take the form of questions. In this book I try to illustrate the usefulness of a few simple questions such as:

(a) What agreements have you entered into, tacitly or explicitly, with yourself and with others?

(b) What rival interests or desires are active in the situation wherein you wish to find the right act?

(c) What are your needs (often quite unlike your desires)?

(d) In what respects are you apt to be deceiving yourself?

Agreements, desires, and needs seem to me the stuff of ethics, the most useful tools of the trade. None of us can disregard his own agreements without disaster. But behind our agreements, maintaining, reshaping, sometimes revoking them, are our desires. If the desires which first made the agreement are no longer alive, it is a mere shell and soon falls to pieces.

Desires, however, are never rightly decisive in the field of right and wrong. For they often conflict, and when this happens no single desire can establish authority over the rest. Our duties, when we find them, turn out to be, as John Dewey says, the acts required by the situation, including ourselves and our ideals. To study the situation and ourselves as part of it, in search of the act just now called for by the facts, is the business of ethical reflection. To the listening mind its environment is vociferous with implications, that is, with its needs and with ours. But one sees these needs in the light of some theory about our human nature and its place in the cosmos. Such theory is the essence of science, of metaphysics, and of religion. Because we know very little in any of these fields, we are very green about our needs and the needs of the world for us. But one thing is certain: we get more light on our needs by using the light we already have. We see deeper into our duties, that is, into our needs and the needs for us, by following the glimpses already given us. Hence the Order of the Day is ordinarily clear. It is to act on the knowledge that we have while seeking for more. When we do that, we get along very well with ourselves and with other people. When we refuse, by self-deceit and by broken agreements, to use the little light we have, we run against moral disaster.

12. The main theses explained in the pages which follow are these:

(a) Ethics, the theory of good and of bad conduct, rests on the study of three principles: consistency, growth, and self-deceit. As man emerges from custom-bound existence he finds that he cannot hold his own unless he learns. Learning has a relatively persistent element as well as an obviously moving element. Some confidence that we can learn and some ability to tell how far we have gone, must abide with us all the way. They persist, not unchanged but constant, like the purpose of a navigator who seeks one port by various means and through many miles of advancement or deviation. So long as one learns, or slides backwards, the same person persists in his purposes. These purposes become agreements with oneself and with others. The doctrine of agreements fills the first two chapters of this book, and furnishes the basis for the morality of veracity, security, understanding, promises, contracts, and treaties.

(b) We are so made that according as we face or ignore facts we grow or degenerate. The attempt persistently to hug our present comfort involves us in slow degeneration. No one wants this. But so long as we try to avoid it we find that we must take our opportunities to learn, that is to grow, by facing facts. (Chapters III to VI.)

(c) We need not face the facts. We can turn away from them, persuading ourselves that the comfortable fictions which we wish to believe are true. Most of us do this at times because it is the easiest thing to do. But we are apt to be driven out of it by finding that in the attempt to preserve our ease we are losing ground, which we never intended. (Chapters XV to XVIII.)

Persistency (or stability) and growth are the principles of right conduct. Persistent self-deceit is the method by which we go wrong. Growth includes persistency. Persistency does not necessarily include growth. We can persistently decay.

Because stability is a simpler idea than growth, I shall describe first the ethics of stability, which we attain and try to preserve by means of agreements with ourselves and with others. As we wake up in childhood, we find ourselves tied into many relationships and subject to various desires which we have not chosen. As time goes on we validate or reject some of these. Thus our character takes shape as a center of branching plans which connect us with other people and integrate our centrifugal desires. When we find that our plans need improvement if they are to live in a changing world and to fit our changing needs, we come to recognize how unescapable is our need of growth, the central need of man, described in Chapters III to V. Our desires are then seen to be good when they are in line with the authoritative need to grow, bad when by self-deceit they diverge from it.

(d) Stability and change, the twin principles of growth, are each so essential to us that they tend to win sway over us alternately. They are the conservative and the radical elements in us, one the champion of security, the other of reform, one urging law and order, the other pressing for freedom. In Chapters XII and XIII I try to bind them in indissoluble marriage.

(e) These principles of right conduct:—stability, and growth, are valueless without application and implementation. They do not apply themselves to improve the habits of man. Therefore in Chapters VII to XIV I suggest some ways to apply the laws of good conduct and in Chapters XIX–XXI some methods to make them take hold of daily actions so as to avoid self-deceit.

(f) Ethics is not the whole of a good life, nor even the best of it. In heroism, research, creative art, and adoration, we forget ourselves. Unconscious of obligation, we drive straight for the best in sight, by a path which I call by the unsatisfactory name of supermorality. (Chapter XXII.)

A. RIGHT

I
PRINCIPLES

CHAPTER I

AGREEMENTS

1. TOOLS AND THEIR USE

Tools are material or immaterial. Both varieties serve our physiological and our psychical needs. A physician at the bedside of a puzzling " case " of illness uses material tools such as a clinical thermometer. This gives him insight into the diagnosis between febrile and non-febrile *fever* disease. He uses also immaterial tools, diagnostic questions, such as: Have you any pain? Where? For how long? Such a series of questions, like the thermometer, is put together in order to throw light on an obscure problem: What is the nature of this patient's disease and what should be done to cure or alleviate it? A well-made question is an immaterial tool of analysis.

In ethics also we face difficult problems and need well-selected tools, mostly immaterial. Ethical problems concern right and wrong, better or worse, what ought or ought not to be done. I suggest that we can best begin the solution of any ethical difficulty by asking:

(a) By what agreements (if any) have I bound myself in relation to the matter in hand?

(b) Have I kept these agreements?

(c) Have these agreements become unfit for the needs which they were originally made to serve? Should they therefore be refitted to the present need?

Such questions as these are *tools of ethical insight*. They are, I think, the best tools to begin with in ethical work. Later on questions about what we desire and about what we need are useful. They will be formulated in later chapters.

How to use the three rough-shaping tools that I have just recommended can be suggested by using them to extricate ourselves from the dilemma presented in Joseph Conrad's story, *Lord Jim*.

Originally Jim came from a parsonage. When his vocation for the sea declared itself he was sent to a training ship for officers of the mercantile marine.

Ever since Jim was a little chap he had been preparing himself to meet dangers on the sea, rehearsing his part in a succession of adventures . . . saving people from sinking ships, quelling mutinies on the high sea, unflinching as a hero in a book.

After two years of training he went to sea, became mate of a fine ship, was disabled by a falling spar, and left behind in an Eastern port. When well again he shipped as chief mate of the " Patna," a local tramp steamer of 1400 tons, " old as the hills and eaten up with rust worse than a condemned water tank." She carried eight hundred Moslem pilgrims bound for the Red Sea. The captain was a renegade New South Wales German who brutalized all those he was not afraid of. " The five whites lived amidships isolated from the human cargo."

In the Red Sea on a calm night the ship struck something, probably a submerged derelict. A big hole was made below the " Patna's " water line, but she still floated, down by the head. One iron bulkhead, very rotten, was apparently all that kept her afloat, and this was expected to give way any minute. Jim felt it bulge under his hand, and flakes of rust jumped off of it. There were three times as many passengers as the ship's boats would hold, even if there had been time to get them in. Jim saw that he could do nothing and thought he might as well stand where he was, waiting for death.

But while he waited, his imagination evoked the horrors of panic to follow if he waked the passengers: the trampling rush, the pitiful screams, the boats swamped. He wanted to die quietly, without added terrors.

Then he thought he could cut the boats loose so that they would float when the ship sank. As he was running up the ladder toward the boats the chief engineer hit him on the shoulder with the boat stretcher, thinking he was " one of them niggers." The other officers were fiercely and blunderingly trying to get a boat loose so as to leave the ship.

Jim stood on the other side of the ship as far away from them as he could get, and waited, without a sound, stiffened in the idea of some sort of heroic indiscretion. The others let him alone and tried to launch their boat. They " had no leisure to look back at his passive heroism." He still kept his distance. He wanted it over. " I loathed them," he said afterwards. Twice he shut his eyes in the certainty that all was over, and twice he had to open them again.

While struggling with the boat George (one of the other officers) suddenly died of heart disease. The others in the darkness did not know this.

Then the ship began to buzz fore and aft like a disturbed hive. The passengers were waking up. Jim found himself stumbling over the legs of the dead man. The others below in the boat, now launched, shouted back to the dead man, " Jump, George, jump!"

" The ship began a slow plunge under me . . . I looked up and found I had fallen across a thwart. I had jumped, it seems. I knew nothing about it." He felt as if all his ribs on the left side must be broken. " I wished I could die." A faint voice said, " She's gone." No lights any longer showed. " It seemed to me I must jump out of that accursed boat and swim back. . . . I had jumped certainly; but I tell you they were too much for any man! " Jim went off with the other officers.

* * *

The " Patna " did not sink after all. She was towed successfully to Aden by a French gunboat which found her the morning after the officers left her.

Jim was certainly in doubt about the right course, both before he jumped and afterwards. Even if in the end he was driven by some sort of blind instinct, there was conflict in him before that. Two possible courses of action were debated in his mind, and may be discussed by us.

It was a conflict about right and wrong, not about methods. The question was not about the best means to some clear end, but about his duty. Should he go or should he stay? That was the question; not how to go or how to stay and protect the passengers.

Was he responsible? When first we face his situation I suppose most of us would say, "Clearly he ought to stay and help the passengers." But could he do it? Could he keep himself from jumping into the boat? Perhaps he did not know what he was doing. He had been hit with a boat stretcher by the chief engineer. Perhaps he was so confused that he was carried along in a daze by his muscles. One does not call a man responsible for what he does if he is unconscious, drugged, the helpless prey of physical forces. If he had no choice about it but went over the ship's side like a piece of baggage, he could not properly be said to have done anything right or wrong.

Is this a far-fetched notion? I think not. He certainly might have been so stunned that he acted like an automaton. Men often behave in that way when they have been "knocked out" in a football game; when we understand what has happened we do not blame them for what they do. If this is Jim's situation, it is a medical problem, not a problem in ethics. Certainly he behaved a good deal like a man in a dream, and there is no right and no wrong for a sleepwalker. If I accidentally fall out of a window, light on a passer-by, and kill him, no one would say that I was either right or wrong, good or bad, in killing him. I could not help myself. The thought of the horrible misfortune might haunt me for months afterwards. But if I blamed myself I should be morbid. It was bad luck, not bad conduct.

Was Jim's act like this? No. For in Conrad's story it was not on the head that Jim was struck. It was on the shoulder. There is nothing to suggest that he was stunned or faint. He seemed to be in good health when the accident happened and after it.

Perhaps, however, he was in the grip of some psychological compulsion, some blind impulse, like the rush of a frenzied mob in a theater fire. He says something to suggest this: " I had jumped, it seems. I knew nothing about it . . . I tell you they were too much for any man." That might mean that he was forcibly pulled into the boat by the others, or that he was swept along by his terrified fellow officers as one might be carried along by a crowd. But the facts are against all these possibilities. He himself says that he jumped. The others had gone ahead. They were now in the boat below and certainly did not pull or push him in.

" They were too much for me " might mean that the Mohammedan pilgrims still below the deck were too many for any one man to save. He could do nothing for them and so might as well save himself. But it seems to me clear that he did not mean that, for later, when in the lifeboat, he was on the point of jumping out and swimming back. Then he saw the vessel sink, as he thought, and gave up the idea.

Psychological compulsion, " temporary insanity," was at one time a common plea for the defendant in murder cases. It has some plausibility. In a sense we can say that anybody in a rage or panic is as helpless, as irresponsible, as if he were insane. But are not most people responsible for getting into a rage or a panic? Unless a murderer has been known to be insane previous to the murder, or has shown other signs of insanity besides his ungoverned anger, he does not often escape by this plea. Indeed the fact that Jim brings up the argument that he could not help himself, inclines me to believe that he really knew he was wrong and was trying to excuse himself.

Questions like this, " Could he help it? " " Was he responsible? " often come up in a discussion of right and wrong, and have to be settled in one way or another before there is anything ethical to discuss. In this case it seems to me reasonably clear that Jim did know what he was about, that he was not stunned or insane, and so ought to be judged, by himself and by us, as either right or wrong. For " psychological compulsion " of the sort that destroys responsibility and wipes out all questions of right and wrong, means some definite type of mental disease such as does not appear suddenly during an accident in a man who has been normal a few minutes before. There would have been other symptoms of insanity both before and after the accident. Jim showed none.

If we try to imagine some purely nervous and temporary lapse, a " brain storm," beginning when the ship struck the derelict, we look for a state of mind quite different from Jim's. We expect to see him obsessed by an idea, possessed by a single train of impulses, carried along like a leaf in the wind. But his behavior does not suggest this. He goes below and examines the damaged bulkhead. He estimates the number of passengers, sees that the boats are too few to hold them, starts to join the other officers, perhaps with some idea of remonstrating with them. Then he walks away from them and stands against the rail, waiting for the ship to sink. At this point his decision to stay by her is apparently firm. Later he weakens and jumps.

I think it is clear, and certainly Conrad thought it clear, that Jim had his wits about him and made up his mind in the ordinary way. First he decided to stay; later he followed his impulse and went. In the moments just before he jumped he did no thinking. But he knew what he was about and where he was jumping, for he landed in the boat, presumably by aim and not by accident. Moreover, just before he jumped he noticed that the ship " began a slow plunge," and decided that she was going down head first. I think we must assume that he knew what he was doing and was responsible [1] both for jumping into the life-boat and for not jumping out of her later to swim back.

Self-preservation might be adduced to defend Jim's course. Can we settle his problem on the biological principle of the desire to survive? The struggle for existence is often said to be the deepest law of life. Whoever or whatever is now alive, we say, has come out on top of the evolutionary struggle in obedience to this law. Can we expect any one to break or to oppose the laws of nature? That would seem to demand a miracle or an act of treason to the march of evolution.

But if self-preservation were the only law of life all heroism would be immoral. Whoever tries to save another's life in fire, storm, or plague disregards the prudent law of self-preservation. Every doctor busy in an epidemic of contagious disease disregards the law of self-preservation and no one thinks him wrong for it. Evidently self-preservation is not the only law of ethics. It describes what people often do, sometimes rightly, but it speaks to us with no exclusive moral authority. The soldier is expected to do all he can to help his country by exposing himself to the risk of wounds and death. If he runs away to save his own life, he is not blamed provided there is nothing else that he can do with his life to help the cause he is fighting for. Who is to decide this? The officers in command, not the individual. Only if there are no orders and no plausible plans for advance, resistance or retreat, only in a situation of *sauve qui peut*, is self-preservation the right or the duty of an individual soldier. National, not individual, self-preservation is his obligation.

In peace, as I have said above, the right of self-

[1] See S. Sheldon Glueck, *Mental Disorder and the Criminal Law* (Boston: Little, Brown & Co., 1925).

preservation is challenged by any obligation,—such as that of a fireman, a policeman, a doctor, or a ship's officer,—which makes one responsible for an attempt at group-preservation.

Many other solutions of Jim's problem could be proposed, such as the utilitarian principle that whatever brings the greatest happiness of the greatest number is right, or Kant's rule, " So act that the rule of your action might be acted on by every one else without self-contradiction." But to try out the main theories of ethics at this point would mean writing volumes on this one case. So I shall apply at once to the solution of Jim's problem the set of mental tools which I put forward at the beginning of this chapter.

By the unwritten law of the sea, clearly understood and agreed to by sailors, Jim was bound to stick to his ship in an emergency such as was now upon her. So were all the other officers. In deserting the helpless passengers they were breaking their agreements. All the more reason why Jim should keep his.

Keep your promises. Abide by your agreements. Fulfill your contracts. Pay your debts. This is the principle which settles most ethical problems. Some agreements are vague and uncertain. But Jim's agreement was perfectly clear. He learned about it and approved of it when he was in training for the sea. It was a tradition known to all British seamen.

But perhaps this rule has exceptions. Granted that " Stick by the ship " should ordinarily govern a ship's officer, there may be some special reason why he should break the rule this time. Is there anything exceptional about these particular circumstances? Apparently not. It seems a clear

case of the situation in which officers are bound to stay by
their ship until all passengers are safely removed from her
or until every effort has been made to do this. This agreement has grown up because situations like Jim's have happened before and will happen again. Just because the sailor
meets special temptations to " self-preservation," that is,
to look after himself and let the devil take the hindmost,
special regulations have been planned to checkmate this
impulse.

It is only natural that each man should think first of his
own safety and try to secure it. But it is also natural that
shipping-companies need patronage. To get it they must
be able to assure prospective passengers that they will be
protected from the risks of the sea in every way that can
be thought out in advance. One of these ways is the rule
that officers and seamen of the vessels shall agree to forfeit
their natural " right of self-preservation " if this sacrifice
is necessary in order to save the passengers. Many, perhaps most, people who take passage on a ship know that
this rule exists. They have heard of disasters in which it
was applied and passengers' lives thus saved. Therefore,
in a sense, an officer like Jim has entered into an agreement
not only with the ship's owners or managers, but with the
public as well, with all actual and possible passengers.
They may have chosen this ship and this company, rather
than some cheaper but less reliable one, because they
trusted " Jim " and the other officers to abide by their
agreements, in other words, to do their duty.[1]

If there were no reliable agreements like this, people
could not coöperate with each other; every one would
have to go his own way, build and sail his own ship, make

---

[1] In the testimony given by the two men at the wheel at the trial after they
landed, it is clear that they had implicit faith in the fidelity and competence of
their officers. Presumably the passengers had a like trust.

all her timbers, rigging, and machinery himself, launch her and man her alone. On this principle no one could get far, hardly farther than the savage who makes a canoe out of a tree-trunk and paddles it himself. We may insist on paddling our own canoe, but we agree to let some one else make it and transport it to our starting point. Whenever we depend on others we depend on the validity of our agreements with them.

Without dependence on others and their dependence on us none of us can get what we want. "We must hang together or hang separately." What each is to expect of the others is fixed more or less clearly in a cluster of understandings, promises, appointments, traditions, rules, laws, all of which I call "agreements." Some of these are:

(a) explicit: spoken, written, sworn to. The great majority are

(b) implicit: tacit, though often well understood.

2. TACIT AGREEMENTS

Tacit agreements are those made and carried out by actions rather than by words. Many of them are implied in our explicit agreements.

"How much to Lynn?" you ask at the ticketseller's window. He names the amount. You take out a five-dollar bill without more words. It is then tacitly agreed that he will not appropriate your bill without giving you your change and one ticket to Lynn. By your voiceless action and by his own he is bound to this agreement. When he slaps down the ticket you are bound not to take it without paying. You would be justly indignant should he simply put the bill in his cash drawer and hand you a ticket without change. Your tacit action was as plain to him as the declaration, "I will take a ticket to Lynn," would have been. Had you several children with you and had you been

talking with them in a familiar way, the ticketseller might
have been in doubt as to the agreement proposed by the
five-dollar bill. " How many? " he might then have asked,
and " How many of these children are under five? " Thus
a clear, explicit agreement might have been built up,
though a part of it would still have remained tacit.

Because the implications of our words and other actions
are so many, the tacit agreements of our lives far outnum-
ber ordinarily the explicit, especially between friends.

" Will you dine with me tonight? "
" Very glad to."
This is an explicit agreement. But the essential part of
it is tacit. A literalist could point out that strictly this is
no agreement at all. The essential words " come " and " I
shall be " are tacit. Strict constructionists might show
that " very glad to " does not say what the speaker is glad
to do, nor who is glad. Passing beyond these absurd liter-
alisms it is also obvious that the friendly guest has not
explicitly promised not to come drunk, not to spit on the
floor nor to eat with his fingers, not to remain obstinately
silent all the evening, not belligerently to attack his friend's
taste in interior decoration nor criticize his food nor look
bored by all his other guests. Yet all this and much more
is tacitly understood on both sides, else he would not be
invited.

These obvious and time-saving implications which
branch out from our explicit agreements, and depend on
our understanding of each other's habits, can be summed up
in the *expectation of good faith*. All the blanket-agreements
of common decency cannot be completely spread out in
advance of each day's work. They are given in a single,
inclusive, tacit agreement to follow the spirit of our fellow-
ship. One will not take advantage of one's fellows in any

underhand way. One will not wantonly or carelessly let an engagement slip.

Tacit agreements are more liable to abuse and to misunderstanding than explicit agreements are. The nod of a buyer at an auction is usually taken as an agreement to purchase; it is more convenient than a spoken word, and nearly as clear. But an involuntary movement or a nod addressed to a neighbor in the crowd may involve the nodder in difficulties. At the end of the auction he may unexpectedly find himself an owner and a debtor. Yet baseball, football, and concerted music are full of just such tacit agreements and wordless coördinations which work perfectly. The members of a string quartette start their music and synchronize their later musical decisions by tacit agreements involving a precision and swiftness of interchange hard to match in any other field. They glance at each other between phrases, but still oftener they "glance" at each other with their ears and so bind themselves together from instant to instant by a process almost as simple as sense perception, almost as swift and smooth as the chemical messages exchanged between the body's unconscious organs to keep them working together. Such agreements are as well understood and as rarely broken as any that I know. The decisions of each player when to begin, how much to vary the time in *ritenuto* or *accelerando* passages, how much tone to use,—all these are tacitly interwoven with the decisions of others. The behavior of buyer and seller or of teacher and pupil ought to be like this, though it seldom is.

"To keep in touch," as our facile, overworked metaphor has it, involves a continuous flow of simple, rapid, tacit understandings, each following close on the heels of the last. This current can be translated into promises and fulfillments. It can be made explicit. But this is needful only for duffers. Any good team of artists or athletes requires few words to direct harmonious progress within their purpose.

I have spoken of tacit agreements in ticket-buying, at auctions, among athletes and musicians. Marriage also involves a profusion of tacit agreements. Not every item of marital teamwork can be anticipated and explicitly provided for. The exigencies of travel, weather, and sickness, the incalculable behavior of nurses, children, and plumbers, leave no time for discussion or even for speech. Then tacit understandings must furnish the basis of such coöperation as we can muster. The closer the understanding the more agreements are tacitly fulfilled. But there are still many which accomplish their ends better when they are made explicit. How finances are to be regulated, what attentions are to be paid to the " in-laws," are decisions best made explicitly during the engagement period and not left as a tacit understanding that each will do what is proper.

Each expects the other to *act in character*. An uncounted multitude of previous looks, words, silences, outbursts, successes, and failures, has conveyed to each an understanding of what the other can be trusted to do or to omit in certain emergencies. Each is aware that the other relies on him to act characteristically, that is, not to violate the spirit of their well-tested understanding. The letter of it has no application in emergencies. What they have explicitly promised to each other is too general to direct their behavior when the house is afire or the family income gone. In such crises the value of an intimate relationship is revealed. What valuable though tacit understandings then spring up in working order? What new rôle does each swiftly assume in reliance upon the support of the other's competence in a different rôle? Can they move in opposite directions, each to his post? Does each select promptly the tool that he can use best? It depends upon the degree in which they have perfected their tacit understandings. If the principle behind their decisions has been explicitly agreed upon, they can serviceably play up to each other, as they act out the new implications of their creed, illumined in the mind of each by the need of the moment.

Around most explicit agreements there is a penumbra of implicit ones. When two friends agree to travel in Europe together, they explicitly agree about steamer passages, dates of starting and returning, and about the main features of their route. But it goes without saying that neither shall incontinently invite a third person to join them, that neither shall suddenly decide to make the journey barefoot, or to take along a pet monkey. The general formula of these tacit agreements is something like this: " I will do and omit nothing which is out of line with the character that you know in me, or with our explicit plan. I will not disappoint your expectations so far as I can anticipate them." Such a broad, tacit agreement is reciprocal, and quite as definite as verbal understandings about dates, prices, and places.

The life of a business partnership has a similarly broad fringe of tacit agreement around the verbal pledges with which they start.

Honest and clear but silent agreements should be distinguished from " virtual," that is, fake agreements. A tacit agreement should be as sincere, as definite, as binding as any other. It is only when actions speak louder, more swiftly, and more precisely than words that agreements should be tacit. The silent understanding should express a positive advantage, not a slump or a blur. "Virtually he promised" may mean that he did not promise at all, though he fooled some one into believing that he did.

Whatever we do with others rests on a framework of such mutual understandings, mostly implicit, a few explicit. Most of us want civilization to go on. We do not want to relapse into savagery. But what we call civilization, in contrast with savage life, is as strong or as weak as the tissue of understandings which link its members together. Appointments, timetables, bargains, wages, prices, families, athletic teams, orchestras, partnerships, schools, churches, governments, theaters, picnics, games, Arctic explorations,—all these rest on agreements. Any day's work is a sample of what we are enabled to achieve because people (ordinarily) keep their word and do what they have agreed to do.

The use of language itself involves tacit agreements. The deaf mute, until he learns that certain signs of the fingers always mean what they are agreed upon to mean, lives in terrible isolation from his fellows. For all of us, words spoken or written would be meaningless if people had not come to an understanding on what they are to mean. If a person suddenly decided to break the understanding whereby his "yes" means assent, and began to use it to mean dissent, we should be at cross purposes with him. He might not be a liar but linguistically he would be impossible.

The first contention of this book is that duty, the substance of ethics, includes the honest endeavor to keep our agreements until they are dissolved by the consent of all concerned. It means more than this, but never less. The central questions of ethics: How can we find out what our duty is? and Why should we do it? mean, How can we find out what our agreements are? and, Why should we keep them or improve them? To the question: Why do our duty? the answer is, " Because otherwise we cannot get what we need." Most people most of the time need to work, play, learn, make love, or do something else that involves getting along with themselves and other people. These needs work themselves out in desires, in understandings, in teamwork. Therefore, if we are to get what we want, we must keep our pledges, or do our duty.

But our agreements are often vague. Hence for the same reason that we need them at all, we need to make them clearer. They are often out of date, clumsy, unsatisfactory, even to those who made them. Then they need to be improved, so as to fulfill more satisfactorily the desires and needs that made them in the first place. They need to be extended, reduced, or modified. They tie us down because we need to be tied in order to get good teamwork. But they can be changed, by mutual consent, to allow for growth, for new ideas, for reform.

The purport of ethics, then, can be summed up provisionally in three rules:—

(1) Make and make clear your agreements.

(2) Keep your agreements.

(3) Improve your agreements along the line of the need that first shaped them.

Agreements, duties, and obligations crystallize desires; they express in tangible, useful ways, what is desired, perhaps desirable. If we revolt against the cramping idea of duty and obligation, we are revolting against our own desires,— a perfectly proper thing to do if it makes more satisfactory desires emerge. But if those desires are to get anywhere, then a revolt against one set of duties or agreements must lead to the establishment of a new set, framed more nearly to meet the heart's desire, and the desires of those one needs to work with.

Jim loved the sea. He wanted a sailor's life. He went into training for it. In that training he made and carried out, I take it, a set of agreements with his parents who paid for his education on the understanding that he would do his work and not loaf, fish, or play cards in the time assigned for study. Persumably he also made and carried out agreements with his teachers, with his fellow students, with his landlord, his tailor, and his fiancée, if he had one; certainly with himself. All these agreements crystallized his desire to go to sea, and worked towards its fulfillment. To question them was either to question the desire itself or to wonder whether he could get to sea in some swifter and less cumbersome way. If he failed to find this, there would be no further question in sight.

3. OUR DESIRES ARE GUIDED BY OUR VIEW OF THE FACTS

We do not always know what agreements we ought to make, keep, or improve, because we are not sure what we want to do or to plan next. How can we find out? By looking about us and seeing what range of possibilities, desirable and undesirable, is in sight. *This is like consulting a bill of fare.* When we sit down in a restaurant and are asked what we will have to eat, we ordinarily ask for the bill of fare. Not until its possibilities are before us can we decide on our desires. It may be that we desire something that is not on the *menu* at all. Still we shall be surer of this after we have seen what is offered.

A person's desire, then, finds itself, sharpens itself, or develops, in view of what he believes to be the relevant facts. When a student selects his courses for the year he usually consults the elective pamphlet, even though in the end his choice may follow some one's advice. His choice is less blind if he has tried to consider all that he might do, and does not hurriedly sign up for the first course that pops into his head. By casting an eye over the whole field of available choices he is more apt to find what he " really " wants, what he wants " on the whole." The better he knows what interests him and the more thoroughly he can discern, behind the opaque course-titles and the teachers' names, the kind of work actually given in the different courses, the more likely he is to be satisfied with his choices as the year goes on, the more " reasonable," as we say, is his final decision.

To " reason " in such a case is to hatch out or to clear up our desires after a survey of the facts, that is, of our own abilities in relation to the available choices. Doubtless there are always some germs of desire in us at the outset, else the facts on the bill of fare or on the list of college courses would have no effect. But until one is roused by sight of the possibilities or by some one's description of them, one may be aware of no desires at all.

It is partly for this reason, I suppose, that many students reach the end of the senior year with little notion of what they intend to do after graduation. No occupational bill of fare is offered them and so no appetite is roused. The various professions and callings are hardly more than words to the student. A well-to-do youth may be in doubt not merely which of the possible jobs he is interested in, but whether he cares to earn his living at all. In this uncertainty he may drift into a hunting expedition, take a year at Oxford, or try a sojourn at the Law School in lieu of a decision.

But whenever a decision is arrived at, desires and facts interact like appetite and a bill of fare. Some glimmering of interest in making our way leads us to notice what occupations keep our friends busy after their graduation. Later, some definite knowledge of what a doctor's, a teacher's, a broker's life is like, rouses live interest, when these jobs are lined up before us as alternatives. Facts appreciated shape desire. Desires make "mere facts" mean something to us. Facts and desires reciprocate in a self-developing spiral, which in a later chapter I shall call our central need for growth.

But why fulfill one's desires? Because only a desire can command or countermand a desire. Nothing but an impulse of some kind can set us in motion. If you don't want to go to sea, what do you want to do? Even a dislike involves a preference, and a preference is a desire. One can desire to do nothing at all and can fulfill that desire in a course of masterly inactivity, if one has the means. For this one may be reproached by a righteous or interfering elder. But if his appeal is to succeed, it must rouse in us some hitherto dormant desire to do something besides loaf. This may be a wish to please the elder or to stop his talking, or to escape boredom, or simply for a change. But whatever in the end moves one, will be a desire to get or to avoid something.

Suppose the prodding elder fails to rouse any desires by his appeal. He may then resort to something more potent. He may cut off the supplies. But if this is effective, it is because it so changes the situation that loafing is no longer desired. In view of the new situation in which one is unable to buy decent clothes, to get any amusement, or perhaps even to get a square meal, the desire to loaf is apt to be superseded by some other desire which under the circumstances is preferred.

The new situation may leave no time for reflection. The loafer may be picked up and thrown out. But in that case he does not act at all, and in ethics it is the validity of *voluntary* activities that we discuss. Leaving out involuntary reactions like breathing, sneezing, and forced motions like those of a captive dragged along by a policeman, the actions of a conscious person always involve desire.

" Why should we do what we desire?" then, is a question which turns out to mean, "From what desire should we do so? " No one does an act that can properly be called right or wrong unless his own will, that is, a desire of some sort, is active. But desires may be good or bad; that is, they may or may not be buttressed by the belief that they stand for what we need or for what our situation and our fellows need of us. Behind our agreements are our desires. Behind our desires are what we believe to be our needs. This is the subject of Chapters III to VI, but will not be further explained here.

4. INTERNAL AGREEMENTS

Our desires issue in agreements with ourselves [1] as well as with other people. The essential element here is a decision binding one's future actions. New Year's resolutions bind one to plans of hygiene, of order among one's possessions, of a better use of one's leisure time, of vengeance upon one's enemy or loyalty to one's friends. Of course many such agreements are soon forgotten. They are effective only in proportion as we turn our ingenuity to finding means to insure their fulfillment and to set in motion, while the resolution is still hot, some machinery to work from that instant toward its fruition.

All sincere understandings with others imply an intention, that is, an understanding with ourselves, to keep the promise. In deliberately fraudulent agreements there is no such intention; but the other party is kept in igno-

---

[1] For a definition and analysis of what is here meant by an agreement, see Chapter II, p. 47.

rance of this, else he would not waste his time in the matter. The good faith on which contracts, understandings, treaties, covenants, and promises of all sorts are based, is an assumption by each side that the other has agreed with himself as well as with his fellows to keep his promise. It seems clear, then, that if we are to fulfill desires which concern others and reach out into the future, we must bind that future to ourselves and ourselves to that future.

Jim had made up his mind before he came on board the " Patna " to be a hero. His idealistic temperament, his unused energies, were not satisfied by keeping his agreements with the company which employed him. He burned to show his capacities for self-sacrifice. Conrad never tells us that Jim shared this ambition with any one else. Apparently it was a settlement made with himself. His daydream ended in something like a contract: " I will distinguish myself; the world shall hear from me." By this rather melodramatic understanding with himself he was almost as much bound as if he had signed and sealed it before a notary. Before the end of his life he made it good.

When his first disaster came and his ship was rapidly sinking, it was in obedience to agreements with himself, rather than with his employers, that he stood stiffly against the bulwarks as far away as he could withdraw himself from the frantic efforts of the deserting officers. This very self-conscious attitude expressed his loathing for their dirty, fear-driven behavior as they struggled to launch the heavy lifeboat. His feelings as well as his principles revolted against the deserters. But he did not clearly understand what he was doing nor why. His attention was caught in his own sensation of moral nausea at the situation, and of contempt for the officers. This emotional blur accounted in part, I think, for the final defeat of his heroic resolve. In the confusion of strong emotions within him, terror and the natural impulse of self-preservation mingled with curiosity to draw him across the vessel's deck to the bulwark overlooking the lifeboat already lowered by the other officers.   Then his distraught consciousness was still further unstrung by a hideous shock. He stumbled over the dead body of the engineer.   Utterly demoralized by this, he moved toward the boat like soft iron to a magnet.   Then the others below yelled for their dead comrade whom they thought to be alive but hesitating on the deck.

At that call Jim finally jumped into the boat without quite knowing that he jumped. He came to himself when the thwarts bruised his ribs.   At this juncture emotions and impulses pushed him about like a piece of wreckage. But his desire to jump out of the boat again, and to swim back to the ship, showed that forces of resistance were still active within him.   Some of these forces sprang, I think, from his agreements with himself, his pledge to heroism.

Such resolutions, which we often call *our " principles,"* *I call agreements with ourselves or internal agreements*.   A person's deliberate but unwritten decision to turn over a new leaf, the less articulate determination to swear off smoking or to keep accounts, are like branches from the main trunk of character.   They bear a family likeness and express a single tendency which grows more definite as we mature. They are explicit or implicit understandings with ourselves.[1]

But are internal agreements really possible? Are they not merely a metaphor? " Agreements are an exchange of commitments between two persons," says a friendly critic. I agree that papers or oaths may be exchanged. By these we try to convey, each to each, the assurance that each will actually do what he has pledged himself to do. But the assurance which each thus gets from the other is no

[1] I return to this subject on page 43.

stronger than the sincerity of resolve within each person. That cannot be exchanged. It lives or dies in each separately. An external agreement is the declared reciprocity of two inner promises. If the agreement were in essence social, its breaking would be so too. It is significant that what two seemed to make, either can break alone.

It is true that in external agreements each party comes to his decision in view of the other's decision. But each decides with his eye on many other facts as well. He reckons with markets, politics, weather, health, his own and others' capacities, too, if the agreement is to have force. If he reckons without them his agreement is worthless. "When the Chinese mayor of Shanghai made a verbal compliance with the Japanese demands [in September, 1931] he doubtless . . . meant what he said. But he reckoned without his inflamed fellow citizens and the large number of Chinese troops in and about the city. It is not enough that spokesmen should . . . give verbal assurances of what China will do. There must be reliable evidence that they speak with full competence and authority." [1] Else their promises are like paper money without real value behind it.

This recent instance and Japan's similar behavior under the Nine-Power Agreement in 1931 and 1932 show how hollow are the exchanges of commitments between two parties unless substance is given to their compact by the sincere and reasonable intentions of those who take part. Sincerity springs from the agreement of all the impulses within a person as he faces a certain situation. If all the elements, bellicose, industrious, canny, sentimental, religious, which exist within a person or a nation, have faced the same body of facts and sincerely agreed about

---

[1] Jerome D. Greene, "Present Troubles in the Orient," Address at World Affairs Institute, New York, March 23, 1932.

the actions called for by these facts, then their agreement is valuable and not a mere form of words. Then it may be reënforced by oaths, penalties, and publicity. But if the agreement is only social, if it rests on no facts except those created by the exchange of commitments between two persons, then it is largely a matter of form, like diplomatic civilities between enemies.

Compare this with a somewhat different situation. When two men agree in an opinion instead of in a promise, the strength of their agreement is obviously not in what they say to each other but in the similarity of the impresssion made on each by a particular set of facts. Both bow to the same interpretation of reality. Therefore they can agree with each other. Reality has the same control when we reach a valid agreement not only in our opinions but in our plans. Then we have:

(a) A set of facts recognized by each.

(b) A similar intention declared by each person in view of these facts.

(c) The record of these decisions by the parties.

The strength of any agreement is not only in the vacillating wills of those who sign it but in the constituency, of facts or of persons, which these wills represent. Does the plenipotentiary accurately represent the desires of his nation? If not his promise is viable only until the next election or the next revolution. Does the intention of the person mirror the facts and impulses in which he is enmeshed, by which he will probably be controlled? If he is swimming in Niagara river one hundred feet above the falls, he may have a sincere intention to come home for tea with his aunt. But this will make no difference in the event. Earlier he could have avoided the control of the current and secured the control of his will. Now he cannot; for free will must be an early bird to catch its worm.

Are internal and external agreements as much alike as I have argued? Can we really have two parties which reach or avoid an agreement within one person? Certainly we have conflicts with ourselves as well as conflicts with others. Why then should we not recognize the agreements within ourselves, which prevent or stop conflict? When this occurs, is the harmony merely a sameness and not an agreement? I do not find it so. You can ask and answer questions, advance and refute views, inside yourself as well as with another person. You can convince, browbeat, haggle with yourself. You can ask some one to arbitrate your internal conflict and can agree to abide by the result. If all goes well, each party within you is modified, gives up something, though each retains the nucleus of its original contention, as people do when they convert each other. Your impetuosity says to your prudence: " In view of your giving up this and I that, our new view is adopted." It combines some advantages of both. It is a net gain or growth, and it is essentially a contractual affair.

The similarity of internal and external compacts seems to me even more obvious because a pledge can be " internal " to a small group (say the Senate of the United States), yet " external " to a larger group such as the House or the nation. The Senate considering a tax-bill finds itself internally divided into " soak-the-rich " and " soak-the-poor " groups. In a similar way any senator may find himself internally divided between his desire to get himself reëlected by pleasing the veteran bonus-grabbers and soaking the rich, and his desire not to be defeated because the rich, who have been soaked, refuse to pay for his campaign. Interests, in the Senate or in the individual senator, may diverge, and then escape divergence by agreement.

One more illustration of the similarity of agreements inside a person and between persons, and I am done with it. We may arrive at an understanding by internal or by external conversation. When we talk with another person there is still a sense in which we are talking with ourselves. For *his words have to become our thoughts* before we can understand them, attack them, agree with them, or modify them. The difference between intelligent talk and intelligent meditation is that when two of us fertilize each other's minds, new ideas arise faster in both, are more interesting and have more emotional color than when we think alone. Whether we think alone or with others, notions arise in our minds, meet and jostle others, are assimilated, rejected, or held in suspense. Not every idea which we entertain in solitude is accepted. We can consider our own ideas and reject them as well as another's. Most that are called "our own" are in fact received from others, though we may have forgotten from whom. Our own ideas are often fragments of old conversations. On the other hand many an enthusiast soliloquizes even when he talks with others. He is warmed by his fellows as he might be by coffee or by spring weather, but he receives no ideas from them. Some of us can hammer our own thoughts out better by discussion, others by writing, by dictation, by walking up and down, or under the stimulus of reading alone. When two hands or two ideas coöperate in a bit of work they may belong to one person or to two persons. It is sometimes a toss-up which way works best. Today the coöperation binds two persons, tomorrow it is concentrated in one, according to the call of the moment. The rare perfection of teamwork by two is often the image of a single person's hands working together. So it is with plans and with agreements.

If it is true that internal and external agreements are so much alike, what differences are left?

(a) Internal agreements need not procure external understandings in order to be useful; valid external compacts depend on internal agreements of the same purport.

(b) In internal agreements the " parties " usually know each other more intimately than in external agreements. Hence internal agreements often work better, because each impulse dovetails better with the others.

(c) Witnesses and penalties are invoked oftener in external than in internal agreements.

(d) In an internal agreement *I* recognize a state of persons and of facts (including my own desires and needs), and bind myself to act according to the opportunity offered me. In an external agreement *we* recognize a situation (including our own desires and needs), and bind ourselves to act out the opportunity offered us. In both cases a recognized opportunity for growth is the essential thing. In good agreements we obey this recognition. In a bad agreement there is no such opportunity because it contains the seeds of its own destruction. It is sick, because it is verbal rather than real. It is flimsy because it is in conflict with the facts. When it knows this contradiction it is dishonest.

This reasoning implies that a *bad agreement*, made without sincerity or without facing the obstacles and treacheries which may be involved in carrying it out, *is really a disagreement concealed by words*. It will not do the work of an agreement. It is counterfeit coin. But do we not break *something* when we break a deceptive or impracticable promise? Yes; we break the screen of words behind which a disagreement was all the time hidden. We pull off the mask which concealed the actual intentions. The truth emerges.

In this chapter I have tried to show that when we wish to decide an ethical puzzle such as Conrad presents to us in *Lord Jim*, a convenient tool is the question: What agreements, internal and external, tacit and explicit were made in view of the facts of this situation? When we have grasped the agreements in the case it is illuminating to ask further: Were they kept? If not why not?

Chapter II

AGREEMENTS AND DESIRES

I have used the word *agreement* an unconscionable number of times but I have not yet defined it. An agreement is *a declaration of intention arrived at in view of an understanding of facts by the various tendencies within one person or by two or more persons.*[1] The intention once defined, promises the united action of the desires or persons concerned. To develop this intention may take years. But its essence is given when the original decision sets up its plan and cuts off opposed possibilities. Then vows, written contracts, penalties may strengthen it.

Mrs. Jones has a tendency to explode in anger when her husband, who is out of work, sits down by the kitchen stove to warm himself and to mope. "He ought to hustle and help with the housework," says the indignant part of her mind. But another part of her knows how helpless and footless he is, and how blue he feels without his regular job. In time these two tendencies in her may come to an internal agreement not to nag him any more until she can suggest something that will occupy him without mortifying his masculine pride. The cellar needs whitewashing, and this job, when she suggests it, appeals to him. From this beginning odd bits of painting and carpentering turn up. In the end he and she come to an understanding that he shall keep himself busy with *something* whenever he can find it, and that she shall not scold him for idleness

[1] Another definition: A meeting of two or more wills in recognition of each other and of their situation, for the furtherance of their common interest. This meeting may be held within one person or between several persons.

at the time when he is at his wits' end for lack of discoverable chores.

1. TWO FEATURES OF A VALID AGREEMENT AND OF THE DESIRES BEHIND IT

Agreements are the crystallizations of desire, and are as good or as bad as the desires. The worth of a desire depends on two essential points, (a) its sincerity and (b) the recognized state of facts behind it.

Sincerity or good faith means that each has made the same agreement with himself that he makes with the other, and intends to keep it. If two nations sign *in good faith* a treaty of peace, then they possess no secret treaty which contradicts their signatures. Hidden reservations, private interpretations, furtive schemes to undermine the agreement are inconsistent with the good faith which each pledges, explicitly or implicitly, to the other.

I recall how in my boyhood the members of our gang watched each other for signs of sly evasions. If one of us made a promise and then muttered the words " Over the left," he fancied himself free to break it. So we listened hard for this ritual. If we crossed the second finger over the first while making a promise we could then proceed to evade it. Sometimes the crossed fingers were held behind our backs and the " Over the left " was whispered very faintly. We were on the watch for such tricks, because we needed to be sure that our open covenants were not canceled by secret treaties.

Good faith does not compel us to keep such an agreement (internal or external) forever; but it can be rightly dissolved or improved only by a new agreement made by the concurrence and conviction of all the desires or interests concerned. When they see a better way to accomplish their common end, when one persuades the rest, or when they mutually persuade each other, then the original decision can be reshaped without treachery or self-contradiction. But if one element revolts and breaks the agreement, disregarding the facts and interests concerned, we have civil war and self-destruction, within a person or within a group. Within a person an impulse of envy upsets his self-imposed standards, say of good manners. Other people may be injured as well, but the certain damage is that done within his own make-up. His conflicting desires have weakened his underpinning.

Beside sincerity in an agreement we need something more. We need to know that it is *a reasonable compact in view of the relevant facts*. Among the facts in view when Mr. and Mrs. Jones declare their intentions are the actions which each expects from the other. It is partly because of these that each desires the agreement. The actual needs, desires, capacities, and opportunities of each give body to their compact and help to ensure its fulfillment. Their promise is good because it expresses the organizable needs of each person better than any other agreement in sight. In other words, their act is one of recognition leading to action. They perceive an area of mutual interest. "We have in common," they might say to each other, "the need to avoid squabbles and to support rather than to irritate each other. This is a fact. Let us catch up with this fact and act on it." The fact of their common need determines the value and permanence of their agreement, and leads to the decision "I will" (or "We will"), which is both a promise mortgaging the future, and a tightening of loose strands within the personality. It is a promise by each to himself as well as to others. It recognizes and then further establishes, in them and outside them, an area of relatively rigid fact which neither of them can change without hurting himself and the other.

The need of soundness as well as of sincerity in an agreement can be phrased as a requirement of *moral collateral* on each side. When my uncle promises (to my surprise) that he will pay my way through college, I ask myself not only, is he *sincere*, but, is it *reasonable* that he should bind himself to such an expense and that I should let him expect me to work hard enough to satisfy him. Is it not more than he can afford? Am I not promising more than I shall perform? He seems to think that I am going to accomplish a good deal in college. Is it fair that I, with the needs and capacities which I have, should accept such an offer and bind myself implicitly or explicitly to make good? Do the facts before us, and the reciprocity of our needs and desires, make this compact a sensible step in the growth of our plans? Is my uncle basing his investment on anything stronger than my unsupported will? Can I show him any fund of solid accomplishment in like conditions before?

If a promise rests on firm moral collateral it is strong with the strength of reasonable probability and inductive science. Then the conflicting elements in a person (or in the various persons in a conference) may pledge each other and witness each other's concurrence with a sense that they are following a desire to face the truth. It is easy to make a temperance pledge with oneself or sign a contract with others. But the virtue of the agreement is not only in the pledge but chiefly in its sincerity and in the soundness of its expectations. For nothing is settled until it is settled right.

Right and wrong seem to depend on making, keeping, and improving agreements, which are the crystallization of our desires. When we have scanned the bill of fare our decision issues in an agreement with the waiter: "I will take such and such food." That is, "If you will have such dishes cooked and served I agree to pay the prices charged on the *menu*." Such agreements, kept or broken, fill our lives.

The survey of moral collateral which fixes our choice as the fruit of a reasonable desire can be suggested by another metaphor,—"four-way reflection." The driver of a motor car in traffic is expected to keep himself informed not only of what is in front of him but of what is behind him and on each side. From moment to moment a sensible decision as to speed and direction depends on foreseeing the consequences of any move, consequences to himself and to others. In making up our minds what we ought to do next, as judged by what we desire on the whole to do, we should look round us and imagine the consequences of turning to the right, of turning to the left, of stopping, or of speeding ahead. Our first impulses are modified, or ought to be, not only by the obvious facts in sight but by some of the possible futures which these facts imply. These possible futures are brought into view by considering what is behind us, because the future can be predicted to some extent from the past. We remember that not long ago our sudden impulse to stop in traffic led to a rear-end collision. The same thing may happen again. Reflection on our desires, then, brings possibly undesired futures into view in the light of the past. But there are other people on each side of us. They also have to be considered. Hence the metaphor of " four-way-reflection " which means considering the future in the light of the past and remembering the other people concerned. In view of all this, one's first desire is modified by reflection, as the utilitarian philosophers have rightly insisted. My immediate desire is perhaps to stop and consult my road-map. But I don't want a collision nor great inconvenience to those behind me. Hence, on the whole, I no longer want to stop just now, but later, when I come to a clearer patch of road.

There is a difference, then, between some desires and others, between a well-informed Will and casual wishes, a difference often marked by the words " right " and " wrong." By a " good " desire, a " righteous " will, we mean one that has been formed in view of all the facts, present and future, that appear to bear on it. Among these facts are our own whims and our own ideals. Naturally we cannot see all the facts, not even all the relevant facts, any more than as we steer our car we can take account of the cars a mile behind us or in front. Moreover we may be in error about the facts that we do see. But no one is responsible for more than he can do. If one has acted with the knowledge that he has or can get before he has to decide, he has done all that can reasonably be expected of him. He has done his duty; he has done right, even though he may have acted on a mistake.

Ordinarily he intends to steer clear of thoughtless or ruthless behavior such as stopping suddenly and without warning in the midst of traffic. This is " wrong." It is one's wish often enough, but not the sort of behavior that one is willing to stand by on the whole, that is, after sensible consideration. Reasonable conduct is guided, one believes, by the needs of the actual situation and not by any casual desire.

The most obvious evidence that an act is *right*, then, is that some one desires it :—

" really."
at bottom.
on the whole, in the long run.

all things, and persons, considered.

in view of all the relevant facts, including the desires of others.

after sober reflection and discussion.

after consulting experts.

after prayer.

as an expression of what we believe the situation (and ourselves as part of it) needs.

Wrong is an impulse which has decided to be:—

a superficial wish not rooted in the main trend of one's plan.

a whim that does not bear full consideration.

a casual, momentary desire that will soon disappear.

a foolish desire, ignorant of what it wants, based on a mistake.

a headstrong, largely emotional, and therefore blind or self-deceiving desire.

These impulses have in common the failure to hold up their heads under consideration. They disappear or they drive along with their heads down, or they screen themselves behind plausible sophistry. When such desires win and are embodied in agreements, the agreements, like the desires, are bad, because they do not bear the light. When faced they contradict the will of the person who made them.

Suppose a fat and hungry stockbroker on a high stool in a restaurant. On the counter before him is a plate of tough and weighty doughnuts which he would remember, if he let himself think, have previously disagreed with him. He grabs one, nevertheless, and dispatches it in a few bites. His desire for this doughnut was a bad one, because it was contrary to his own needs, as, in his proper senses, he knows them. It is an odd psychological process by which he thus contradicts himself. But every one knows it well enough in himself. We all know what it is to act as if we did not know what in fact we do know. The characteristic mark of this stockbroker's bad desire is that, though perfectly harmless under different conditions, it is bad just here and now, because in a stout, tired, elderly man, aware of the sources of his own chronic dyspepsia, this doughnut blocks the way to his own more permanent and characteristic interests. He will have indigestion and perhaps waste the rest of his day.

The essential trait of " badness " in an agreement, in an action, or in the desire which creates them, is self-contradiction, which leads, when it is realized, to self-condemnation: " I was an idiot to eat that." But who is it that has been contradicted? Who now condemns the doughnut eater, and by what right? An idiot is an idiot once for all. He cannot be otherwise. But the dyspeptic stockbroker is not an idiot, though at times he acts like one. Now and then he goes off on tangents, but usually he keeps a fairly straight and reasonable path. His associates can count on him. Like most people he has a recognizable individuality made up of characteristic gestures, habits, ideas, prejudices, and principles. When conscious of these he can condemn his own lapses because he has something to lapse from. The crazy longing for the doughnut was contrary to what he knew were his main needs; but he succeeded in hiding from himself. (See Chapters XVI to XVIII.)

A bad agreement, then, or a bad action is one which contradicts the person who made it and denies the situation in which he finds himself. Other people and their interests are part of that situation. They are among the facts in view of which he acts. He shuts his eyes to them and acts as if they did not exist, thereby deceiving himself and denying truth that he knows.

In this discussion of right and wrong I am purposely beginning at the surface and working inward towards a central principle. I do not believe that any simple com-

mand like " Keep your agreements " is the whole answer
to the question, What is a man's duty? But it is the most
immediate answer and is included in the truer answer which
I am leading up to. Behind agreements are the desires
which make, remake, or break them. Behind desires are
the facts in view of which these desires grow up. Well-
informed desires are better than casual desires. But desires
themselves are not the last word in ethics. We must believe that they fit our needs and the world's needs if we
are to follow them as our duty. In Chapter III I shall
come back to this point.

When desires conflict, organization is better than suppression because almost all our impulses have *some* sense
in them. Though we may rule a desire out of court and
reject it as " bad " because in its present shape it conflicts
with our accepted plan of life, " bad desires," like " bad
men," usually have something good in them. Ordinarily
it would be wrong for a clerk whose hours run from nine
to five to fulfill his desire for a ball game on Wednesday
afternoon. But his desire for baseball games is not in itself
bad. It is out of place on Wednesday afternoon, but, ordinarily, in place on Saturday afternoon, because his contract
of employment prescribes no work after one o'clock on
Saturdays. He wants to keep his job. He also wants to go
to ball games. He can fulfill both these only by confronting
them with each other and assigning to each its place in
view of what he wants, " all things considered." The
right place for a " bad " desire often turns out to be:—

(a) Not now but later,—Wednesday's lust for baseball.
(b) Not here but elsewhere,—a desire to sleep or to read newspapers
in the shop.
(c) Not in this form but in another,—a desire for power that leads to
" bossing " instead of to preparation for leadership.

Desires are good except insofar as they fail to take account of other desires and to attempt a synthesis with them. Entire suppression of any desire or of any man is a last resort when we can find no place for them. But I do not expect this cursory statement to be clear or convincing. I shall come back to the subject later. (Chapters XII and XIII.)

When organized, our desires and those of our neighbors make the "rules of the game." Finding in ourselves and observing in others (a) a recurrent set of hasty, unconsidered, obviously foolish or undesirable ways, and (b) a set of habits that will prevent these lapses, the more sensible of us accept agreements which correspond to the rules of a game. Such are the rules of good manners, the rules of sound business, the rules of the road for motorists. Some of these are printed and have the force of law. More of them are established by mutual understandings which only a "hog" will deliberately violate, though no punishment is attached by law.

Conversation, entertainment, family life, office routine, business, education, war, in fact almost everything that people do together, comes to have its own set of rules, which help most of us to get what we want-on-the-whole. Such rules are meant to control our rebellious tendencies to go straight for what we want when we want it, irrespective of what is ahead of us (consequences), or behind us (lessons of experience), or on either side of us (other people and their desires). To guard against such anarchy there grow up trade agreements, treaties between nations, college rules, codes of ethics, laws.

2. AGREEMENTS NEED TO IMPROVE AS DESIRES DEVELOP

When social regulations grow rigid, mechanical, and lifeless, when they cramp our freedom and spontaneity, we rebel and challenge their right to govern our actions any longer. "There ought to be some allowance for exceptions," we say. "We need to keep abreast of the times. No rule was made by all-wise people and none should be immortal." Such a protest sometimes voices a blind desire to smash things and to do as we please, regardless of others' rights and of our own permanent interests. But when it expresses a recognition of new items on the bill of fare, or of new desires born out of the old, in short of mental growth, it represents the same human need that made the rules in the first place. It has therefore every right to remake them now. The need to improve our agreements is a branch of our fundamental need to grow, and, as a means to that, to remake what we have made. Football rules, trade agreements and health laws are revised from time to time and genuine improvements have been registered in such revisions. Traffic rules are extended or modified as traffic increases and population shifts. International law is changing, we hope improving, as the nations find better ways of dealing with each other.

When these changes express the urge for true growth and not merely a restless craving for novelty, the fundamental reason for them is that men and women have seen further into their needs, thus far but partially revealed in their desires or ideals. A person sits down to write an important letter to a friend. He knows in a general way what is needed, but by the time he has written out a first draft, he finds that he has left out some of the most important points. When he has added these and reread the letter, he sees that its tone is wrong. It is formal and argumentative. It is too long. It is dull. Yet it expresses something that must not be lost sight of when he rewrites it. His main point is there, though clumsily expressed. So he launches himself upon the third writing. This time the result is on the whole better; it is nearer to what he meant to say in the beginning. But he now sees that his meaning has offshoots that he was quite unaware of before. Has he, then, abandoned his original intention and run off on another track? No; that original intention is still there. But it has a life of its own, and therefore it has grown with each revision.

Any one who has tried to write, to organize a business, to carry on a friendship, or to plan a summer camp finds that it takes a long time to see the needs of the situation. They involve much that was at first overlooked. As long as a soul is alive and growing it comes upon surprises inside itself as well as in the world outside. We never know exactly or entirely what we want. We are always finding out more about it. It is an ideal sought as well as a knowledge possessed. Most of us get into trouble because of our lack of imagination or our failure to use our imagination to picture our own future and the feelings of other people. We cannot always play safe. We do not want to keep out of every adventure that may develop unforeseeable difficulties. Marriage is such an adventure. Industry, travel, scientific research, portrait painting, the study of philosophy, the attempt to write poetry—anything worth doing —is such an adventure. It can be counted on to grow upon our hands and so to spring surprises on us. But imaginative anticipation of these surprises is one of the powers most capable of training and most valuable in maturity. "Put yourself in the other man's place," we implore each other. But it is just as important to put oneself into one's own maturer future, to see its events, to hear its conversations, to taste its tang. Imagination is part of good work in ethics as well as in art and in science.

3. ALL DESIRES ARE CONDITIONAL,—EXCEPT ONE

But no one's imagination is strong enough to foresee how his purpose may need to be deflected as it crosses the current of others' needs. Hence concrete agreements should be conditional, not absolute. The only agreement that can rightly be absolute is the agreement to face the facts and to do our best. I made an engagement the other day to talk over some hospital cases with an assistant at four in the afternoon, and at half-past four to consult with a publisher about the arrangements for printing this book. About half-past three a message came over the telephone that one of my oldest friends, who had been ill for some weeks, was now believed to be close to death, though still quite conscious. It was her wish and that of her family that I should come at once to the suburb where she was and play to her some of the music that we had played together in old times. Of course I went although this meant breaking two engagements, as I could not reach by telephone either of the persons concerned. It seemed clear that their desires, like mine, would be to have those engagements broken, because there are matters of life and death that most people agree to put above all other claims. Naturally nothing of this kind was provided for when the appointments were made. But it was in the spirit of our agreements that if certain emergencies arose the appointments should be canceled. Our business could wait. My old friend's need could not. As it turned out, inconvenience was not only tolerated but welcomed by both of those whose appointments I broke, in view of the greater need.

Obviously not every new and urgent claim justifies us in breaking an earlier promise: only such claims as we reasonably believe are provided for in the spirit of the original agreement.

I have analyzed duty so far into:

(a) The keeping of agreements, and

(b) The correction of their letter in obedience to their spirit. But agreements must be *made* before they can be kept, broken, or improved. This point comes late in my argument because it is often slow to appear in actual life. We find ourselves carrying out, for better or for worse, agreements which we have never made. We seem to have been born or dropped into them, without any clear acceptance on our part. We find ourselves members of a family, students (or loafers) at a school. We have friends and enemies before we have consciously done anything about it. We never definitely or explicitly bound ourselves to any of these people. We wake up in the middle of a game which began before we knew much about it.

Then as we become more aware what we are about, our likes and dislikes assert themselves. We more or less consciously approve or disapprove of what has been done for us by parents and teachers. We rebel, play truant, or run away. We get tired of our acquaintances and drift away from them. Or if we reject none of our family's customs, it may be merely from inertia. We are used to the familiar arrangements at home and have never considered any alternative. Simple individuals and simple races go on in this way, I take it, for a large part of their lives, content to accept without consciously approving or disapproving the habits in which they have grown up. Ethics hardly concerns them.

But some day a crack appears in this smooth surface of habit. An outsider questions it. He asks you why you stick to those silly old customs, and of what use they are. He champions another set. You have always paid cash for what you bought, eaten pie for breakfast, and voted the party ticket. Your friends do the same, so that every one knows what to expect of his neighbors. It seems as natural as the seasons. But when your new acquaintance, from Missouri, asks who put you into this strait-jacket and why you stay there, you realize for the first time that you have some control of such matters and might rebel.

Or you may wake up when some of the familiar demands begin to seem to you exaggerated. More party loyalty, more college spirit, more family obedience, is demanded of you than you have bargained for. You resent it. Then comes the awareness that you don't know exactly why you do anything. Bewilderment and a general sense of dissatisfaction lead to questioning and so to thinking. This suggests more definite agreements and, still more, more clear-headedness about them. So we validate or reject the customs of our breeding. What remain are agreements made with ourselves or others and ethically binding as the old habits could not be.

But often we do not know what rules we are living under or why. Or they conflict and we are confused. Consider the following occurrence as an example of the need to make and to clear up some agreements.

> A policeman in uniform called at the house of Mrs. X, a rich widow. He had tickets for the annual policemen's ball, one dollar each. Obviously it was not expected that Mrs. X would go to the ball, but only that she should buy some tickets for her maids, who possibly might want to go. Mrs. X had the feeling that if she failed to buy she might not be treated quite as cordially by the police or even be as safe. Accordingly she bought three tickets.

In this story one seems to be groping about in a room full of steam, on a floor of cotton-batting. Nothing is clear. Nothing is solid.

(a) " It was not expected that Mrs. X would go to the ball." Who did not expect it? The police, the maids, the widow herself? And if it is not expected, what of that? Does she need to do what every one or any one expects, or to avoid doing anything that some one, sensibly or foolishly, does not expect her to do? How does she know that it is not expected? How can she find out? Presumably by asking those who are supposed not to expect it. Then why doesn't she settle that point?

(b) She " had the feeling " that failure to buy might be risky for her. Well, what then? Does the feeling rest on facts? Why not find out? Common sense depends on asking and answering such questions as these. But no one speaks. Every one tiptoes about, finger on lips.

(c) Do the maids want to go to the ball? It is assumed that they do, but we do not know. No one has inquired.

(d) Has the old lady ever given them to understand that she will give them tickets to this ball, in case they want them? Probably she does not know. But she can find out.

(e) If the policeman knows perfectly well that the old lady will not go to the ball, which is one of the settled points in this wilderness of uncertainties, why does he offer the tickets to her and not to the maids?

(f) Does he believe that the maids do not care enough for the ball to pay for tickets themselves, but will be pleased with him for getting the tickets free, by inducing the old lady to pay for them?

(g) Is the policeman offering these tickets, not because he believes that the old lady or any one connected with her wants them, but because he has found that she and others like her are afraid to refuse, lest she receive less vigilant police protection? This may seem far-fetched, but members of my classes have testified that their parents were in fact governed by just such fears, and have bought such tickets in consequence. The question is, does this particular policeman know and use these fears? We do not know, and we may suppose that the old lady does not know.

(h) Are there any grounds for these fears? I have heard it said on what I believe to be fair authority that there are such grounds. I have also heard it denied. I doubt if the old lady knows any more about it than I do. I assume that she is groping in a mist of ill-grounded suspiciousness, of hearsay, intellectual impotence, and general discomfort.

(i) Whether such fears are groundless or not, there remains the question whether the policeman has any right to be selling these tickets. He comes in uniform. Is he not supposed to be on duty at this time? Has he left his beat and its responsibilities in order to sell these tickets?

(j) But if he is not on duty but is selling tickets in his leisure time, should the city which employs him permit such use of his time and of his uniform? The tickets state that the proceeds of the ball are to be used for death benefits and for the relief of disabled and superannuated policemen. Does the city, any more than the widow or we ourselves, know that the money is actually spent for this purpose?

(k) If the money is spent on what are virtually pensions for policemen, should not the city and its citizens prefer to establish a municipal pension system and to support it out of taxation? Is it defensible to allow the police officially to persuade or tactfully to coerce a fraction of the city's population into providing a pension system which should be paid for by all citizens?

(l) Is the city providing for its police a scale of wages which is so insufficient that the police are led to beg charity from the same persons who are paying these insufficient wages, though they probably have no idea what the wages are?

(m) Is the old lady merely trying to save money when she hesitates about giving? Does she really prefer to ignore all these questions and to buy the tickets because the police perform heroic acts of service from time to time?

Our first need, if we are to guide ourselves intelligently toward right action, is facts, facts about our own desires and ideals, facts about the people around us; and our second need is more facts. Without the answers to such questions as I have asked in the preceding pages, conscience and good will are useless.   There are no reasonable agreements to be kept or broken because no one knows the essential facts. No ethical decision, right or wrong, can be made in such a situation.   The next event will be a drift, a lurch, or an oath, rather than a decision.

Before we can make even a guess as to whether the lady ought to buy or refuse the tickets, we must answer most if not all of these questions. When we have answered any one of them,—say the question whether the maids want to go to the ball,—it will be possible to take the next step. The old lady can then decide whether she has already given her maids to understand, in more or less similar cases, that they can expect free tickets. This would be some reason, though not necessarily a good reason, for her buying them.

There would still remain the question whether she had any right to buy the tickets at all. If she decides that the policeman is not trying to intimidate her or to practise a kind of covert blackmail, and if she concludes that policemen are as good an object for her charity as any that she can think of, she may feel an obligation to buy the tickets and so to give her maids a spree. There would still remain the problem whether as a citizen she should help to perpetuate a system of inadequate wages (if they are found to be inadequate), or to postpone the establishment of a municipal pension system, by buying these tickets.

As one thinks over the situation it appears to call for three steps: (a) Systematize or organize these vague understandings until they do not contradict each other. (b) Make definite agreements on the basis of adequate information. (c) Act. On reflection the obligation to make her maids a present of the tickets because she has intimated that she would do so, might contradict the obligation not to encourage the police in blackmailing the community. Or if she decides that there is no blackmail about it and that the police give just as good service to non-buyers as to buyers, another question is still open: Does she prefer to give away her surplus dollars in this way, or is she simply taking the line of least resistance, as most of us do, I fancy, when the policeman calls? Is she only trying to save herself the discomfort of imagining how stingy the policeman will think her if she refuses, and how promptly he will share this opinion with the maids?

Suppose she concludes that this is not her state of mind and that she really has a (more or less vague) plan of charitable giving to many objects, among them policemen; suppose she reasons that this plan is properly embodied in a habit of buying policemen's ball tickets once a year. Her problem would then remain: Does my supposed obligation as a charitable person conflict with my traditional obligations as a citizen who is bound to stand for good city government and not to help perpetuate by my gift an inefficient system of underpaying the police? If she decides that this last obligation ought to cancel the habit of buying the tickets, it will remain doubtful whether she can accomplish anything toward abolishing a bad system and setting up a better one, unless she is ready to take some further steps. She might try to initiate municipal action by gathering signatures for a protest to the authorities, or by requesting her local representative in the city's affairs to move for an investigation of policemen's wages, perhaps for a system of municipal pensions.

The probability is, I suppose, that she will decide (a) that she has not the strength or the influence to start such a movement, (b) that her refusal to buy tickets would only annoy the police, and perhaps the maids, and that therefore, (c) all things considered, all her agreements cleared up, collected and systematized, she may continue with clear conscience to buy the tickets.

Many of us, I suppose, are often in such a muddled state of mind as this. Our question is not whether we shall do the right thing,—keep, break, or improve our agreements. Our question is where to find the right course among a dozen vague, overlapping, jostling, or contradictory claims. To straighten out the tangle is our first duty. But, as I have said, we usually begin to wonder about it, and finally to think about it, after muddling for years through a confusion of half-perceived and half-kept agreements, the very existence of which is dubious.

(a) To make or clear our agreements.
(b) To keep them.
(c) To revise or improve them in view of new facts.

This summarizes in logical order the points which I have tried to bring out through the analysis of the policemen's ball (making clear), of *Lord Jim* (keeping), and of rewriting a letter (improving).

Is it ever a good plan to leave our agreements vague? The unwritten constitution of England, the long unformulated Common Law, Theodore Roosevelt's " gentlemen's agreement " with Japan, seem to indicate that there are advantages in not reducing our understandings with each other to exact, written form. Sometimes the spirit of a compact seems to be more conveniently maintained if it is not embodied in any rigid form. Such elasticity seems to suit the English temperament better than it does the French. The main point seems to be that the agreements should not be made clearer and more rigid than the desires and needs behind them. When we are in a tentative and dubious state of mind we should not make binding promises. When our views are swiftly changing, it is foolish to act as if we had come to a conclusion. Some understandings should be tied up as tightly as legal documents can bind them, else no one will know what he can count upon. Between this and the other extreme of utter fluidity there are tentative, partial, conditional understandings, all useful. But we must be clear about the degree and the area of unclearness that we sanction. Few of us want to tie ourselves to perfectly definite engagements several years in advance, but we need to be very clear about the limits of this freedom. If there were any danger that a friend would count on finding us at home on the Sunday after next Christmas because he found us there last Christmas, we should want to *make it clear that we are not clear* about our plans so far in advance.

1. In this chapter, after defining agreements, I recalled the obvious fact that they are the children of our desires and inherit their parents' qualities, good and bad.

2. A good agreement, based on a good desire, is *sincere*. It contains no secret reservations.

3. Moreover it is *sound*, because it has grown up during and after an effort to face the solid realities within our own lives and outside us.

4. During this effort conflicting desires may come to light. We find ourselves wanting to eat our cake and have

it too.   When it is possible to avoid head-on collisions like this and to carry out both desires by adjusting their claims it obviously wastes less energy than if one of them has to be suppressed.

5. Such adjustments of conflicting desires are the rules and laws of society and play the same part as the rules of a game.

6. Yet though they are useful in keeping order and in settling disputes, they need, like the rules of the game, to be revised from time to time as fast as improvements appear.

7. Hence all our agreements, like all our desires (except one) are conditional.   They are valid until we see a better arrangement,—" we " meaning all those concerned.   Only one desire is absolute and unconditional in its authority,—the desire to learn, to see the facts as they are and to act accordingly.

8. But agreements, like desires, are often muddled.   To make them clear to ourselves and to others is often the first need, though it is apt to occur to us late in the day.

CHAPTER III

NEEDS

In the last two chapters I have tried to show that when we are in doubt as to what we ought to do, the most serviceable tool is the question: What are our promises in this matter? If we find a binding agreement we can usually see what to do next; for the intention to carry it out is ordinarily implied in the decision to make it, as the intention to go up the escalator is implied when we step onto it.

But not all agreements ought to be carried out forever. The persons who made them may later see good reason to remake or abandon them. Perhaps they were made under a misapprehension. Perhaps two or more of them contradict. So to test our agreements we need a second tool, the question: Do they now express the well-considered *desires* of those concerned? For whatever desires once made, more reasonable desires may properly remake. The advance from agreements to desires and thence to better-considered desires brings us one step toward the ultimate reason for good action. But certainly the desired is not always the desirable. There must be some source of authority deeper than desires themselves, even the best considered of them.

1. WHAT IS AN AUTHORITATIVE DESIRE?

The direction in which to look for authority has already been suggested. Our clue is in the words *really* and *on the whole*. If we are sincere when we ask ourselves what we " really " desire among the casual impulses which arise

in us some evening after dinner, we proceed to get an
answer by soaking ourselves in the relevant facts of our
situation. Here we are in a certain latitude and longitude,
bounded by yesterday and tomorrow, by other people
and their desires, by our money, our time, our ideals,
and our capacities. These facts cannot " make " us desire
anything or do anything. But they offer us a preferred
opportunity, which we shall miss, unless we study it.
This leads us to further questions. In view of our make-up
and our situation what may be expected to happen if we
carry out the desire that now is in the spotlight? What
have others to say for or against it? Is this particular urge
for a drink of whiskey, for a place to sleep, for a job, for
marriage, for the abolition of slavery in Arabia, for humanism in America, in line with what we want on the
whole, that is, with our central and permanent needs?

2. AN AUTHORITATIVE DESIRE IS ONE BASED ON THE CHARACTERISTICS OF OUR MAKE-UP

" The ultimate basis of all authority," says Professor
Whitehead, " is the supremacy of fact over thought." [1]
I shall assume that this is true and that the best way to
search for clues about the right is to compare our desires
with the durable structure of facts, first in our own nature
and then around us. This was Aristotle's plan. He advised
us to consult the structure of the universe when we need
guidance on right and wrong. The structure of the universe takes a special form in man. Parallel to man's
build is man's function. Our mandate from reality is
built into our capacities. Why not say, then, that the
good man (like the good poker, newspaper, or ship) is he
who does what he is built to do? It seems reasonable.

[1] A. N. Whitehead, *The Function of Reason* (Princeton University Press, 1929),
p. 64.

To find the use of anything we look at it; we inquire what it is made for. You can use the toe of your boot to poke the fire; but it was not made for that and so it suffers. A poker does the work better and is none the worse for it. You can use a man as an adding machine, as a beast of burden, as ballast, as cannon-fodder. But he comes off the worse for it, because only a small part of him is functioning. No power especially characteristic of him then guides the use to which he puts himself. If he smokes like a chimney, drinks like a fish, or drifts like a cloud, it is reasonable to suspect that something is wrong in him because he is not a chimney, a fish, or a cloud. If he guzzles like a hog, snarls like a wolf, or baulks like a mule; if he is as ruthless as a tiger, as imitative as a sheep, as mean-spirited as a cur, he is fighting the main trend of his own nature, laid down in the structure of his body and of his mind.

The substance of Aristotle's advice is this:—Be guided by what you are, follow the lines of your make-up. Therefore, act like a human being, not like a stick, a volcano, or a butterfly. This principle leads us to finer distinctions, as we follow up the branches of a species. A bulldog does not excel if he tries to behave like a greyhound. He is not built for it. There are similar subvarieties under the *genus homo*. The man of action, when he discovers what he is, should be directed by the facts of his make-up to plan a life of action, not a student's or an aesthete's career. He should pick his job and shape his training for action. Then his duties will not need to be improvised; they will spring from the original bent of his nature.

But men of action are not all alike. The principle of distinction which identifies one first as human, then as man of action, leads logically to more individual choices. Granted that he is a man of action, what next? Is he an executive, a pioneer, an organizer? What ideas or energies are native to him? In what company does he feel most alive? What biographies most appeal to him? By such tests a person finds himself and his duties.

Following Professor Whitehead's suggestion that all authority rests in the supremacy of fact over thought, following Aristotle's principle that the function and the " good " of anything can be found by studying in its make-up *what it is good for*, we may surmise that the source of authority over our desires can be found by studying the facts of our human nature. Our bodies and minds are built on a plan distinguishable from that of the rest of the world. Perhaps, then, the facts of that ground-plan are authoritative, when their relatively permanent trend is contrasted with our multifarious and shifting desires. Suppose we say that these structural facts represent our *needs* and that our desires are right when they correspond to our needs, wrong when they diverge.

But the facts within us, the facts of our make-up, inevitably call our attention to the facts outside us. We need other people, we need food, we need the assistance and coöperation of reality in a thousand ways. We need to be stimulated, aroused, interested by the world around us. Bereft of such stimuli we lapse into vacancy as an idiot or the blind-deaf child does. We live by the bounty and by the calls of our environment. We need to be needed. But this aspect of our authoritative needs can better be postponed for a few pages till our structural needs have been more thoroughly canvassed.

The authoritative facts about the human nature to which we find ourselves heir, exhibit a set of trends or capacities which Aristotle celebrated as the guides to right conduct, that is, to conduct befitting a man. This idea has led us naturally, I think, to distinguish within human duty the guidance of our individual capacities as a hint to our individual duties. By finding what he is especially fit for, a person finds his chance to be of use, to earn a living, and to make a place for himself, economically and socially.

3. A CHARACTERISTIC OF OUR MAKE-UP IS OUR NEED TO HANG TOGETHER

An authoritative fact about our human make-up is our need for integration. It is a commonplace that human energies cannot survive without working together. This is as true inside the individual mind as it is in society. Our muscles need to be coördinated if we are to stand without falling. But they win this complex integration without consciousness or discussion. The conscious personality of any single man must be at pains to *bind itself* together; otherwise its individuality fades out and is overwhelmed by the powerful persons or forces around it. The man who wants to please everybody, who tries to be " all things to all men," who agrees with all that you say and all that your opponents say, collapses gradually into " a mush of concession."

Such a being is neither good nor bad, right nor wrong, because he is committed to nothing. Dante put him into the lowest hell. But he is to be pitied as well as blamed. He has stunned himself by butting into the rigid facts of his own nature, not as he would like it to be but as he finds it. We find our will impotent when physical forces control our bodies and quench or twist our thoughts. We meet another type of control in the laws of implication and contradiction. We are not free to do as we like when our will strikes against these laws. We must integrate ourselves in accord with them or cease to exist as persons who control a future and obtain what they desire.

The authority of the moral law, then, has one of its roots in the superiority of coherent life over a scatterbrained existence, of sanity over insanity. If your life is a going concern, it is so by virtue of the internal integrations, the plans and principles of action, that you have made, kept, and improved. If my life is a thing of shreds and patches, of inner conflicts and distrust, it is because there is nothing to hold it together and to feed its coherence, as the giving and taking of promises does.

It is a not improbable speculation that the imperative need of each of us to hold his life together with a plan of action is the conscious form of our biological organization.

4. TO HANG TOGETHER PSYCHOLOGICALLY MEANS TO BE ORGANIZED AROUND A PLAN AS BODILY ORGANS ARE

The ooze on the floor of the ocean, if it could organize itself, as was once believed, into amoebae and other simple forms of life, would be fixing in tissue what a person's internal agreements fix in plans. The heap of molecules would tie itself up in a plan: "You stay there at the surface and make a skin; I'll go inside and attend to our nutrition and locomotion." The body of a living creature provides its self-maintenance and resists its devouring environment because its organization settles a division of labor. There is between its parts a coöperation which, if it became conscious, would be like the plans round which a man needs to organize his life. I do not mean to assert that there is consciousness in the heart, stomach, and liver, or in the lower forms of life, only to suggest that what distinguishes life from inorganic matter is the clearer evidence of a structure in which parts are unconsciously integrated for nutrition, reproduction, and self-defense. A *conscious* plan is a kind of integration, always with one-

self and usually with others as well. In the life of man such
plans are his psychical organs.

The new-born child has no conscious plans. An idiot is
one who never grows beyond this condition. A person
without conscious internal integration would be an idiot.
But even an idiot forms habits, and habits are an early
stage in our evolution toward conscious integration. To
dress and undress mechanically is to follow a plan which
if conscious would be an internal agreement. Even to get
oneself a meal involves internal integrations. It appears
to me, then, that the moral law (Make, keep, and improve
some set of agreements and opinions) has the authority of
one's psychical integrity, which demands organization
and resists destruction even by ourselves. The authority
of the moral law is the energy of the will to live and to
learn. If you are to have an individual existence that you
can call your own, you *must* continue to recognize something in it that develops in spite of wear and tear.[1] If your
purposes were of one sort today and wholly different tomorrow, you would be nobody at all, even though your
flesh held itself together and lived on. By all the life-force
that dreads insanity and repels moral disintegration, our
minds are bound to that recognizable and persistent core
which feels the moral law of integrity.

Here we see the foundations of moral authority, the need
behind desires. No one likes to be told what he must do.
But since it is our own desperate hold on personal individuality that says, " I must get a plan of life and develop it
or go to pieces," we cannot reasonably complain of restraint. Agreements cement our life structure into a plan.
They bridge the stream of time to give us passage to the
future, support in the past, and confidence in the present.
They peg down the flapping edges of our will. Till we

[1] See Chapter VI.

agree on some project and commit ourselves to it so that we and others can know where to find us, we have no security when we go to sleep at night that we shall find ourselves again in the morning. We might miserably find somebody else. I know no worse nightmare than that. We approach its terror when we try to rebel against our vital need for an integrating plan of life.

Agreements made, kept, and improved have authority, then, because self-dissipation, which means slow psychical death, is the alternative. Goodness and badness are not frills on a conscious being's life. They are the core of that conscious life, and if one asks, "Why should I submit to the regulations called morality? Why shouldn't I do as I please?" the answer is: Because you prefer conscious, intelligent life to mental suicide or chronic somnolence. To develop this life you have to make and apply a set of regulations, that is, a morality, to yourself. For you cannot live without some semblance of a consistent purpose. You can complain to yourself and order it changed, if it does not suit you. But you cannot reasonably do as you please when the pleasure contradicts your own plans. A person who is pleased to saw off the branch that he is sitting on cannot long continue to do as he pleases because his desires cancel each other. To get what he wants, to be free, in fact to continue psychical life, a person needs to organize his life in view of the realities inside him and around him. That organization is morality, good, bad, or tolerable.

5. OUR INTEGRITY SURVIVES BY FACING REALITY, THAT IS BY DOVETAILING WITH THE FACTS AROUND US

So far this chapter has asserted that the human needs which are authoritative over our vagrant desires and so give us ground for a moral law, are to be found in the struc-

ture of our organism, (a) in its special capacities and
(b) in its inherent urge to avoid psychical disintegration.
But it is only by an abstraction that we can separate our
lives from the world around us. Our earliest and most
obvious needs are for food and for the help of other people.
The authoritative facts, then, by which we ought to shape
our desires, are outside us as well as within.

Man's structure is made to fit his environment. His
integrating function, which, could we find it, would have
authority over his chance desires, cannot be identified
without looking outside him as well as inside. He is made
to eat, to breathe, to talk, to move about on a planet that
supplies his food, his oxygen, and the opportunities to
which his muscles, guided by his senses, can take him.
Within this environment he is in a certain situation (family,
job, state of health). Perhaps he can govern his desires by
the authority of that situation which meets one of his
impulses half way but discourages the rest. Then the
" act that meets the situation " would be the right one.
Professor Dewey tells us so, and I accept his verdict as
soon as I see that he means to include our desires and ideals
as part of our situation and capable of molding it. The
" situation " includes our capacities as well as our old
friend the " bill of fare," in view of which we can choose
better than by our unguided feelings.

What we " really " desire, what is desirable, what we
need, is what we desire in view of all the facts that our structure and our situation bid us take into account. This is in
line with the ideas of Freud mentioned in the Introduction.
Whatever we do, none of us wishes to be deceived. Our
authoritative desire, if we can find it, must be one which
avoids the internal pitfalls dug by our sophistry. If we
know by heart the ancient mantraps along the road of
self-deceit (see Chapters XV to XVIII) we can help our-

selves to distinguish our "real" desires by hugging reality and banishing our "rationalizations."

In another tone Gandhi tells us the same thing. We deceive ourselves, he says, in supposing that we want to
crush our enemies, because in fact we haven't any,—*once
our eyes and theirs are opened.* If we knew them and they
knew us, there would be no more hate in the world. To
know all is to pardon all. Good desires, then, are those
founded on the truth; evil desires, on stupid illusion.
Gandhi does not expect to convince us of this. He asks
us to convince ourselves by trying the experiment; but
few are ready to risk it.

We are more nearly in the mood to accept the adventure
when we have been studying delinquents. For we find
that many of them,[1] like the neurotics and like the German Emperor in July, 1914, get into trouble because they
try to live in a world of their own, insulated from the real
world. The Kaiser on his yacht flatly refused to confer in
1914 with the representatives of other nations in hope of
preventing war. He thought he could go it alone. He
thought so because he refused to face the facts.[2]

6. BUT HOW CAN FACING REALITY CHANGE OUR DESIRES?

Our desires spring up and die down *in view of* a certain
state of things. When we find on study of the situation
that our desires are senseless, they begin to die out or to
correct themselves. For example, we often wish and sometimes try to be in two places at once; but we do not keep

[1] A remarkably accurate picture of one is "Danny" in *Mothers Cry*, by Helen
Grace Carlisle (New York: Harper & Brothers, 1930), p. 129.

[2] When Grey, the English Secretary for Foreign Affairs, tried to bring about a
conference of the nations most concerned, the Kaiser penciled on the dispatch:
"I will not go into it, . . . In matters of honor and in other vital matters one
does not consult others." (*Ich tue nicht mit, . . . In Ehren und vitalen Fragen,
konsultiert man andere nicht.*")—Emil Ludwig, *Juli 1914*, (Berlin: Rowohlt, 1929),
p. 86.

at this occupation long after we see what it is. We fume
or gloom for a time and then telephone or write a letter,
salvaging what we can of a badly-made desire, abortive
because it could not really become a plan. Any desire
tends to die of starvation unless it can be nourished by
facts. Viable plans are built up when desires come to terms
with fact, and find out what they can do. Much that is
bad in our desires is simply stupid, ill-informed, illogical,
shortsighted. In our folly we try to upset the universe
though we do not often see our attempt on so large a scale
as that because we do not think it through. Of course the
facts which our desires try to alter are not always un-
alterable but we can alter them only by knowing their
structure. Nature has a grain like wood or stone and if we
are to split it we must follow the grain. Or if we decide to
go across the grain we must find a set of tools adapted
to that particular task.

We Americans desire an orderly community where murders and motor accidents do not happen. But we have not
achieved it because we have not collected the essential
facts. We have as yet no real knowledge of the American
hoodlum, rich or poor, no understanding sufficient to
manage or to convert the wayward currents of his folly.
Our desire remains impotent for lack of tools to drive a
tunnel through the mountain of our ignorance of human
nature. We must go across the grain of its structure, but
as yet we have nothing but splitting tools in our hands:
laws, sermons, hopes.

7. WHAT SORT OF FACTS DO WE NEED?

When we ask how to distinguish what we happen to
desire from what we ought to desire, or, what gives authority to any urge within us, the answer seems to be:
Congruence with certain facts in our nature and around us.

That seems to be part of the answer suggested by Aristotle, Gandhi, and Freud. But it is still vague. Granted that ignorance is partly to blame for our shortcomings, we need to be more specific. Ignorance of what? Not of astronomy, of foreign languages, of ancient history. It is a more particular blindness that concerns us. It is an inexperience of ourselves and of our own needs. Nothing is more helpless, nothing less authoritative than a desire which is ignorant of what it needs to know. Such a desire wrings the hands of parents at the crib of their sick child. It needs something, it is crying for something, and they too. But what it needs can be known only by elaborate studies of other children in similar trouble. A doctor is supposed to stand for the focussed conspectus of such studies, accumulated in many hospitals through many years. He knows the essential facts and so the needs of action in this illness. The child's mother longs to take it in her lap and comfort it. But perhaps it needs to be let alone. She is ignorant of what she needs to know.

8. WE NEED THE FACTS WHICH KEEP US FROM GOING TO PIECES AND LINK US TO OUR FELLOWS

I believe that these examples support the thesis stated tentatively on page 72. If we ask, What is the difference between the desired and the desirable? the answer is that our desires sometimes ignore our main need. Reality enlightens them provided reality is understood to mean something that we can freely coöperate with before we learn our business from it, something that we can add to, confer with, improve on; not something that we must bow to dumbly. For any one can escape slavish submission to reality by suicide, and in hard pressed countries people do so terribly often. This proves that some desires, at least, must be satisfied if we are to take facts as a guide.

Unless reality can rouse some desire in us or link up with some desire already in us, we have no use for it. But I believe it can. It can satisfy our main need because it created it.

Our needs, then, are the tie between ourselves and the realities which feed us. Our needs orient our self-evident but unauthoritative desires. The moral law bids us follow our needs.

This law is authoritative (a) because it keeps an individual from going to pieces; and (b) because it holds social groups together. The human race must early have discovered that the " sacredness " of some promises, treaties, charters, is a matter of life and death to its members. It is necessary as well as virtuous. It is part of success in the struggle for existence. In primitive societies vital interests are nailed down by iron customs which compel hospitality to strangers, protect the life of those who flee to a shrine, and forbid marriage within the clan. These rigid rules exclude individual freedom of opinion. You and your group want to live. This central desire creates the group's unanimity and decrees the fixed customs into which its members are born without a chance, perhaps without a desire, to disagree. The real needs and the supposed needs of the *group* settle its customs and the behavior of its members. In later stages of human evolution status becomes contract. Customs become agreements.

As a member of a family, a gang, or a tribe, as a student, even an E student, as an inhabitant of a particular country and town, our habits bind us into a bunch of vague understandings, which we may keep, stretch, loosen, shift, or break, but cannot altogether escape except by shuffling off this mortal coil. Some of these understandings we recognize and validate as we grow up. Somewhere between babyhood, when conscious agreements are practically nil, and adult life when almost every word and plan tightens a structure of recognized understandings, a person goes through a stage when he has few definite engagements because he has not found himself and has not made up his mind. He suspends judgment and looks about him. One ought to be in this state about particular matters all one's life. But for the indecisive type of person it is dangerous luxury. With him any choice, even a wrong one, may be better than none. For he can usually correct a wrong choice, but he cannot improve the shape of his life till it has some shape to improve.

9. ANY AGREEMENT HAS SOME INTEGRATING FORCE; A FACT-CRAMMED AGREEMENT HAS MOST

I have tried to show that morality is authoritative because we need to bind ourselves to plans and agreements *of some sort* on pain of being gradually snuffed out if we do not. This need holds us even to bad agreements, until we have given notice that we disapprove of them and have done our best to convince all the interests concerned in them. Till this is done any agreement is better than none. But a reasonable agreement, that is, one made face to face with the facts of our situation, is more authoritative than an ill-considered one, no matter how good the intentions which made it. I sympathize with modern Italian "realists" about justice, freedom, and democracy, insofar as these skeptics mean that all promises are insecure unless they express the actual state of wills and conditions. A mere good resolution is almost as weak as a pious wish. Man is not apt suddenly to change his love and hate, nor his deep and ancient habits, by a word or a promise, no matter how idealistic and well meant. Realities are in the saddle and ride mankind. They say to us, "Don't promise more than you can perform. Don't overstate or exaggerate your ability to change swiftly the average of your previous behavior. What you can perform depends on what you are, and are growing to be. Don't speak as if you, a diplomat, could deliver the deeds and dollars of multitudes merely because you are convinced that you are right."

" He that is a liar speaketh of his own." He that is a diplomat may represent no will but his own. The actual state of things which he is supposed to represent includes public opinion, well or badly instructed. It includes national and nationalistic aspirations, as well as mystical impulses like polar exploring, personal loyalties like those to Jesus or to Mohammed, a sentiment of justice like that of Socrates refusing to escape from prison. These realities decide whether our well-meant agreements are precious or cheap. Any sincere agreement, any pledge made in recognition of what we take to be truth is better than none, but I am convinced of Professor Whitehead's thesis, already quoted, that the ultimate basis of all authority, moral or scientific, is the supremacy of fact not only over thought, but over our willfulness or our cheap optimism. When an agreement like democracy, or a treaty at the end of a war, stands for a true account of what those concerned now desire and can count on themselves to keep on desiring for a considerable period, then it is momentous and authoritative. But if it stands only for our good intentions or for the fiat of power, then it is a levity. It trifles with great issues.

When the " realities " on which our agreements rest have no more authority than the Monroe Doctrine or our American traditions about entangling alliances, or our common prejudices about leprosy, we have no reason to bow to them. When currents of feeling are swerved by fashion, by propaganda, by forgetfulness, or by a wave of mob-passion, the agreements to which they have led us have no authority and deserve to be changed by mutual consent. Habit and inertia may hold them for a time, but in moments of absent-mindedness these bonds relax and, unless we forestall it by reform, disintegration occurs.

10. THE AUTHORITATIVE FACTS HAVE TO BE DISCOVERED AS WELL AS OBEYED; OUR PLACE AMONG THEM HAS TO BE CREATED AS WELL AS FOUND

I phrase the nature of moral authority, as congruence with the structure of our own psychical existence and with our need to be needed by our fellow men, but I am keenly aware that I am writing in the midst of a period when a considerable slice of humanity finds no need for its services. Conceivably this might become permanent and general. Conceivably our planet might have been made so that if a man tried to follow Aristotle's advice he would find that he is of no use to his fellows. There might be no place for him, no call for his services, no job and no friends for him. Then his hand might well be against every other man's and every man's against him, as in Hobbes' "state of nature." I suppose that is what many a person feels when first he tries to practise Aristotle's advice even in the best of times. He seems to himself born in the wrong century or on the wrong continent. He finds no place that fits him and is forced to take a second or third place or to look on while others play the game. So far as his job is concerned he is always a misfit. In an industrialized country like America, a fair share of us are forced to seek for our own life, the life that develops the best in us, during the hours after work is over.

But any one who watches his fellow men with interest must be amazed, I think, to see how many seem in their maturity to have found and made a position almost as individual and characteristic as their features. One can almost recognize a friend's shoes or his coat after he has worn them a while. They grow to share his individuality. So it is with the other possessions into which he settles as he matures. His work, his way of amusing himself, his friends grow to fit him with surprising accuracy. A trade or a subspecies of trade that hardly existed before, a need that no one recognized tends to develop, with his efforts, around the man who is fitted to fill it. I do not believe that a place for every man exists ready-made and waiting for him to step into it. But I do think that such an opportunity is ready to be made. It develops around almost any one who keeps trying for it. Supply and demand gradually create fitness in each other.

R. L. Stevenson wrote of Burns that he died not so much of disease and unhappiness as of being Robert Burns. The habit possessed and finally overcame him. But he also lived by being Robert Burns. The combination of occupations by which he managed to make himself acceptable to his contemporaries was unique. Plowman, poet, and Don Juan might well seem incompatible ingredients. But Burns made a living of them. Emerson earned his bread by writing down stray sentences on all sorts of subjects which occurred to him as he wandered in the Concord woods. Later he packed these sentences into lectures and finally into essays, though many a sentence was, as he said, " an infinitely repellent particle." [1] Sir Harry Lauder with his contagious laughter, the women who do shopping for the rich, the personnel workers in shops and factories, those who provide storage for furniture, those who raise funds for colleges and for other miscellaneous causes in which they are not interested, the professional social workers and professional hostesses, the professional flea-

[1] *The Correspondence of Thomas Carlyle and Ralph Waldo Emerson, 1834–1872*, Charles Eliot Norton, ed. (Boston: Houghton Mifflin Co., 1894), Vol. I, p. 161.

killers and rat-killers,—all these people have invented a profession or practise one quite recently invented. New machines, radios, aeroplanes bring out marketable qualities in men. In a similar way, qualities looking for an outlet work up a demand for their employment.

I do not say that every one finds his place. I should rather say that no one ever finds it, except approximately. What usually happens is that after experimentation we settle down with some job, some mate, some set of habits for which we are not violently unfitted. Then the work, the persons and the neighborhood around us begin to develop or to ossify us according to our choice. There results a personality in a job, both colored individually.

But aren't there some real failures, people born without the intelligence or the drive to make their capacities tell? It sometimes seems as if there were hardly anything else. There are many whose individuality their fellows never discover. But the essential point, I think, is not the degree of our success or the tragedy of our failure in finding our opportunity, but the necessity of making a life out of the attempt or not at all. Yesterday's conversation with a friend, today's reading of the newspaper, the dollar you may earn tomorrow take whatever reality and value they have from the degree in which some one's thought, some one's effort there finds its place to grow and to be of use.

11. THE CENTRAL NEED TO FIND AND MAKE ONE'S PLACE

If a person's main need is the better expression of what he really is, and if it points to what he can do best both for service and for his own development, a bad desire is one that even its possessor knows is leading him away from the main need of his nature, namely, to find, make, keep, improve, and enjoy his place in the world, or more briefly, to grow. Good agreements are those which maintain and encourage growth. Our central need condemns some of our wishes as bad because they contradict others. It is the individuality of each man expressed in his desires to learn, to possess, to explore, to enjoy, and to share. It is his central self in the process of growth. Each of us finds it by looking for the relevant facts, that is, for his own capacities as his opportunities suggest them to his mind, and for the opportunities which the world offers him when he looks for them, but seldom presses upon his attention. These opportunities suggest ways in which he might spend his time, occupations he might choose, friends he might cultivate, clothes he might wear, amusements he might seek, books he might read, interests he might further develop. Among these are some labeled " yours," vaguely when you are vague about yourself and your desired opportunity, distinctly when your main tastes and talents are clear.

" Here's *your* colors," says the impartial vendor of red and of blue flags at a Yale-Harvard contest. He wants to make his wares attractive by describing them as already assigned to meet your individual need, already tagged with your name. More realistically the boot-seller tries to find " your " size in the boots which only use can further individualize until they are uniquely yours. So one looks for a job nearly one's size, with the hope that one can make it fit by working up in detail the demand that presents itself roughly sketched in. With the same hope employers look for a man approximately fit for the need they have to supply. They expect the candidate both to develop the job and to be developed by it.

Beside this sort of exploration, the other way to find one's chief need is by thinking about it. Reflective imagination brings relevant facts into view; it also brings the thinker into a state that is sensitized to see them. Is it time for you to leave college and go to work; to settle on a ranch in Canada; to marry against your parents' wishes? You seek an answer by reflection: In view of the future as you trace it in imagination; in view of your past and of the characteristics which seem to have led you to the present situation; in view of the probable effects of your action on the people nearest you: what next? Looking about our world as if it were a " bill of fare " helps us to discover what sort of choice is called for by our needs and by the need for us. The search concentrates interest when perhaps we thought we had none. Reflection criticizes, tests, and creatively develops the applicants for our attention after search has lured them from their hidingplace.

12. IN SEEKING THIS WE STUDY NOT THE WHOLE WORLD BUT OUR OWN SITUATION

Of course we do not try to look the whole world over whenever we come to a decision on what we need. We survey only as much as we think concerns us.[1] When a man says, " Well, *all things considered*, I have decided not to do any choral singing this winter," he does not mean that in coming to this conclusion he has considered all the subjects treated in the *Encyclopaedia Britannica*. He means that he has thought about, say, half a dozen ways in which he might divide his time, and decided that for the present there is no room among them for singing. He has looked over his inclinations, as he ranges the possible winter's programs before him. He has also looked to see what change, if any, comes over these inclinations as he recalls the path by which he became involved in the various activities, including music, which filled his time last winter. Into which of these was he drawn almost acci-

---

[1] The art and need of finding this slice of reality is discussed further in the next chapter.

dentally, because he was going about with a certain group of men who no longer interest him? Which of last year's doings are still in line with what he has planned for this year and, vaguely, for the years to come? He pictures the probable events of the coming winter, first with and then without membership in the choral club. He considers how his different plans would affect his ambitions, his particular friends, his parents.

When all this is done he finds, perhaps, that the singing had better be cut out for this year. On the whole he would rather not go into it. But " the whole " means the whole of a small group of considerations called up when he looks over the map, not of the world but of his neighborhood.

To guide one's desires, to combine them as best one can into a working whole, one thinks over or discusses with a friend " the facts " about one's capacity, one's apparent strengths and weaknesses, and then the facts of one's environment. Some people feel much surer about these environmental facts than about their own likes and dislikes, tastes and ideals. With others the emphasis is reversed. Most of us, I take it, would say that we have " inside knowledge " of our desires which no one else can attain. But about the facts of our own fundamental needs, and of the world's needs into which ours might fit, we have no certainty. For every such fact is seen through a theory. It is not grasped immediately like desires and sensations.

13. WE NEVER FINALLY DISCOVER OUR JOB BUT ONLY OUR NEXT JOB

A plan for the year, with its inclusions and its exclusions, is never wholly satisfactory. There are compromises in it. There are makeshifts, approximations, patches to cover a hole where nothing worth while has been thought out. It is not our chief need that is seen in this winter's plans, but its more or less satisfactory representative.

If one says that every person's central need is to grow by finding and making his place in the world, still it must be confessed that no one knows, either at the beginning of his life or at the end of it, exactly what his place is, who he wishes to be, what he wants to amount to. Progress consists in finding the next stage in one's work and in acting on what one finds. Theodore Roosevelt was more of a man when he was President of the United States than when he was a tenderfoot ranchman in North Dakota or an amateur "Rough Rider" in the war with Spain. But he would not have been satisfied to remain indefinitely in the White House, even if he had thought it politically feasible or good for the country. Into each of his adventures he threw himself with so much zest that each was for the time his job, the representative of his central need. The presidency was on the whole the most satisfactory representative that he ever found. It is true that in his later rôles, as leader of the Progressive Party, or as prophet of disaster during the World War, he showed trends in his nature not so clearly revealed during his presidency. But it is not clear that he was growing through these ventures. I think that he was marking time until he should discover his next opportunity. But death found him first, and he left the stage with much of his life still unlived.

Any distinguished man has a good deal more in him than ever gets expressed. His life means more than any or all of his representative attempts in work, play, love, and worship. His efforts indicate a direction. At best he makes masterly sketches, at worst caricatures, of that which can never be completed and never ought to be.

14. OUR PHYSICAL NEEDS ARE CONDITIONS OF OUR LIFE BUT
ARE NOT AUTHORITATIVE MORALLY UNLESS WE FIND SOME-
THING WORTH WHILE IN LIFE ITSELF

I set out in this chapter to find some authority among our
desires. I find it in certain features of our human make-up,
some of which bind a person together while others point
to our need to grow by finding and improving a place for
ourselves where we can be of some use to our fellows and
earn our way. These features I call our needs.

It might be objected at this point that if I use the word
need to label our tendencies, to capitalize the distinctive
qualities of our human make-up, and to mark a place among
our fellows, I should pay more attention to the obvious
and primal needs of food, sleep, and shelter. For these
biological needs seem to present a perfect example of
authoritative fact when they run against the current of
our desires.

A child *desires* to put a caterpillar into his mouth but he
does not *need* to do it. A baby needs its proper food. But
it may not desire food at all. It may have to be fed in spite
of its resistance. The neurasthenic adult especially needs
food, but usually has no desire for it, has in fact a repugnance for it. If he forces himself to eat, it is not from appetite but from a reasoned belief. He accepts the fact that
his organism needs food. It is hardly true to say that he
desires " on the whole " to eat. He does not desire that
under any conditions. But he believes that if he now eats,
he will in time regain his appetite. He says to himself,
" I want to get well and I am convinced by what my
physician says that, if I am to recover, food is what I
need." Under these conditions his desire to live involves
not a desire to eat but a decision to eat despite repugnance.

A nurse needs sleep after she has been on duty for thirty-six hours. But she may have no desire to sleep. She may have tired out her capacity to feel fatigue. She may be "running on her nerve." She knows what she desires without a ray of doubt. But she may not know her needs; she may have to be persuaded by friends that she needs sleep, and so ought to go to bed.

The biological needs which we know best are a bunch of *conditions without which life cannot continue*. Our economic needs are almost as imperative. Civilized men cannot live as they want to unless they can use each other's supplies. Economic needs are the hypothetical results of a desire to live decently. If we care to live we need to be nourished. We need to get up and work if we are to keep our job. We need some knowledge, if we are to get along, though we only desire it from time to time when we are in difficulties or when we are inspired by others' wisdom.

These examples seem to show that all our "needs" issue from a central authoritative urge, the will to live, which does not fail even if we have lost our appetite for food or for sleep. This conclusion is in line with an impressive ancestry of beliefs. That *the central object of life is "life itself,"* and not any single element in it, such as virtue, knowledge, beauty, pleasure, harmony, or reason seems to be the verdict of many of the wisest men in history. Jesus came, he said, that we might have more *abundant life*. Schopenhauer found us dominated by the *will to live*. Herbert Spencer and the biological tradition which follows him, makes self-preservation or "*survival*" the main urge in evolution. Bergson called this urge the *élan vital;* Freud, the *libido*. Guyau, Croce, Unamuno, and John Dewey appear to me to agree that "*life itself*" *is the fundamental need of man and so his most authoritative desire.*

In this chapter I have tried to show that our agreements need to be standardized by something more authoritative than our own desires, some of which cannot stand up under criticism. I have proposed the hypothesis that *our needs* supply the authority required. But so far I have not tried to define a need nor to give any definite account of what it is that we need. When speaking just now of our need for food and for sleep, even when we do not desire them, it appeared that what we *then* desire is life. In arguing that we need mental integration to preserve ourselves from mental death, and that we need to join forces with our fellow men if we are to preserve our civilization, have I not shown that behind all our needs, uniting and characterizing them all, is the will to live? Can we not say with truth that we have but one authoritative need, one central desire,—to live? Is not life itself our dominant need?

The idea has great attraction. It jumps with current biological beliefs: that the mind is part of the body, and the body part of nature; that through contact with nature in science and in art our minds can take their proper place and so can develop our civilization; that we are at our best when we " feel most alive." " Life " is something that every one can recognize as in some sense his need. It is not a priggish or a snobbish ideal. It does not ignore either the physical or the mental element in us. It does not isolate us as ascetic ideals do, from nature, for surely we are kin to all that lives. When we exalt " life itself " as our central need we take in the impulses for knowledge, for beauty, for freedom, and so for joy.

15. THE SEVEN SPECIFICATIONS FOR AN AUTHORITATIVE VALUE IN LIFE

" Life itself," then, seems to include much of what we need as our authoritative aim. It is:

1. Catholic enough to take in all the powers of all sorts of people.

2. Biological enough to link us to nature and so to science and art.

3. Enfranchising and so enjoyable.

But there are two specifications of a main need which " life itself " does not meet.   Among other things we certainly need:

4. A source of authority over particular desires.

5. A medicine for self-deceit.[1]

We need an object *in* life by which we can steer ourselves. We need an antidote for our poisonous tendency to fool ourselves.   Suppose then we say that our main need in life is to " face reality."   There we have a phrase that meets these two specifications, as " life itself " does not. But the five specifications so far listed still fall short of what we most need in our *Summum Bonum*.   We need also:

6. A principle of rebellion and reform.

7. A recognition of individuality.

16. THESE SEVEN ESSENTIALS ARE COMBINED IN THE IDEA OF GROWTH

I can share the modern enthusiasm for the idea that " life itself " is the authoritative object in life, provided I am allowed to go a step or two behind the words towards what I think they mean.   Without this, the belief that " the object of life is to function " [2] seems to me too hospitable, too soft, and too lifeless.   We are not eager to encourage *all* life; some of it is clearly bad.   The mob spirit can be very lively at times.   So can the bacteria of disease, the fleas, the cockroaches, and the rats.   Men are seldom more alive than in anger, in war, in panic, or in jealousy.   They function actively enough then.   But we

---

[1] That this is one of our central needs will not be clear until we reach the chapters on self-deceit (Chapters XV to XVIII).

[2] See Hornell Hart, *The Science of Social Relations* (New York: Henry Holt & Co., 1927), Chapter III, p. 15.

prefer other functions.   For an authoritative object *in* life we cannot choose life itself.   Its abundance must include not merely survival but selection.

Selection involves discipline as well as spontaneity; rejection as well as acceptance.   We prefer civilization to barbarism, though both are " life."   In the biological sense life is shown in degeneration as well as in progress. Insanity, idiocy, chronic disease exhibit as much life as their opposites, but not the *kind* of life which we believe to be good.   Life, vitality, or health is like a crude ore from which we can extract the metal that we value.   What we care about in life is not merely fecundity or survival, but progress in certain directions which seem characteristic of humanity at its best.

We do not always desire life, nor desire it at any cost. Otherwise there would be no wars, no suicides, and no heroism.   We desire and respect a particular element in it and that element I believe is growth, progress, development, in every individual along the lines indicated by his powers as well as by his relation to other people and to nature.   In these ways reality guides us.   Life is at its hottest when we are gaining on chaos.   We want abundant life, but " abundance " does not mean a huge quantity. It means more of the right kind, and that is the kind which furthers every man's growth.

A good desire then is one which pushes us on through agreements one step into the needs,—our own and other people's,—which our situation just now presents to us. These needs are always for self-maintenance through growth, because, as I shall try to show in Chapter V, the attempt to stand still and take things easy produces a decay which we all abhor.   The right, the desirable, the standard by which we may improve our agreements and test our desires is the action in line with the characteristic needs of our mental and bodily structure in its relation to our environment. I have suggested, without trying yet to make it plausible, that *the need to grow* is the center from which all our special needs branch out. In the next chapter I shall describe four invitations in response to which our sense of what we need becomes vivid. Here I end by defining a need as a form of growth.

Chapter IV

THE REVEALING OF NEEDS

Our sense that we have any particular needs (beyond food and shelter) is not always awake. Desires are self-evident. Every one knows whether he is hungry, whether he is sleepy, whether he wishes to loaf, to go home, to get away from home, to get a job, to get married. But needs, and especially our central need of growth, with the assertion of which I ended the last chapter, are not self-evident. Only a piercing experience brings them to the surface of consciousness. In this chapter I shall describe four searching experiences which find in us what is often deeply hidden. Our needs are revealed and our desires shrouded: (a) in emergencies, (b) in scientific truthseeking, (c) in creative art, (d) in education.

1. THE STIMULUS OF AN EMERGENCY

Few things impress me more than the power of certain emergencies not to paralyze but to rejuvenate us. In a fire, in an earthquake, in an epidemic, some are incapacitated by horror and waste themselves in outcry or ineptitude. But if any leadership springs up, the majority of us are at our best, not only in strength of will and muscle but in readiness to take a risk, because the emergency makes us feel others' needs as our own. If there is time to think of oneself at all, one's dominant feeling is, "This is the real thing and I'm glad to be in it. Pain here is better than pleasure elsewhere." One forgets that one has a body, a tempted and a resisting conscience, a checkered past and a dubious future. One finds oneself at last a "going concern."

Of course no one can live in a perpetual crisis, and no one wants to solve his problems at the cost of others' suffering. I recall the experience of response to emergencies for the light it sheds on duller days. At such times there is no leisure and little choice of path, because our latent need to be of use then becomes dominant, responds to others' needs, and for the moment overshadows our individual preference. We are simplified in a like way by the zest of sharing an athletic game, where little emergencies keep arising. There we can throw our strength into a single endeavor because in the heat of play our internal conflict, our doubt of the future, our regret for the past are forgotten as they are in emergencies. Selfishness and unselfishness are transcended because each man wins in the victories of his team-mates or suffers in their defeats. No wonder that athletics dominate the other activities of college life. The athlete feels in the game an obvious need for what he can do instead of a traditional demand that he shall develop himself for educational goals that he can scarcely see at all.

Needs, when we realize them, are imperative and authoritative. They show up the weakness of ethical theories which base duty solely on the ideals or desires of the better self. Such self-initiation sounds too easy and soft. It hears no commands from reality outside us. Wordsworth described a different experience when he called duty " stern daughter of the voice of God." Any one who shies at Wordsworth's theological terms can find the same austerity in the morals of polar explorers. Robert Scott's forlorn five, stumbling back half frozen and half starved from the South Pole in March, 1912, obeyed a command as stern as any which a theist hears in the voice of God. They kept step with a dying comrade on the march though they knew that to match his painful slowness might cost them their lives, as in fact it did ten days later. But they also knew that it would be base to leave him. They stayed with him till he died, almost in his tracks. Such a situation issues commands. And if we believe that it is some need of the world that calls us, what more majestic voice could we hear? If it is not God's it is the same voice with another name.

Heroism meets us in almost every newspaper. Almost every screaming fire-alarm rouses latent heroism in some one not otherwise remarkable. In a collision, June 10, 1930, between the steamer "Fairfax" and the tanker "Pinthis" the "Fairfax" caught fire off Marshfield, Massachusetts. Some of the passengers leaped into the sea in terror of the flames. The crew were disorganized. Lester Kober, a "wiper," went to the deserted engine room. Ordinarily it was not his duty to be there. He was not supposed to understand the duties of a fireman. But just then there was danger that the boilers would explode. At the investigation the following facts came out:

> "There was lots of smoke in the engine room, wasn't there?"
> "Yes, there was."
> "And it was dangerous to remain there, wasn't it?"
> "I don't know, sir. I'm no judge of that."
> "But you stayed, didn't you?"
> "Yes, sir."
>
> He said that he could not tell why the fireman and oiler could not have stayed as he did. When pressed to state whether he stayed from a sense of duty or because he did not have more sense, he answered simply, "I saw that someone was needed there." [1]

What call is there for heroism in ordinary "unreligious" men? *The call of need.* You have no desire for a risk that may cost your life, but you hear the voice of the situation:

[1] The Boston *Herald*, June 19, 1930.

" Here is your job. Take your place." Ordinary inclinations have nothing to do with it. This need is of another kind. It is a pull from something outside you, independent of your likes and dislikes. Some one must take this risk and you are the only one in sight.

But who knows that the call of need is a fact? It does not really speak. Well; the physiologist treats organic needs as facts, though no one can see, hear, or smell them. The need of an injured heart valve calls leucocytes out of the bone marrow and the liver, calls the heart muscle to thicken itself and carry a heavier load of work. If unconscious amoebae and muscle cells can obey the call of need, why should not a conscious human being risk his life when he sees the need? Sometimes it moves us; anyway it pushes against us. And when it is felt not only as a push but as an impulse, it has roused a desire. But this is a desire of a peculiar sort. It ignores our pleasures or convenience. It feels like an impulse rooted in forces outside us! Yet it is not really outside us. It must be inside us or it could not set us in motion.

One's obedience to the need of an emergency is free. It is not the push of slavish fear nor of sheer compulsion; there are almost always respectable ways to ignore it. Nor is it a reflex action like a wink. It is a conscious decision, though no one stops to ask himself whether he wishes to go on. The element of desire emerges chiefly when any one else tries to hold us back. Then our urge to get on with the job rises to a passion. Hamlet throws off the friends who try to stop him from following the command of his father's ghost:

"Unhand me, gentlemen!
By heaven! I'll make a ghost of him that lets [hinders] me!" [1]

[1] *Hamlet*, Act I, Sc. 4.

2. THE CALL OF TRUTH

We understand better the pull exerted on us in emergencies by the world's needs, if we recall how men have felt the need to live and perhaps to die for the truth. Men have borne torture and death rather than deny their beliefs. A good many men would bear torture rather than let the good name of one they love be smirched. Here is no emergency, no human life to save. It is only the truth that calls; yet we should loathe ourselves if we denied it. With self-respect gone, life would not be worth living. We are not anxious to die, but will not avoid it at such a price.

In modern times martyrdom for truth is usually gradual, not sudden. When a man of science slowly wears out his life, as Darwin did, in the pursuit of truth, his sense of imperative need at critical stages of his research is almost a tyrant. It banishes opposing desires; it makes a monk of him; it gives him almost superhuman endurance. Yet if one were to ask him, "Exactly what are you after this morning?" he might say, "I don't know. I want *whatever turns out to be the truth* which this crucial experiment will reveal. It may be a flat denial of what I have been looking for. It may explode the beliefs in which I have been working, or show at least that in this field of work there is no sign of their truth. If so, *that* is what I want to know." Negative evidence satisfies a positive desire because it turns one off to look elsewhere. It shows that our present road is the wrong one. Pasteur's experiments showed that spontaneous generation of germ-life in a lifeless fluid like sterile milk did not occur, as had previously been believed. The gradual appearance of life out of the lifeless, as the current theory of cosmic evolution still seems to demand, found then and finds now no support in experimental science. That negative goal Pasteur won; and it was the goal of his desire.

This desire, to find and to record whatever the evidence seems to prove, is fairly common among laboratory workers. But it is a very queer sort of desire, for it is actuated by nothing definite. It wins even when it loses. Whatever the evidence shows, life to one's hope or death to it, that is what this odd desire seeks. Its preference seems curiously like indifference. All " personal " interests are so irrelevant to it that scientific men are apt to say that in their work they are governed by no desires, no wishes, no values. Truthful, not wishful, thinking is their goal. To describe and organize facts, they tell us, is the whole of their business. Others may pursue subjective ideals. In this mood they forget their one dominant desire, to learn something. This ideal they prefer to their minor wishes. But what is a desire that is not a personal desire? *It is, I think, a sense of need freeing an elemental impulse to grow.* We call it familiarly enough the " desire for truth." But we scarcely realize how strange it is that anything so bloodless can rouse us to lifelong effort.

Certainly there can be a sort of bloodlessness in concentrated scientific work. Pasteur spent his evenings pacing the corridors outside his laboratory, meditating on what he had recently found and planning new experiments. Though his wife and children lived on the same floor of the same building, he hardly saw them except when they acted as laboratory assistants. Yet what a furious flood of energy poured out of him! For weeks at a time a single question would bore into his mind and dig out one ingenious laboratory experiment after another. The whole series floated on a current of energy such as few can house in their tenement of clay. Pasteur's energy flowed out in response to his sense of need. Yet he was hardly aware of any desires of his own. He believed himself the servant of science. The need of more truth governed his thoughts and his hands, so that his center was outside him, yet not in any tangible object or place. Like Garrison when the mob threatened him with death because he would not stop attacking slavery, Pasteur knew what he had to do. The needs of his time, his country, and his work were rooted in his life. They were his will. Yet he was doing what he preferred to do. His choice was free. His desire to learn was unconditional.

It seems, then, that the energy to find truth and the impulse to do whatever is needed in an emergency, have something in common. In both a man feels himself commanded by a need. The scientific bent gradually creates a person who must hunt the answer to his questions. His aptitudes and the call of the situation make research his job. His " personal " desires are not altogether abolished. The hope to verify his own pet hypothesis, the itch to have his name known, still spring up around the main need. They may crowd it out. But in the better type of scientist they are dominated by the urge to learn.

Given this unconditional desire, he can take his orders from facts; he can be glad even when they disappoint him, glad not at the moment but soon after. This apparent contradiction is familiar enough. If a stranger roughly pulls you back after you have started to cross a street, you are indignant until you see the motor-truck from which his quick jerk saved you. He gave you the truth about the traffic and saved you from the consequences of your mistaken hypothesis. So nature frustrates the investigator who starts off on the wrong track, and in the end he is thankful for the check.

3. THE NEED TO EXPRESS TRUTH IN ART

Creative work in art frees a similar sense of need. It commands us; it is also ourselves. Sincere artists, when they are not potboiling, try to be candid, that is to say, they mean to express the truth, not by copying anything but by fidelity to their vision. They set down what they see whether others like it or not. The right phrase, the right notes, the right line come out of a sense of necessity. They need to be thus and not otherwise.

The test of a writer proposed by Thackeray in his preface to *Pendennis*, is this:—"Is he honest? Does he tell the truth in the main? Does he seem actuated by a desire to find out and speak it? Is he a quack who shams sentiment and mouths for effect? Does he seek popularity by claptraps or other arts. . . ? *I ask you to believe that this person writing strives to tell the truth.*" (Italics mine.) This artist like many scientists felt himself commanded by a need to express the truth. But unlike the scientist, this artist looked not only at his fellow creatures but into himself and his own emotional experiences as he faced the universe. He was true to these. He felt their need to issue in a piece of work that added something to the world. As in an emergency or an exploration he heard the call of adventure.

Of these three basic and permanent human adventures, heroism, scientific ardor, and creative art, I shall have more to say in the chapter on The Supermoral. Here my point is that in them personal desire is concealed by a telescoping of fact and act. One does as the facts bid and does not bother about one's own desires. By a similar tropism less vividly felt, simple, hard-working people carry on much of the world's daily routine.[1] They seem

---

[1] " Without these cannot a city be inhabited, . . . they will maintain the state of the world."—*Ecclesiasticus*, 38, verses 32 and 34.

hardly aware of any desires of their own. They do what is to be done. More self-conscious people feel the call of need as a will of a higher order. Whatever the need requires, whatever the truth may be, wherever perfection lies, that is desired.

4. THE NEED OF EDUCATION

In these three urges we feel our central need. We recognize it distinctly when the revealing invitation comes to us. In others we can be less certain about it. But in the tremendous business of *education* we venture to be certain of children's needs even when they themselves are in the dark about them. We are even surer about buried needs in the sick. We dig for them beneath the surface of obvious facts and desires. When we try to find a sick man's organic needs, when we try to follow in his needy tissues the call to which his desires no longer correspond, when we persuade him to be pinioned on his back in a plaster cast (for spinal tuberculosis), or to give up the food he most craves (in diabetes), our faith in these apparently cruel procedures rests on confidence that we know his body's needs. They are not obvious. The sufferer has no inkling of them. They are unconscious physiological events hidden in his tissues and recognized by his doctor only in the light of other cases studied, some of them years before or in far-off countries.

As in the sick body, so in the educable urchin. No desire for learning is evident in him. The need of it is hidden deep in his nature. Probably he needs education, discipline, and hard work. But he does not long for them. He wants to play. You send him to school. How then can you defend such unnatural compulsion? By logic something like this: (1) This child has the usual human capacities. He is not feeble-minded or diseased. (2) Experience shows that normal children usually profit by education which they do not desire. (3) Therefore, probably, this child will. (4) Therefore he must go to school.

Centuries of experience with all sorts of normal children have convinced us that they have valuable capacities: curiosity, imagination, appreciation of beauty, courage, and self-control, which they do not dream of and so do not desire to develop. It may take years of work and faith to get the development which they need and which others need from them. But the experience of the race proves that it is worth while to dig for this gold, by faith in the child's capacity. Education is like boring for oil. Experts tell us that others have drilled into strata like this and have been rewarded. So we spend money and energy without immediate reward, believing that in this year's lot of school children, deeply concealed beneath the surface of their childishness, there is capacity to be interested in history, in music, or in physics, and a need to develop this capacity.

This drilling process which we call education needs faith in the unseen, based on experience. Good teachers insist on believing that scholars need much that they do not desire. Yet this educational faith rests on a theory not verifiable in any child when his work starts, seldom completely verified in any one, owing to lack of time, poor backing at home, poor teaching, and perhaps poor material in the person himself.

As we grow up we take charge of the digging ourselves. We know that our parents and grandparents have found themselves when they shouldered the responsibilities of self-support, marriage, and citizenship. Therefore we believe that we can. Do we itch for these responsibilities? Not at all. We hardly know what they are. But we itch to amount to something; we intend to hold up our end as well as the next person. Most of us can admire some-body or something, and whatever we admire exerts on us a pull in that direction.

Bound up with the dim sense of our needs there is an urge, not for concrete enjoyments or achievements, but for emulation and so for standing among our fellows. We hope to be of use somewhere, to take part in the world's work, in short to find out where we are needed. Where this hope will lead us next is all the more obscure because it will certainly be along a path that no one else can follow as well. If we are really needed, despite the crowd of other probably abler people who now jostle around us, it will be because at some crucial point we differ from and so can excel the rest. Faith that we are individual, though we seem just like every one else, is logically and vitally neces-sary though hard to maintain. We make our start in baby-hood very much like every one else. Our differences gradu-ally emerge till before we die we may be painfully aware of them. But before that there is a long period when we see no trace of originality, no particular capacity, or special perceptiveness in ourselves. Yet we need to find it. Our livelihood, our capacity to make ourselves agreeable and to find zest in life, depend upon discovering how we can supplement others by seeing freshly into the needs, tastes, and opportunities around us.

Our needs, then, are obscure. When not revealed by emergencies or by a strong natural bent, they have to be sought below the surface of what we facilely desire,—sought by the process called education:

(a) Because we are human and so need in our growth the accumulated heritage of the human race, if we are to find a place abreast of our fellows.

(b) Because we are *uniquely* human and so must find our vocation on a path which no one else can show us.

In this chapter I have set down a group of basic experiences which seem to me to have one character in common: they search us to find in us the act which needs to be unleashed. In each case the actor feels a sense of relief, when his occasion sets him free. It is essentially the same need, I believe, that calls us and is called on in us in all these cases; namely, our need and the world's need for growth. To grow we must live. When fire, flood, or pestilence endangers lives which our act might save, the world's need of life boils up in our muscles. For each person who is in danger looks forward with hope to a future; he clings to life for what it still may bring. He may never think of his own growth. He would be rather priggish if he often did. But he grips a hopeful future, when he can work out something new and good for himself and for those dear to him. Such a future is what I call our growth. Because of such possibilities we care for life, our own or others'. In emergencies human possibilities are on the edge of disaster. We too are human. We feel a stake in others' lives, because any life is valuable. That stake becomes the sense that we are needed.

The urge to find truth whether it disappoint us or not, voices man's deep need to learn, and to push on the world's knowledge. Scientific ardor is one of the urges of growth by which our love of life pushes us on, governing individual whims and wishes like a master. Martyrs have died for truth as they saw it. Investigators wear themselves out for truth as they find it. The world's need has become their root desire.

It is less clear perhaps that the sincere artist tries to meet the demand of truth; for he does not copy actuality. But he is true to his own feeling, and that feeling, when he is sure of it, governs his will. He cannot change it; he obeys it and by such obedience he creates something new.

A child's need of education is obviously his need to grow. Our only doubt is whether there is anything there to be educated. We take generous chances on this because we are certain that nothing else is so important as the measure of development,—great or small,—that may be called out by an effort based on faith. This development is *the* good, so our efforts say. It is the central human need, the unconditional or authoritative desire.

In emergencies, in the search for truth, in creative work, in creative education, the vital need of growth commands our other desires. In athletics and in any congenial job the need which we answer is a need for fun or for skill rather than for progress. But the pleasure of using this skill is kept alive by new tests. When work and play become mere routine the zest usually goes out of them. They are continued as duty not as fun. Maintenance as well as novelty is necessary in growth; but when the fire of life begins to cool, maintenance may be all that we are good for. Then we keep our agreements though we cease to improve on them. That is the beginning of stagnation, which is slow death. Stronger life will soon have to push us out because we have ceased to grow. Till that happens we must hold on, supporting or encouraging others' growth, preparing to die as decently as we can, when we are needed no longer.

The theme of this chapter is that the need for us is revealed afresh when life, and with it hope, are at stake, when we can serve truth or beauty, and when we can further another's growth in education or anywhere else. In the next chapters I shall try to say what growth means and why it includes all our other needs.

Chapter V

THE AUTHORITATIVE NEED,—GROWTH

Say that our all-inclusive need is *growth*, and I think we can make it fulfill the specifications of an authoritative aim in life. The word may have to be stretched somewhat, but it will not burst. Growth presupposes life and is, I believe, the act and consequence of facing reality. But, further, it is the life of the learning self and so it takes a reforming attitude towards reality, at any rate in ourselves. Live creatures sometimes stagnate and so degenerate. The only way to conquer decay and to avoid stagnation, itself a slow decay, is by growth. We need to go forward by learning. For this end we need to face reality. But what then? Having faced facts we must take our part in developing them.

To grow one must survive. Self-preservation, with the physical needs that it entails, is a condition of any other work for a living organism. But the only self that we can preserve is the learning self. "Facing reality" is the dullest and vaguest phrase on earth if *any* reality will do. The reality that we need is that which recognizes our individual needs and issues to each of us the command: Come my way from the spot where you are.

Nothing could be triter than the assertion that we ought to grow. I am not saying that. I say that we cannot *intend* anything else. When we try to stand still or to fool ourselves, we go backwards, which no one intends. Therefore the only motion we can fully intend is onwards. What we mean by "onwards" is the next subject in this chapter.

1. MAN IS DISTINGUISHED BY AN EXCEPTIONAL CAPACITY TO LEARN AND BY A TENDENCY TO SWIFT DECAY

It is generally agreed that man is built so as to express in his mind and in his body certain functions related to his environment. His needs are these functions. Beside other creatures he is distinguished by some of his needs; linked by others. He needs oxygen not because he is man but because he is a living aerobic creature. He needs tools because without them he cannot manage the sort of life which distinguishes him from other animals.[1] He needs education if he is to be civilized. Without it he remains a savage.

What we believe to be man's needs will depend on how we interpret the data of anthropology, psychology, philosophy, and history, so far as we know them, and on what we think of human nature as we see it in our fellow creatures and in ourselves. From the study of historic human trends and of outstanding men and women, from whatever we know of human culture, and from our reflection on what we see around us daily, we can hardly fail to draw some conclusions about the needs of civilized man.[2]

As we emerge into civilization we seem to me distinguished by the capacity to learn and by the tendency to decay. Civilized man can gain indefinitely, not in stature, weight, or strength, but in knowledge of his world, in affections, aesthetic appreciation, and in the organization of his energies, individual and collective.[3] He can also fool himself more and degenerate faster than any other creature.

---

[1] I do not assert that no animal except man uses tools, but that the habitual use of varied tools is characteristic of man.

[2] I realize the element of bias or of error inherent in any one's attempt to say what men chiefly need. Another looking at the same facts might see no trend in them. Or he might say: " Not growth but happiness is what we most need. We are best adapted to our world when we are happiest." But on that principle I do not believe we should ever have emerged from savagery.

[3] " What distinguishes men from the animals and some humans from other

Our senses, our emotions, our thoughts, our impulses offer us something to learn from week to week. Thus urged we have built institutions, sciences, arts, skills, intimacies, appreciations, which conserve our connection with the past and welcome the teaching of the present. (a) *Whatever conditions surround the use of our capacity to learn* (for instance, warmth, food, water), and (b) *whatever forms our learning capacity assumes* in response to appeals from experience, forms such as work, play, love, humor, suffering, joy, beauty, religion, science, art, *are what I call the needs of human life.*

Even before we reach the rudiments of civilization, our impulse for self-preservation becomes the hope of something beyond bare existence. Carried along with our desire to live is some " standard of living." A standard of living implies a critical attitude about our use of time. In prison men " do time "; in fashionable clubs they kill time; while waiting for trains they waste time. But our need to grow expresses itself in our restlessness when we think we are not getting anything out of our time. We try to turn a prison, a college, or a spare hour into something worth while because growth or the means to growth (rest, relaxation) is what we seek. When no purpose is advancing, when time does not bring progress in something which we care about, our central need rebels.

2. THE ATTEMPT TO STAND STILL PRODUCES PSYCHIC POISONS: SELF-DECEIT AND ISOLATION

In support of the belief that our inclusive need is to learn (or to grow) by facing facts, it may be said that if we do

humans is the inclusion in their natures, waveringly and dimly, of a disturbing element which is the flight after the unattainable, that touch of infinity which has goaded races onward, sometimes to their destruction."—Whitehead, *loc. cit.*, p. 51.

not learn we are apt to be slowly eliminated. Time and the human organism will not stand still. Life sprouts new threats to existence, new diseases, new insect-blights on crops, new automobiles, new excuses for war, new economic catastrophes. The Esquimaux and other isolated races may avoid them for a time. But even they are in danger. The old ways are no longer secure. Any race that is not to be eliminated (and no race desires it) must defend itself by shifts and devices that are pretty sure to develop brains of a certain sort. Nothing nobly ethical about this so far. But brains of any kind have limitless possibilities not only for foxiness but for constructive thought, for imagination,—in short for growth.

Of course we manage to resist a great deal of the growth that is implied in our impulses, our ideas, and our plans. But our world is pretty sure to prod us if we live, not in Tibet or in Timbuctoo, but in civilization. It urges us to move on. Our neighbor stirs up our dormant ideas because he thinks differently. He may be as lazy as we are, but not in precisely the same place or at just the same time.[1] When we fail to learn from the experience which confronts us, our neighbor is apt to jog our elbow because we are in his way. Our archaic opinions or our immobile conduct plague him until he protests.

Or the jog to our inattention may come from within. A new mood, colored by the " internal weather " of body-chemistry, reveals our familiar habits in a new light. Then democracy, sex, war, and education look different to us, and if our organic obstinacy does its part in presenting our old view side by side with our new one, a growth and not merely a shift of prejudices may occur. Thus time itself calls to our drowsy ears and presses on us

[1] In a society of savages or feeble-minded people the *focus* of many persons' laziness coincides.

our need to learn. We resist, but it forever threatens our defenses because it has a confederate within the walls, a crescent tendency within us which conspires with the stimuli outside.

Of course this urge does not always win. We have ample capacity to forget, to drowse, and to fool ourselves. We loaf, we drift, we explode, we repeat ourselves, we become alcoholic. Thus we absent-mindedly pull down a structure which in fact we do not want destroyed. But we do not often notice this destruction. We usually keep it out of sight, though it still works away there to undermine us.

A special outgrowth of the laziness which resists our growth and threatens our neighbors is self-deceit. Our civilized brains give us a remarkable capacity to deceive ourselves, which is quite as characteristic of modern man as its opposite, the capacity to learn. Self-deceit expresses the resistance of " the flesh " to the urge of " the spirit." The adult body survives the attacks of climate and the inroads of bacteria because it can preserve or restore its balance. " Homeostasis " [1] the tendency to resist change, is the principle of bodily health.

The normal body absorbs enough to maintain itself and stops there. Its ideal is to stagnate. But stagnation ossifies and desiccates the mind. It becomes more mechanical and less mental if it is not vitalized by learning something from day to day. We cannot think the same thoughts, see the same faces, and run through the same habits week after week without going to sleep mentally; and sleep, beyond our daily allowance, is mental degeneration. In mental life homeostasis is the devil. It is represented there as the desire for mental comfort. We fool ourselves because it is

[1] W. B. Cannon, *The Wisdom of the Body* (New York: W. W. Norton & Co., Inc., 1932).

easier to do so than to face the facts. The notion that our shabby behavior is inevitably forced upon us, that there will be plenty of time later to do what needs to be done now, and that other people do not need our help because they are not really suffering much,—comfortable homeostatic notions like these favor our laziness and resist the urge to grow.

Balance, the virtue of the adult body, is thus the vice of the mind. What preserves the body destroys the mind by weakening our specifically human capacity to outstrip ourselves. The boundless truth around us presses in upon our ignorance. But if we let it in, we may disturb the comfort of our stagnation. Growth may involve growing-pains. Keep disturbing facts out of sight and we can live easily, cosily, pleasantly. So we deceive ourselves by turning our attention away from the reality of our shortcomings. If we face it we cannot help growing. But we can veil our faces from it by daydreams, by recklessness, or by any other sort of self-deceit. Still the facts and our own central need are at work and produce obliquely their effects in us.

In the attempt to shut ourselves away, we can say: " I am not at home; I have taken a vacation from ethics" (the moral alibi, p. 285), or " This is not my office hour; come back later " (procrastination), or " I'm here but I can't see you. I can see no further than the door " (selfishness). " No duty to learn need apply. I see no such need." Thus laziness, sophistry, spurts of recklessness slip in by the back door while we shut out facts at the front. (See Chapters XV, XVI, XVII.)

Self-deceit is favored, as already suggested, by the special capacities of a *civilized* brain. So is growth. It is after our intelligence has developed beyond the feeble-minded and our economic requirements are decently provided for that growth (or decay) can be rapid. So long as our brains and energy are used up in keeping us alive we do not learn much else. The stagnant people are those who are isolated by feeble-mindedness, by geography, by economic necessity, or by all these conditions at once. Such people are relatively untouched by time because they see in their routine so little that has not happened before.

The dull, the isolated, and the self-deceivers can avoid growth as the insects seem to have avoided it for thousands of years. The non-human world moves but slightly, backward or forward. Even within the human race progress is not clear except in periods and in races strongly tinctured by the desire to learn. Civilization grows as knowledge grows. It does not long remain civilization unless it keeps learning. In his more sensible periods man accumulates and passes from generation to generation a part of his gains. He also destroys, forgets, suppresses truth, murders his own soul. Even in the midst of plenty he can degenerate faster than any other mammal because he is built to grow and not to attempt stagnation, which kills him. Thus good which is growth, and evil which is self-deceit, fight it out in us.

3. FORMS OF GROWTH

The ways and the conditions of growth are man's needs. They are as many or as few as we care to distinguish. He can grow in knowledge, in skill, in the capacity to experiment, to appreciate, to enjoy and to create beauty, in self-guidance and self-organization, in sympathy, in imagination, in serviceableness, and in many other ways. But since each of these interpenetrates the rest it is arbitrary how many we name. Among the conditions of his growth, as already suggested, are physiological, economic, and psychological supplies, food, water, shelter, a temperate climate, and other people. These special needs, the conditions plus the forms of his growth (which are also his duties), express his central need to be what he was made to be.

A. In what may be called " *logical growth* " we:—

(a) See something that starts up a purpose or an idea in us. (Premises.)

(b) Act on this. (Experiments, conclusions.)

(c) See something more as a result.

(d) Get a further idea or plan.

(e) Act on that; and so on.

To " see " includes being roused by interesting facts. These include, as already said, (a) one's own agreements, affections, capacities, desires, one's stage of growth, personal equation, and bias; and (b) the opportunities offered by the situation, as it is or can be made, including its history up to date and the present facts about the people or things concerned.

Action in view of this includes (a) making plans, contriving experiments or hypotheses to develop the ideas which one's knowledge of the situation suggests; and (b) putting questions, verifying hypotheses, building something, framing legislation, and minding our own business. This is scientific progress; it is also moral progress.

After some advance has thus been obtained one takes another observation and the process starts afresh. Such a spiral type of growth, which uses the same dodges again and again as it goes on, characterizes any lively conversation. Each listens to get the point to which the other has brought their common topic. In view of that, he says something to develop it further. Then he listens again; and so on. The dialogue may be question and answer, or a series of suggestions each based on the last and trying to carry it further. In a talk that is worth while something develops. Each grows, at any rate in knowledge of the other. If the interchange is especially fruitful each learns more about the subject in hand.

When a scientific investigator works on his problem he sees something, plans, acts, sees more, plans better, acts again, and so on. Pasteur, after reading up and verifying by experiment the chemistry of the tartrates, had an idea about the difference between the tartrates and the para-tartrates and the reason for their different behavior toward polarized light. Acting on this notion, he planned an ingenious experiment which verified it, advanced our knowledge of these salts, and suggested the new science of stereo-chemistry. Then some germs got into one of his tartrate solutions in which two sorts of crystals had been precipitated. Soon after the arrival of these germs (*penicillium glaucum*), one set of crystals was found to be gone, presumably eaten by the germs. In view of this fact and of all that had preceded it in his research, Pasteur framed fresh ideas and new experiments about the appetites of germs and about fermentation. In view of the results of these experiments there grew up in him new ideas about the cause and cure of anthrax, a disease then rapidly killing off the French farmers' sheep. These ideas he verified by experiments, and so stopped the epidemic of anthrax. With the new knowledge gained in this campaign he planned further research which laid the foundation of aseptic surgery and led him later to find a cure for hydrophobia.

Through the growth of Pasteur's chemical, bacteriological, and medical knowledge he advanced from seeing new facts to imagining probabilities, and from this to trying them out. Thence he won new facts and so new ideas, new verifications or disproofs. By this logical method he worked on, until his growth was checked by old age.

In the growth of competence in any field of work the same spiral ascent can sometimes be traced. Smith's blundering attempt to speak in public leads to criticisms and so gives him clearer knowledge of what he lacks. In view of this, he practises in private. Then he tries public speaking again on the basis of increased practice and clearer awareness of his faults. Partial success and partial failure redirect his effort to eliminate particular faults; then comes a new venture, and so on.

B. *" Jumpy," rhythmic, or intermittent growth.* The logical unrolling of an inductive science is not the commonest sort of growth. The increase of skill or of affection often moves by " jumps." A head of pressure accumulates unnoticed till suddenly it forces us on. Looking back we can see the growth. Something like this happens when after long staring at a geometrical demonstration we suddenly see it. Sometimes we jump backwards. Many of our advances have considerable elements of retrogression in them, caused by error or by wrongdoing, by suffering or sacrifice. In the development of a poem or a melody the writer makes false starts, writes and destroys, develops luxuriantly, prunes, reshapes, shifts phrases about, though a single developing " idea " links the whole process together, as it does in experimental research. But because suggestiveness is of the essence of art, the artist, unlike the investigator, does not try to develop all the implications of his idea; but leaves each appreciator to develop them in his own way.

Ideas like skills or appreciations may develop in secret and then " jump." The " jump " to a new idea is sometimes precipitated by chance, as it was when germs happened to get into Pasteur's tartrate solution. But the " jump " will not come off unless thought and keen hunger for truth have prepared a special resiliency.[1] Then mind and circumstances jump together.

C. *Coöperative growth*. The development of good team-work in industry, in athletics, in friendship, or in marriage has been best described by M. P. Follett [2] and those who have followed her advice. Elliott D. Smith [3] has formulated her idea in two maxims to prevent industrial conflicts:

(a) Get together.

(b) Get the facts.

By " Get together " he means: Listen to the other party's views as a means to developing your own, and present your own as a means of developing his. This process, by which people mutually evoke the deeper layers of each other's experience, works well only when a common interest has brought the group together and underlies the discussion of their difference. Because this common interest exists industrial conflicts are more preventable than political conflicts. Two political opponents cannot both be elected. Their interests are opposed and their desire is not to get together but to find out which can eliminate the other. So it is in most debating contests. But employers and employees may find a solution which profits both. A shortened working day is presumably such a solution in certain industries.

When reasonable men differ, each of them supposes his opinion to rest on facts. But if they are facts for one man they should be facts for the other. They are not supposed to be private because they are supposed to be true. But

---

[1] " In science chance favors only the prepared mind." R. Vallery-Radot, *Life of Pasteur* (Garden City Pub. Co., 1926), p. 76.

[2] M. P. Follett, *Creative Experience* (New York: Harper & Brothers, 1928), Chapter VII.

[3] Elliott D. Smith, *Psychology for Executives* (New York: Harper & Brothers, 1928), *passim*.

each party may be looking at a different set of facts. Therefore when people differ and when both wish to get the truth, they may come to agree if they have the common sense to pool all the facts appealed to by either side. When scrutinized in common some of them will be found untrue, others will be verified; still others reinterpreted. Facts do not contradict; and so when a residuum of verified data is finally reached it should govern the opinions of all.

In medical disputes we say: " Get the microscope; demonstrate your specimen." When the disputants have both had a look they often come to agree. So in other matters when opinions differ and when we pool all the facts on which these differences rest, we find that to " get the facts " is to get together in opinion. This in turn brings better acquaintance between the parties and so assembles a new set of facts: the qualities of your group, their strong and their weak points, their habits of mind, their field of experience, what they take for granted, where you diverge on fundamentals, where you can hope to agree. If things go well you find out also more about yourself. You discover which of your ideas are peculiar, which are trite, which are illogical, which are convincing, which fall on deaf ears. You also see more deeply into the ramifications of your own ideas.

In profitable discussion each member discovers gradually which part of his idea is essential to him, and which can be eliminated without serious loss. An idea has a " soul " and a " body." There is (a) a vital nucleus and (b) a part which can be dropped without disaster. Two clashing ideas can unite, as two germinal cells join in the process of fertilization. Their two nuclei mingle to make a single fresh nucleus which intertwines strands from each, arranged in a new pattern. The protoplasm around the nucleus of each then falls away and a new cell-body is sprouted by the new nucleus.

So when men hold opposing opinions about their common enterprise each can:—

(a) Discover the vital nucleus of his own belief.

(b) Unite that with the corresponding center of the other's belief.

(c) Work out from that point a plan to develop their common offspring.

Here is an example of two plans apparently irreconcilable, yet ultimately united by discussion. In 1922 a negro student applied for a room in the " Freshman Dormitories " at Harvard, obeying the rule which requires all freshmen, except under special conditions, to live there. His Southern white classmates objected that they should not be compelled by the rule of residence to live at close quarters with a colored man. There seemed to be a deadlock. Harvard did not wish to abandon its rule as to freshmen's residence. The Southern whites argued that in joining the college they did not expect that this rule would compel them to live at close quarters with a colored man. The nucleus of the colored man's claim was his right to live in the freshman dormitories. The nucleus of the Southern whites' contention was that they should not be compelled to live beside a colored man.

Reduced to these essentials the two ideas were not incompatible, and a plan satisfactory to both was found. In one entry of a dormitory tenanted chiefly by Northerners the students were asked whether any of them objected to having a colored student in that entry. None had any objection. The negro was accordingly assigned to that entry, out of contact with any student who objected, yet in enjoyment of the same privileges as the rest. The college authorities took care to select one of the best and

most popular dormitories so that no one could say that
the negro's quarters were inferior.

In this settlement each side secured essentially what it
desired and neither surrendered anything vital. Had the
negro insisted on the right to choose any room that he
could pay for, even if it was next men who objected to
him, or had the Southerners insisted that they would not
live near any building which housed a negro, then the
two contentions would have been incompatible. But because both sides were reasonable enough to yield in non-
essentials, they secured a settlement agreeable to all and
superior to either of the conflicting claims as they at first
appeared.

In such a growth of better coöperation, whether in friendship, in industry, in a musical organization, or in athletics,
I have often verified the three simultaneous and reciprocal
activities suggested by Miss Follett.[1] Simultaneously

(a) the persons come to *understand* each other better,

(b) they become *united* more closely, to push on their
common task;

(c) they *evoke* each other's
powers to think and to act,
because they strike sparks from
each other.

Thus the whole endeavor
grows.

No one of these elements
precedes the rest. Each works
in an organic or functional relation to all the rest simul-

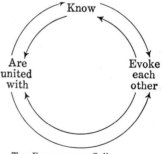

THE ELEMENTS IN COÖPERATIVE
GROWTH

taneously. The members of a congenial group of people
working together get to know each other better as they
grow more united in the service of their job and become

[1] In unpublished lectures.

more united as they grow more intimate. Their mutual stimulation of one another's ideas knits them more closely into a working team and increases their understanding of one another. Their greater intimacy and closer integration multiplies their power to call out one another's best.

Another chapter in the history of such a coöperative growth begins when the total group of, say, five members breaks up into smaller parties of two or three, more stimulating, intimate, or united in certain respects. These intimates talk over the problems of the whole group. After such subcommittee-work the whole committee moves on faster when it meets again. So it has often happened in the work of the League of Nations. So a football team often splits into smaller groups which rehearse with captain, coach, or special partner their particular part in the game. Even in solitary practice a member may come to better understanding of his own strength and weakness and so to a better integration of his faculties, till each calls the rest like a physiologic hormone. Then each has grown and can better contribute to the growth of the team.

Finally the team as a whole develops by meeting the challenge and learning the ways of other teams. Leadership is here largely mutual but there is nothing to exclude the continuous and special leadership of some individual within the group or outside it.

D. In the New Testament the idea of growth appears in the metaphor of sowing seed and reaping the harvest. "Whatsoever ye sow that shall ye also reap." Sometimes the harvest comes as a surprise. We sow suffering, mourning, persecution; we reap not more suffering but increased power to bear it, a power developed out of adversity, as muscle grows out of physical toil. The link between seed and harvest is the fact of growth under the stimulus of attack. In biological terms, immunity is built up as the organism resists invasion.

Sometimes growth is the direct increase of seed sown in fertile soil. Sow insult and you have two angry men instead of one. Sow mercy and you receive it. Sow " the sword " and perish by the sword. This is not the development of an immunity, as in the Beatitudes, but the growth of a contagious vitality or a contagious evil, caught by other persons. Growth under stimulus, germination in good earth, and the rapid but feeble shoots from shallow soil are contrasted with degeneration, but not with passive stagnation. Passivity, as in the fate of the man with one talent, issues in the loss of what he tried to keep.

Is growth too hospitable and undiscriminating an idea to stand as the moral standard? Weeds grow as fast as flowers. The skill of pickpockets, the mutual jealousy of nations, and the rapacity of "veterans " seeking a bonus grow at least as luxuriantly as intelligence and good will. But of the human forms of accretion just listed none is an example of growth under my definition [1] because they are predominantly self-destructive. The " self " destroyed is the integrating agreement between desires within a person, between a man and his fellow men, between nations or between groups. If any one does not like to call such incarnate desires a " self," he can call them agreements instead, and say that none of these cases portrays growth because they all destroy agreements, whereas growth constructs and maintains agreements.

When these disqualifications are clear I see no case of growth that is not good, and I see nothing absolutely good in the world except growth and the means to it. Any single form of it may have to be suppressed (like laughter

[1] See Chapter VI, p. 149.

in church) because it interferes with another form more essential to the life in which one has agreed to take part. One cannot do everything at once. Perhaps the best form of growth is that which makes two purposes grow where only one could grow before. This is the organization of contrasted purposes into mutually supporting harmony. Such organizations are the state, the family, the orchestra, the university. When a man helps to build such a growing organism of growing parts he reaches his highest achievement.

Summary. When we say that the object of life is " life itself " we mean that the object of life is growth. We achieve it by facing reality and drawing its power into ourselves. Our make-up fits us peculiarly either to grow by learning from reality or to decay through an attempt to rest in self-deceit. The slowest form of decay is stagnation, which is a virtue in the non-human world, including our own bodies, where it supports the growing parts of us. The most stagnant races are those most isolated by geography, climate, or mental limitations. But contacts with others lead many to degeneration, not to growth.

We have as many needs as we have capacities that can develop. Our needs are as similar and as unique as we are.

Outstanding forms of growth are:—(a) inductive reasoning, (b) the " jumpy " accumulations of skill, (c) the coöperative mutual development of a working group, and (d) the germinative character-reactions described in the New Testament.

In the next chapter I shall analyze more closely the elements of the idea of growth so as to arrive at a definition.

Chapter VI

GROWTH AND TIME–CONSCIOUSNESS

Growth is, I believe, the most characteristic aim of civilized man. He cannot help meaning to recognize things and people as they are, unless he commits intellectual suicide. But for a creature with memory " the things that are " refuse to stay the same. They are always being added to, even if he chooses to shut his eyes and keep them shut. In harmony with these facts, a creature with human eyes and a human brain is a creature built to learn. When he refuses to learn he pulls himself down. But no such rebel, I believe, intends to commit *slow* suicide. The act is swift when it is intended.[1] At any rate, the person who closes his eyes to facts does not intend suicide. But if he keeps them open he can aim at nothing but new experience. So far as I see, then, growth is the only thing we can *intentionally* aim at. We can aim at ease *per* stagnation or self-deceit; but that results in slow extinction, which we do not intend.

The will to face any sort of reality turns out, then, to involve the will to grow. This intent is latent much of the time, but it can be dug out and roused to an unescapable desire like the love of truth and justice.[2] Many of us are often only half awake. But in proportion as we are " all there " we know that the desire to see what is before us and to learn from it where to go next, expresses our central need. Without this we should be mentally dead; our minds

[1] The political prisoner's hunger strike is an exception; but he has a cause to die for, and lives in his growing cause.

[2] See Chapter IV, " The Revealing of Needs," and Chapter XXII, final page.

live because we desire it and we desire it because they live.

Apparently, then, the only sort of life that we can seek with any chance of getting it is the growing life. The remaining questions are how, in what direction, how fast, how continuously we choose to meet the inevitable challenge of time. Individuality and environment supply the answer, whether we hear it or not. The fit growth for each one of us is the growth of his nature from where it now is to what it now lacks.

1. FIVE FEATURES IN THE IDEA OF GROWTH

The notion of development implies that something hidden, as in a seed, a child, or a musical composer, gradually emerges. In this process I see five characteristic features: (a) A thread of continuity between what emerges and what stays behind. (b) Something new but (c) not predominantly self-destructive. (d) A change that meets the need of the situation just then present in an individual and around it. (e) Furtherance through success and through failure. I will comment on each of these features.

A. *The continuity of a plan.*

When we reap what we sow we gather up not merely the seed itself (as the words say) but a harvest of new grain integrally connected with the seed by *something which persists despite changes or because of them.* What can such a thread of connection be? So far as I see, it can only be a purpose, followed out by our mind or by our tissues, though in the latter it is by faith, not by sight, that we onlookers can grasp the thread. The growth of habits in a person, of institutions in a society, if they are growth and not mere " happening," are, like invention and scientific progress, the fruit of turning attention on what was not noticed before. Attention creates new life, because thought is

part of life. The grip of Pasteur's attention on his purpose
to understand the development of living microörganisms
and their relation to disease and death, gave continuity
to his growth and developed new life in his own character
as well as in the laboratory where he worked.

When we say that a character develops, we mean that
in the realization of some purpose the person is going
forward. In the " growth " of cities, on the other hand,
it is hard to tell progress from disease. They often enlarge
and degenerate at the same time, like the human body
when pituitary disease increases it to a giant's size. The
larger the giant, the sicker. " Growth " in weight due to
dropsy in heart disease is ultimately fatal to the sufferer.
If there is purpose behind these changes we do not see it.

In like ignorance of any rational plan we gape vulgarly
at the tallest building or the biggest fortune on earth; we
quake stupidly at stellar space. It is as cheap to wonder
at the bulk of the universe in time and space as it is to be
thunderstruck by the number of square feet of canvas in a
painting. If the universe were merely vast, we should be
mean-spirited to wonder at it. Its huge size might be a
gigantic idiocy. So it is with our " bigger and busier "
cities. No continuous or reasonable purpose is served by
such weedy " growths " as these. Their visible enlarge-
ment is no more proof of growth than an increase of rust
or of rubbish.

The continuity of purpose which is an essential part of
the idea of growth is never visible. When we speak of any
visible growth we can mean only a visible increase, which
may in truth spell degeneration and death to the creature
concerned. The only growth that can be distinguished
from its opposite is that of a known intention. Even in
the " growing " body of a child, an animal, or a tree,
though we hope that some aim is being fulfilled, we cannot

be certain of it. Their tissues *may* be running wild like the cells in a tumor. Only in our minds and in mental products such as institutions, sciences, works of art, and games, can we trace evidence of growth without obvious limit. In the human body we see no reason to believe that its function is to go on gaining in temperature, moisture, size, or weight indefinitely. But unlimited gain is just what we see called for in the nature of our minds and by their relation to the learnable truth, the appreciable beauty, the admirable traits about us.

The continuity of growth, then, is not something immediately visible, audible, or appreciable by any sense. It is an interpretation of what we see. We might have seen, during Gandhi's twenty-one day fast in 1924, that he was taking no food. But we could not have seen that this fast carried out the central and continuous plan of his life, which did not then need food, though his body did. To regenerate human nature in himself and in his countrymen, he needed just then to fast. But only by knowing his purpose could we know how he then needed to act.

Nevertheless growth, if we are to believe it genuine, must have some tangible results. When a person has the habit of going into trances he may protest that through these trances he is growing in wisdom and in virtue. But we are not convinced, unless words and behavior give us some tangible evidence of it, in him or in others.[1]

B. *The appearance of novelty.*

When any creature grows, something new emerges. His present stage is not a new appearance of an unchanged character taken out of a box or unwrapped, as in the metaphor of evolution. If you tie a string to a stone and let

---

[1] Akin to the loose use of the word " growth " to mean a quantitative increase and nothing more, are the still looser phrases in which we say, for example, that it is " growing dark," when all that we mean is a gradual change, not a growth or a decay.

it swing back and forth like a pendulum or make it re-volve in a circle about your hand, there is constant change but no growth because there is no new expression of purpose in it. Yet the swing of a fashion from shorter skirts to longer, to shorter, and so on, or the swings in govern-mental control from strict to loose and back to strict again, sometimes lure the unwary to fancy that the form of growth called " progress " is going on, especially if one fixes attention on one relatively short phase of the cycle. From the veering of fashions, from the shifts of the seasons and the variations of the weather, we distinguish the growth of knowledge, of character, or of a melody because something believed to be no repetition or cycle but a genuine novelty appears, without losing continuity with what has gone before it.

C. *The purpose continuously expressed in the new stages of any growth cannot be predominantly self-destructive.*

If this were not so we should call the process degenera-tion or suicide. But there is always loss. The later stages of growth rarely if ever include all the earlier ones. It is not simply a process of accretion. Parts of it are destruc-tive. (" *La vie c'est la mort.*") I suppose the most perfect growth is that of a mind following out logical implica-tions of an idea through reflection and experiment. But in the growth of character we see only approximations to logical growth. Even when logical implications [1] are de-veloped it is not the truth that grows; it is the person who

---

[1] *Implicit.* " Said of an element or character of a representation, verbal or mental, which is not contained in the representation itself, but which appears in the strictly logical (not merely in the psychological) analysis of that representation. When we think of the Antarctic continent as real we do not stop to reflect (or go on to realize) that every intelligible question about it admits of a true answer. But when we logically analyze the meaning of reality, this result appears in the analy-sis . . . Whether what is implied will or will not be suggested by the contempla-tion of the phenomenon in question is a question of psychology." —C. S. Peirce, *Dictionary of Philosophy and Psychology*, ed. James M. Baldwin (New York: The Macmillan Co., 1911), Vol. I, p. 525.

comes gradually to see them. Suppose the person is an ideally logical one. Then his very concentration on his problem involves for his growing mind the loss of opportunities in other fields. He may lose his sensitiveness to music or to literature, as Darwin did. Perhaps a life that keeps all its old interests alive in some form when it adds new ones, grows more truly than one which drops some of its earlier interests entirely. In the better types of growth the older interests survive at least in specimen when they are displaced by new ones. But in any case there is much loss.

Self-destruction, then, goes on in us side by side with growth. Loss and gain are not alternatives. Both go on at once in consciousness as they do in our tissues. In hepatic cirrhosis tissues are destroyed in one part of the liver and rebuilt in another simultaneously. It is a race between life and death. Can new cells be turned out and fitted into position faster than their fellows are destroyed? If so the organ and its possessor survive. Otherwise they die. During the years 1915 to 1917 the destruction of English shipping by German submarines and the simultaneous building of new vessels in English and American shipyards raced each other, as disease and repair race in the cirrhotic liver. Doubtless the life of any human being presents to the clear-seeing eye this momentous race of creation and destruction.

Here are some of the losses involved in the attempt to grow:—

(a) We clear the ground in order to get started on a new enterprise. We cut forests, burn underbrush, drain swamps, kill bacteria and counter-revolutionists. We clear away wretched slums to start a building reform. We banish our random thoughts and impulses. Sometimes we destroy more than we create.

(b) Even when growth proceeds steadily there is destruction bound up with it. In the child's apparently growing body, countless cells die daily and the new material of its food comes from other lives destroyed. Presumably it is the same with his mind.

(c) Growth in knowledge or in character involves some purposeful forgetting of items unessential to its aim. It is three steps ahead and one backward. In waking hours no one forgets everything; but there is much that one intends to forget, like newspaper items or faces in a crowded street, because they give us nothing to take hold of, nothing to work into any plan. Memory is highly selective. It intends to drop much that it holds for an instant. But when it *drops what it intended to hold* it drops one part of us into the grave. Because such dying is apparently a part of every life, our life-gain is net, not gross.

But if we are right in believing that we have grown in our knowledge of medicine and of mathematics, in our sensitiveness to suffering and in our mutual understanding of each other across economic barriers, then there has been net gain despite our loss. In medicine some valuable knowledge in diagnosis and in treatment drops out and is forgotten in every decade. But more is added, and so it is reasonable to believe that our medical resources are growing.

D. *Timeliness.*

In the idea of growth we need to recognize, beside the elements of continuity and of novelty, beside the predominance of gain to purpose over loss to purpose, *a fourth factor which I shall call timeliness*. It is the person's obedient but original response to the needs of the moment both in his own mind and outside him. Timely recognition of just where we are and what we need *now* in order to carry on the particular projects already started in us, is an essential element in growth, because the next stage in each individual's development is linked up with two moving series of events,—one inside him and one outside. To grow he must make his acts fit into these two moving series as they are at each moment of his action. In the time-context or history of his growth there is at each moment a step to be taken now because it is called for by the logic of the present. In view of what this instant presents to each of us *and to him only*, the next step is to be planted thus and not otherwise in the moving series.

I shall exemplify this first in the series outside us, beginning with a case in which misfortune leads a person to miss his step. The blind man who tries to step up again after he has reached the top of the staircase is not advancing. He is not carrying out his growing purpose but only something like it. For his self-defeating purpose includes the image of a pseudo-environment (another step) which is not there. He takes a step when he does not mean to take one. Like him is the deaf man who talks loudly when he means to whisper. He is getting in his own way as well as troubling others. The blunderer who is blind to the social atmosphere, to the political situation, to the awful *faux pas* which he is making, puts his foot in it and is caught in the trap. He does not find *his* opportunity though he has taken a step. His individual purpose is not the reason of his act, as in moral growth it must be.

But growth includes not only the power to shape an act in view of one's unique situation as it is, but to reshape it after a blunder. A singer who tries to give intelligent pleasure may find that he gives only pleasure, or that he gives pleasure only to himself when he wishes to give pleasure to himself and others. His purpose is so far baulked. But if he grasps the situation rightly he can undertake another venture with better aim. He can grow in his professional aim.

We grow when we know enough to grasp our present opportunity and switch the forces of nature into the service of our purpose. In these acts we take up into our purpose energies and elements from our environment as we take in our food and drink. We do not grow unless we understand, not only our own persistent purpose, but the material world around us and in our bodies so that we can see new ways to fit each into the other. The inventor and the artist are not only possessors of inspired ideas but shrewd and penetrating students of the materials available around them and in their minds and muscles. To face the reality in ourselves and the reality outside ourselves, and then to burrow into the nature of each so as to fit it to the other, is an essential for virtue, for growth, and for any creative work. When we see that our ideas have reached a point where they fit into some of the currents of opinion, of electricity, of trade, of other people's educational needs, we can take part in them and they in us, each forwarding the other.

I will take as examples of this interchange our utilization of

(a) gravitation,
(b) respiration,
(c) habit,
(d) vocabulary.

We keep our aim steady and are enabled to approach it in part because we are physically so heavy that we are not blown away like dead leaves. Perhaps if we were as light as they we might in time find ways to tie ourselves down or to do our tasks on the wing. But it is convenient that we do not need to. We have learned to take advantage of gravitation and to get its aid in our plans, though on long marches or on steep climbs it handicaps us.

The fitness of our bodies for life in an atmosphere like ours is another advantage that our efforts have often very little to do with. Most of the time we do not control our breathing. If we try to quicken it, to slow it, or to stop it except for a short period, nature calls a halt on all our purposes by making us unconscious. Ordinarily it serves us so long as we submit to its habits. But when one plays a wind instrument or uses a mouth-suction pipette, the particular relation of our lungs to the outer atmosphere is made to subserve the purposes of our art. In this case our development is possible because with the aid of our weight, our breathing, the heart's action, and the repair of tissue during sleep, our flexible purpose bends itself around, over, or under obstacles, and so coöperates with a group of physiological processes almost inflexible in their habits. We favor or impede these useful processes, though we cannot guide them in detail. Most of their work for us is a free gift or a necessary condition of our physical existence.

We voluntarily surrender to habit, or to the working of physiological linkages outside our conscious control, a large part of our locomotion and nutrition. Once as children we picked our way among alternative ways to walk or eat. Now we choose only the main design. The detail is carried out unconsciously. By choice, then, a large part of our history is habit-bound. So far as we know, this has to be so in order to set the higher command free. If most of our attention went into managing our arms and legs, the materials of action as well as the action itself would have to be shaped by us. But it is one of the conditions of growth that the shaping purpose shall have some materials to shape, some resources accumulated by past growth and not the issue of that moment's energy. One is free to write out an original idea because one does not have to make the muscles, blood, nerves, senses, the language, pen, ink, and paper with which it is written.

When we write or speak we find our materials because we profit by past growth, others' or our own. Every crescent act lays an egg. These past gains are at hand for our omelet. Our "own" words which we choose, combine, emphasize are the tools of our trade. We have learned to use them. This means that they are in our vocabulary. Our vocabulary, like our trained muscles, is ready at call; but our words and gestures do not automatically force themselves into our sentences as a manic patient's words do, often to his surprise, sometimes to his distress. Our words are at hand, but they do not force our hand. Our vocabulary means our accumulated experience filed away in verbal symbols, ready for use. It is like a nail or a hammer, made by another, capable of being used by others and for other purposes. But we can pick it up, and when we have learned its use we can make it serve our purpose in an original design. So we pick up a handy word, not ours except that, like the nail, we have it at hand. We have learned how to find it and how to use it. That learning is itself also our tool and so part of the material of free action.

In such acts we rise on stepping-stones of our dead selves. By means of thought-habits no longer consciously directed, we direct the conscious thoughts of the moment to create a new fragment of life. Yet our materials and our habits are not dead because they are still controlled by us negatively. If a serviceable habit came up in the wrong place so as to block our dominant purpose of the moment, we should still recognize it and check it.

These examples show how the growth of any creature depends on absorbing the energies and getting the directions which he needs from the world around him. Through his lungs, through his stomach, and through his five senses, he picks up from moment to moment what his purpose just then requires from animate and from inanimate nature. When he is healthy and wide awake he aims to feed himself from the supplies, physical, economic, intellectual, aesthetic, religious, which he needs for his growth. To get isolated physically is to starve. To get isolated economically is to starve. To get isolated socially and intellectually is to starve. But no one wants to starve. Our central need to grow, then, requires us to absorb and transform the particular realities which are arranged around us, into flesh and blood, into the knowledge, character, beauty, or skill which are the next stage of our growth. The need issues in science, in morals, and in art.

Even Crusoe on his island faced the central need to keep himself alive by plans and undertakings. But under ordinary circumstances mental growth comes chiefly when our minds are penetrated by the minds of others. We get much of our mental fiber, not by solitary browsing on the nonhuman world, but by fertilizing our gains with those of other people. Much as we are members one of another in our economic relations, we are still more closely intertwined in the process of growth, of enjoyment, and of invention. One person's mechanical invention, his musical theme, his philosophic idea, his good spirits issue from another's. Each lifts part of the crushing weight of ignorance; together they roll it away. One gets the trick of invention from another's invention. When we see another do his bit of imagining, or of generalizing, when we watch him pull out a plum or catch a fish, we are roused, not always to imitate him, sometimes to vary the trick and to try it ourselves, in accord with our individual capacities. When we write original music, verse, or prose,

when we plan a crucial experiment, when we give a truthful answer on the witness stand despite a temptation to lie,
the purpose which at that moment represents our character
is married to this moment's opportunity and issues in a
fresh bit of reality.

So far I have drawn my examples of the organ of timeliness in growth from our success in fitting an idea into the
physical and physiological environment, or, as we say,
in seizing our chance. *But our chance has to be pursued
within our own minds as well as outside them.* Within each
individual the sensitive spot which can recognize his
own needs at each individual stage of his growth, is the
growing edge, the sapwood of his development. Yet it is a
very elusive spot. Most of the time it is lost. To know
exactly where he stands at any moment, what he knows
and what he does not know, what he loves and what he is
indifferent to, what jokes he sees, what work rouses his
energy, what persons he can look up to, is for each man the
center of his need, the greatest thing in the world, but one
of the most difficult to grasp. For it is new and strange
even to the man himself. " When good is near you, when
you have life in yourself, it is not by any known or accustomed way; you shall not discern the footprints of any
other; you shall not see the face of man; you shall not hear
any name. The way, the thought, the good will be wholly
strange and new." [1]
In the adventure of growth it is life or death for a man to
know exactly where he is. Yet this place, which sounds ab-
surdly simple to find, is missed by most of us most of the
time because we are afraid to stand alone there. Perhaps
no one else sees it. We may be mere fools in thinking that
we see it. We all fear ridicule and loneliness and so we seek

[1] R. W. Emerson, *Essay on Self-Reliance.*

shelter in familiar commonplaces which because they are common are not ours. Yet unless we know just what place we have reached in knowledge, in power, in control, we do not know what to do next.

I once watched a feeble-minded child trying to find the one crescent-shaped hole in a board containing several holes of various shapes. He had a crescent-shaped block in his hand and for nearly a minute he tried to jam it into a lozenge-shaped hole. Then his teacher called to him sharply: " *See what you have in your hand.*" He looked at it dazed, surprised, then enlightened, and almost at once he found the crescent-shaped hole and fitted in his block. The hole was not the block but it fitted it. This dilemma and the escape from it seem to me symbolic of the central drama of each person's growing life. If he can see what he has in his hand,—interests, capacities, opportunities,—if he can see his own present situation, he can find the next step in his growth. When he looks for facts to fit (or refute) an hypothesis, success depends on having an exact image of what he is hunting for. That gives a clue to the sort of experiment that will verify or upset it. It is a sort of foreknowledge because it issues out of a past of the same sort and clears the track for the next station.

If we make the sharpest picture we can of what it is that we want to find, then nature is full of suggestions that verify or refute it. Then luck helps us because our minds are sensitized to see what others would not notice. Because of this, the person who asks advice often finds his answer as soon as he sits down before the wise man and formulates the question. Till that moment nothing drives him to picture exactly what it is that he wants to know. Probably it is already in his own mind, in a nook, round a corner. Roused by his own questions and by a good listener he can step round the corner of his mind and find his answer there. We know (obscurely) what we are going to know (clearly). So our search and our growth give us a grip upon the future. When we have learned this by experience the whole process of search is lighted by the zest of pre-attainment.

But a man cannot carry on his simplest daily routine, far less grow, without fidelity to his own private vision. Of course he needs to be enlightened by all he can get from others, but in the end he must judge whether they are wise or not. He can escape this only by hiding his head in the sand. If he accepts the help of others he is no safer than the wisdom of his own judgment that they will guide him truly. It is our own sense of the fire's heat that tells us when we are getting too near it. It is by the sensations in our own feet and leg muscles that we walk without stumbling on rough ground. It is by our own share of humor that we see or fail to see a joke. Others may be keener but they cannot do our laughing for us. No one can laugh for us, learn for us, or grow for us. That is private. Faithfulness to the private message of our senses, of our sense of humor, of honor, of beauty, of probability and reasonableness,—that is the key to our growth. We begin to degenerate as soon as we lie to ourselves about such matters or about any matters.

In view of these facts the interest of our life, which is our growth, is bound up with the unconditional desire: so to lean on experience that we always know where we are in it. When a man pauses in his reading, it is of vital importance to him to be able to find his place again, provided his book is worth reading. Without that he cannot go on. To defer modestly to another's judgment on the question, "How far have I yet read?" would be impertinent. Your friend could find out only by asking you, even if you were a dunce and he the wisest man in the world.

Your life or mine is like a book in which we have read a certain distance. Unless we know exactly how far we have gone in it and what is still blank or vague to us, we cannot use what we know and we cannot learn more. We have some ideas about marriage, industry, baseball, Shakespeare, aeroplanes, war, sex, crime, education, the negro, the Republican Party, and the blacking on our shoes. If we know where our knowledge stops, what we believe, what we do not believe, and where we are uncertain, then we can grow from that point. Otherwise we cannot grow, and if we do not grow we degenerate, which no one desires.

E. *The energies of growth find furtherance and gather headway through success and through failure.*

(a) *Success.* As we grow we are getting what we want. To know this is to enjoy it and ourselves. It is contentment, satisfaction, pleasure, happiness, joy, delight, rapture, ecstasy. Physical pleasures, the joy of art, love and beauty, the solid satisfaction of success, the delight in victory, reflect in various colors our sense of attainment. For the time effort is relaxed and we rest in security. In such moments our sense of time is dimmed or lost. Hours hurry by. We seek no future; we recall no past. The present possesses us, though within this present our minds run back and forth as they do when we take in all at once the sounds, smells, and colors of early morning at sea. Another characteristic of our moments of happiness is their heightened sense of life. Our minds and bodies live more intensely than usual because they share the heat of other life around them.

Ordinarily this joy in attainment as a phase in growth is sandwiched in between two periods of hard work. We keenly enjoy our food and our rest when we have earned them by labor. We enjoy the game when we have put our best into it, because the pleasure of attainment is not merely a contrast, as when hot water feels good to cold hands, but a sense of fulfillment. The significance of every phase in the race reaches its height in the victory because the satisfaction and the work done to gain it are parts of one process, which starts afresh when a new effort is aimed and fired by the success or by the failure of the last one.

So at least it should be. But there is in almost every one a deep-rooted inertia which hopes to rest in attainment, to fasten on joy and drink its sweetness forever. "*Verweile doch, du bist so schön.*" Why is only the transient beautiful? Why should most of our joys be brief? Because when we are wide awake we know that we are meant to turn each climax into the energizer of another adventure. Joy recharges our batteries and flashes up the green light on the road ahead. We know it well enough in our hearts. But we are as lazy as we are ambitious and so we try to fool the universe and to stay rich without working for it. For a time we succeed in this because much joy *is* given us free, without effort or desert of ours. Often enough the world hands us a gift of working capital without our doing anything to earn it. In the tropics nature is rash enough to give us almost all that we need for physical existence and so we are apt to stagnate and to degenerate there. We begin to live like the simpler animals and plants and so to merge back into them. Even in sterner climates nature still gives us the beauty around us, the love from our parents, the strength and sensibilities in our bodies, even when we do not pay our board and lodging.

But I suppose no one gets the best out of these free gifts or continues long to feel how good they are, unless he pays something toward the world's housekeeping. The delight that comes to us, free or by labor, goes stale unless it issues in fresh effort and so brings new vision. By the structure of our bodies sensation is planned to lead to motion, feeling to effort, vision to action. But not to *any* action, not to mere explosions and " barbaric yawps," and not to the reveries of Narcissus. Success is a stage in growth pointing on to the next one. To be aware of one's virtue is to be a prig. To be aware of one's learning is to be a pedant. To wallow in one's pleasures is to be a hog. Prig, hog, and pedant are mired in their own attainments, trapped in the cave where they meant only to camp over night. But when one has grown to know something about the stars without priggishness or pedantry one faces one's ignorance about them and so is spurred on along this track to further knowledge. To delight in one's health is to feel fit for further work and, if all goes well, for further enjoyment. The logic of our nature as beings *built to learn* issues in the alternation of attainment in joy and of action springing from it.

But not only in their alternation. When life goes well, delight in what we see, and labor to see more interpenetrate. There is pleasure *in* effort as well as *after* it. The heightened vitality of success builds up a head of pressure which starts the new advance. As we read verses that we know well, the vista ahead is lighted by the perfection of the moment. There is delight in each phrase for itself, for what it issues from, and for what it leads to. Familiar music is delicious at each instant for what it is, for what it leaves, and for what is coming. A bit of its past and a little of its future are felt in its present, even by amateurs. Mozart could hear his whole sonata at once ("*gleich alles zusammen* ") before he began to write it out.[1] Action that

---

[1] *Life of Mozart*, by Marcia Davenport (New York: Charles Scribner's Sons, 1932), p. 283.

is voluntary and vigorous is warmed by a continuous sense of its worth. If it is action in *progress* its "end" guides us now to the right, now to the left, past obstacles and ir-relevancies. The motive is also the end. It is grasped in imagination before it is attained in fact. Otherwise the single steps on the sidewalk, the single sentences read or written, the single acts of plowing and planting, buying, selling, cooking, eating, and sleeping would seem as cheap, and be done as half-heartedly as the "work" of college loafers or the "hard labor" of prisoners who see no future and no point in their efforts.

In moments of attainment our supratemporal meaning is clarified and our life with it. In hours of plodding it is clouded by our blindness and our ignorance. The finished artist can paint for hours with continuous joy in the moment. But because we are not artists we have to build up our powers by periods of plodding, dimly known to be worth while but far from pure joy. From drudgery to delight there is a continuous increase in the sense of attain-ment and so a diminution in the sense of effort.

When we find what we have long been looking for, the supratemporal element that guides all search comes swiftly into focus. Like the peculiar zest of responding to a crisis it expresses the outburst of an energy which has been long accumulating. A long past is fulfilled in this instant. Like other delights, the joy of an emergency spans time and is not all caught in the temporal instant. Rupert Brooke greeted the war as many a man has greeted first love, because it fulfilled what he had long foreknown, waited for, sickened for lack of. So Plato embraced new truth as he recognized its birth in his mind. In a former existence, he thought, he had known it. Now he reknew it.

All search contains this supratemporal element. We could not look for God, Augustine says, unless we already possessed Him, not the whole that we are looking for, but some part. Any sensible man knows what he is after. Yet it is possible to forget it and so to fail in one's search because one is vague about its goal.

(b) *There is another element in progress: failure and the awareness of it.* We work ahead not only because we see a good but because we hate an evil. The pleasure of pre-attainment lures us along; the rebounding wrath of failure kicks us ahead. In some keen experiences of defeat we demolish one obstacle in the way to success and so see more clearly where we want to go. To take a wrong path, return, and seek the right one is progress provided we are sure that *some* path leads to our goal, provided our goal is not a lazy self-contradiction such as wasting our time and hoping to save it too. That sort of laziness every one can avoid if he chooses. It is the fate of those who do not care enough for progress to get their goal.

No one enjoys death, but something like death is inherent in all the progress that we have any experience of. Children mature and we are glad of it on the whole. We do not want them to remain children as long as they live. That is the fate of the feeble-minded. But we need not hide the fact that when children grow up they are inferior to their own past in beauty, in grace of movement, in resistance to many diseases, in capacity for sound sleep, in sensitiveness of hearing, in the capacity to be delighted, in whole-hearted intentness on what they are doing. If we love these things in a child we hate to see them lost when he grows up. Something dies and is not reborn.

This is as inevitable as grief for the death of a child we love. For joy and sorrow spring out of the same root,— love. What cannot die does not often keenly rejoice us. Because we love music, children, bird-songs, the swift dash of a sprinter, the fragile beauty of spring, we do not want them to last forever, not at any rate in that form. Its profusion of *passing* beauties is one of the special charms of childhood as it is of music. Its very rapidity of movement is part of what we prize in it. Slow it down and it is spoiled like the slow-motion pictures of a high dive or like a *scherzo* played *adagio*. We want these things to flash by us, even though they flash out. Yet when they die, part of us dies with them, because our memory cannot hold it. Something, doubtless, we retain. We love the world better because it has given us such memories. We are quicker to welcome anything else of the same sort. We know more of what there is in human nature at its best. We have more human sympathy for others in similar loss. But all these are general. They have no sharp outlines. Those are gone.

Doubtless some of the losses of growth are due to our stupidity and should breed not resignation but revolt. Such revolt has already begun and has won something. Among the rich, at any rate, children are not now robbed of their childhood so early nor so completely as they used to be. Perhaps it is not inevitable that we should grow so much clumsier as we grow bigger. Need we be more easily bored as we get brainier? Some people seem to keep their eagerness and their grace despite "the ignominy of being grown up." [1] Better medical work, better education, more shame for our ignominious maturity may salvage much that is now lost. But much beauty will always die, and for that, if we are not callous, we rage or sorrow.

We cannot say without perversion that we are glad of any sorrow. But we are glad of fresh life which involves sorrow not merely as an accident but as an inseparable

---

[1] S. M. Crothers, *By the Christmas Fire* (Boston: Houghton Mifflin Co., 1911).

part of love. We do not want to avoid sorrow by insensibility. When we are poignantly aware both of beauty and of its transience, we understand Francis Thompson's somber assertion that, "The tears of joy are salt as well as the tears of sorrow. And in that sentence are many meanings." [1]

There is tragedy as well as sorrow in progress. When we choose progress (as we must to live), we are fools unless we face the tragedy as well as the success of it. People come to grief for no fault of their own, or to a degree of grief quite unrelated to their faults. Their very strength fells them when it collides with greater strength which they cannot see. The moth in the flame, the fish in the net are no more pitiful than Shelley fighting the marriage laws of England or Roosevelt baulked of his chance to go to war in 1917. But it seems inherent in growth that ardent vitality like theirs should sometimes blindly obstruct the march of progress and beat itself to death by strength that we honor, against strength that we honor still more.

There are still blacker tragedies: Beethoven's deafness, Keats's death, Lincoln's assassination, Mary Lamb's insanity, which have no visible connection with progress. They ought to stimulate the advance of medical knowledge. Meantime it is in spite of them, not because of them, that growth lures us on.

2. THE DEFINITION OF GROWTH

What I describe in these chapters under the familiar name of growth has received many other titles. Most of them emphasize a certain *type* of development or a particu-

[1] *The Works of Francis Thompson* (New York: Charles Scribner's Sons, 1913), Vol. III, p. 15.

lar formula for it. In "growth" I wish to include features
from all of these. The peculiar waddle of the Hegelian
dialectic, the ponderous organization of Spencer's formula
for evolution, the profound subtleties of Professor A. N.
Whitehead's "Process," the tortuous progress of Goethe's
Faust, the ascetic austerities of Gandhi's spiritual emergence, all illustrate, I suppose, parts of what I here call
growth. We can grow through hardship without insisting
with Browning's *Rabbi* that we must "welcome *each* re-
buff." We can grow in culture without stiffening into
Kultur. The Christian's "hunger and thirst after righteousness" can live at peace with the neo-Hegelians'
"self-realization," with Bergson's "*élan vital*," with Miss
Follett's "creative experience," and with Keyserling's
"*Schöpferische Erkenntnis*." To distinguish the sort of
growth that I mean, I define it as *the fresh expression of a
purpose (or of an idea), which keeps such continuity with its
past and suffers only such losses by the way as it can bear without
losing its identity*. In decay and in self-deceit as in growth
we have continuity and novelty, but these are governed
by a predominant self-destruction. An alternative definition follows:

*Growth is the combination of a particular identity with the
special novelties which from moment to moment are essential
in the realization of a purpose.*

3. GROWTH AND THE CONSCIOUSNESS OF TIME

The various elements emphasized in these definitions
seem to be united when we relate growth to the idea of
time or at any rate to one of the ideas of time. Growth,
like time, issues from a past, is surveyed and oriented from
a present, and reaches into a future. To be growing, which
is what I mean by being ethically right, is to be conscious of the three phases of time included in one's time-

experience; it is to live by the reality of the past, of the present, and of the future.

When we remember to abide by the relevant elements in our past, we act honestly or in accord with our agreements. When we grasp our present we know where we now stand in thought, in affection, in sensation, in desire, in commitment to others and to the past, and so in opportunity for the future. To know our present is to grasp what no other human being can see as well. To face the future is to create and to welcome what is new and, by integrating it with the present and the past, to grow. Facing the present, its insights and its opportunities, we make agreements. Facing the past, we keep them. Facing the future we improve them. Facing all three we possess as much of reality as we have earned the right to.

When we do right we are time-conscious. When we do wrong we try to annihilate or to ignore a part of time. When we break a promise we act as if our past had no existence and no claim on us; we do what we can to abolish it. When we are any less clear-sighted than we can be about our present situation, its opportunities, its logic, and its commands, when we fail to assert what we know must be asserted or to decide what we know must be decided now, we try to deny our present. We fail in what Emerson called " self-reliance." When we refuse to look at new beauty or new evidence, when we refuse to admit that we may be stuck in a rut or mistaken in a belief, when we take failure or success as ultimate, we are trying to ignore the pressure of the future that ought to be upon our present as it is. In the momentary joy-of-attainment which characterizes certain stages in our growth, the awareness of time almost fades out. But what one sees from this hilltop sends one on again into work, guided, as before, by the suggestions of past, present, and future.

Growth is *in* character, not *towards* character, *in* learning, not *towards* learning.   We could never discover how to undertake our journey of experience unless we were already on the road.   And if we ever could reach an end of it, it would have no meaning for us.   Growth has no end and no cause.   It is not towards any attainable finish.   It is not a means to anything except further growth.   It is what we desire all the way along, when we are not deceiving ourselves.   We desire, of course, to reach the next stage in our advance and we fix our minds on this because it shows us our direction and is a sample of what we need.   Such stages are our special goals.

All this is clear if we do not forget that whenever we learn anything it is a fair specimen of what we mean by growth.   No one wants to grow towards learning but only in learning.   We want to approach particular milestones along the way, but we do not approach learning because we always know something, and we do not approach the end of learning because it has no end.

One gets to the same point if one considers *experience* as a sample of growth.   We do not grow towards experience; we grow in it, and so long as we are time-conscious creatures we do not get to any end of it.   We first found ourselves in it and we can never find ourselves anywhere else.   But we can try to shut it out as we do in any of the forms of self-deceit to be described in Chapters XV and XVI.   That effort is itself an experience, not of growth but of degeneration.

It is as easy to overestimate as it is to deny our growth. When we fancy ourselves growing we are often in fact repeating our old ideas, smiling our old smiles, or copying unconsciously another's theme.   At any moment no one can be certain how original he is.   Later reflection, the comment of friends, old notebooks may be needed to settle the question. But they do not always settle it against our hopes. So far as any one knows, some of our acts do climb up over the bodies of slave-habits or slavish imitations and plant their flag at a new height.

II

APPLICATIONS

CHAPTER VII

HONESTY

I have now finished what I have to say on the principles or distinguishing marks of right conduct. Before I describe the characteristics of wrong action I wish to make some detailed applications of the principles worked out in the last six chapters. I shall begin with an account of honesty, because if this word is taken to include straight dealing with oneself it covers almost the whole of applied ethics.

By honesty I mean keeping our agreements, spoken, written, or tacit, until in the march of development they are dissolved by mutual consent or until we have done our best to get this consent. The subject divides itself into three parts:

1. Honesty with ourselves.
2. Honesty with others.
3. The types of reserve or of secrecy which need to be distinguished from dishonesty.

1. HONESTY WITH OURSELVES

Of being true to ourselves I have already said enough. It is even more fundamental than a virtue. It is psychical self-preservation. In this it is unique. To deceive others brings us no immediate or invariable punishment. We may never be found out. But when we deceive ourselves we are always and instantly caught, for we destroy in the act a portion of our own substance, and so have just so much less self left to deceive again.

2. HONESTY WITH OTHERS

Honesty with others includes (a) veracity (verbal truth-fulness), (b) uprightness in action. We convey impressions, true or false, not only by words but by silence, by a nod or a gesture, or by any action which validates or breaks our agreements. Cheating at cards, theft, forgery, adultery, murder can be committed without speaking or writing a word. But they all involve deception in some form. A lie is an intentional verbal deception without consent. It is not a misstatement made in good faith nor a mistaken scientific observation, nor a slip in arithmetic, though any of these may deceive us. They are inaccurate and they may convey an impression which is false; but no one considers them dishonest because no deception was intended. The intention is everything, not for efficiency but for honesty. Even if no one is actually deceived, the attempt to deceive is a lie.

But one further condition must be added. To be a lie the deception must be contrary to the other's wish. In football, in card games, in legerdemain, in the drama, we are there to be deceived if the performer can do it. We expect it. The full definition of a lie then is: an intentional verbal deception, actual or attempted, and without consent.

Honesty is doing our best to keep a promise or a contract, to stick to an understanding, to be loyal to a friend, to play the game according to the rules. So long as flood, earthquake, and other natural disasters do not interfere with it, the world is as stable as the agreements in it. So long as people believe that business compacts will be lived up to, business confidence is maintained, initiative is encouraged, energy is called out, and business credits are piled one on top of another like the stories of a skyscraper. But at the bottom, supporting the whole structure, is some one's confidence in some one else, confidence that a bank is solvent, that a debt will be paid, that a government will not repudiate its obligations. A little honesty goes a great way. Despite all its graft, business survives by virtue of the " gold basis " of upright men and fair transactions in it.

It is no exaggeration, then, to say that there must be a deal of honesty in our society else it could not hang together at all. If people did not play fair oftener than they cheat there would soon be no one left to cheat. Stubborn resistance is offered to our natural dishonesty by the logic of our need to trust and to be trusted if we are to coöperate at all, and of our need to coöperate if we are to enjoy the measure of civilization so far attained. Out of these needs there springs a power not ourselves that makes for honesty and cudgels us when we get very far out of the straight path. We deserve no credit for it but we may thank our gregariousness that it is there. Even the buildings in which business is done stand up because of the honesty that went into testing their materials, into calculating their strains, into planning, constructing, and inspecting them. We do not think of this as virtue. It is a matter of habit and routine. But at a hundred points the job could have been faked, scamped, neglected, so that the buildings would be unsafe.

At the time of the Italian Renaissance, when most people had ruthless enemies who might do away with them by poisoning their food, the honesty of one's cook and of all those who had access to one's food was a very important defense. Nowadays we need not worry about such things. We can assume honest behavior in the processes of growing, packing, preparing, cooking, and serving our victuals.

The adulteration of food, the watering of milk, the menace of dangerous germs in meat or canned goods are kept at a negligible minimum in most parts of the United States by government inspectors and by the fear of public condemnation.   In some transactions, though not in all, honesty is the easiest way to get along, because dishonesty so often brings, by one or another path, its own punishment. After minor experiences with deceit in childhood or youth, most people find this out and settle down to a fair average of uprightness.

In international affairs we have, I suppose, more dishonesty than elsewhere, first because it is easier to conceal it here than in business, and then because nations have thus far got along with far less teamwork than is essential in business.   Coöperation demands honesty, and when nations coöperate they can afford dishonesty as little as the tradesman can.

I am here describing honesty not as a virtue but as a logical and therefore practical necessity of working with others who need to know what to expect of us and where to find us. Good faith is actually assumed in a large area of our daily transactions.   This is not wholly because of the virtue which we attribute to our fellows.   It is rather because we believe that most of them have discovered that dishonesty usually leaks out sooner or later with humiliating results and that they cannot expect to be fairly treated, as they need to be, unless they treat others so.

3. TRAPS FOR LIARS

This basic drive toward honest dealings among men is reënforced by the power of three useful traps for liars. Without these traps there would doubtless be far more cheating than we now find. By these traps nature strikes back when we try to make a lie pass for the truth.

First, through the defects of memory: liars have to remember just in what words they have previously lied; and this is difficult. A lying witness whose answers have been recorded in shorthand finds it hard to match the stenographic record when, after an interval, he is asked the same questions again. A truthful witness forms his statements on both occasions by recalling the same events, and though his memory may drop details or add embellishments, it will not often make the sort of ingenious invention that a liar does.[1]

This trap for liars is built into the structure of memory. The trains of association by which we recall the details of past events run along the same tracks again and again. When we recall our impressions after an interval we find them essentially the same, blurred here, developed there perhaps, but not falsified. The liar is often quite unable to remember his own lie, and especially to remember it automatically when he is caught off his guard by a skillful cross-examiner. Here are some instances:

1. " Do you still maintain the truth of what you have sworn to at this trial as to seeing the nurse let the patient fall backward four or five times and pick him up and laugh at him? "

" I certainly do."

" I read you a question asked you by the coroner [several days earlier]: Did you at any time see Hilliard fall or stumble: Answer: No, sir. I never did. . . . [The contradiction is obvious]

2. " You said in your affidavit [made last week]: The blood was all over the floor. It was covered with Hilliard's blood and the scrub woman came Tuesday and Wednesday morning, and washed the blood away. . . . "

[1] The truthful but confused witness, frightened by court procedure or misled by crafty lawyers, often makes statements contrary to what in his right mind he knows to be the fact. But he is not lying, and his misstatements have not the self-defending character of the perjurer's.

" Yes, sir."

" But I understood you to say that you didn't get up till noon on Wednesday."

" I didn't see them Wednesday morning; it was Tuesday morning I saw them scrubbing."

" But you seem to have forgotten that Hilliard didn't arrive at the pavilion until Tuesday afternoon at four o'clock." . . .

" Well, there were other people who got beatings besides him."

" Then when speaking of Hilliard's blood upon the floor you meant beatings of other people? "

" Yes, sir—on Tuesday." . . .

By this time the witness began to flounder helplessly. He contradicted himself constantly, became red and pale by turns, hesitated before each answer, at times corrected his answers, at others was silent and made no answer at all. Though ordered by the court to return next day, he was never seen again at the trial.[1]

A second trap for liars is the difficulty of getting them all to tell the same lie. They do not learn their parts in time. Sometimes they do not know that they are to appear on the stage at all. They have not been notified of their part in the plot. The following experience brought home to me this difficulty for liars.

One evening a group of physicians at a small medical club were discussing the nervous affections of the stomach. One of our members said that a woman in his clinic was sure that she had a lizard in her stomach. We laughed over it and speculated as to possible ways to persuade her of her mistake. Then up spoke one of the elder men in our group, saying, " I'll fix that woman; you send her to me! " So said, so done. The unfortunate female appeared at his clinic within a few days. Our friend the doctor listened with great attention to all her symptoms, nodding his head gravely from time to time. He entered a lengthy account of the case upon his records, and meditated sagely for a time when she had finished. " Yes," he said, with a sigh, " there is no doubt about it; it's a clear case of lizard in the stomach. It is no use concealing the truth from you any longer; you have every symptom of the disease. But we have made a good deal of progress

[1] F. L. Wellman, *The Art of Cross-Examination* (New York: The Macmillan Co., 1903), pp. 242, 244.

within the last few months, Madam, in the treatment of that trouble, and while I cannot make any promises (for no honorable doctor can do anything of that kind), I think I can give you good hope that you may be relieved. A medicine has recently been discovered which, in the majority of cases—not all cases, mind you—will dissolve lizards in the stomach and allow the resulting substance to be excreted by the kidney. As I say, Madam, I cannot promise a cure, but this I can promise: within a few days after you have taken my medicine you will be absolutely sure whether or not it has proved effective. In case it should prove effective, you will notice within forty-eight hours from the time you take it an extraordinary change in the color of your urine, which will be tinged some shade of blue, or green. In case the medicine fails, as it is quite possible that it may, there will be no change whatever in the color of the urine. The medicine will be contained in three capsules, for which I have just written a prescription; they can be obtained only at one apothecary's in the city, as the medicine is difficult to procure and known to but few. I have written his address on the prescription."

The doctor then handed her a prescription for three-grain capsules of Methylene Blue, a substance which, when taken into the stomach invariably produces a deep blue color in the urine. The woman took the medicine, perceived to her amazement and delight that a blue color was imparted to her urine, recognized that the lizard must have been dissolved, and was at once freed from all her symptoms.

Now this is the end of the story as it is usually told; but there is a sequel. Within the course of three months another lizard grew. This time the poor lady had no more faith in Methylene Blue as a permanent cure, and turned up at still another Out-Patient clinic under the charge of a very honest physician, to whom she told her story. He said of course that it was ridiculous and impossible, because lizards couldn't grow in people's stomachs. "Oh," she said, "you know Doctor Blank, don't you? He is a good doctor, isn't he?" "Yes." "Well, he told me I had all the symptoms of lizard in the stomach. He wouldn't tell me a lie, would he?"

"Well, anyway, you haven't got a lizard in your stomach now." From this the doctor went one step further than any one had gone before; he investigated not only what was *not* the matter with her, but what the trouble actually was. He found that she had an excess of muscular activity in her stomach, the irritation of which gave the gnawing and scratching feeling which she attributed to the presence of a lizard. Having discovered this fact he proceeded to treat her for this trouble, which he succeeded in curing, and after that the lizard never grew again.[1]

This story exemplifies an " honest lie " told with excellent motives. Its frustration illustrates the point that honesty is defended not merely by the good intentions of individuals but beyond these intentions by the impossibility of getting into the plot all the persons who must be in it to insure success. Some one is forgotten or cannot be reached in time, or will not come into the game. Some one forgets his part and innocently blurts out the truth.

A third familiar snare for liars is their tendency to quarrel and then to take an easy revenge on one another by peaching. A large part of our present knowledge about labor spies came out when one of the spy-corporations quarreled with another and brought a suit, in the course of which some professional secrets were ventilated.[2] Quarrels between thieves work out like quarrels between liars. Thieves of public money who have won control through corrupt politics cannot always agree on the distribution of the loot. They quarrel and so the public discovers their peculations. When the Tweed Ring controlled New York City, soon after the Civil War, they managed to steal some thirty or forty million dollars. One member of the ring, ex-Sheriff O'Brien, claimed $350,000 as his share. Boss Tweed refused him this, whereupon O'Brien obtained copies of the account-books disclosing the frauds of the Tweed Ring, and sold them to the *New York Times*.[3] This evidence led to the downfall of Tweed and his group.

[1] R. C. Cabot, *Social Service and the Art of Healing*, Dodd, Mead & Co., 1909, p. 163.
[2] Sidney Howard, *The Labor Spy* (New York: Republic Pub. Co., 1924), pp. 169, 170.
[3] D. T. Lynch, " *Boss* " *Tweed, the Story of a Grim Generation* (New York: Boni & Liveright, 1927), p. 362.

4. PSYCHOLOGICAL FORCES WHICH WORK FOR HONESTY

Seconding the aid given to our natural or acquired tendencies to be honest by our need to trust and be trusted in the inevitable teamwork of civilization, and reënforcing the good work of the three liar-traps just described, there are some familiar psychological forces which work automatically for honesty. Some of us are too lazy to be dishonest. In others habit makes ordinary honesty almost mechanical. In many the recollection of shame and disgrace on being detected in some youthful lie persists as an instinctive disinclination to do anything that might expose us again to such humiliation.

Subtle forms of imitation also help to develop, maintain, and increase honesty. Not from conscious admiration or imitation but instinctively, people of an impressionable type can hardly help falling into the ways of those whom they strongly like. A shady character comes to know and to like a person of unusual honesty, who does not preach about it but takes it for granted in himself and in his friends. Some of this honesty the weaker man assimilates like a fashion.

As I list these quasi-automatic aids to good faith I do not mean to suggest that there is nothing in us that *consciously* works for honesty. Any one who has felt and hated in himself the insidious curse of self-deception longs to be free of it, and there is no important difference, so far as I know, between hatred of self-deceit and love of honesty within ourselves. This in turn leads us to see that we cannot deceive another without deceiving ourselves in the process. For when we get ready to cheat a person we look at him through the wrong end of a psychological telescope so that he seems very small and insignificant, indeed so small that a few lies cannot hurt him. But all the time we know perfectly well that they do, and that the psychological telescope is one of our own pet tricks to fool ourselves.

As we come to realize this, our positive zest for life and all that we want to do with it, our positive affection for our friends, are focussed in an attraction for free and open dealings with ourselves and with others. We like to see where we are and to clear fogs out of the mental atmosphere. The more we love the actual things and people in our world the more we want to see them clearly and to be seen clearly by them. Dishonesty works best in darkness. Daylight is its enemy, and because we love life we come to love clearness in the media through which we see.

5. ARGUMENTS FOR ABSOLUTE HONESTY

All this is obvious, perhaps trite. But does it follow that all dishonesty and all lies are wrong? Most people hesitate to say so. Part of their doubt about pledging themselves to absolute honesty under all conditions vanishes when distinctions are clearly drawn, first between lies and innocent errors, next between lies and the mutually permitted deceptions of strategic contests such as games and war, then between lies and conventional misstatements such as begin and end our letters, and finally between deceptive concealment and reserve. But even when all these distinctions have been admitted, honest people will usually stand up for a certain amount of dishonesty. They will usually defend a moderate number of polite ("white") lies, of medical lies told with a kind motive, and of lies told to help or to shield some one else. I shall not discuss this matter in detail here because I hope to devote another book to it. But I will sketch the main arguments for the principle of absolute truthfulness.

(a) No one wants to be called a liar or to plead for general mendacity. It is a limited group of lies that are defended. But can one " localize " the habit, as Germany hoped in 1914 to localize the dispute between Austria and Serbia? Success turns out to be almost or quite impossible. A single lie spreads. It is difficult to draw the line around it. It spreads in the habits of him who tells it and it spreads in the community as soon as it is openly defended. Self-permitted lying tends to spread beyond the limits allowed. Pious frauds are easier the second time; found convenient here, they are temptingly handy elsewhere. If one lies to the insane, shall one lie to the neurasthenic, to the irritated, to the prejudiced, to the unbalanced? But who is unprejudiced? Who is perfectly balanced? When shall we lay down this terribly convenient tool? Need we lay it down at all? It is much easier to hold onto it.

(b) It is easy enough to defend a single lie on a particular occasion. But when one asks, as one properly may, what principle governs the judgment that this particular lie is a good thing, it is hard to get an answer. A polite lie under a set of peculiarly difficult conditions seems easily excusable. But if we ask: " Will you say, then, that whenever you wish to avoid hurting some one's feelings or whenever you are in a bad fix socially, it is right to lie," few are content to answer " Yes."

Or suppose we maintain that a doctor should lie to his patient when the truth about his illness might discourage him and so hurt his chances of recovery. Shall we say then, A doctor should lie to his patient whenever a lie seems medically useful? How about those sick people who prefer to face the facts? How can the doctor distinguish them? And if he does not distinguish them, is he not assuming a dangerously autocratic attitude in his work?

(c) When we lie to people the act assumes either that they are enemies or that they are weaklings. Have we any right to make either assumption?

(d) What seems to me the best argument for absolute honesty was pointed out long ago by St. Augustine in his essay *De Mendacio*. Whoever candidly avows his belief that lies should be told occasionally, conscientiously, under special conditions, puts us on our guard against his own attempts to lie under just those conditions, and so makes it difficult for himself to carry out his policy effectively. Dr. Joseph Collins argues for kindly lying to patients with chronic disease.[1] Every page of his argument strengthens the already strong popular tendency to discount what he and other doctors say about the prognosis of disease. A popular writer defends lying under certain conditions. His wife of course reads his books and knows this doctrine. On a visit to Boston she happens to consult me as a patient and confesses that though he is the best husband in the world she never can tell when he is handing her a benevolent and conscientious lie and when he is adhering to ordinary honesty. She knows that he intends everything in the kindest possible way, but she cannot reap all the benefits of his devoted kindness because she cannot tell when to believe him.

A great English surgeon addressing a graduating class of medical students said, in 1902, that they must always appear perfectly certain of their diagnosis because patients do not like any appearance of uncertainty in their doctors. Now the fact is that most intelligent doctors are often in doubt about what ails their patients; so that this famous man's advice was a veiled counsel of mendacity. It got unveiled within a few months and stirred up indignant comment in the daily papers. Then a notable public character was taken sick and the same great surgeon signed daily bulletins about his progress. The newspapers, how-

---

[1] Joseph Collins, M.D., " Should Doctors Tell the Truth? " *Harper's Magazine*, August, 1927.

ever, discounted the favorable news of these bulletins because the surgeon who signed them had given public notice that he believed in lying sometimes, perhaps here. Of course he intended to define rigidly the rare conditions under which he believed lying to be a duty. But how could any one be sure that he was not conscientiously lying just at the moment when he defined these conditions? How can we ever be sure where a conscientious liar will draw the line?

It appears to me, therefore, that the doctrine that it is sometimes right to lie can never be effectively asserted. For our hearers take notice and so make ineffective our subsequent attempts to lie. I recall a sick man who ordered his physician never to tell him the truth in case he should be seriously ill. Picture the state of that sick man's mind when later he hears his physician's reassurances. " Perhaps he doesn't consider this sickness a serious one. Then he will be telling me the truth." How can the sick man know? If he asks the doctor whether he considers the disease serious and gets a negative answer, how is he to interpret that answer? If the doctor did consider the disease serious he would be bound to say " No," and if he did not consider it serious he would also have to say " No." His words have become mere wind. No one can interpret them. His reassuring manner, his smiles, his cheering tones may be true or they may be lies. Who can say?

Suppose the disease comes to a point which demands operation. But to mention operation is to let the patient know that his trouble is serious, and that is forbidden. Shall the doctor therefore let the operation go and let his patient get worse? Whatever the doctor does or says his patient has grounds for fearing the worst. No reassurance can be taken at its face value. The most trifling ailment must be suspect; good news may always mean bad.

Here then is a self-enforcing moral law. "Thou shalt not confess to a belief in occasional lies." But to conceal such a belief is to deceive in a way and to a degree that most people would admit to be bad. For the very conscientiousness of conscientious lies depends on their being known to be exceptions to the rule. No one can be a universal conscientious liar. Suppose, then, that the occasional philanthropic liar is asked the question, "Do you consider lying ever justifiable?" If he answers "No," when in fact he is concealing certain exceptional instances in his mind, he tells a lie that it is impossible to defend. But if he answers "Yes," and defends, for example, polite lies, lies to the sick or to the insane, lies to defend a woman's honor, his dilemma is twofold. First his hearers are put on their guard against his benevolent mendacity, and so he has checkmated himself in the very field where he intended to work. Secondly, his hearers have no way to be sure that he is not lying at the very moment when he delimits the field.

Beyond this his hearers are left to wonder who else agrees with him. Who else is apt to lie in those same embarrassing situations? By one man's acknowledgment that he thinks lies sometimes right, confidence is impaired not only in him but to some extent in others. The fear of lies thus spreads in two directions. It diffuses from the confessed occasional liar to others, who may or may not believe in lying under the same conditions. Also it extends from their defined conditions to other possible occasions. For how can we tell that the time for benevolent lying was itself veraciously specified by a person who has confessed that he sometimes lies on principle?

So far as I see, then, the conscientious defense of lying is impossible. But suppose it never becomes necessary for us to defend it. Suppose no one asks what we believe about it, and we keep our beliefs to ourselves. Then that in itself is a plan to deceive, when the time comes, those who still trust us to be truthful. One cannot silently harbor a belief in conscientious lying without being an *unconscientious* liar. One cannot confess it without undoing oneself, yet one cannot conscientiously keep it to oneself. Hence one cannot hold the idea at all without being *ipso facto* a traitor to society. One seems to be in a fix.

6. TYPES OF RESERVE OR OF SECRECY TO BE DISTINGUISHED FROM DISHONESTY

Concealment may deceive. Conscious reserve is concealment. Hence one who considers lying bad because it breaks promises is apt to be accused of decrying all reserve. A lie can be told by silence; but not all who withhold facts are liars. When is reserve truthful? When it violates no explicit or implicit agreement to tell. To sit silent and hear a friend or an enemy falsely accused is treason to unspoken pledges. But to express in conversation no opinion about the character of a slight acquaintance, even though we may happen to have quite a sharply-cut idea about him, is a reserve which ought to be commoner. Doctors are rightly reserved about their patients' affairs, lawyers and social workers about their clients, priests about their privileged communications. Moreover the effort to " burn our own smoke " by concealing discouragement, fear, worry, annoyance, suspicion, or boredom violates no promise to pour out all these misfortunes upon our friends. They have never asked or desired it.

Secrecy or reserve is a public benefit:

(a) When it minimizes the spread of evils which no one needs to share. If the house is afire every one in it, except the baby, needs to share knowledge of that disaster at once. But no one needs to share the smoldering of our anger, the flames of our jealousy, the smoke of our despondency. Frankness on these matters may be only a mean self-indulgence. They ought to be held as private property.

(b) It is good to conceal one's erudition and to curb one's volubility when they are prone to bore or needlessly to alarm. A nurse is apt to pour out her hideous hospital experiences simply because she is full of them. A sympathetic but apprehensive patient tips her up with a rash question. A stream of horrors runs out, and is avidly absorbed by a mind that can make no use of them and so is haunted later by their ugly company. Here again frankness is a vice.

(c) It is well to conceal one's nakedness when others find it dangerously provocative. It is fashionable just now to assert and to practise the contrary because sexuality is an obsession of our time. If our climate were hot enough to make clothes a burden instead of a convenience we might get as used to doing without them as Central African tribes do. But the facts being what they are, nakedness is selfishness because it pretends to ignore bad consequences to other people.

(d) Frankness is usually a vice and reserve usually a duty about information received by us in confidence. But, in rare cases, professional secrets, legal, confessional, medical, *may* represent a conspiracy against the public. When crimes are concealed and the innocent falsely accused because information has been locked up in confidence instead of being passed along to the public prosecutor, we have a typical abuse of secrecy. When a doctor, a lawyer, a priest receives such confidences as this, they are essentially like stolen goods. No one had the right to give or to receive them. Tacitly they have been repudiated in advance. To receive them breaks a previous (implicit) promise to society.

But if there are confidences which one has a right to receive, in the hope of helpful advice or action for one in trouble, one has obviously a duty to keep them from all except those to whom the secret was (implicitly) given in the first place. It is understood, or should be, that medical secrets are usually shared by medical assistants whose help is essential in carrying out treatment. So it is with legal secrets and with those imparted to social workers. One deals usually with a team of workers, rarely with a single individual.

(e) Secrecy in games, in the strategy of war, business, or diplomacy is like " secrets " and other surprises at Christmastime. They are expected under the " rules of the game " and are as good or as bad as the " game " itself. It is of course essential that every one concerned should know the rules of the game and should be willing to play the game under these rules. Secrecies outside the rules are what we mean by cheating. Within the rules they are implicitly desired even by those whose will they foil. I want to find out my opponent's secrets in a game of cards, but I like the game itself and want it to go on under the rules which permit him to keep me in the dark. Without these there would be no fun in the game.

War is today one of the " games " that civilized mankind is trying to abolish. But until it is abolished we cannot blame any nation for playing it with all the secrecy that its strategy demands. Frankness would here be treason against a previous agreement with one's own nation.

(f) Secrecy or reserve is a good thing for us and for our neighbors when it concerns " half-baked " ideas which will be needlessly misunderstood if blurted out or pulled out of us prematurely by another's questions. When the evidence is not all in, the judge or the laboratory worker reserves his judgment. He may have a guess, a suspicion, a half-formed belief, or even a tentative conclusion on which he will rest, in case all the later evidence supports that which has appeared thus far. But anything that he allows himself to say about these unfinished approaches-to-an-opinion is apt not only to mislead others but to warp his own mind by fixing in words what should still remain in the fluidity of surmise. At this stage reserve is a duty and frankness is a vice.

Experiences of beauty, of religion, or of difficult resolve are sometimes cheapened by the attempt to share them with others, because our inadequate words may push out the experience itself and take its place in our minds, just as a cheap nickname clings to a person instead of his real name. Adequate words for an experience of beauty are what we mean by poetry. Far from cheapening the experience they increase its value. But though most of us can get delight from beauty we make a mess of it when we try to describe it.

(g) Finally, reserve is the only reasonable policy about any subject, when we know that to mention it is to start a riot. If we agree that mob-spirit usually upsets all sensible plans, it follows that we should be reserved when our reserve may help to prevent war, drunkenness, panic, group hysteria, or whatever sets free the spirit of destruction. A wrangling family, a quarreling committee, any group of people who have lost their heads is a small mob. Experience teaches us that to touch certain subjects in it produces mob-spirit and so explodes people's self-control as a match explodes a powder magazine.

Much " frank talk " and " frank writing " about sex has this effect. It fools people into thinking they are facing facts when in reality they are basking in daydreams that lead to no defensible action. The " conspiracy of silence " about syphilis and gonorrhea was a cowardly and stupid refusal to face facts and to act on them. Frankness is doing good here. Concealing physiological facts about reproduction has done appreciable harm, and perhaps it may be possible to show that good has resulted from the current publicity about the subject. But most of the ponderous or trivial "frankness" now current about sex has, I think, no beneficial intention and no good result. It is a touch of mob-spirit, that is, of unguided emotion, which makes fools or beasts of us when we indulge in it.

I have tried to show that veracity and honesty are absolute obligations. They are forms of the central absolute obligation to face and to love reality, that is, to learn, to act and to create the truth. In this the only perfection that we can attain is that of intention; but we need not fall short of this. No man is infallible, and no one can be perfectly accurate nor promise to attain fact. But any one can be perfectly honest and perfectly veracious if he chooses. I believe that these qualities are always in place and that we can never get too much of them. When it seems as if they could be overdone it is because we mistake them for something else, sometimes for mere loquacity or tactlessness, more often for brutal frankness. Unlike honesty, frankness is as often bad as good. It is good whenever it fulfills a pledge, tacit or open, to let others know what is in our minds.

Concealment is often proof of wrongdoing, sometimes of rightdoing. Proper reserve conceals what has been promised to no one and is, we believe, needed by no one. The secrecy essential to lying, to theft, to most sexual faults, to most murders is a concealment which breaks promises implicit or explicit. Such crimes express our desires but not our needs or any one else's.

A few definitions will sum up the chapter.

(a) Honesty is doing our best to keep our agreements until they are dissolved or improved with the consent of all concerned.

(b) Veracity is verbal honesty.

(c) A lie is an attempt to break an agreement without consent, that is, without the convention that makes us expect to deceive and be deceived in games, in drama, or in war. This convention may itself be good or bad.

(d) Frankness is saying whatever is in our minds.

(e) Confidential agreements are pledges to limit frankness.

(f) Proper reserve, or proper secrecy, means withholding ideas or facts which would violate previous agreements if shared.

(g) Mob-spirit is uncontrolled contagious emotion. Frankness often sets it loose, especially in talk or writing about sex.

CHAPTER VIII

KEEPING AND BREAKING AGREEMENTS

When one tries to apply the principles explained in the last seven chapters, difficulties arise. Are agreements all absolute or are some or all of them conditional? If conditions are legitimate can they be known in advance to those concerned, so that in case they arise the agreement may be abandoned by mutual consent and without rancor? Is there a difference in obligation corresponding to the distinction between the spirit and the letter of a contract? Can an agreement ever be rightly broken? If so when? What of our legal obligations? Are they agreements? If not, what authority have they? Should one feel bound by customs in which one has silently acquiesced? In the next two chapters I shall try to answer these questions.

1. CONDITIONAL AGREEMENTS

Are any or all agreements conditional? Nothing destroys more completely the mutual confidence on which our civilized affairs rest than secret reservations because of which a person may later claim the right to break a promise. If a person goes into marriage or into a baseball game with secret personal reservations unexplained to his partners, he is essentially a liar, and a more dangerous one than if he did it out loud. But in contrast with secret and therefore unfair reservations there are, I believe, in almost every promise limitations which ought to be known to those concerned but are rarely explained as explicitly as they need to be. Our ancestors used to add the condition "D.V." (God willing) to many of their promises. They pledged themselves to keep their engagements *provided* illness, death, or other accidents did not arise. We know as well as our grandfathers did that some catastrophe may interfere with the fulfillment of our promises. But when we gave up saying "D.V." we put nothing in its place, and this sometimes leads to trouble, for not every one understands these silent reservations alike.

Perhaps the most definitely conditional formula that is still popular is the accountant's "E. & O. E." written at the foot of his sworn statement as to the accuracy of a balance sheet. This means that the accountant stands responsible for the figures, *provided* his unintentional "Errors and Omissions" are "Excepted." He will not swear that his statement is correct, since it may contain errors and omissions, but only that it is veracious, because he has done his best to make it correct. He swears to his own truthfulness, not to the inerrancy of the figures. By this phrase, as by the use of *Deo volente*, we pledge our intentions. If we fail to do what is expected of us, it shall not be by our own will but only by our helplessness. Accidents may happen to our bodies or to our mathematical calculations. All that we promise to control is the spirit and the effort. For reasons beyond our control the performance may nevertheless fall short. The words "to the best of my knowledge and belief" at the end of an oath have the same intent. They foresee possible inaccuracies and give warning in advance of human fallibility. There is no agreement to be correct, but only to do one's best in that direction.

A second group of accidents which may prevent the fulfillment of an agreement is the sudden emergence of some previous agreement which is generally recognized to have the right of way. Fire engines and hospital ambulances have the right to displace other traffic and so perhaps to break people's agreements by delaying the delivery of goods contracted for at a certain hour. A municipal traffic ordinance about fire engines is recognized as something to be obeyed even if it compels us to break a business engagement. When a policeman finds it difficult to make an arrest and calls on a passer-by to help him, the passer-by has no legal right to plead other engagements. He must get in and help. These cases show that we recognize a right of way for civic business when it conflicts with industrial or personal engagements.

In view of these examples it begins to appear that we make very few absolute agreements, because we have but few unconditional desires. In one respect or another almost every engagement that we make is conditional. This means that both parties tacitly or explicitly agree that it ought to be broken under certain conditions, though with due notice, if that is possible. Such conditions and exceptions are written into many formal contracts which describe in detail what both parties believe is the best way to behave in certain contingencies imagined. In the contract these beliefs are made binding. They do not impair but strengthen the validity of the tie. The flimsier kind of understanding is that in which exceptions are *not* thought out or provided for in advance. Informal compacts are often made to contain an inclusive but tacit condition something like this: Whatever unforeseen event may disturb the plans which we have made together, whatever impulse may tempt either of us to twist our understanding to our private profit, we will act as if in each other's presence and in accord with the spirit of our agreement, which is the desire for mutual benefit. The will to agree shall persist.

2. PREFERRED CONDITIONS

An *order of precedence* is recognized among certain of the agreements which we assume. It is generally understood that professional obligations take precedence of social engagements. A physician's duty to his patients, especially to those critically ill, is agreed to be so imperative that when they need his presence he is bound to leave his meals, his night's rest, his holiday, or to break any ordinary social engagement with family or friends. They do not expect him to keep a dinner engagement or to go, as he had agreed, to a theater-party, if he suddenly receives from a patient a call that only he can properly answer. Of course he is bound to give warning of this as early as he can. But people usually know enough about sickness to forgive him readily because they realize that if they were sick themselves they would count on their doctor's help in need, even if he had to inconvenience his family and friends by coming. In serious illness he is owned by his patients rather than by himself or by anybody else.

But his patients' claim on him is not absolute or ultimate. National obligations precede professional ties. In time of war a conscription law may oblige him to leave family, friends, and even patients. This priority of claim is not often explained or even realized until war comes. But when it comes, the nation's need is usually recognized, not only as traditional but as reasonable, unless one objects conscientiously to all war.

Even the claim of the nation, however, is not absolute. The individual conscience may repudiate it. Most of us respect the "conscientious objector" to all war, and applaud his refusal to serve. In the war of 1914–1918 the English conscription law of 1916, and the American law framed after it, expressly excepted from combatant service Quakers and members of any other religious sect which forbids war, provided they had not hastily joined this sect after war was declared. Provided, then, that the nation believed their objections to be sincere and not a pretense trumped up to cover " slacking," it respected such conscientious objections.

Not every one agrees to the justice of this last zone of conditionality in our agreements. Some believe that a nation's claim over its citizens is absolute and has no exceptions. But enough has been said, I think, to show that most of our agreements, if not all, " have a string to them " and are not so absolute as they sound, even in the minds of those who make them.

Summarily, then, it appears that when we say, " Yes, I shall be glad to dine with you tonight at seven, " we add tacitly, " You understand, of course, that you may not see me: (a) if illness or accident should keep me away; (b) if a professional, civic, or religious duty should arise as an emergency voicing the call to which I am at all times subject. In any such case I will give you immediate warning if I can."

I think it would be better if such tacit assumptions were oftener stated explicitly. Not all persons understand implications to quite the same degree or in quite the same way. The authority of a nation over conscience and *the individual's right to rebel openly* when his conscience commands it are especially vague. Whewell thought they should be left vague because if we stated the conditions under which revolution is justified, revolutions would occur too often. He recognized that the right of revolution exists, but thought it dangerous to define it. I disagree. Men are not tempted to break a contract merely because they have taken pains to insert in it beforehand the conditions which may make it impossible or undesirable to fulfill it. Provided the parties agree to such limiting clauses, much is gained and nothing lost by inserting them. So it is with conditional agreements to obey all the laws, wise and foolish, sound or self-contradictory, which our fellow countrymen make through their elected representatives in Congress assembled. A formidable foreign power or a formidable money-power might cow Congress into passing iniquitous and self-destructive legislation. It would then be the law of the land. But all good citizens would openly revolt against it and go to prison provided they could not get it repealed.

3. TARDY PERFORMANCE

The delayed fulfillment of agreements may not only inconvenience some one but may impair general confidence in a person's reliability. If a time limit has been definitely stated beforehand, and if none of the natural disasters or superior claims just mentioned have intervened, a failure in punctuality is a broken agreement. The legal " statute of limitations " expresses no ethical principles but merely the inconvenience of trying to pursue by legal action a claim that is covered by the dust of seven years. Morally seven years or any other period has no effect. I ought to pay my debts if I can, after seven or after seventy years. " If I can " means unless it is reasonably clear that I am not bound by any other obligations recognized to be even more important than the debt. If I should pay installments on the debt at the cost of depriving myself of necessary food or of ruining my means of livelihood, the chance of my paying the rest of the debt in the future is impaired. I am unfair to the creditor to pay any part now, if by paying nothing now I might later pay the whole.

4. VICARIOUS AGREEMENTS AND DUE CARE

Are we bound by the promise of another acting in our name?
When an extravagant collegian runs up bills in his father's
name and without his consent, is the father morally
bound to pay? Most people would say, "Yes, if he has
the money." But suppose the student is an orphan and
charges his purchases to his uncle or to his cousin or to a
friend who is no relation. Then the duty to pay is not
nearly so clear.

An essential tool for decision seems to be this: Has the
tradesman taken care to find out whether the boy was
authorized by his father, his other relatives, or his friend
to run up bills in this way? If despite reasonable precautions the tradesman has been deceived, the burden of loss
should not fall entirely on him. Suppose the student
exhibits to him a skillfully forged letter authorizing the
recipient to charge his purchases to his uncle. If the forged
signature agrees closely with the uncle's real signature
kept on file in the store, the uncle should pay, I think, at
least part of the bill. How much he should pay would depend on a fair balancing of the hardships imposed by the
forgery on the uncle if he pays, or on the store if he does not.

"Due care"[1] on the part of a tradesman obviously
does not bind him to be so cautious that he excludes all
conceivable objections before extending credit. He is not
bound to guard against an epidemic of forgery among college students. It is too improbable. But if he has taken
reasonable precautions before he allows a student to start
a charge account, it seems fair that a loss due to the student's dishonesty or recklessness should fall rather on the
student's relatives than on the tradesman who is no relation to him. If (in the case just given) the uncle is really

---

[1] See below, p. 194; also Chapter XI.

no more to the student than various other relatives, and is no better off than they, it might be fairer to divide the bill by mutual consent between them, rather than to inflict the whole sum upon one.

The ethical decision here rests first on the assumption that somebody must bear a loss. Presumably the goods cannot be returned, because they have already been damaged or consumed. Next it is reasonable to believe that the student's own relatives are bound to him by tacit agreements and therefore are responsible for his doings as strangers are not. Most people's relatives will admit this. If, then, a boy's father or other relatives wish to cut him altogether adrift and to acknowledge no responsibility for his debts, they are bound to notify in advance any tradesmen with whom they may reasonably expect him to deal. Without this, a father's silence gives the tradesman the moral right to suppose that the son's debts will be paid in the usual way.

5. REPUDIATION OF AGREEMENTS

A peculiar type of broken agreement has to be dealt with when a national government repudiates the debt incurred by a previous government. The Russian Soviet Republic acknowledges no responsibility for debts incurred under the Czarist régime. The Soviet might now say that any one foolish enough to trust that the corrupt government of the old régime would last forever or would be succeeded by one in sympathy with its obligations, should be punished for his folly. No one can collect a gambling debt by force of law. It should never have been incurred. According to Soviet Russia, whoever dealt with the Czarist régime was a gambler and any agreement with the Czar was a bad agreement.[1]

---

[1] The actual reason given by the Soviet government is that repudiation is part of its war on capitalism (that is, on all other nations), and that the Soviet will

Against this it can be said that the Russian monarchy did not seem any nearer to its fall in 1914–1915 than for many years before that time, and that new governments have often assumed the debts of their predecessors even when they heartily disapproved of them. Unless governments could bind their successors, even their probably dissentient successors, no nation could negotiate a long-time loan. Most governments need now and then to borrow money. When the Soviet government needs a loan, it must be ready to bind whatever successors it may have on Russian soil; but in view of its own repudiations this may be difficult and so the loan may not be forthcoming.

When a government repudiates the borrowings of its predecessors it weakens not only its own credit but the credit of all similar governments. The Soviet's repudiations have not substantially weakened the credit of most other existing governments, I take it, because they are too different from them in standards of national morality to be affected by what the Soviet has done. But if any other state, say Turkey or China, should set up a dictatorship of the proletariat and then try to secure a government loan, the behavior of the Russian Soviet might stand in the way.

The continuous responsibility of a nation is comparable to that of a business partnership. New personalities entering a firm do not weaken its credit unless their previous record has shown their unreliability. Legally and morally, the members of a firm are responsible for their predecessors' engagements, no matter how they may differ from their policies and principles. Theoretically, a government, like a corporation, is as continuous as a single human

continue to repudiate its debts "until the complete victory of the international revolt of the workers against the yoke of capitalism." *Constitution of the Russian Socialist Federal Soviet Republic*, Sec. I, Chap. II, 3, d. Quoted by Walter R. Batsell, *Soviet Rule in Russia* (New York: The Macmillan Co., 1929), p. 82.

personality. No man repudiates last week's debts on the ground that he was then another person and that he does not now approve of what that other person did. Repudiation is regional suicide, like cutting off one's arm. That power cannot be restored.

6. THE RIGHT TO BREAK AN AGREEMENT

When should agreements be broken? Never by one party alone, until every attempt has been made to convince or at least to warn the other persons concerned. What diplomats call " unilateral action " by any party to an agreement tends to destroy the validity of all similar compacts. In the great majority of cases agreements cannot be rightly broken except by consent of those who made them. Even this unanimity is not always enough. All those concerned indirectly, as well as those who made the agreements, should be considered and, if there is doubt of their opinion, consulted. But there are occasions when there is no time or no way to reach the partners of an agreement. Their willingness may then, in exceptional cases, be assumed. Postponing this matter for the moment, I shall next consider occasions when agreements ought to be broken by the consent of all concerned.

(a) *When there was no serious agreement in the first place*, this fact may need to be made clear to one of the parties who tries to maintain the opposite. A binding pledge is one made seriously. A vow of marriage made in a theatrical performance, made as a pure joke, made by six-year-old children, made by persons who are insane at the time of the vow is not a valid agreement in law or in morals. Yet one of those concerned might conceivably wish to hold the other bound. The other is then not bound legally or morally, because he never intended to be. If both wish to be bound, then a true agreement should be made under

other conditions, outside the drama, before witnesses, in
sane, adult life.

(b) *Contracts made under force or fraud further exemplify
transactions which are not an accord but an extortion.* The law
justly assumes that those who enter a binding agreement
ought to be " on an equal footing," that is, in a position
to understand equally well what they agree to. One of
them may be wise and the other foolish, one rich and the
other poor, yet both should be equally competent to settle
their common business. But if a bargain is urged on B,
who is drunk, by A, who is sober, the law will not enforce
the contract, especially if A got B drunk in order to obtain
his consent.

Ethically this case is not quite so clear, because it is
usually fair to assume that though one may be irresponsible in drunkenness, he was responsible for getting drunk,
and so for the consequences that could reasonably be foreseen from drunkenness. Does this mean moral responsibility for whatever irrational deed he may do when drunk?
Not if in all his previous experience (fortunate man!) he
has never done anything irrational when drunk. He is
responsible only for what he can reasonably foresee. In
most cases, however, I think the plea of drunkenness as
an excuse for breaking a promise is advanced only when
one finds the later results of his promise inconvenient.
Ethically one ought to repudiate equally an advantageous
promise made in drink.

Simpler cases of *unfair agreements* are those in which one
person takes undue advantage of his special knowledge
and of another's confidence in it to procure his consent to
something entirely against his interest. Doctors sometimes
persuade patients to undergo expensive operations for
diseases, such as " chronic appendicitis," that do not
exist, and which these doctors know do not exist. If the

doctor has made a mistake in diagnosis, despite careful examination and consideration, the case is quite different. He cannot then be rightly blamed even though his mistake brings financial or physical disaster to his patient. But when he knowingly misleads his patient in order to get money, the agreement to pay is a fraudulent one and should be broken if the fraud is discovered in time.

A treaty made *à force majeure*, that is, under a threat of forcible coercion, is exemplified in the Chinese-Japanese agreement of 1915, giving Japan control of the Chinese province of Shantung. The Chinese signed this, as the Turks signed the treaty of Sèvres in 1920, not from any free consent to its terms but under coercion. The Japanese terms were presented as an ultimatum. Japan had the upper hand. China, helpless, submitted. It was an agreement like that by which a citizen surrenders his purse to a robber who points a pistol at his head. He takes the lesser of two evils, desiring neither.

Such a treaty, however, should not be recklessly broken by the injured side. It should endeavor to convince the conquerors that the treaty is certain to lead to trouble for all concerned and that it is for every one's interest to change it. If this fails the injured nation should appeal to whatever justice can be obtained through the League of Nations or through any group of nations representing a relatively disinterested international public opinion.

Does China's situation differ from the plight of one who agrees to pay a high price for food in a place where food is scarce? There is a sort of coercion in both cases. But in the latter it is at least possible that the seller as well as the buyer is coerced by circumstances and is not merely asserting his own superior power. If there is but little food to sell and he must live by the sale of this small quantity, he may, like the buyer, be forced to charge high prices in order to live.

The evil of an agreement accepted under the threat of coercion is that, like the international treaties just mentioned, it is in fact a disagreement masked by words. Hence it tends to upset itself as soon as the party coerced feels strong enough to revolt. It tends to break down in bitterness, not to improve itself in good feeling. Some of the peace pacts by which the nations of the world have improved their relations since 1920 tend to strengthen themselves as time goes on. But a " peace of victory " tends to break down. One cannot say that a pact signed under compulsion ought to be broken, but only that it is likely to break. It ought to be improved by voluntary arrangement.

(c) *The pseudo-agreements of childhood* which are more properly not agreements but customs, should later be validated or revised. Customs such as cleanliness and table-manners a child often accepts on authority or because of affection and trust. These are not genuine agreements. They are customs passed on by elders and impressed as habits. Not understanding them the child may forget them without any fault. His elders may properly remind him without blaming him or accusing him of breaking his word when he fails. In babyhood such habits are rightly enforced by parents without the hope of understanding or voluntary coöperation by the child. But his deviations from orthodox behavior in these matters are not breaches of an agreement. They may properly be repressed but not justly blamed.

As soon as children can understand, and often much sooner than their parents think so, the vague pseudo-agreements about washing, dressing, eating, keeping clean, punctuality, sharing, making a noise when elders want to be quiet, should be cleared up. Some of these the child will see the need of and will agree that he ought to keep. Some he may succeed in persuading his parents to give up. There will remain a residue which he sees no sense in but submits to for the time, as we submit to the wrong-headed ways of the party in power at Washington. We hope to change them some day. Meantime we prefer obedience to revolution.

In some families the bonds are so tightly knit that it is fair to say that each child makes a blanket-agreement to obey his parents. In other families the children have understood from early years that they are not under military rule but under a constitutional monarchy. The parent's powers are limited. He may give bad orders and the child is accustomed to distinguish them. For instance, the command to love and caress a member of the family to whom he is indifferent, may be issued on the general theory that any close family relation demands affection and its expression. I have heard a boy scolded because he did not try to carry out such a one-sided and unreasonable understanding. There is here no break of an agreement, only a disobedience by one side to what the other side has chosen to consider an agreement. But when the child has decided to disobey he is bound to give notice of it. Otherwise his silence means consent.

A similarly one-sided agreement often leads to trouble when the poor ask aid of a charitable organization. Perhaps the breadwinner is out of work and one of the children is sick. The social-worker may begin at once to make plans to help the family out of difficulties, forgetting to consult the persons most concerned, the members of the family. She may arrange to send the sick child to a hospital, telling the mother about the plan, but not discussing it with her or trying to show why it is safer for the child. Often enough the rather inarticulate mother says nothing at all at the time and is therefore assumed to have agreed to do her part in carrying out the plan. When she later fails to bring the child to the hospital, she is blamed or called " uncoöperative." But perhaps she never intended to coöperate, though she was too embarrassed or too inarticulate to say so. If it was a tacit agreement, it was vague and badly made. The situation would be better, of course, if the mother had voiced her objection at the start. But if she merely says and does nothing, the social-worker has herself to blame. Tacit agreements with those who are habitually tacit, or who are tacit because they do not know how to express themselves without giving offense, represent, I think, a blunder on the part of the more glib and self-conscious party.

7. THE VALIDITY OF AGREEMENTS WHICH PROMISE SECRECY

One may unwittingly accept a confidence involving a promise which one would not have agreed to make had one known what it involved. For example, a physician is consulted by a patient, makes an examination, and discovers smallpox, which requires notification to the board of health and so some publicity. The patient objects to this because he has given the physician confidential information, believing that it would be kept secret. Inconvenience and expense will be incurred if the secret becomes generally known. But the physician has previously pledged himself to obey the state laws enacted in order to protect the community in just such a case, by keeping all contagious patients isolated under the supervision of the board of health in their own homes or elsewhere. If the patient remains at home, the board may fix a placard on his house door warning every one of the contagion within. Such a warning is disagreeable and many families resent it. They implore the physician not to " betray " them.

They assert that he is threatening to betray a sacred confidence trustingly reposed by them in him.

His answer is that he never intended to receive any such confidence. He assumed that the patient would not ask him to break his previous implicit promise to the state; hence he cannot rightly be said to be betraying a confidence. So far as smallpox is concerned, few physicians in this country would now dare to break the law. With syphilis and gonorrhea they more often violate the law requiring a report to the board of health. The physician's duty, however, is perfectly clear in all such cases. He has agreed tacitly to obey the law and should do so unless he thinks it his duty to start a public revolution against it and go to prison as a martyr for his disobedience.

The same ethical problem is presented in a less serious form when some one tells you of an engagement in marriage and then tries to pledge you to absolute secrecy. This may be impossible without lying. If when asked, "Is So-and-so engaged?" you refuse to answer, you reveal the secret as much as if you said "Yes." If you say "No," you break your implicit pledge to your friends and acquaintances not to lie to them.

If a person unguardedly gives a general promise of secrecy before he is told of an engagement in marriage, he should at once explain that he understands his promise (like his visitor's desire) to be conditional. He is sure his visitor does not wish him to go to the length of telling a lie in order to keep the secret. In my experience the visitor then hastily assents, though he may rue it later. Should he demur we should try to make it plain that an unconditional promise of secrecy about an engagement in marriage may turn out to conflict with a previous implicit agreement of truthfulness which is not likely to be violated once without starting a wave of uncertainty about all sorts of statements, made either by the person telling the lie or by others. If still your visitor insists that he wishes to hold you to your promise of secrecy at all costs, the right course, I think, is to give him notice that you consider yourself bound by your previous tacit agreement of veracity with all persons, and that as you had no right to make another agreement violating this, and had not intended to do so, you do not feel bound by it in case it turns out to involve you in lies. No man has a right to assume that you will violate your general tacit agreement of veracity, any more than to assume that you will perjure yourself on the witness stand, or that you will steal or murder to oblige him. The secret of some one's contagious disease or some one's betrothal may have been deposited with us like stolen goods. One may buy a fur coat or receive one as a present, not knowing that it has been stolen. The agreement of sale or gift is then a bad one, though entered into without blame. It must be broken and the coat returned when the rightful owner is found. It is not ours to keep in contravention of our previous explicit or implicit agreements with society.

This case illustrates the principle already mentioned that agreements which contradict a previous agreement are bad and should be dissolved by the consent of those concerned. When the United States was ready to build the Panama Canal in the early years of this century, England had rights on the isthmus established by the Clayton-Bulwer Treaty of 1850. To secure a modification of these rights John Hay, President Roosevelt's Secretary of State, negotiated in 1902 a new treaty with England providing that " The Canal shall be open to the vessels of all nations . . . on terms of entire equality, so that *there shall be no discrimination . . . in respect to the charges of traffic* or otherwise." (Italics mine.) In direct violation of this treaty,

Congress passed in 1912 an act exempting American vessels engaged in coastwise trade from the canal tolls charged to the ships of other nations. Great Britain naturally protested, and in 1914 President Wilson induced Congress to break this bad agreement with our coastwise shipping and to keep its previous compact with England. The exemption act of 1912 was repealed. Obviously this was the only fair thing to do. It was like the act of a man who having inadvertently made two engagements for the same hour breaks the later one, after confessing and apologizing for his stupidity. But I think we have never confessed our fault nor apologized to England.

The agreements of criminals with each other, against the public, should be broken for the reason just given,—because they violate previous civic agreements, tacit or implicit. For example: the secret rebates promised in 1870 by the Lake Shore Road to the Standard Oil Company [1] stood for a promise to carry their oil cheaper than the oil offered by other shippers, and were therefore paid in violation of law. The rebate agreement violated a previous promise to favor no single shipper. Discriminations in rates to favor one shipper would give a railroad power to make or break any of its customers. The law prohibited this, and the Standard Oil Company, as an incorporated body, had agreed to obey this law.

8. INVOLUNTARY CANCELLATION OF AGREEMENTS. WHO SHOULD BEAR THE LOSS?

When war breaks out, when fire, earthquake, flood, or pestilence devastates a country, it may be quite impossible to do what had previously been promised. An impassable river may separate a contractor from his job on the date

[1] Ida M. Tarbell, *History of the Standard Oil Company* (New York: McClure, Phillips & Co., 1904), Vol. I, p. 49.

when he had promised to carry out his contract. How should the resulting loss be borne?

Early in 1914 a gas company contracted to light the streets of a town on the east coast of England. When the war broke out and bombs began to fall from aeroplanes in night raids, all street lights were prohibited by law. The contract could not legally be fulfilled. In this case there was no ethical question of a right to keep or break an agreement. The town was not free. Wars and earthquakes abolish agreements by the dozen. Under the conditions the contracts become meaningless. No one has broken them though the law sometimes rashly says that an " act of God " has made their performance impossible. Physical forces have produced disaster. The only discussible question is, who should bear the burden? Early English law punished the contractor who could not reach his job on account of a flooded river. This is manifestly unjust. But it seems almost as unfair that those who engaged him should be penalized, as in some cases they would be, because of the contractor's failure, even though he could not help it. Suppose a plumber has agreed to come at any time in answer to an emergency call to mend a leaking water-pipe. An accident unavoidably detains him, and no other competent person can be found to stop the leak. The escaping water undermines a wall and part of a house falls down. Who should bear the damage?

The best answer, I think, is suggested by a parallel to the laws now widely prevalent in this country for compensation to workmen accidentally injured while at work. It is often impracticable to settle how far the workman, his fellow workmen, or their employer may have been responsible for the casualty. If every one concerned has been obeying the laws intended to safeguard workmen in their employment, it is better to assume that, under the conditions, such a misfortune could not be foreseen or prevented. It was, in short, an accident and no one's fault. The insurance company then pays compensation and so the burden is shared by a considerable portion of the community. When a road is washed out or a bridge broken down by a flooded river, the expense of mending is still more widely shared. Taxation divides the expenses; every taxpayer pays part of them and so no one is unfairly burdened. In the case of a workman injured in a factory, the community is not so obviously inconvenienced as by a washout. But it is just that a good many people should share indirectly the burden of compensating the workman and his family, because the community has been hit, in the person of one of its members, by an accidental occurrence, which apparently is no one's fault.

If the injury is obviously due to the workman's own carelessness, it seems unfair to burden his employer with the cost of his disablement. But is it not equally unfair to burden the worker's wife, his children, his relatives and friends with this cost? In such a case the workman cannot bear the whole cost of his carelessness. Others must share it, others who are as little to blame as the employer. It will do no good to penalize the workman's family. So by insurance or through taxation the burden is justly shared by many.

9. ACCIDENTS AND DUE CARE

When " unforeseeable " events, such as a tornado, an earthquake or a war prevent us from keeping an agreement, it must often be admitted that they were not strictly unforeseeable. Earthquakes happen more frequently on the coast of California than in many other places. After the very serious earthquake of 1906, there was talk of rebuilding the city of San Francisco in some safer place. Strictly this would not have been impossible, only enormously expensive. If this seems preposterous, consider the villages built high up on the volcanic cone of Mount Etna, which is always active and which every few years emits destructive lava streams. It is not absurd to say that these villages ought to be removed, even at considerable hardship to their people. Disaster is not for them unforeseeable. It should be foreseen and prevented. At the other extreme is the situation of a state like Massachusetts, repeatedly shaken by slight, so far harmless, earth-tremors; never, I think, by a serious one. No one would say that Boston should be moved to a safer place for fear of a serious earthquake.

Problems like those which come up in this chapter are bound to arise even in the best regulated families, groups, and societies, because we cannot get on without agreements yet can never be wise enough to make them watertight and fool-proof. Any person's life and growth depend upon the crystallization of purposes into agreements which connect the days, acts, feelings, plans of any one individual, so that he hangs together and is not hysterical or irresponsible. They also make it possible to work, play, and be friends with other people.

But agreements are the children of desires and inherit their parents' failings. When desires are ill-considered or self-contradictory, the compacts which represent them may need to be broken. Not every one who starts on a journey finishes it. If it turns out a fool's errand one stops and turns round. Of course one cannot be perpetually revoking one's desires. Unless most of them are carried out a man has no continuous life and society falls to pieces. But because we are neither angelic nor devilish we find that we can live by many of our agreements but not by all.

The gist of this chapter seems to be that:—

1. Very few agreements are as absolute as they sound. The parties usually understand that under certain conditions (not very definitely grasped) a prior engagement, professional, civic, patriotic, conscientious may emerge. This is understood to take precedence. But the exact order of precedence is not always clearly understood or similarly understood by the persons concerned. Such matters should be more thoroughly talked out at a time when no crisis is at hand.

2. Unexcused delay in the fulfillment of a compact weakens confidence in the individual and to some extent in all individuals. The legal statute of limitations about debts has no ethical force.

3. We are bound by the promise of another acting in our name if we have, tacitly or explicitly, allowed him so to act.

4. National credit depends on the understanding that a government will honor the debts of its predecessor even though disapproving of its policies.

5. No one should break an agreement without an effort to get it modified or abandoned with the consent of all concerned; this effort should be as persistent as the conditions permit.

6. Such consent should be sought:

(a) When one of the parties had never intended to make any such agreement.

(b) When the agreement was not valid at the outset; for example, a compact made in joke, by minors, by the insane.

(c) When it was made under force or fraud.

(d) When it contradicts a previous agreement.

7. Agreements may become impossible to perform because of some unforeseen catastrophe, such as war, fiat

money, earthquake, fire, flood, illness, or accident. If this involves a loss of property, the burden may properly be shared by others exposed to similar risks.

It must be recognized, however, that very few accidents are as accidental as they appear. Many of them challenge us to convince ourselves and others that *due care* has been exerted in the effort to prevent them. I shall return to this problem in Chapter XI.

Chapter IX

THE VALIDITY OF CUSTOMARY AND LEGAL AGREEMENTS

1. THE DECISION TO REJECT A TRADITION PREVIOUSLY ACCEPTED MAY REQUIRE DUE NOTICE TO OTHERS CONCERNED

Traditions, as for example, those of the sea, are not all of them binding, but due notice should be given when we decide to break them. What I have written so far about the tools to be used for unearthing what is right and distinguishing it from what is wrong, may sound as if each of us should mine his gold and settle his principles without considering any one else. It seems inevitable that each of us must make up his own mind in the end, and do as he thinks best all things considered. But among the things to be considered are the usual ways of the world, the feelings of those about us, the traditions of the past, and the fashion of the present. None of these can make up a person's mind for him. But they hand us facts which we need to reckon with.

In any epoch which thinks of itself as an " age of transition," clever people rebel against duty, morality, and the idea that there is any good sense in the word " ought." Against these old ideas they assert the individual's freedom to do as he likes. In our time this takes form as a revolt against "Puritanism" or "Victorianism." In such protests, sense and nonsense are intimately mixed. But I am interested in what I take to be the sense of the mixture.

No tradition which people have obeyed for years or centuries has any right, so far as I see, to command assent from any one of us unless we have allowed others to believe that we accept its authority. Age and respectability entitle a tradition to be examined with care, because what has suited the last generation *may* still suit this generation. There is no good reason to believe that men's desires and preferences change so rapidly in a single generation that no important identities survive. If our fathers believed in marriage, in honesty, in nationalism, and in " free competition," some value probably remains in these notions. But how much? One can find out only by asking oneself as thoughtfully as one can whether they still express human needs.

Jim accepted the traditions of the sea when he joined the " Patna " in Conrad's story. Perhaps he tacitly acquiesced in customs which he had never questioned. On discovering this he might decide to rebel against them. But granted that the dead hand of the past had no right permanently to hold him, the question still remains: should he reject it *instanter*? Is it our duty as well as our right to throw off any dead tradition as soon as we discover that, for us, it is dead? If so the customs of the sea ought, perhaps, to have had no authority over Jim. He might properly refuse to acquiesce in the nautical tradition which bound him to stay on his ship in case of disaster at sea. *But at what date had he a right to refuse?* Having gone aboard the ship tacitly agreeing to the old tradition, could be rightly repudiate it as soon as his more wide-awake consciousness discovered its absurdity? Suppose he had suddenly come to consider it positively mischievous that a man's hands should be tied by this tradition. What then?

A man is not bound, as Emerson says, " to drag along forever the corpse of his dead self." If he has seen the error of his ways, he should change them; *but with due notice.* When he finds himself sailing in the wrong direction it is ordinarily sensible to stop at once and turn round. But if he discovers his mistake at a moment when other vessels are clustered thickly around him, he must not attempt to turn round as soon as the thought flashes up. Others should be warned so that they can get out of the way without collision. If Jim changed his mind about the traditions of the sea, he must still admit that he accepted his position as mate as if he had no objection to the duties traditionally associated with it. When he came aboard without objection he committed himself and involved others, the shipload of Mohammedan pilgrims in particular. Therefore during the life of that understanding, that is, for the duration of this voyage, he is bound by the traditions which he did not overtly repudiate at the start. When next he wants to go to sea, if he still believes that the traditional *mores* of the sea have no foundation in human needs, he can explain that in case of a disaster he will recognize no responsibility for the passengers or cargo. Then his employer will have the option of refusing to employ him or of taking him with the understanding that if anything goes wrong Jim will look out first for himself.

"Thou shalt not murder thine agreements," seems to be a commandment implied in making them. We are not bound to abide forever by every custom to which we have been somehow committed. But when we decide to change, we are expected,—indeed we have tacitly agreed,—to remember the traffic around us. We must give due notice of our new convictions; else we become a menace.

2. WE OFTEN DEPEND ON TACIT "BLANKET-AGREEMENTS"
　　BY WHICH WE GIVE AND RECEIVE ASSURANCES THOUGH WE
　　MAY NOT NOTICE THEM

When we visit a foreign city, play a new game or a new piece of music, we "catch on" to its ways by watching others and by sensing its spirit. So it is that we " catch on " to the ways of our own community, turn to the right as we pass people in the street, lift our hats on meeting a lady known to us, drop our dimes in a slot as we enter a subway. No thought is given to such matters. We fall into the ways of others because it is convenient, because it avoids collisions, and because we want to " play the game " in which we find ourselves.

When we do this our behavior gives, and other people silently take assurances. We expect and lead others to expect that familiar customs can be depended on. Such assurance does not hold good in all parts of the world. In a remote corner of Borneo, of the Cameroons, or of Chicago, where the customs of the place are not known to us, we may be uncertain whether it is safe to go alone and unarmed. Our very presence may unwittingly challenge all and sundry to come out and fight us. On the other hand, in the Champs Élysées, on London Bridge, in the 42d Street depot in New York, the chance of being attacked is so small that we are not aware of it. Pockets may be picked but life is safe. The general population in such a district rests its security on the existence of a tacit blanket-agreement to live and let live. For some, this understanding is valid only because they are afraid to break it. No universal good will controls them. But under the local conditions of publicity and police protection one is safe in assuming that those we meet intend to live and let live.

If any one challenges this assumption and asserts that he has never made any such agreement, it can be pointed out, first, that when an alien receives citizenship in this country he swears to " bear true faith and allegiance to " the laws of the United States; and further, that all parents are legally responsible for the lawful and orderly behavior of their minor children. The ordinary adult citizen makes no such promise to be orderly or to obey the laws. But surely we expect at least as good behavior of him as we demand of the newly naturalized alien.[1] Most of the adults who are not immigrants have never explicitly declared their intention to respect the laws and duties of citizenship as set forth in the laws of the land. And even if they have so declared, the oath often has little or no force because it is made in a perfunctory way. There are vast numbers of laws that scarcely any one has heard of or could possibly remember if he had read them. The agreements which actually work in keeping the peace are largely tacit and half-unconscious. They represent an attitude, mental and habitual, an intention to behave decently, either because one is used to doing so, or because one fears the disagreeable consequences of misbehavior. Few people want the dislike of their fellows, the reputation of being queer, unreliable, or cantankerous. No one wants an inconvenient and conspicuous conflict with the police.

Ordinarily we live under tacit blanket-agreements which include obedience to well-known laws unless and until we are ready to rebel publicly. But the laws actually passed may include such as H. L. Mencken describes: "A law is something that A wants and can hornwoggle B, C, D, and F into giving him, by bribery, by lying, by bluff and bluster, by making faces. G and H are therefore bound to respect it, nay to worship it. It is something sacred."[2] Of course Mr. Mencken knows well enough that *some* laws represent what he and all of us desire to have enforced. He intends to wake us to the need of defiance toward

[1] Any one who makes this assumption, as I do, is apt to be accused of believing in Rousseau's *contrat social* and other legends of imaginary history. But the accusation, like Rousseau's theory, is absurd.

[2] Quoted by G. B. Munson in *Humanism and America* (New York: Farrar & Rinehart, 1930), p. 246.

certain notoriously bad laws, and of skeptical inquiry about others. But no intelligent study of laws can escape the attempt to distinguish good laws from bad.

Tacit blanket-agreements regulate our ordinary behavior in the streets, in trolley cars, schools, colleges, factories, theaters, churches. There is no law and no explicit compact about lining up in the order of arrival before a window where tickets are sold. But the indignation vented on a late comer who tries to slip in at the head of the line shows that we expect him to catch on to this customary agreement by native intelligence, and to abide by it in common decency. To take off one's hat in a Christian church and to keep it on in a Jewish synagogue are customs which all decent males are expected to obey, though no oath or law enjoins it upon them. The ordinary man may see no good reason for either custom. He is not expected to, and, if he is wise, does not always expect to. It is only when law is put behind a custom, as in the traffic regulations, that we hope to discover a good reason for it.

3. SUCH UNDERSTANDINGS SAVE TIME AND LABOR

We need such tacit blanket-agreements. They are convenient, labor-saving customs. For their network of expectations given and received we take no credit to ourselves and desire none. They are convenient, not virtuous, —convenient because they let us focus attention on more interesting affairs without need to worry about personal safety, without fear that others bear us ill will, suspect us, or plot against us. How much energy these agreements save, how much unhappiness they prevent, we realize only when we are deprived of them. When one is grabbed by the throat or swallows something the wrong way, one becomes aware how precious is breath. How precious is our ordinary confidence of security we realize only when we see the terrified neurasthenic or the bewildered immigrant choked by fears of what people may be thinking of him, suspicious that he is being watched, despised, or laughed at, fearful for his own safety.

4. THEY ALSO SAVE WORRY

Customary agreements save anxiety by providing security. A suspicion of insecurity makes us miserable. It also blocks our plans. Not only war, but any approach to war conditions (that is, mutual suspicion, espionage, hate, violence, eagerness to deceive and to outwit), blocks the trunk line over which our ordinary plans travel towards their destinations. It is no particular pleasure to be secure on our feet because of the pull of gravitation and the balance of our muscles. But unless we have this security we cannot do anything. We do not often rejoice in the law and order of our town or in the fact that we pursue our interests unhampered by racketeers or the fear of them. But we depend nevertheless on law and order as a basis for the activities that make our lives worth living. The convenience of the understandings which underlie our confidence in each other, the saving of pain and energy, the enfranchisement of our minds for work, for enjoyment, for friendship, and for creative planning,—these facts make blanket-agreements important in civilized life.

5. DUE CARE IN THE APPLICATION OF CUSTOMARY AND LEGAL AGREEMENTS

Official devotion to regulations about law and order sometimes means brutal repression of free speech and rigid defense of things as they are. Any innovation tends to upset the old order in a hospital, a college, or a business office. The old order naturally resents being upset, and so the maintenance of routine strangles improvements as well as crimes. To rigid minds the desire to improve things and the desire to smash everything look much alike. Their surface must be broken through in either case. It is broken from without by the burglar or the murderer. It is split from within, like the egg of the emerging chick, when an inventor, a reformer, or a reorganizer gets to work. He breaks up the old shape of a law, of a building, of an economic order, or of a religion so as better to express the needs which first produced that shape.

Destruction and reform often go together. A surgical operation intended to improve life may extinguish it. An emigrant who pulls up stakes and abandons his old life, hoping to better himself in a new country, may never succeed in his ventures. The betterment intended by surgeon and emigrant may end in ruin. Because of this, timid people even the " timid good," may become, as Theodore Roosevelt said, the enemies of the public. Grasping security and quiet, they vote down reasonable reforms or stigmatize them as revolutionary. On the other hand, the temperamentally restless, the habitually discontented applaud every proposal for a change whether it gives evidence of being an improvement or not. To such people all law-and-order is a ruler's pretext to perpetuate iniquitous old customs. To the conservative, all who attack the established order are criminals.

Despite these misunderstandings it is obvious that *some* degree of law and order is a means to improvement as well as to stability. The order which makes a place safe for a conservative to live in also insures safety to inventors, creative artists, municipal reformers, and educational reformers, while they labor to change that place for the better. It ought to be made dangerous only for those who plan violent destruction.

Our blanket-agreements are useful then. But they must be made and remade to fit the needs of our growth. Our tacit compacts to maintain each other's safety and to let each other alone when we want to be let alone, work most of the time because " we " agree fairly well in a local standard of taste and manners. But this is not always so. What seems a decent reserve to us may seem an inhuman frigidity to a stranger. What looks to traveling Americans like a free fight among the boatmen of Tangiers or the porters at Alexandria seems to them, I suppose, only a lively emulation. Tagore has told us that Hindus do not object to a good deal of disorder and dirt. Consequently they hate the English for spending so much tax-money on cleanliness and order. One man's order is another man's chaos. In each case " order " or " safety " means *such* a degree of coöperation (or of independence) as suits the purposes of those concerned. In one town it means pretending not to see strangers when we meet them and giving each as wide a berth as the traffic permits. In another it includes loud yells, fiery looks, furious gestures, fierce jostling, but usually stops short of bodily injury. A pack of hounds pressing to get out of their kennel when the door is opened, tumble over each other chaotically but without mutual hostility. Some men feel quite orderly when they are behaving like that pack.

Chapter X

THE INTERPRETATION OF AGREEMENTS

To distinguish the spirit from the letter of laws and of other agreements is an unescapable need, (a) because we are so much clearer in our desires than in our expression of them in agreements, (b) because we forget, (c) because we grow, and (d) because nearly all our desires are conditional.

The virtue of an agreement is to be clear and binding, within the period of its intended life. It takes human relations out of vagueness. It prevents disputes about what we can rightly expect of ourselves and of each other. But the phrase, "spirit and letter of agreements," seems to bring back the vagueness which agreements were planned to abolish. The word "spirit" has misty associations. What is to become of the solidity of our understandings if one can interpret them in terms so fanciful and so arbitrary as "spirit"? The answer to this objection is that we are forced to depend upon this spirit because many an agreement, written, spoken, or tacit, does not interpret itself in a changing situation. Some one has to decide what it means. Who? If possible, the person who made it. No one knows its significance as well as he, for he knows the purpose (or spirit) that made it. Our purposes are among the clearest items in our consciousness. Far less plain are the words in which we express them. Most of us know what we should like to accomplish, but few have skill to express it in accurate speech, or in understandings with ourselves and others.

1. LETTER AND SPIRIT; A DISTINCTION NEEDED BECAUSE WE ARE MUDDLED

Hence the need to revert now and then from the letter of an understanding to its purpose or meaning is as unescapable as the meaning itself. So long as we have so much more skill in knowing our own minds than we have in conveying their substance to others in lucid words, we shall be occupied off and on with the ancient task of construing today the text of a law, a constitution, a treaty, a spoken or written promise, in the light of what we know we once meant, or believe that some one else meant. The labor of interpreting rigid words in the light of growing purposes is a perennial human task. Nothing speaks for itself, not even the precise symbols and figures of mathematics, far less the data of physical and social science. None of them keeps up with our growing knowledge of facts and of our own meaning.

2. BECAUSE WE ARE SHORTSIGHTED AND FORGETFUL

Agreements are no more secure than the memory and the imaginative foresight of those who made them. We forget part of what we meant. Our minds weather like trees and our meanings with them. We fail to imagine the probable or possible future. "And to thee only do I promise to keep myself so long as we *both* shall live." When that promise is spoken, neither bride nor groom imagines the possibility of another marriage in case one of them should become hopelessly insane. They feel that they are united to each other and to no one else so long as *either* of them shall live. Later in married life one of them may change and the other may persist in this wedding-day's vision of marriage as eternal. Whether by growth or by deterioration we often change our minds about such matters. To the one who remains faithful to their pledge as they both ardently understood it at the outset, the other whose mind changes may seem unfaithful to the spirit of their agreement.

I know no way to rule out such difficulties as this once for all. If we succeed in freeing one or two of our agreements from any shade of obscurity, we shall neglect others. In some of them, the divergent interpretations of later life will certainly raise difficult problems of mutual charity and forbearance. So far as I can see, there is no cure or prevention for this. It is inherent in the precious but sometimes tragic facts of growth and of individuality. But with forbearance and mutual charity, and with willingness to discuss what is now reasonable as well as what was once said or written, we can still persist in the spirit of our agreements despite our differences.

3. BECAUSE WE GROW

The spirit must remake the letter again and again, not only because we forget but because we grow. We can keep our agreements alive and growing only by exercising them frequently in the light of our present. The spirit that originally made a partnership, an institution, a marriage may have grown or changed so much within a few years that unless we bring it up for discussion frequently, we who made it may differ about what we made and what action it now calls for. Witness the disputes about the Monroe Doctrine, the freedom of the seas, the Sherman anti-trust law, or the definition of an amateur athlete. We need to appeal again and again from the letter of these agreements to the needs which made them and to the history of those needs down to the present moment.

The spirit of any agreement is thus disconcertingly wider and deeper than its letter, because both are parts of the human spirit, a network of interweaving purposes aware of but a fragment of its own implications. Its purposes are not sharply or permanently outlined. They grow as it grows. They find meaning after meaning hidden like a nest of Chinese boxes inside the one that they start with. They are also in constant danger of disintegration through forgetfulness and through their distracted imitation of other people. Ethics deals not only with agreements but with the desires which give birth to them, and with the needs which have created these desires. We can be saved from a rule-of-thumb existence because our desires, flooded with new experiences of fact, emotion, and speculative thought, confront us with the need to remake them. We desire to make a living; but find that we need to make a life as well. We desire to be up-to-date in the political life of our time, and find ourselves engaged in the formidable study of history. We desire to understand our friends, and find ourselves thus pledged to study their interests, their psychology, their ancestry, their religion.

In this growth we are in line with modern jurisprudence which shows us how great judges, in their conscientious attempt to expound and to interpret the law, have for centuries been adding to it, cautiously but helpfully. Judge-made law is no longer a bogey to us. The spirit of the Common Law, of the English Constitution, or even of the written Constitution of the United States is something to be learned, but also something to be cultivated and to be created. It is like the spirit of science, through which a scientist masters the discoveries of his predecessors and then, carried on the current of their spirit, makes discoveries of his own.

We are all judges, especially about the developing significance of our own affairs. Hence each of us should do his bit of creation in ethics. Human relations and the interior relations of our own minds are fields of art in which each of us has a chance and a need to do something creative. Conversations, week-ends, vacations, partnerships, industries, friendships are works of art in which we are drawn to attempt improvisations upon ancient themes. Sincerity urges us to say what we see and what we think, and every time that we are veracious we are original. Even in the dullest and laziest of us this process is started by our central need, to grow.

Then, if we are at all sincere with ourselves, even the most familiar of our ideas come to be combined in new ways and colored with new shades of meaning. The ancient endeavor to make a friend and to be a friend is forever renewed because we and our friends are growing individuals who never before occurred upon this growing planet. The world we live in has changed since Jonathan and David, even since Roosevelt and Taft essayed to build a friendship. We see friendship in our own terms and we desire to make it somewhat different from the friendships that we have heard of. We face new possibilities outside us and new impulses within us. These are the spirit of our endeavors. By them we make a series of sketches which gradually fix themselves in understandings with ourselves or with others, understandings which are crude with our crudeness, stupid with our stupidity, but able to remold themselves again and again to make their letter more nearly fit their spirit. We are not without guides and precedents in ethics. We get hints from history and suggestions from our contemporaries. But when it comes to the final stage, the stage of action, we must go it alone. In our daily dealings with our jobs, our pleasures, our friends, and our own ideas, no one can tell us what we prefer or what we mean.

4. BECAUSE MOST DESIRES AND SO MOST AGREEMENTS ARE CONDITIONAL

So far in this chapter I have been trying to show three reasons why the bright red tape of agreements has to be untied and retied again and again, because they do not contain all that we meant when we made them, because we degenerate and forget part of what we meant when we made them, and because we grow.

But there is a fourth reason. Though our desires are among the clearest parts of our consciousness, *few of them are unconditional*. In speaking just now of our agreements I recalled three familiar facts: (a) that any doctor's social engagements are made subject to his patients' professional needs, (b) that he ordinarily thinks himself bound to leave his patients if he is conscripted for the army in time of war, and (c) that if he conscientiously objects to all war, he may break even his agreements with his country in order to do what he thinks right. Parallel to this series of agreements,—social, professional, civic, conscientious,—each conditioned by those of a higher order, there is a series of conditional desires.

We desire to lie in bed so long as there is no reason to get up; but when the family's convenience needs us, then we need, and should desire, to get up. The family's claims are matched by our desire to answer them until business demands our efforts. Because we desire to make good in business, our domestic comfort is not what we desire when it interferes with business. Our ambition for business, however, is conditional on our not being needed for national service in a crisis like war. But even to the nation we owe no absolute allegiance. Only when a man feels that the State has *rightly* called on him, as it might in time of famine, earthquake, or flood is he bound to take his part in the common service. He may well feel a keener zest for such a job than for any other. But for a war which he believes unjust, the nation's order arouses not his desire but his loathing.

Man rightly desires ease when it interferes with no other claim. He desires family life provided it does not upset his business, business provided it does not cancel national service in a genuine crisis, and national service provided it is in line with what he believes to be true and right.

5. THE UNCONDITIONED DESIRE AND THE NEED BEHIND IT

His ultimate loyalty, then, his only unconditioned desire, is for whatever the truth as he sees it may reveal for his guidance. If it be possible, he wants to follow this along a path that does not cut him off from his friends, from his business, from family life, and from simple pleasures. But no one can make up his own mind for him, and to be true to what he sees as the truth is not only his right and duty, it is his only security against mental annihilation.

Our only unconditional need, with which our desire must come to agree on pain of death, is for such experience as will enlighten our ignorance. We need all that forwards this growth, and we need nothing else. Our best service to others is to fertilize their experience with ours and ours with theirs. Friendship and marriage, industry and government are built up by such mutual fertilization. But we have nothing to give unless we have been truthful with ourselves in acknowledging both what we see and where our vision stops. This takes courage, especially when we happen to see what others do not, or fail to see what is evident to them. It is especially by the exercise of such courage that we can be of use to our fellows. It is by the differences in our brains and in our fields of experience that we contribute something to the common pool.

Hence our particular desires and agreements all need to be conditional. So far as they are for anything that cannot deepen or widen the experience by which and through which we may contribute to the world's progress, they are nothing that we need and should be nothing to us. Pleasure, pain, sleep, food, solitude, sociability, travel, comfort, poverty, work, play, love, worship are desirable and should be desired so far as they go on from the place where we last stopped reading in the book of experience. We keep the spirit of our agreements when we are obedient to the spirit of growth which lives in them and in us. Internal honesty is the food of this spirit.

Chapter XI

DUE CARE

1. LEGAL ASPECTS

It has long been recognized in the Common Law that society expects each member not only to abstain from maliciously injuring another's person, property, and reputation, by aggressive action or by breach of contract, but to exercise " due care" in the fulfillment of his obligations to other people.

In trying to settle ethically or legally how to divide the burden of disasters, actual, foreseen or only dimly conjectured, one faces the problem of what kind or degree of care constitutes " *due care.*" After a disaster at sea we inquire whether any one has been careless, perhaps criminally careless. Granted that one did not foresee and was taken by surprise so that no ill will entered into the disaster, should one have foreseen? The attempt to answer this question leads me to consider situations in which there is, admittedly or possibly, a partial responsibility for the breaking of a promise, not complete disability or powerlessness, though an element of accident is admitted.

In 1854 [1] a man leased a piece of land with an option to buy it at a certain price. Gold and silver were then legal tender and no other form of money was known to the landowner to be contemplated. Nevertheless in 1862 Congress made " greenbacks " legal tender. The lessee exercised his option and tendered the price of the land in greenbacks,

---

[1] This case is taken from G. L. Clark's *Principles of Equity* (Columbia, Mo.: E. W. Stephens, 1924).

worth then about half as much as gold. Should the owner be forced to sell on those terms? The court held that the hardship was too great and that he should not be compelled to sell. Ethically this seems fair. The war and the desperate financial expedients adopted by Congress to pay its expenses could conceivably, but not probably, have been foreseen by the landowner in 1854. Circumstances, and not his carelessness, led to his difficulties. The letter of this contract was broken for him, not by him. The court decided according to the spirit of it.

It seems clear that relief from the obligation to keep a promise " because of changed conditions " should depend ethically on whether or not the change could reasonably have been foreseen. Conditions can be counted on to change somewhat between the making of a promise and the time of its fulfillment. The weather will certainly change, the conditions governing prices, markets, and very probably wages. Other opportunities and invitations will probably be shifted. The law and the customs of society do what they can to discourage gambling in business, in contracting marriage, or in a bucket-shop. But they do not wish to penalize genuine hard luck brought on by illness or pure " accident." That would increase unavoidable hardship.

An unforeseen and disastrous change of conditions is the essence of the " great hardship " which has been considered by the courts a sufficient reason for allowing a person to break his promise. For similar reasons our law does not allow a bankrupt to be deprived of the tools of his trade, even though his creditors seem to have a right to them. The community has a prior agreement with each of its members not to deprive him of the means of making a living, both for his own sake and in order that he may not become a public burden. This agreement foresees and discounts in advance the claims of creditors based on the bankrupt's debts. They cannot rightly expect him to carry out promises to them as creditors, in contradiction to the promises which as citizens they earlier made to him and to all men in the laws about bankruptcy.

2. ETHICAL ASPECTS OF DUE CARE

Let us consider some cases in which the obligation of due care is clearly an ethical as well as a legal question. If a doctor has assumed the medical care of a sick man and if the patient dies, suit for malpractice may be brought by his relatives in case they believe that the doctor was careless. In such a suit the doctor cannot escape by showing that he wished the patient no ill and did nothing to injure him. He cannot escape by proving that he visited the sick man and prescribed treatment. He must also prove that he was not careless either in what he did or in what he omitted to do. He must show that he used due care.

What is due care? Three examples will bring before us the factors and the problems involved.

(a) An epidemic of diphtheria broke out in February a few years ago in a part of Alaska to be reached at that season only by a dog-sledge journey. A wireless message was sent out asking that antitoxin for diphtheria be sent as fast as possible by dog sledge from the Health Office of the nearest city. It was so sent and on arrival was administered to a considerable number of children. A large proportion of them died immediately with symptoms suggesting that the serum had in all probability caused the death.

On investigation it was shown that other portions of the same lot of antitoxin had previously been used with excellent results under the Health Board which sent it, and that stock samples of the same make were still (in animals) curative and not poisonous. It was also shown that during the dog-sledge journey the bottles of antitoxic serum sent to Alaska *had been frozen*. But when thawed out again before administration there was no alteration in their looks or odor. They were apparently unchanged and had therefore been administered,— with the fatal result already told.

Was the Board of Health morally wrong, criminally careless, in sending the serum? Should they be punished for the death of the children?

The intentions of the Board of Health were obviously good. The ethical question is, Were they careless? Should they, or their agents, have tested this particular lot of serum after it arrived in Alaska and before it was administered? Such is not the custom when batches of serum are sent out from a state laboratory and used in nearby cities applying for it. Antitoxic serum has been found to keep well, and in the Alaska case the retesting of other specimens which had been manufactured at the same time as the fatal bottles showed that it *had* kept well. In animals, the serum had all its curative properties. (Naturally it would not have been proper to test it on human beings.)

Was the Board of Health or its agents negligent in not packing the serum so as to prevent its freezing? Assuming that such protection against freezing is practicable under the conditions of a sledge journey to Alaska, which seems rather improbable, there still appears no reason why any one should have anticipated that freezing would do any harm to an antitoxic serum. In preserving such material ordinarily it is heat, rather than cold, that one avoids. We keep it on ice in the laboratory, cool though never frozen. Moreover, the ordinary changes in appearance or in smell to be expected if the serum had deteriorated were not found in this case.

The Board of Health and its agents, then, do not seem to have been careless or in any way blameworthy. On the basis of previous experience they could not reasonably have expected that freezing and subsequent thawing would render diphtheria antitoxin poisonous. Only the subsequent animal experiments have recently proved that this is actually the case. We now know that a fresh, potent, curative antidiphtheritic serum becomes a poison if it is frozen and then thawed. *But this is a new fact.* It was unknown to science until brought to light by this tragic accident and by the experiments which followed it. No blame, therefore, should be attached to the Board of Health, though it was only natural that the parents of the unfortunate children should demand punishment for those who furnished a serum which killed their children. The members of the Board were not careless. They exercised due care, though despite it, tragedy occurred.

It is certainly a sobering reflection that fatal accidents like this can happen in connection with the administration of a remedy which ordinarily saves hundreds of lives a year in every great city of the United States. The weight of responsibility which, as this accident shows, now rests on boards of health and on all who under their supervision prepare and administer diphtheria antitoxin is really terrific. For they exercise coercive powers. Children taken sick with diphtheria in the congested tenements of a city cannot always be allowed by the health board to remain in their homes, even when the parents wish it. The difficulties of procuring proper home care for them and the danger of their infecting others sometimes make it imperative to take such children to a hospital. But once in the hospital, diphtheria antitoxin is almost certain to be given, and its administration, as this case shows, has had dangers that no one could foresee. Parents therefore have little choice but to allow their children to be subjected to certain risks which no one can yet accurately measure.

Any one who takes a railroad train, a motor car, or even an elevator runs a risk to life and limb. But it is a small and a reasonable risk known to all, and the individual is under no compulsion to take it. Strictly speaking, I suppose, the parent of a child taken to a municipal hospital to be treated for diphtheria can refuse to allow this remedy, often life-saving, occasionally dangerous, to be given to his child. But under conditions as they exist, parents have neither knowledge nor power which would lead them to interfere. When an epidemic has broken out, they and their children are obliged to trust the vigilance and the skill of the men and women officially in charge of the city's health. On the whole there are extraordinarily few accidents in this field of work and the community has good reason to be satisfied. But a little carelessness on the part of any member of a large group,—laboratory workers, technicians, pharmacists, physicians, internes, nurses,— may have fatal results. Even without any carelessness deaths may result (as in the Alaskan case) simply because medical science is still young.

Let us take another medical case.

(b) Mrs. Jones was ill with pneumonia in a private hospital in which the charge is $100. a week. Nurses were in attendance day and night. On the night of December 18 the night nurse, having had no rest during the day, was unable to resist drowsiness and finally fell into a deep sleep, during which the patient became delirious, got out of bed, jumped from the window, and was killed. Was the nurse to blame?

Can one resist drowsiness? Is there a point at which sleep is as irresistible as the current of a swift river? I have heard it said by a cavalry officer of the English Expeditionary Force which retreated from Mons in August 1914, that after five or six days without any sleep, except in very brief snatches, his men would often doze off on horseback. Some of them fell to the ground, and even after this, with full knowledge of the risk, would again go to sleep in the saddle and again fall off. They knew that such a

fall might mean serious injury and that, if the horse escaped, they would be captured by the enemy. Nevertheless they slept and fell.

It seems fair to say that under these conditions men cannot help going to sleep and cannot justly be held responsible
for any harm which occurred to them or to others. Is the
nurse's case parallel? She had had no sleep during Decem-
ber 18th. But for most adults to pass one night without
sleep is not at all impossible, even if they have had no
preparatory nap during the preceding day. This nurse's
situation is not to be compared with the plight of the
British cavalry during the retreat from Mons. But how
can we be sure that this particular nurse had the average
powers of keeping awake? She may have been by nature
an exceptionally sleepy person. In that case should she
not have known it and so have refused to go on duty,
especially in a case of pneumonia, with the well-known
tendency of that disease to make patients dangerously
delirious at night?

Moreover sleep comes on us gradually, not suddenly as
a rule. With the responsibility of a case of pneumonia on
her hands this nurse might have called for help when she
felt herself getting drowsy. It is hardly probable that she
could not have secured assistance without leaving her
patient. Doubtless some of her superiors in the hospital
hierarchy would have been angry. She might have been
scolded or even discharged. Quite possibly the fear of
these consequences prevented her calling for help. Or she
may have thought she could keep awake. She may well
have been too ready to take a chance. But if she did this
knowing, as the average nurse is bound to know, her own
physical powers, and knowing as she ought the responsibilities and dangers of nursing a case of pneumonia at
night, then she was careless and to blame.

(c) Our customs regulations explain that if the inspectors find in a passenger's baggage any dutiable articles which he has not mentioned in his declaration, he must pay the penalty even if his omission to list them was in good faith; that is, even if he did not know what was in his baggage. This rule is, I think, quite just, and such an omission seems to me ethically wrong unless the customs regulations are obviously obscure. For one ought to know what is in one's baggage if one signs a declaration about it. Even on one's first ocean voyage one should have asked advice about such matters and taken measures to prevent mistakes. Forgetfulness is so common that in any such situation it should be expected and guarded against in advance by keeping a list of one's purchases or of the contents of one's baggage.

3. THE LIMITS OF DUE CARE

One is responsible morally as well as legally for blunders: (1) up to the limits of average intelligence, or of the intelligence to be expected in the individual concerned; and (2) except in situations which one could not reasonably have been expected to foresee and prepare for. Any one responsible enough to travel can keep a notebook.

Certain sorts of knowledge are as much one's duty as honesty in one's job. But we are prone to deny this responsibility.

> I didn't know it was loaded.
> I had no idea I had spent so much money.
> I didn't realize that I was driving so fast.
> The overcharge was due to the error of a subordinate.
> I've not had time to answer your letter. I haven't got round to it.
> It was lost on my desk.
> I was suddenly called away.
> I couldn't reach you. The line was busy.
> I never heard of the regulation.

Such phrases are familiar and usually sophistical. We may grant that in a rare case any one of them might constitute a valid excuse. Ordinarily we know well enough that in point of fact they do not. If the item forgotten was, say, an old weather bureau prediction, which nobody could reasonably be expected to remember, if the accident (an earthquake) could not have by ordinary prudence been foreseen, if the time elapsed was so short that no one could be expected to finish the task in question, if one were called away so suddenly and so imperatively that only one with superhuman calmness could have remembered to notify the friend at the other end of his engagement, if the customs regulation was a new and outlandish one, then perhaps no carelessness can properly be alleged. But it is a duty to possess and to mobilize *some* knowledge. Some efficient provision against familiar accidents and probable lapses is to be assumed in all adults who are permitted to be at large. Without it we cannot do business. Careless, criminal ignorance, as well as criminal negligence, is unfair to others.

4. DUE CARE CONCERNS THE WAYS AND MEANS OF MORALITY

Like honesty and decisiveness, due care is a virtue that is bound up with our very existence as rational creatures. It may be defined as the application of such brains and such power of attention as we possess to maintaining the life of our agreements by putting them into execution. It is a division of the department of ways and means in morals. It is ethical efficiency. It is what logically follows when a desire comes to grips with the world where it is to be carried out. Carried out from whence? From the region of latent desire and decision, invisible to others, into the world common to us all. A person with a good " poker face " can carry on an active life of desire and plan, unseen, unheard, altogether unknown to others. But at a certain moment the creations of his psychic life are " carried out " onto the open table of the card game, where any one can see them.

Due care, then, is one of our logically necessary agreements with ourselves. It is the virtue of self-consistency or honesty-with-ourselves, become operative in the outside world. If one has made any agreements (as every one has), due care in acting on them is logically implied. Otherwise the agreement would have no meaning or value.

Energy and attention first shape our plans and maintain their internal integrity. Then this same energy and attention " follow through " the stroke which begins in desire and emerges in decision. One form of this " following through " is due care. It is here that honesty, good intentions, eager hopes, enthusiastic impulses no longer suffice. So far as we truly want our ends, we want whatever may turn out to be the means to them, as we trace it continuously, watchfully, tenaciously, like a dog on a scent. For the sincerity of a person's agreements and desires is shown in his actions. If he is genuine, if he " means business " he shows care in the execution of his plans. If he is careless so much the less energy of desire is then at work. Honest agreements, with ourselves and others, correspond to the making of a contract and the intention to fulfill it. Due care is the delivery of the goods. It is a later stage of what the agreement meant in the beginning.

These later stages carry our psychic life out into the world, linking it up with the physics, chemistry, biology, psychology inside us and outside us. You decide to go to town. So far you are in the thought world. But if you are not merely " entertaining the idea," you take steps to that end. To " take steps " is, first of all, to deal overtly with the physical laws of muscular work, of balance, fric-

tion, gravitation, and geography. At this critical stage
you need to take care that you do not slip on the stairs,
stumble over the doormat, or take the wrong road. In relation to our central need of growth, due care is a part of
what, in Chapter VI, I called *timeliness*. It is knowing
where you are and what you are about so that you can
move to your next step without losing touch with your
last and without flying off at a tangent.

How much attention, how much care is enough? The
answer seems to be that, in his ordinary affairs, each of us
has already learned how much care or attention suffices.
" Due care " means the amount and quality of attentive
effort which previous experience has taught a person that
he must expend in order to succeed. If I were put into an
aeroplane and told to pilot it with due care, the amount of
care that I ought to give to it would rightly be zero. I
ought to climb out at once, because I ought to realize that
accepting the job would launch me on the hopeless and
criminal task of knowing what I cannot possibly know, of
trying to anticipate what I cannot anticipate, and of avoid-
ing dangers which I do not know enough to avoid. Therefore due care would mean leaving the machine *presto*. So
long as I stayed in it there would be no such thing as due
care, for no previous experience could teach me what care
is due.

In a new type of action a man can do no more than *grope*
for the sort of attention that he needs for success. His
only clues are whatever he has previously done that is
like this new venture, and what his friends can tell him
of their experience in similar attempts. When you first
try to skate you mean, presumably, to " be careful " and
not to fall. But how can you? You do not know what to
guard against. You try to use such faculties of balance,
such counter-leanings and defensive contortions as you

have previously learned from slippery floors or from experience on stilts. But skating is so different from either
of these that you cannot know much at the outset about
how to take care of yourself. Your due care can only experiment.

About many of our affairs, about spelling, about appointments and punctuality, about hygiene, about hurting
others' feelings, about the choice of a doctor, we are in a
better position to be careful than we are in our first attempt
to skate. We have learned by experience in these matters
what sort of mistake we are apt to make. Not to make the
same mistake again is in most instances the essence of due
care. But against new dangers it is relatively helpless.
Each careful person needs to learn his own particular weaknesses, the thin places in his own individual suit of armor.
Naturally absent-minded, sophistical, or clumsy people
find that until they have formed better habits they must
expend more energy and attention than their spryer neighbors in order to accomplish simple plans without mishap.

5. ONE MAN'S CARE IS ANOTHER'S NEGLECT

Obviously, then, due care is an individual matter. It
means for each of us the attention that he has learned by
experience he usually needs for success in the kind of plan
now in hand. Under what special circumstances, when
tired, hurried, hungry, preoccupied, when in crowds,
under pressure, when suddenly freed from pressure, on
convivial occasions, in the early morning is he more than
usually fallible? The quality of attention that would carry
A through his day's work without mishap will not suffice
B. It cannot be measured, but each person can find out by
experience what he needs, and hold to it. If he is nevertheless upset by a catastrophe, like the freezing of diphtheria serum into a poison, a reasonably careful person

does not blame himself, but plans to exercise in future the particular care that will prevent diphtheria serum from freezing, and to retest serum that has been subjected to any drastic change of conditions.

In legal procedure due care is estimated by rougher standards. The jurymen cannot see into a man's mind as he sees into his own. For them the due care of an engineer, a pilot, or a plumber must mean the average care taken by that kind of person with the experience which he may be presumed to have had. They judge him to be careful or careless, diligent or negligent, after inquiring whether he has shown evidence of taking as much pains as a " reasonably prudent man " of his experience would take under similar conditions. The law expects more wariness of an adult than of a child, more skill in an experienced physician than in a neophyte. The legal standard is the average person of each type.

In ethics, however, no one can take himself as an " average man." Each of us knows best his own individual powers and failings, here greater, there less, than the average. It is by an individual standard, here as throughout ethics, that we judge ourselves duly careful or culpably careless.

I have completed with this chapter what seem to me the essential points in the application of the principles discussed in Chapters I–VI. But beside *misapplication*, ethical theory is prone to another vice, which can be called *fragmentation* or the tendency to break up into useless fragments. The attempt to prevent this vice will occupy the next three chapters.

Chapter XII

SOME CONJUGATE PRINCIPLES IN ETHICS [1]

1. FREEDOM AND RESTRAINT

Any one who honestly looks into himself sees certain facts. Among these he sees some of which he is ashamed. This proves, I think, the essential truth both of "ethical monism " and of " ethical dualism." Sometimes we hesitate between opposed desires. That is dualism. Sometimes we recognize that the conflicting desires are our *own*. That is monism. An insane man also sees conflicts within him. But he often is too sad to feel any concern with them; or he is carried along by currents of destructive energy that submerge all conflict and all regret. When he smashes things or attacks his nurses he feels as much outside his acts as if they were the shattering of waves on rocks. But healthy people's minds do not work thus. They are both in their conflicts and above them.

Ethics must deal both with the obvious fact that our desires conflict and also with the unifying force introduced by our agreements and by their growth. These are data of ethics which any sincere person can easily verify in himself. Neither need be denied merely because we are certain of the other. The gospel of spontaneous self-expression, of naturalness, vitality, freedom is a true assertion of the fact that we have various desires all of which push for their own satisfaction, and some of which give us ecstatic delight when they are expressed. But our inhibitions are

[1] A phrase suggested by President A. L. Lowell in his *Conflicts of Principle* (Harvard University Press, 1932), p. 39.

just as natural as our desires. We have a vital need to breathe, and, when choking, an overwhelming desire to breathe deeply; but we do not desire an indefinite orgy of it. Deep breathing carried on forcibly beyond the inner check of discomfort throws us into a fit or into a faint. Nature does not want an indefinite supply of oxygen in our tissues; so she supplies restraint when twenty-three per cent. of the oxygen in the air has been taken in. The remaining seventy-seven per cent. she rejects.

Almost every muscular movement is a combination of impulses and inhibitions, of " go-it-now " and " stop-here." A " free " action cannot launch itself without the aid of restraint. Impetuously you spring from bed; austerely you restrain yourself from falling on your nose. Had you stayed in bed you would have avoided the need for inhibiting certain muscles in your staggering legs. But the act of getting up has involved you in inexorable restraints. Once up, dressed and fed you can board a bus in cheerful spontaneity; but obligations follow. You must pay your fare or be thrown off.

It is as difficult to live a life quite without restrictions as it is to paint on a canvas without limits. There is no such canvas. There is no free action without a " Thou shalt not." If you start to shin up a tree *thou shalt not* relax the grip of thy legs on the tree trunk until thine arms have secured a good hold above. So and not otherwise canst thou shin, though it is easy enough to slither down to the ground. Positive attempts involve negative precautions. We walk successfully along the cross-beam in the barn high up over the hay because the conscience of our watchful muscles restrains incipient lurches while it releases the right motions.

Discipline and restraint are as *natural* as free impulse because they are part of the same choice. To say, " I will have freedom but no restraint," is like saying, "I will always relax but never contract my muscles." But in fact it is almost impossible to relax one set without some contraction in another set. When you turn attention to one matter you turn it off others.

The genuine issue between "freedom" and "restraint" is between (a) a *positive joined to its own negative* and (b) a supposedly *pure negative*. Here the contrast is really between two kinds of restraint. One can restrain the impulse to eat bread because one wants to get thin, or one can, it is said, restrain appetite because one respects restraint itself. Sooner or later every one has to do much that he does not wish to do. But is it ever duty for duty's sake, pure self-sacrifice, discipline accepted without a glimpse of gain? It sometimes sounds like that. Passages can be quoted from Kant to prove that an action done because of anything that we desire has no moral value. But if we listen longer to Kant or to any other defender of nose-to-the-grindstone discipline, there emerges from the wood-pile a dusky angel of desire. The ascetic who seems to court pain, the "Puritan" who is reported to frown on harmless pleasures, the humanist who insists on discipline are like athletes training for a race. They give up much that they desire for the sake of a preferred Desire.

The ascetic courts union with God, or the peace that passeth understanding. To attain that he mortifies other desires. The athlete and the laboratory worker mortify the desires which interfere with their Desired Goal. The Puritan desires a special type of perfection so hotly that he welcomes discipline as a means to it. The positive value is often kept in the background; but it is still the power behind the throne for ascetic, Puritan, and humanist.

The negative is there also for every libertarian. He runs, leaps, shouts, sings. Without restraint? No; but sometimes without *conscious* restraint. When he was learning to walk, to jump, to sing, he was aware of the constraints which he was obliged to put on himself, the same constraints that the Puritan, the humanist, and the ascetic obey because they are still in the learning stage of life. The essential difference is that the enthusiast for restraint is concerned for growth and therefore for discipline in new projects. The enthusiast for spontaneity relies on his past achievements, which can be run off again and again without difficulty. He lives in the present and lets the future take care of itself.

Again and again this ancient dispute about the positive and the negative elements in action emerges, now in ethics, now among artists and men of letters, now with the educators. Usually the issue is joined in a way to make agreement impossible. Shall we have discipline or freedom, spontaneity or restraint? Neither alone. Both joined. Pure restraint is a cramp. Pure freedom is an explosion. No one wants either the cramp or the smash. We want spontaneity prepared for by labor. We want restraint when it is called for by the goal that we desire.

2. OBJECTIVITY AND SUBJECTIVITY IN ETHICS

Is there anything " objective " about the restraints (or agreements) that a free man adopts as part of his freedom? Granting that when we prefer one way of living we turn from another, does the check come from anything outside us? Yes; but with our connivance. In self-restraint we use facts that we did not invent. We did not create the facts of our own psychology. We might have framed them very differently if we had. We must accept some of them or die; but we individualize them. We must walk by muscular contractions and relaxations or give up walking altogether; but each of us has his individual gait. Everybody has to rest somehow. Effective people find out their own way of resting and their own dose.

Ethical laws are as objective as the physiology of motion and rest. It is an ethical law that every choice limits us. If we choose to lie on the witness stand we must face the chance that cross-examination will bring out the falsehood. Peace of mind about possible detection is attainable if there is nothing to be detected, not otherwise. If the liar had made the laws of his own ethics he never would have included this annoying objective check. He would have arranged to get the advantages of lying and enjoy the immunities of the truthful.

The logic of any agreement is as objective a fact as the logic of the multiplication table. You can keep out of partnerships in business, in athletics, in marriage. But you cannot enter any partnership and then be treated as if you had not; objective fact forbids. Almost every one relishes the rewards that come with labor,—rewards such as skill, competence, and responsibility. But many of us try to break the logic of this situation and to get the rewards without the labor. We crave the love that comes with fidelity in a personal relation, but we act at times as if we hoped to win the prize without running the race. Then we run against the laws of ethics, that is, of human nature.

No set of social rules lasts forever. But each code has the objectivity of its own logic. Each invites us to take or make some shape for our lives. Any shape that we take involves promises to ourselves and to others. Any promise is contradicted by actions that break it. No understanding expresses all that we meant to put into it, and, because we need to grow, we must improve it or find ourselves tied to a clumsy old version of what we desire.

Here we must obey a state of facts which we did not invent and against which we sometimes rage. We obey it or suffer the consequences of trying to break it. Yet individual invention is called for because the logic which binds us was put on us by our own desire, and that desire cannot help growing and sprouting new agreements if it is individual. Two honest men are as different in their honesty as their individuality commands. Yet they obey identical laws of moral logic. Washington, Lincoln, Roosevelt, Wilson were, I think, exceptionally honest men. But the law of honesty led each to a sharply different administration.

3. ETHICAL OBJECTIVITY IS PAINFULLY OBVIOUS WHEN PEOPLE HAVE TO LIVE AT CLOSE QUARTERS

Ethics is objective, then, because we did not make and cannot abolish the logic of agreements nor annul our need to grow by improving them. This logic may be painfully objective when we are living at close quarters with other people. There is a common fund of food on the family dinner table. Each wants a great deal and needs his share. But the shares are, or ought to be, individual. A hungry boy feels as if he needed the whole of the sweet pudding provided for the family. But physiology and family economics have also something to say about his needs. His mother may have had convincing experience that if he ate all that he would like, it would upset his stomach. More probably his stomach could stand it, but the family budget could not. For the other children feel just as he does.

He needs (and in all probability wishes) to live with his family. But if so, the logic as well as the affection of family life involves sharing fairly whatever is not to be had in indefinite quantities. If on the whole he would rather live at home than elsewhere, he must abide by the consequences of his acquiescence in a plan of sharing, or run into conflict with it. There is not provender enough to fill all the children's stomachs as full as their appetites demand. Any child who is not feeble-minded or extraordinarily callous, wants a share for his brothers and sisters. How then shall the family's supply be divided? In the end all will probably agree that the best way to divide it is to give the bigger children and the parents more than the smaller ones.

The space in the house, the jobs to be done, the money available for fun or for education have likewise to be divided up according to the logic of sharing which we call justice. A good deal of "morality" issues from this *logic of sharing* and from the difficulty of getting it into our heads. Most of us like to live with other people because we are gregarious and affectionate or because we see no other way to get along. But it is easier to accept this promise than to live up to its conclusion. Sometimes we try to behave as though we expected to combine the privileges of a hermit with the opportunities of family life. We admit if questioned that others should have their share, but we also grab for ourselves all that there is in sight. We want every one else to take part in the household chores. But when it comes to applying this rule to ourselves we prefer to drop out of the game. We ignore the disagreeable jobs and so thrust them on some one else. It is not that we clearly intend to load all the burdens on other people's backs, especially if we are fond of the other people. But our affections are shortsighted and intermittent.

The logic of sharing is not the whole of ethics. Sensible rules of close-quarters-technique sometimes assume that existence at close quarters is ideal and permanent for us all.

Then the ethics of security begins to exclude growth and extols the life of the ant-colony. Such overemphasis on the logic of sharing cheapens morality by ignoring the ethical issues that do *not* center in the art of living close together. Sometimes the crowded quarters are unnecessary; sometimes they are not so narrow as popularly represented. Then children perceive, often sooner than their parents, that the time has come to break away from family life. Ireland found this out long before England did. England resisted the separation but, I suppose, is glad of it now. Nevertheless a life at close quarters and a consequent cramping of each person's development may be the best choice in sight. The alternatives may be worse and there is much gain in sharing difficulties and in adapting oneself to them.

But the time comes when the morality-of-close-quarters consists not in making the best of them or in unselfishly taking one's part in their burdens, but in breaking away from them or in applying our brains to make the quarters less close. Until recent times children's indoor energy had to be suppressed on rainy days because their elders could not stand it. Yet there was often some unused space at the top of the house. The idea of making this attic space into a playroom for children is quite a modern one and even now is much neglected. Quarters need not always be so close as our thoughtlessness allows them to be.

4. BIOLOGICAL ETHICS OFTEN OVEREMPHASIZES THIS SORT OF OBJECTIVITY

What we may call security-ethics, or biologically-based ethics, emphasizes the need of adapting ourselves to close quarters assumed to be fixed. The " bad " person is one who objects when he finds that every one is expected to clip his wings and stay inside the fence. He is an " agitator " because he wants either to get out of the group or to reorganize it.

Obviously there can be little growth, reform, originality, or creative work in a society where people are " good " in the biologic sense. We approach such stagnation in the small, rigid towns where " Main Street's " opinions rule every one's behavior. Some good qualities are developed, perhaps overdeveloped there. There is beauty in a family group where smooth teamwork is evolved, where all are content with what they have, where each member knows where he can be of most use and acts on his knowledge, where no one is selfish and every one is busy. But please read over that sentence, applying each phrase to an ant-colony. Ants are far better adapted to their environment than we are. They seem more socially-minded and less selfish than we. They give each other far less trouble than men and women do. They are more industrious, punctual, steady, faithful, and apparently contented.

Until recently moralists were ready to accept this comparison with insect life. The sluggard was bidden to emulate the ant. It needed Fabre's common sense to point out that extraordinary stupidity goes hand in hand with the accurate work of wasps. We now recognize the blindness and the stagnation as well as the inerrancy of such a group, whether it is an affectionate family, a contented factory-population, or a hive of bees. If the difference between good and bad were merely the difference between the socially-minded and the non-socially-minded, then ants, bees, and wasps would be nobler as well as more efficient than men. The biological point of view appreciates one part of morality,—its orderliness, its unselfishness, its capacity for self-maintenance and for teamwork. But it neglects choice and growth. It makes for permanence and reproduction but not for improvement or discovery. It emphasizes usefully an objective element in ethics, namely, our need to adapt ourselves to a social group which is necessary to our existence; but it neglects an equal need to reform ourselves and our environment.

5. OBJECTIVITY OF THE ETHICAL RESOURCES ACCUMULATED IN THE GROWTH OF CIVILIZATION

Another objective element in ethics emerges when we try to see afresh what we desire and need, by looking over the resources of civilization. To stare at one's own behavior, to consider its alternatives or combinable elements is only part of the process of making an ethical life-plan. A larger part is exploration. We are born on an estate, the heritage of civilized man. We are not bound to stay there, nor, if we stay, to leave things as we find them. But because centuries of work by thousands of people have explored and improved the situation where we are born, common sense leads us to look over the estate thoroughly. Our inheritance is what has survived to us out of man's achievements in philosophy, science, art, industry, play, religion, government, and human relations. These are ancient interests. They are inherently human. We are human too. Is it not probable, then, that we can create, within or near these interests, the individual variation of them which will suit us? What we desire to do with our lives will be found somewhere near what others have found, created, loved, imagined. Naturally, then, we look about us.

After trying an enormous number of edible plants, roots, fruits, and animals, man has found some that suit his stomach. He does not try to eat dogs, crows, locusts, and grass, unless he is starving. His diet has reduced itself to a few staples. Each of us makes his choice among these staples and then tries to have them cooked and served to suit his individual needs. No one is so foolish as to insist

on starting where the cave-man did and tasting every discoverable animal and vegetable for himself. We accept
the dietetic heritage of our race, not as a terminus but
as a starting point. We have modified the diet of our ancestors, perhaps improved it. We prefer cooked meat to
raw, sugar to molasses, tea and coffee to other herb in-
fusions. But we still try the traditional foods. We even
acquire a taste for some that we do not like. Why? Because
we want to test any food which many others have found
pleasant and nutritious.

In the field of art we try similar experiments. Here is a
group of staples on which our branch of the human race
has nourished itself generation after generation,—the
works of, say, Euripides, Dante, Shakespeare, Bach,
Goethe, Velasquez, Leonardo, Cervantes. Shall we slav-
ishly accept all that our fathers accepted? No more and
no less than we do in diet. Probably our taste in art is not
entirely inhuman. It is fed on material akin to that which
has satisfied others. Then it seems sensible to find out
what we like and need in art by trying the main foods of
the human spirit thus far.

We do the same in science. Nobody sets out to conquer
astronomy or bacteriology single-handed. Neither does
he swallow all that the books tell him. He gives himself
the benefit of what others have done; he listens to their
reports before he makes his own. He does not have to invent the culture-tube or the thermostat for himself, nor
to discover afresh that the sun does not circle our planet
as it seems to do. He climbs to the end of the path which
others have made up the mountain side. Then he goes on
for himself.

These points are obvious in diet, in science, and in art.
Why, then, should any one think it necessary today to

build up his own ethics, despising what others have quarried out in that field? In ethics, as in diet or astronomy, so much has already been explored that it is foolish to ignore it. No one thinks it necessary to discover cookery or calculus over again for himself. Yet every year we see amateur moralists trying to study the ethical heavens without a telescope, and the psychological bacteria without a microscope, because they have never heard of these instruments or because they think them old-fashioned.

It is foolish to make up our minds about right and wrong, about our desires and our needs, about the best ways to treat each other and to develop our capacities, without surveying, as carefully as our time and talent allow, the ways in which others have solved and are solving these problems. Each of us is in charge of an individual life and must steer it by his own senses and by his own ideas. But you and I are not the first travelers over the road. Job, Plato, Jesus, Paul, Augustine, Spinoza, Kant, Montaigne, Mill, Emerson have explored the ethical difficulties that we must pass through. Our scene has changed a good deal since their time. But the main features of the land, its mountains, deserts, canyons, rivers, and swamps are still on the map. The climate has not essentially changed. Some of the snakes and wolves have disappeared. Some new bacteria have come out of hiding. Still we can learn from the old pioneers. We shall do our own bit of exploring, but we still can use their maps.

Every individual has non-individual traits. He feels the pull of gravitation; he needs food and shelter like others. To make up a language of his own would not help him to grow. Babies do something like this and later abandon it because communication, which they naturally want, involves a non-individual language. Living with others furnishes the raw material out of which the individual is to make his own life. From the raw material of language, which is no more individual than a dictionary, each of us makes tools to communicate his own thoughts and to share the ideas of others. Each person's speech is characteristic, in its tones if not in its vocabulary. Yet we all use the same speech and through it take our places at the common tasks. It needs to be said again [1] that imitation trains us for originality. Among the most original things about us is our handwriting. Yet we acquired this after imitating the script of other people. The most original composers of music are those who have soaked their minds at the start in the music of the older masters.

How are we to find "good models" in ethics, in thought, in art? By studying those considered good by people in whom we have confidence. So we choose our diet and our vocabulary, our clothes, our games, and our camping outfit. We still retain our right of independent judgment. No one can compel our love or do our hating for us. But persons whom we consider competent can give us something to start from.

To get our bearings and to get suggestions from others' standards saves valuable time in morals as in science, diet, and government. No one has time or brains to invent a new substitute for clothes, for meals, for hygiene, science, and religion. And it shows no excess of modesty to admit that we could not do it if we tried. We need all the brains that we have to make our own choices and to add our personal notions to what civilized man has invented in 6000 years. To have time for this we need to borrow all that we can from the common storehouse of civilization.

[1] Though J. M. Baldwin and Josiah Royce have abundantly proved it.

6. PURE ETHICAL SUBJECTIVITY IS IMPOSSIBLE, FOR TO BORROW
NOTHING IS TO BORROW ALL

The bold man who decides to owe nothing to the achievements of others sentences himself to a queer punishment. He is condemned to have a strait-jacket fastened upon him in the dark. If this sounds improbable, consider what happens to the man who refuses to follow good standards of grammatical speech. He does not invent a new syntax nor omit grammar altogether. He unconsciously picks up *bad* grammar from his neighbors. Because he will not choose a good standard, and then perhaps improve on it, a bad one is fastened on him while he sleeps.

If an oarsman despises the task of learning good form, (or one of the good forms) in rowing, he does not free himself from convention. He cannot row by pure inspiration from moment to moment. He accepts from his own clumsy muscles a hippopotomoid style which insures quick fatigue and slow progress. Or consider the medical student irritated by the task of learning the conventional scientific methods of diagnosis. He refuses to be bound by old-fashioned rituals. He will gather, sift, and interpret facts in his own way. I have often watched the result. He settles into diagnostic habits which are familiar and bad. He acquires an ancient method certain to lead him into avoidable errors.

Suppose we are opposed to introspection. We refuse to stare into our own minds. We will have no psychology that is not the objective record of visible, audible, or tactual data. Do we therefore escape the difficulties inherent in the queer process of studying the mind by the use of that mind itself? No. We merely record a set of unconscious introspections which we have not arranged or interpreted because we are not aware of their existence.

We reject the tyrannous rules of harmony in music and refuse to learn them. The result is that we pick up and use a set of stale second-class harmonic habits which has happened to stick in our minds from some of the music that we have lately heard.

" No philosophy for me," says the artist, the economist, or the historian, and then he proceeds to walk the streets of his chosen profession with fragments of various philosophies sticking out of his pockets and clinging to his boots. He is apt to make the loose metaphysical assertion that " There is no sense in metaphysics "; or to assert the hasty moral judgment that " Moral judgments on other people's behavior are all bunk."

The upshot of this is that when a person makes up his mind about the ethical problems before him, he needs to have it stored with memories of what the men whom he most esteems have done in similar situations. I venture to say that no one who is in doubt as to how he should treat his parents can fail to get help if he recalls how James Barrie treated his mother, how Edmund Gosse parted from his father,[1] how Stevenson viewed the tragedy of father and son in *Weir of Hermiston*. We could not copy any of these, even if we wanted to. But they enlarge our vocabulary of ethical expedients, as Shakespeare enlarges our stock of words. A box of carpenter's tools and a pile of lumber will not build a house for us. But when we are going to build, it is well to have a kit of tools and to know their use. It is handy to have some lumber and not be forced to cut and shape it in the forest.

I do not know which is the more foolish, to copy the past, to follow the decorous forms that we were taught and to believe all that we were told about good morals, or

---

[1] *Margaret Ogilvy*, by James Barrie; *Father and Son*, by Edmund Gosse.

to carve out our own way regardless of old-fashioned rules. Shall we take a middle course? There is none. Each must think for himself with materials which he does not create.

Emerson seemed to contradict this when he denounced *all* conformity.[1] He was an original writer. But he wrote his essays in language which conformed to the ordinary spelling, grammar, and vocabulary of his time. He invented no new words or new syntax. He conformed to the old custom of using a pen, modified, though not by him, from quill to steel. He conformed to the banal habit of sitting on a chair at a table. He wore clothes, he paid taxes (unlike his neighbor Henry Thoreau), he bought land and lived in a house like other people. He traveled in the customary conveyances by land and sea. He learned German at Carlyle's behest and tried to use traditional arithmetic when he kept Carlyle's publishing accounts in this country. In short, *he conformed in all the matters which he thought of minor importance* compared to religion, politics, literary judgments, friendship.

Every one must do likewise. We have no time to make up our minds or to be competent in our jobs unless we accept, unreformed, many customs of our tribe. Even in important matters we suspend judgment, if we are wise, until we have taken time to understand them. This is hard for most of us because we are afraid to look into some matters (such as Bolshevism, Spiritualism, Cubism) for fear we may see good in them and be converted. To give up a prejudice is as painful as to have a tooth drawn. But the alternative may be worse still.

Shall we accept the restraints of tradition? No. But we cannot avoid the self-restraints which apply themselves to us whenever we pick out an act and plant it exactly where

[1] R. W. Emerson, *Essay on Self-Reliance.*

we think it belongs. Shall we learn the rules which society lays down? No. We shall learn the rules of the material in which we work, and of the human nature with
which we work. Our task and our nature lay down and
work out our rules. What should we do alone? Much of
our thinking, inventing, planning, repenting; certain
kinds of practising and experimenting. But most of us
soon reach a point where solitude is no longer of use because we need the stimulus of others' criticism or approval.
Without this we cannot even work out our own ideas.

If we discard the simple formula that goodness is conformity and badness is revolt, what can we supply in its
place? The standpatters provide for self-maintenance; the
reformers provide for growth. We need both. Biologic
ethics provides for cohesion in the group. " Free " ethics
provides for individual initiative. One provides for
discipline, the other for enjoyment. There is no contradiction here, but only a one-sided emphasis first on identity,
then on difference, which always belong together. Every
one wants order, security, persistence, amid the flux
of change. But what is worth maintaining? Surely not
all that the past has given us. We want order, but
not any order. Slavery and piracy have each their form
of order. " Anything so long as it is fixed and predictable," is as bad a motto as " Any change so long as it is a
change."

Freedom? Yes, but freedom to do what, freedom from
what? Freedom to express, each of us, himself, herself,
and itself? But has each of us but *one* self to express? Are
all our capacities equally glorious and perfect? Granted
that every human activity should give joy, is one joy as
good as another? Are there to be no preferences among the
ways that our muscles can contract? To search for something new is certainly our job. But scientific experiments,

which have pushed on the most successful search that we know, differ from careless drifting because they start with discipline, a method, and a body of tentatively established truth. This truth and these methods they set out to modify and to develop.

To give sense to the watchwords of either camp we need a principle of choice. What kind of order, permanence, freedom, joy is desirable? *Such order, permanence, freedom, joy, such well-tested principles, such new discoveries, such conservatism, such radicalism, such familiar virtues, such departures from old virtues, as enable each person to grow,* that is, to make and improve his place in the world. Thereby he attains his greatest usefulness and his greatest joy. In our social teamwork everybody's behavior should be as different from everybody else's as every one's face is different. Yet all can act on the same principle. There need be no conflicts; because every one needs the growth which belongs properly to him alone, but is best developed by intimacy with what others have.

Bad behavior is inhuman behavior, it lacks choice, it puts a man where he does not belong,—in the place of a log, a dog, a savage, a child. Or it attempts to make him some imaginary and impossible creature,—a person who " has it both ways," who expects the rewards both of the unscrupulous and of the trustworthy, who hopes to get skill without working for it, who disregards others yet counts on their help. For a time and in every one's eyes but their own, people seem to achieve these contradictions. Despite their inner decay they get along because most people are too intent on their own affairs to spend much ingenuity in detecting others' fakes. But the longer the farce goes on the greater the chance that the cheat will be discovered, and the greater the final crash that involves cheat and cheated.

Summary. This chapter aims to show that (1) *objectivity, and with it security, in ethics, rest on:*

(a) Agreements.

(b) Our unescapable need to learn.

(c) The logic of living at close quarters.

(d) The customs and institutions presented to us by civilization as a starting point.

(2) *Subjectivity in ethics, and with it progress, rise from:*

(a) Our individual ideals of a better life.

(b) Our creative impulses in science and art, and

(c) Our miscellaneous, shapeless desires for freedom, for life, for happiness.

Growth unites facts with ideals, and is what we mean by goodness. Badness is self-deceit either about the objective or about subjective elements in moral experience.[1]

Facts as they press themselves upon us through the restraints of society, correspond with the need for security in ethics. Ideals as they press upon these facts, selecting, combining, and emphasizing certain elements, give us the reforming impulses which break out of us now and again. In the next chapter I shall further contrast and attempt to integrate these factors,—our permanent need of security and our endless need of reform.

---

[1] I hope it is obvious that I do not take the distinction of subjective and objective very seriously. Every experience contains both; neither has meaning except when married to the other.

III
INTEGRATIONS

CHAPTER XIII

ETHICAL SECURITY AND ETHICAL REFORM

Continuity of purpose through non-contradictory change is growth. But it is hard to grasp both the continuity and the change at once. We are prone to drop either one or the other. Drop the emerging novelties and we have left the tight security of mental hygiene, of bureaucracy, hard-boiled experts, and rigid ecclesiastics. Drop the continuity of present, past, and future, and we have left the spasms and shifts of the " wild-eyed reformer," the yearning searcher, the opportunist, and the time-server.

With these dangers in sight we need, not a safe middle course but a marriage of apparent opposites. It is easy to follow the average. It is easy to smash everything in sight. It is easy to let our habits harden into dogmas about " law and order." It is easy to trust the latest headlines. But the proper business of ethics is the interpenetration of stability and novelty. In this chapter I shall describe the interpenetration of these elements, after picturing the failure of their attempt to live apart.

1. THE BIAS TOWARDS STABILITY OR ADJUSTMENT IN THE PROPAGANDA OF MENTAL HYGIENE AND ELSEWHERE

Security divorced from reform appears in what we may call " the Gospel of Standpat " as preached by (a) the psychiatrists, (b) the bureaucrats, (c) those entrenched behind scientific expertness or behind ecclesiasticism. Mental health, says a popular writer, is " the adjustment of human beings to the world and to each other with a maximum effectiveness and happiness. Not just efficiency, or just contentment, or the grace of obeying the rules of the game cheerfully. It is all of these together. It is the ability to maintain an even temper, an alert intelligence, socially considerate behavior and a happy disposition." [1]

This is a definition of mental health, not of ethics. Probably the writer would disclaim any intention to speak on ethics. He might even doubt its existence. But he considers mental health a desirable form of behavior, which means ethical behavior. If one said, " Mental health, as you define it, is highly undesirable; let us prevent it if we can," Dr. Menninger would certainly take issue. Hygienic behavior is the sort that he hopes to make dominant so far as he can.

But will it serve? Its watchwords are efficiency, adaptation, happiness, and obedience-to-the-rules-of-the-game. But these can easily lead us to subserviency. Defined as above, the ideal of mental health is the gospel of " normalcy," of Babbittry, of slavery to the past and to the respectable. For mental hygiene the important fact about good people is that they give no trouble. The bad interfere with the plans of their fellows at home or abroad. Parents bring their " bad " children to a " habit clinic " because they are troublesome. By " good " children they mean the ones who " never give their mothers an hour's worry." They are clean, respectable in dress, punctual at meals, ready to go to bed when the time comes, ready to eat what they are bidden, pleasant-mannered, helpful, sufficiently studious, and never in mischief. " Bad " children, on the other hand, will not trot along in their harness. They have plans and ideas of their

[1] Karl A. Menninger, M.D., *The Human Mind* (New York: The Literary Guild of America, 1930), p. 2.

own which interfere with the comfort of those around them. They are "independent," noisy, impertinent, hard to keep clean, careless in dress, speech, and table-manners.

So the human race is split into two groups, the trouble-makers, and the rest. It is customary to label the trouble-some group as unsocial, or antisocial. It resists social authority. Psychiatrists, psychologists, anthropologists, and other biologically trained people are usually content with this description. It involves no difficult thinking. It is true so far as it goes. It is simple and clear. In police records, census statistics, ethnological studies, and in other mass dealings with humanity, it is often sufficient. It is especially popular among French writers on ethics. What it lacks is interest: (a) in individuals, (b) in im-provement. It forgets the need of every individual to grow by finding fresh chances to learn and to serve. If sheep-mindedness is a curse and conformity only a caricature of teamwork, then the contrast of " good " and " bad " is not the same as the distinction between social and anti-social.

Imagine yourself telling Emerson, Carlyle, Garibaldi, Luther, Joan of Arc, or Cromwell that to be mentally healthy they must be socially considerate, obey the rules of the game as they find it, be happy and even-tempered! Would that soothe Carlyle's " divine discontent " with the abuses of his time? Would Emerson recant his declara-tion that " whoso would be a man, must be a non-conform-ist "? Garibaldi and Joan of Arc were socially most in-considerate persons. They refused to obey the rules of the game as they found it. They were often unhappy. They were not even-tempered. On principle they were un-adjusted to the world as they found it. They were deter-mined to rebel until they could change it. Would we had more of them! They were genuine instruments of reform.

The United States would never have freed themselves from England, slavery would never have been abolished, tuberculosis would never have been curbed if men had gone on adjusting themselves to each other and to their environment without a rebellious effort to upset and so to improve the world. Energy to improve things comes out of discontent with things as they are. No reforms would ever take place if mental health, as Dr. Menninger defines it, became general.

George Bernard Shaw is, I think, an exceptionally healthy-minded individual. Nevertheless he puts into the mouth of *Undershaft* in the third act of *Major Barbara* a trenchant statement of the degradation which " mental hygiene " as now preached would bring into industry. " The Salvation Army," says one of its members, *Cousins*, addressing *Undershaft*, a ruthlessly exploiting employer, " makes men behave themselves." *Undershaft* heartily agrees:

Cousins: It makes them sober.
Undershaft: I prefer sober workmen. The profits are larger.
Cousins: Honest.
Undershaft: Honest workmen are the most economical.
Cousins: Attached to their homes.
Undershaft: So much the better; they will put up with anything sooner than change their shop.
Cousins: Happy.
Undershaft: An invaluable safeguard against revolution.
Cousins: Unselfish.
Undershaft: Indifferent to their own interests, which suits me exactly.

Shaw makes us ashamed of our civilization, with its poverty, crime, disease, cruelty, injustice, brutality, and ignorance. He arouses us to abolish the state of mind in which we contentedly obey the rules of the game. He does not decry sobriety, honesty, family life, happiness, unselfishness. But he says that they narcotize us unless they are supplemented by the reforming spirit.

How does it come about, then, that experienced psychiatrists, enthusiastic for mental hygiene, are content to describe civilization in phrases that kill reform? Why do they frown on all discontent? I think the answer is that they spend their lives in treating the mentally diseased. The psychiatrist's mind is organized round the need to calm disturbed patients, to soothe the chronically irritable, to cheer the habitually discontented. His chief business is to make sick people more content with their lot. His foreground is full of people who are rebellious and unhappy because they do not receive enthusiastic applause three times a day; who hate the world because their steampipes occasionally crackle, who are miserable because the sun does not always shine, who are chronic kickers, hopeless soreheads, angry every day in the year. Busy with patients who are rebellious from disease and not from " divine discontent," the psychiatrist is prone to formulae which imply that *all* rebellion is disease and should be suppressed. Psychiatric patients do not often like the " rules of the game " in a sanitarium or anywhere else. Naturally, then, psychiatrists are strong on obedience to rules. Discontent is common in their patients. Hence industrial and political discontent looks to them like a psychopathic state. The radical is a troublesome person. He would be safer in an institution.

The mental hygienists have no wish to block reform. Their phrases are only a trade-mark, like the bronze tan of the pilot, or a trade-habit like the rolling gait of the sailor. A trade-habit, valuable in their parish, leads them to say to all the world: " Calm down, keep quiet, don't quarrel with your lot."

2. " DESIRE ONLY WHAT IS ATTAINABLE "

A second form of the standpat ideal is expressed in the maxim, "Limit your desires to what is attainable." [1] This could mean, " Turn your attention toward something that you can at least try for." In this sense I heartily agree with it. To wish you were beautiful when you are ugly, to wish you could bear a son when you are past the child-bearing age, to hanker after the life of the Middle Ages, to burn with zeal for reforming people by telling them their sins,—this is useless enough. But in most fields we cannot say what is attainable until we have tried for it. Hence the maxim, " Desire only what is attainable," is easily twisted to one of cowardice. To try for nothing except what is within our known reach, condemns us to decay. To demand certain success before we put forth effort is to be bored, to be despised, and to dry up. We owe most to those who plan campaigns quite uncertain of success though quite certain that it is worth while to push the attack for all it is worth.

3. " BE SOCIALLY CONSIDERATE "

Finally, I wish to criticize the phrase, " socially considerate behavior," a favorite among the mental hygienists. The phrase rightly bids us to consider others before we act. *But which group of " others " shall we consider?* The nihilist with a bomb in his hand is considering the cowering millions whom he hopes to free by his act. The Bolsheviki when they murdered the Russian aristocrats were socially considerate towards workmen and peasants.

We cannot consider every one, unless by " considera-

---

[1] Walter Lippmann, *A Preface to Morals* (New York: The Macmillan Co., 1929), p. 191, and Robert C. Givler, *Ethics of Hercules* (New York: A. A. Knopf, 1924), p. 187.

tion " we mean only the bare acknowledgment of his existence. In practice, social consideration means helping one group without consciously hurting any other. In this hope the social-worker tries to aid the poor, the sick, the ignorant in her own city, without knowingly harming those in any other. But she cannot know the distant effects of her action, which may, as some Socialists think, hurt the whole community by postponing radical economic reform. When a social worker is considerate of the sick poor she is (rightly) somewhat inconsiderate of the struggling doctors whose income and prestige she impairs by steering the sick to medical experts in free hospitals.

Almost every one has to be considerate of somebody. Hence the injunction to be socially considerate gives us no clues for action. In relation to one group of people Emerson was socially considerate when he deliberately avoided most of the social reforms in his day. He had " his poor " to aid and his " imprisoned souls " to free by his writings. He stuck to this job and I believe he was right. His chance to be of use was not in work for the needy or for the unfortunate but in writing and lecturing for those who especially needed what he could say. If Emerson had been " socially considerate " in the ordinary sense he would have deserted his post to follow popular clamor. It is always easier to respond to the " nearest need," that is, to the one that others have already found, than to discover one's own work.

4. " LAW AND ORDER "

Next to the mental hygienists the strongest advocates of security-ethics are those holding political office. This is only natural. Some " law and order " must prevail if government is to go on. Most laws exist, (1) to secure our repose and safety, (2) to protect life, property, and reputation, (3) to prevent perjury and fraud. Until the present century there has been little attempt to better the existing order through legislative action. Those who oppose the government, that is, the " outs, " the reformers, and the radicals, are eager to upset things as they are. But when a political overturn brings the radicals into power, it is notorious that they grow conservative. How else can a government be " strong " enough to maintain itself at all? We all need some degree of " law and order " if we are to carry on our business, enjoy our recreations, maintain our homes, pursue science, art, education, or religion. We want these ends; therefore we do not want to be interrupted by robberies, murders, and riots, nor distracted by financial uncertainty and the fear of rebellion.

Militant reformers are bad for business. They discourage investment. If their reforms succeed they dislocate industry, and so upset the schools, laboratories, and churches, which depend on business for the sinews of war. To avoid this possibly serious inconvenience, mayors, judges, and employers often stretch law and order to cover the repression of free speech. Radicals who want to advocate a new system of property-holding are " dangerous men " and should not be allowed to speak. If they are indignant about evils or passionately eloquent for reform, they have lost the happy adjustment to their world which is essential, we are told, to mental health. They are fanatics, probably unbalanced. It is safer to keep them quiet.

No government can recruit soldiers for war and also allow pacifists to attack war in front of the recruiting stations. Polygamy is prohibited by law, and polygamists are forbidden to enter the United States. So it seems natural to suppress books and lecturers who attack monogamic marriage. Thus the very existence of government tends to overemphasize the blessings of security. For government must defend itself; and that seems to involve defending the *present* government. Hence any suggested improvement in government is apt to be treated as revolutionary. If we favor an amendment to the Constitution of the United States, we are charged with attacking the Constitution itself. Those who wish to amend the " rules of the game " (1933 edition), are thought to be attacking all rules.

Stability is essential. Government, law, and business cannot exist without it. But stability and stagnation look so much alike that when we defend stability we seem to favor stagnation. In " The Rising of the Moon," [1] an Irish policeman describing his duties says, " It's those that are down would be up and those that are up would be down if it wasn't for us." From this standpoint one is bound to assume that whatever government does is right. Whoever is in power ought to be in power, presumably forever. Whoever is weak or powerless ought to stay so. The police are to keep him so and to defend his masters. No one seriously defends such a view of government. But much that is done and said in the name of law and order appears as a readiness to suppress free speech among radicals with no better reason than that of the policeman in Lady Gregory's play.

It is often charged that the Christian Church supports things as they are, because it defends a revealed gospel, and because its financial support comes largely from those whose careers might be wrecked by important change, good or bad, in our present economic institutions. Doubtless this explains the attitude of some clergymen toward economic and political institutions. Nevertheless there

[1] Lady Gregory, *Seven Short Plays* (London and New York: G. P. Putnam's Sons, 1909).

was a fair number of pacifist parsons in 1917, and their beliefs cost some of them their jobs. There is a respectable minority of Christian Socialists, equally objectionable to most Christians and to most Socialists. The Christian Science sect was founded on opposition to " things as they are " in orthodox medicine. The Quakers oppose war. The Methodists and Baptists oppose the drinking of alcoholic liquor. Some Southern churches oppose the doctrine of evolution. These instances prove that the churches sometimes attack strongly entrenched forces. Nevertheless I believe it is just to say that the Christian Church has oftener been on the side of security than on the side of reform.

5. EXPERT OPINION

Do American colleges oppose innovations? Only so far as innovations contradict expert opinion. Expert opinion in science, history, economics is built up on a wide survey of the evidence thus far available. In the majority of instances, the opinions which oppose it have been carelessly arrived at. Hence experts are used to the task of controverting cranks, quacks, sensation-mongers, and sentimentalists. It is partly because experts do this job so well that public confidence goes to them. But like the rest of us, they form mental habits and use preconceptions, based on their experience. Most bright new ideas that have been brought before them thus far have turned out rubbish. After finding rubbish in fifty successive cases it is hard to look quite open-mindedly into the fifty-first. Now and again a new " cancer cure " is exploited by a druggist. Can a lifelong student of cancer investigate this " cure " quite impartially when he has seen so many well-supported claims upset by the test of experiment? The druggist may be right, but it is vastly improbable.

College professors are often the wisest people available

to answer a difficult question. For the reason just given they are apt to oppose innovations until they have been well tested. But when well tested they are no longer innovations. Hence the influence of colleges on the public is now on the side of the psychiatrists, the lawyers, the business men, and the churches,—that is, against innovations. And since reforms of all sorts are innovations during the period when they are fighting for their lives, it seems fair to say that innovations in ethics are not likely to come from college authorities.

6. BIOLOGICAL ORTHODOXY

One more group, small but very influential, remains to be mentioned: the biologists. To the biologist, life is the organization of the forces which make for survival in bacterium, starfish, tiger, or man. Life is self-maintenance against forces tending to destroy it. Self-maintenance is also the essence of standpat-ethics. It is only natural, then, that economists, historians, philosophers, and physicians who are trained to view human behavior in terms of biology, find themselves most at home in standpat ideas about ethics.

7. WHO IS FOR REFORM?

Against the biologists, the psychiatrists and psychologists, against the entrenched forces of government, business, the churches, and the colleges, who stands for reform? No profession is organized for this end. Social-workers, perhaps, come as near it as any group. They see so much unhappiness that they are apt to become reformers, though they are also attacked, with some justice, for their indifference to political reform. If we leave on one side the promoters of single causes like peace, prohibition, birth control, and free speech, the most effective reformers are the Socialists, with a sprinkling of journalists and novelists. Some of the most energetic drives toward reform are started by men fired, like Emerson and Theodore Roosevelt, with a passionate certainty that things are at bottom so good that present evils can be overcome. Articulate idealists like these, find so wide a response from the dumb idealist in us all that their influence weighs more than that of the habitual critic.

In America we have several journals committed to a policy of reform, chiefly in politics but also in morals, education, and other matters. The ability and high character of their editors have made these journals serviceable. No one can rightly suspect that their pages express any selfish or corrupt interest. Their honesty makes them authoritative for many who trust neither the news columns nor the editorials of the average American newspaper. Yet they exemplify a bias as serious as that of standpat ethics, a bias in the opposite direction. Standpat ethics puts forward, chiefly in action, the stupid thesis that " whatever is is right." But it would be just as stupid to say that " whatever is is wrong." These journals do not say so but they imply it, and give their readers that impression. Thaddeus Stevens' watchword, when he helped to perpetrate in our Southern States the tragic era of Reconstruction, was " Thorough." He was bound completely to extirpate the slave power, pledged to cut out the corruption from the bottom. Such ideals are supposed to be characteristic of a fearless type of reformer. But surgical metaphors should remind us that radical surgery often kills the patient. A fund of good life fit to survive and to extend the benefits of a temporary insult to live human tissues, is the necessary basis for good surgery.

If this country was as desperately ill as E. L. Godkin [1]

[1] Editor of the New York *Nation*, 1865–1900.

implied that it was, during the last quarter of the nineteenth century, there was no sense in trying to improve it. One does not try to cure a dying man or a dying nation. But the journals that I refer to have pictured so much rottenness and so little soundness in this country that we are not encouraged to do anything about it. It is bad enough to urge the reform of a country consistently described as moribund. But the climax of folly is reached when this hopeless venture is urged by means of three psychologically sterile devices: scolding, ridicule, and contempt. Subscribers are entertained by these antics of clever editors, but meantime their fine honesty and their excellent brains do little service to the country. We have learned that " ordering and forbidding " are useless, but we still encourage the reformer to scold, while reform loses its chance.

8. SECURITY AND REFORM REQUIRE EACH OTHER

It is hard to hold two contrasted complementary ideas in mind at the same time without letting them neutralize each other. Security and reform are relatively sterile ideas until each fertilizes the other. This is trite and therefore we do not learn it. Physics is not trite and so we learn bits of it quickly. But ethics soaks in slowly because it is so obvious. When part of a wave curls over into a rowboat with a well-corked drain-hole in its bottom, one learns quickly that one cannot get the water out by removing the cork. One does not need to experiment about that again and again. But in ethics, points just as obvious still remain in the field of discussion. Such a point I am laboring now: that to cherish the good and to reform it are inseparable acts. The contented consciousness of virtue is vice. But the irritated consciousness of evil is almost as bad. One who usually finds things bad and usually says so is a scold and therefore a public enemy.

Dr. Menninger's definition of mental health given a few pages back needs fertilization by its opposite if it is to do any good. Content about some things is necessary if we are to be effectively discontented about many others. Discontent is also useful; but it becomes useless when it is pervasive. We must be content enough with the moral law and the solar system to use them as a springboard into efficient discontent. We must conform to the habits of our time in minor matters like grammar and taxes, in order that we may effectively resist the rules of the game in important matters such as religion, education, politics, and smuggling. On ocean steamships it seems to be the rule that first-class passengers try to cheat the United States customs and to smuggle in purchases contrary to law. This custom is so general that one who obeys the law is considered fanatical. Nevertheless this rule of the game is, I think, a good one to break.

Is efficiency always desirable? Only a stagnant person can seriously maintain it; for we are efficient only so long as we stick to what we have already mastered. When we learn anything that is new to us, we court, for the time, inefficiency. Public school teachers are efficient, I take it, in teaching the three R's, because they are learning nothing new about them. But the hope of the country is with the inefficient children. They are growing; that is to say, they are inefficient readers, writers, and cipherers. When they begin school they are efficient and secure in walking, sitting, and using spoons. From this security they can dive into fresh inefficiency in reading, writing, and arithmetic.

" I never want to do anything unless I can do it well." A good number of neurotic patients have said that to me. Fortunately they belied themselves. They were not such sworn foes of improvement as they said. They aspired to worship the god of a ready-made perfection. But in practice they did not shut their eyes to the glory of the imperfect. They could feel (though they denied it) the zest of being a duffer for progress' sake.

9. PROGRESS IS LIKE WALKING ON TWO LEGS BECAUSE IT CONTAINS BOTH A STATIC AND A DYNAMIC FACTOR

Enthusiasts for progress insist on the dynamic quality and forget the static element. Yet it is an obvious fact that you cannot walk far or fast with both feet off the ground. One foot must be static while the other moves and so prepares for a new position. The dynamic leg cannot move without the support, the push, the balance, and the security of the static leg. One foot must stand pat. It must be conservative so that its fellow can be radical.

Walking has other static elements: its general direction, and its instruments. If we take a step ahead and then one backward, or if we trot round in a circle, we are dynamic but not progressive because we have no fixed direction. As we walk, our legs stay largely the same. They are far from perfect; on the average they are clumsy, ill-developed, badly appointed. But we cannot reform these imperfections much while we are walking.

The conservative, or standing, foot cannot walk alone. It can hop; it can be carried by a moving staircase, a moving train, ship, or globe. But alone it cannot walk. It must be linked with a progressive, up-to-date member which cuts loose from its mooring and takes the risk of finding no further rest. It may veer off its course; it may go in a circle; it may go backward, or stumble. It is subject to all the winds of heaven.

The static foot avoids these dangers. It is safe and sane. It stands: a model of law and order. It cannot stumble or fly off at a tangent. Its owner can point with pride to its substantial achievements, while he views with alarm the movements of the radical leg. The well-planted foot bears weight; the moving foot bears none. The grounded foot gives security. You know where to find it. It is firmly rooted. It does not try to reach the stars. It is content with the station in which it has been placed. It cannot kick anybody. But when the radical leg leaves the firm earth it loses touch with firm realities. It is up in the air. Aspiring to kick the stars, it may injure some innocent banker or helpless flapper. For it too flaps loose in the air. It needs to come down to earth.

I confess that the standing foot is unprogressive. It stands for things as they are. It gets nowhere. It accumulates fatigue. It is actually beginning to decay, because its position favors congestion and varicose veins. But is the aspiring foot any better off? Of itself it is quite unreliable. Deprived of wholesome contact with mother earth, unhampered by the weight of established things, it is exposed to deflection by the veering currents of its environment. It may go chasing wild geese.

The psychiatric ethics of adjustment and the revolutionary ethics of reform are each like an attempt to walk with one foot. Each falls into absurdities without the other. Yet even in conjunction they may fail to progress. For the combination of rest and motion is not enough. We have this when we stand on one foot and wave the other; but that is fancy-dancing, not progress. Neither immobility nor change, nor both together, give us progress. We need a third element. A combination of rest and motion in our arms, legs, fingers, tongue is progressive only when it is attaining some valuable end. As much motion, as much rest, as the development of the situation requires: a motion in the direction and a rest in the place required,—these make up progress. At a series of shifting points security should give way to adventure, as diastole yields to systole in the heart. Each is good when it fulfills the need of the organism which contains it.

Static and dynamic, content and discontent, efficiency and inefficiency, conformity and revolt, all are neutral ethically, like black and white, tall and short, solid and liquid. Yet each is necessary to carry out any valuable idea. What this value is in ethics I have tried to show in Chapters I to VI.

10. THE EQUIVOCAL WORD "SERVICE"

One final point. In the vocabulary of standpat morality and also in the ethics that I am trying to defend, the word "service" is a favorite. We find our place in the economic and political order, in a family, a neighborhood, and a job, where we can be of some use. There we respond to a need for what we can furnish, because we need to be needed. This is obvious and trite. But we need also to question the credentials of what is called "service"; there are impostors about. To give people what they want at the back door or at the front door, in shops, theaters, books, schools, colleges, churches, and political administrations is often taken for "service." In reality it *may* only pamper people's weakness, flatter their self-complacency, hand them a swiftly-earned, cheap, and worthless diploma, tempt them to waste their time on flashy, sensational books and shows, encourage them to buy a drink or a useless luxury.

One seems to give "service" in such ways; for actually there is a demand for what one supplies. But one may be giving disservice. One suits the public taste, one is popular as a writer, preacher, shopkeeper, vote-getter, if one supplies some demand. But any flatterer or gambling-house keeper, any sycophant or opium-seller does that.

The more demand there is for one's services the more harm one may be doing. Service is measured as truly by unpopularity as by popularity. To be popular, as Lincoln and Lindbergh are, does not prove them wrong. But Benjamin Butler and yellow journalism have been popular too.

Service is giving people what they need. This *may* correspond with what they demand. But their demand is only one piece of evidence in that direction. Children do not demand education. Their fathers do not demand taxation. Children demand candy and many of their fathers demand rum. But neither a demand nor its lack guides us clearly to what is needed. Nothing can guide us except a study of human powers in the light of a respect for what we believe men are fitted to become. What we desire and what we ask for, throw much light on what we need, especially if we can read off our desires at the moment when we are most alive, most in touch with past, present, and future. But we still have desires when we are drunk or silly, when we are mindless and distraught. Those who cater to *these* demands have no reason to call it " service."

It is often impossible to know much of other people's needs. It is hard enough to get glimpses of our own. Much of the time each of us must paddle his own canoe and make his own mistakes. My present contention is simply that to supply what people demand is vastly easier than to supply what they need; true service is hard to come at, easy to miss. It is as hard as prophecy or disarmament or the sight of people's true nature through their disguises.

" Service " is a neutral word, good or bad according to its associations. It is just now the watchword of those who are more eager for security than for reform. To be a serviceable reformer, to respond to the changing needs now for attack, now for defense, is the task of any one concerned above all for growth. Order must be forever establishing itself and dissolving itself in new order. History seems to show that we have more bias for security than for reform. Laziness is commoner than energy. It is right, therefore, that the right should be perpetually astir against things as they are, more alert for reform than for security, though each always needs the other.

In the next chapter I shall finish my attempt to integrate some of the loose fragments now cumbering the field of ethics.

CHAPTER XIV

DISLOCATED FRAGMENTS OF ETHICAL THEORY

1. MOTIVES AND CONSEQUENCES

A motive is a desire. If we imagine the desire fulfilled then it becomes the "end" of the action, as well as its origin. The motive of presidential candidates is, ordinarily, their desire for election. Their "end" is election. Motives, desires, ends are in themselves neither good nor bad. Human agreements and human needs give them ethical color. Ordinarily it is good to desire knowledge, but not when this leads us to open private letters. Then it is bad because we have agreed (tacitly) not to do this.

Can we judge acts by their consequences? Yes, if they are not merely sequences. Consequences which we intend are part of our act. Sequences which we did not intend and could not avoid, have no ethical connection with us. They follow, but we are not responsible.

Does the end justify the means? The means are part of the end, that is, of the articulated act. They are as good or as bad as the plan that they execute. But ordinarily if we say "the end justifies the means" it is a fraudulent statement because it suppresses so many important words. Written out without suppressions the phrase runs: "My good end justified my using bad means in your affairs without consulting you." "I, a clergyman, have the ' good ' end of keeping my parish happy. For this I use the (admittedly bad) means of preaching comfortable doctrines in which I disbelieve. I have not consulted my parishioners. I should not dare to." Every case that I have heard of in which the end is said to justify the means comes to this. The motto is not invoked if one's means are good or if one intends to consult one's victims.

Means and ends, motives and consequences are fragments torn from their context. To judge an act we need to know intention-plus-effort. Intentions alone are not enough. Intentions carried out in genuine effort are all that we can control. If we do our best and fail, we succeed morally.

2. QUANTITATIVE ETHICS

Moral preferences are often phrased in words which sound quantitative. We " weigh " people's conduct; we " measure " the moral gains and losses of sex education; we " sum up " the advantages of family life; we see " more " reasons for honesty than against it. Moreover, when we try to make ethical standards clear and definite we hope to see them rise out of inexactness into precision, and exactness reaches its acme in figures. To be punctual, to pay one's debts, to give even-handed justice are virtues which appear measurable.

Our ideals of control, order, and balance in the conduct of life further suggest that science, with its measured exactness, has entered ethics. Above all, the democratic habit of settling moral questions like polygamy, prohibition, and child labor by majority vote, seems to imply that we can find out what is right by counting opinions.

But I find it hard even to make these ideas sound plausible. What we need when we seek for ethical truth is to settle a group of facts and to evaluate a group of desires. If we reach the truth about a moral question it is because we have found the agreements which bind us, or the needs of human nature, or the resources of civilization available for our choice. These facts are not quantitative. No more are the desires which spring up in view of them. Desires sound quantitative. We desire "this more than that." But when we look at this phrase more closely we find that in ethics we prefer and reject alternative actions absolutely, though this word sounds dangerous. We prefer life to death, honest shopmen to dishonest shopmen, faithful service to slipshod work, absolutely, not relatively. We desire no forgery, no incest, no counterfeiting. Here we abhor moderation and measure.

Majority votes keep the peace. They settle matters which would otherwise be decided by force or fraud. They tell us what the law will allow us to do, but they decide no moral question.

The calculus of pleasures or of happiness has measurable elements in it. Money values can be balanced and some of our desires along with them. We spend money for food and shelter rather than for luxuries. But when J. S. Mill introduced into the pleasure-economy the doctrine of higher and lower kinds of pleasure, he followed common sense but shattered the quantitative basis on which hedonism and eudaemonism (pleasure-ethics and happiness-ethics) rest. Kinds of pleasure, types of happiness are incommensurable. Pleasure is the sign of attainment or of a satisfied physical function. But some attainments are nobler than others because they are consistent with our agreements and with our structural bias towards growth.

"Nobler"? Is not that a quantitative test? No. It expresses a decision in which, when once the elements are clear, we see that one and not the other alternative is what we believe about this matter. Sir Walter Scott had promised to pay his debts; by huge labor he did it. The nobler act was logically evident, not quantitatively determined. It followed from his honorable nature. It was not added up. There were quantitative elements in it as there are, I take it, in every matter in heaven or on earth. But they did not settle right and wrong for Scott.

Progress sounds quantitative. It is a march along a road and so it should be measurable. So it is, once the right road is decided. Decide that you ought to educate your children or develop your muscles, and the distance gained along your chosen path can be measured in dollars, hours of work, foot pounds of energy, inches of circumference. But the direction selected at the outset is not a quantity because your choice dealt with truth or error about agreements, about growth, about beliefs. In these matters quantity is irrelevant.

3. EGOISM, ALTRUISM, AND MUTUALISM

Ethics built on needs and agreements, recognizes no duty owed either to oneself or to others. Duties like other facts are verifiable and public. They exist for no one person's sake. They are for all or they are nothing. But we are shortsighted about all kinds of facts, including the facts called duties. Everyman knows most about the facts of today and hereabouts. He is most ignorant about what is distant from his own life, in space or time, because he is intellectually shortsighted. He is eager and alive about the needs of his own organism, and dull about others'. But he knows that they are as real as he is, just as he knows that past and distant facts are as real as those which are here and now. Because facts and needs live for us all, if they are real at all, we try to verify, share, and publish facts; we try to verify, share, and publish duties.

What is the duty of Europe and of America about lending each other money in war and about paying their debts afterwards? If there is any duty at all in these matters, it is not egoistic or altruistic but, like other facts, public. If these countries have a common interest in war or in peace they ought to behave unitedly. If they have no common interest they ought to behave dividedly. It is all a question of facts. If America altruistically lends money to France and has nothing to gain and everything to lose by it, France will soon lose too, because the two of them depend on each other's prosperity. Who then gains and why should the money be lent? If America selfishly bars the goods of France and yet expects, as it does, to sell its goods to France, its own selfishness hurts itself, and who then gains?

In a recent interchange of newspaper comments between France and America it was assumed by France that America is now selfish but ought to be altruistic, and that France had been altruistic but had better have been selfish. American editorials on the other hand assumed that we were altruistic when we lent the money but should now be selfish because a debt is a debt and should be paid even if it ruins the debtor. It is a tissue of absurdities. Any country which hurts itself, altruistically, to help another, hurts the other country too. Any country which selfishly hurts another country hurts itself, in the long run, too. This reasoning assumes that the two countries are in some way dependent on each other. If they are isolated from each other as the Esquimaux are isolated from most other people on the globe, can any obligation exist between them? I have no duty to recognize a fact if I do not know its existence. So I have no reason to act on an Esquimau's needs unless I know that he needs me. If I clearly see that he needs what I can give without neglecting my other agreements, then I give. But I give because his need of, say, food, and my need to express the sympathy that I feel for him coincide. It is still mutualism not altruism. If it were pure altruism it would be wrong. If I gave to the Esquimau without feeling his need as my need it would be because some one told me to give, or because it was respectable, or because I hoped for some reward here or hereafter. There is no altruism and no virtue in any of these acts. Altruism in the strict sense is either stupid or selfish, that is, in either case a blunder, not a recognition of truth.

The authority of duty is the authority of facts in the form of agreements and needs. If I act against recognized facts I do wrong. If I act on recognized facts I act because of *them* and not because of any person, myself or another. It is wrong to act solely for any person, myself or another. To act for private ends, my own or another's, which represent no mutual agreement and no reciprocal need is to act contrary to the facts on which social duties rest. The prime fact is that we are members one of another by reason of the interdependence of our needs. This is obvious among any small group of people who know each other and care for each other. Common needs, common desires are there the outstanding facts. No one is selfish or unselfish to those he loves unless he utterly forgets the facts which join them, and then he knows that he wounds himself as well as them.

Towards distant, largely unknown people like the Tibetans we feel, most of us, no duties. Were we in contact with them as we are with European nations, or were we traveling among them, we should use such minds as we have to get onto good terms, that is, to find mutual interests. We should try to act neither selfishly nor unselfishly but in line with whatever common needs we could find.

All this is, I think, clearer in the relation of employer and employee. When an employer raises wages we do not praise him for altruism; when he defends the raise at a stockholders' meeting and says that it is good business, we need not conclude at once that he is greedy and selfish.

We say that good business is good for all concerned, that in the long run, which means in fact now, what is good for a buyer is good for a seller too. *To find and to enlarge the areas of mutual interest is the whole duty of man in industry, in international life, or in the closest friendship.*

If we suppose that men's interests are really opposed, then there is no ethics between them. They are like two experts who believe the opposite about the same matter. On that matter there is for them no truth. They are in different worlds. Now transfer the situation to the field of ethics. Suppose two men swimming for one plank which will float either but not both. If they care nothing for each other they have no duties about that plank. Either might heroically refuse to take it from the other. But that would be because one of them cared so much for the other's life that his greatest need was in the other. No one could say that duty points out which man ought to give up to the other. There is no such duty. If one says the stronger should give up to the weaker, what of the weaker's right to accept? He can be justified only if he sees a common ideal fulfilled by them both in the other's sacrifice,—an ideal difficult to visualize, but I think not impossible. That would furnish a basis of mutual interest and so of duty. Without that the problem is insoluble. Ethically the two are in different worlds.

4. SACRIFICE AND SYNTHESIS

Sometimes ethics involves choice and sacrifice. We take it or leave it. We go one way or the other. Sometimes the right is synthetic. The nuclei of several " rights " are to be found and commingled. Forking situations occur when we reach our limit or run against our limitations. One cannot both lie and not lie, steal and not steal, be faithful and treacherous to the same person about the same agreement, jump into the water and keep dry. Often one sees advantages in both alternatives but it is physically or logically impossible, so far as we see, to combine them. This is the " old-fashioned " morality of temptation, resistance, sacrifice, or submission. That such problems often face us is just as certain as that we are finite beings. In thought we can be in two places at the same time; we can run with the hounds and with the hare. But in action we must choose. We keep our agreements or we break them or we change them with the consent of all concerned.

But when we try to improve an agreement there need be no total rejection of the alternatives discussed. We hope to keep the good hitherto won and to develop it. When we discuss industrial agreements, educational enterprises, or civic plans with a view to improving their provisions, we try to combine the suggestions of many minds. We integrate the best of the old ways with something new, because we have learned something. What I called " cooperative growth " in Chapter V is ethical synthesis. Better use of time or money, if it *is* better and not merely different, joins the central purpose of the old ways to something new.

5. FORCE AND HATE

We apply force *to ourselves* whenever we act. Without applying the forces of gravitation and heat, without starting the pulls and pushes of muscles on bones, we cannot do anything. We rightly apply force *to others* with their consent in games and in surgery. With their anticipated validation we force children to go to school. With their implied consent policemen force on the public any annoying law like traffic regulations or parking regulations. The force that we call " brutal " is that which is applied without any consent, explicit, implied, or anticipated. Without consent, no agreement; without agreements, no rights towards each other.

When we use force in *self-defense* it may be in accord with a tacit or explicit agreement which the other has forgotten in panic, rage, grudge, recklessness, or insanity. Then we carry out his will and our own in accordance with our prior agreement. Or we defend ourselves in accord with an agreement to fight, as in prize fighting or in war. This may be a bad agreement but there is no treachery and need be no malice in fighting under it. We have the right to defend ourselves against a murderer or against the kidnapper of our child (still possibly without hate) either on the ground that he has authorized the use of force against himself by his previous acceptance of legal protection or because we believe he does not realize what he is doing.[1] An act that violates fundamental, though perhaps tacit, agreements should be resisted, by reason if that is possible, by force if we believe that this is for the interest of the attacker as well as the attacked. John Brown showed no desire to resist the law under which he was hanged. Probably he thought it in accord with his own ideals and those of the country that, since his attempt to end slavery had failed, he should die. The country acted against him in self-defense and he submitted.

Murder is the extremest violation of another's rights, because it breaks the agreement on which almost all other agreements rest. It is the supreme denial of another's worth, when we know it to be as great as our own. We kill other animals, especially insects and bacteria, without compunction because we assume that they are less valuable than we. Murder denies in act the difference between a man and a mosquito though the murderer does not doubt it in fact.

[1] Of course we do not think of this at the time. We act without much thought.

Capital punishment is defended as a method of self-defense carried out by the community. When we oppose this argument we doubt whether it actually defends society; we assert that it makes it impossible for us to right a mistake in judicial process when later evidence proves the victim innocent; or we may doubt altogether the State's right to punish. *Killing in war* is defended, rather feebly, as national defense, or as a choice of evils. We may believe that to kill men is preferable to allowing them to enslave us or to oppress other men. When a nation goes to war willingly or even gladly it is unfair to call war murder. It may be the crowning human stupidity; I think it is; but it need not involve the treachery and the malice of murder.

Malice or hate is the denial of another's value so far as emotion can do it. The ultimate moral loyalty is to act on the truth which we know and thereby to know more of it. Hate denies known truth and so destroys our grip on reality so far as our impulse can do it. But the impulse may be very superficial. In a moment of anger, a flash of hate may come and go without harm to others and with little harm to ourselves because our habitual sense of values returns so swiftly. Chronic smoldering dislikes or indifferences poison their possessor and their objects far more seriously.

6. CONSCIENCE

When we feel or think about the behavior which follows from our agreements, our needs, and our chosen relationships to the people and things around us, conscience is at work. Like every element in ethics it can harden into tradition or prejudice, or it can fail ever to emerge from them. It can be hedged off as a special faculty like intuition, genius, or reason. Then its " voice " becomes a monologue or a nuisance because the beliefs which it announces are not informed or reformed by reflection and criticism. We are no more infallible about right and wrong than about any other basic belief. But we must trust the best knowledge that we can attain, else we dissolve in indecision.

Men have sudden, vivid impressions about morals as they have about business ventures or about other people's character. If these impressions sum up long thought and experience they are valuable. But their clarity and urgency are no more proof of their value in morals than in sickness or in politics. Feeling has no more reason to speak *ex-cathedra* about morals than about any other subject.

When we are sincere in the desire to find the truth,— physical, philosophical, historical, ethical,—we soak ourselves in the available facts, we take time to let them mature in us, we discuss them with the best critics that we can get, we try to allow for any special biases which we recognize in ourselves, we gather all our results together and wait in the presence of all the truth that we know for its answer to our demand for light on our next step. No single act in this series can rightly monopolize the name of conscience. Any act in it could be called prayer. The whole process gives us such light as we can obtain about right and wrong or any other matter of fact.

7. VIRTUES AND VALUES

The familiar " virtues " are branches of our central need to grow by taking reality into our lives. As we gradually learn to face and to act on the fact that we are members one of another we are drawn into what is popularly called *unselfishness*. We know perfectly well, though we often find it pleasanter to forget it, that what is desirable for ourselves is desirable for others similarly placed, and that another's good is as desirable to him as our own is to us. Henry Sidgwick, Whewell, and other writers on ethics have called this knowledge a moral intuition. But it seems to me nothing more than an application of our central need to learn, that is, to catch up with the facts and avoid self-deceit. "Unselfishness," the "Golden Rule," or the "sense of justice" is our main need and our central desire when we open our eyes to the facts called "other people," facts which sympathy reveals but which our laziness urges us to ignore.

So it is with the other virtues. *Courage* means acting on what we believe to be the needs of our situation, despite fear. *Temperance* means calling drunkenness and gluttony by their right names and acting accordingly despite a tendency to call them "high life" and so to please the fancy of the moment. The terrible New Testament command, "Be ye perfect," means, I think, that we are to keep on growing through obedience to commanding facts which we know but are too lazy to face.

How many virtues, values, or needs shall we distinguish? It depends on the purpose in hand and on whether we tend to be "splitters" or "slumpers" in our habits of definition. In a college curriculum we cut up the whole field of knowledge, the disciplines of aesthetic, physical, and professional training into as many parts as we find convenient. But we know that these are arbitrary divisions of the single purpose to grow or to be educated. The capacities and the plans of each individual should determine how far he goes in each subject or how he combines them so as to learn several at once.

As with needs and virtues, so with time-honored schedules of values or attitudes. Everett's table of values,[1] economic, bodily, recreational, associational, characterial,

---

[1] W. G. Everett, *Moral Values* (New York: Henry Holt & Co., 1918), p. 182.

aesthetic, intellectual, and religious, seems to me as serviceable as most. It can be adapted to express all the forms of man's need to grow if we take Everett's " bodily " values to mean the conditions which our relation to an environment of air, water, and food, to climate, to gravitation, and other forces, makes essential to physical life, which in turn is essential, so far as we know, to growth. The values conserved in governmental institutions are included by Everett under " associational."

Spranger's *Lebensformen* [1] gives us a table that differs only in detail from Everett's, though Spranger's emphasis is on " attitudes " rather than on values. The items in his schedule,—theoretic (intellectual), economic, aesthetic, social, political, and religious,—can easily be stretched so as to include bodily values under economic and recreational values under aesthetic. Everett's " characterial values " correspond to all Spranger's types melted together. [2]

So much for the principles, applications, and integrations by which one may answer the question:—What is the meaning of the adjective *right* when applied to human conduct? In the next four chapters I shall analyze what we mean when we call an action *wrong*.

[1] Eduard Spranger, *Lebensformen*, translated by P. J. W. Pigors under the title *Types of Men* (Halle: Max Niemeyer, 1928), Part II.

[2] Under various titles almost every writer on psychology, sociology, anthropology, ethics, or government, catalogues the resources of mankind. Anthropologists call them institutions; sociologists speak of trends, interests, wishes, cravings, or social forces; in ethics the term "values" is becoming more popular than "goods." Economists are apt to list demands. In the budgets of American cities the taxpayers' money is divided to pay for what are supposed to be the city's needs: education, police protection, transportation, health, recreation are the main divisions.

B. WRONG

Chapter XV

FIVE FAMILIAR TRICKS OF SELF–DECEIT

When a person does wrong but has no inkling of it we call him stupid or insane rather than immoral. To achieve immorality he needs also a queer sort of blindness. In the end he is deceived about the matter, and may fancy himself quite a hero. But at the start he is a party to his own deception. Wrongdoing contains first a recognition of what is right, and then a willfully achieved blindness to it. If one asks for evidence of this, one has only to look into himself or into the pages of William James's *Psychology:*

Where . . . the right conception is an anti-impulsive one, the whole intellectual ingenuity of the man usually goes to work to crowd it out of sight, and to find names for the emergency, by the help of which the dispositions of the moment may sound sanctified, and sloth or passion may reign unchecked. How many excuses does the drunkard find when each new temptation comes! It is a new brand of liquor which the interests of intellectual culture in such matters oblige him to test; moreover it is poured out and it is sin to waste it; or others are drinking and it would be churlishness to refuse; or it is but to enable him to sleep, or just to get through this job of work; or it isn't drinking, it is because he feels so cold; or it is Christmas-day; or it is a means of stimulating him to make a more powerful resolution in favor of abstinence than any he has hitherto made; or it is just this once, and once doesn't count, etc., etc., *ad libitum*—it is, in fact, anything you like except *being a drunkard*. *That* is the conception that will not stay before the poor soul's attention. But if he once gets able to pick out that way of conceiving, from all the other possible ways of conceiving the various opportunities which occur, if through thick and thin he holds to it that this is being a drunkard and is nothing else, he is not likely to remain one long. The effort by which he succeeds in keeping the right *name* unwaveringly present to his mind proves to be his saving moral act.

Everywhere . . . the function of the effort is the same: to keep affirming and adopting a thought which, if left to itself, would slip away. It may be cold and flat when the spontaneous mental drift is towards excitement, or great and arduous when the spontaneous drift is towards repose. In the one case the effort has to inhibit an explosive, in the other to arouse an obstructed will. The exhausted sailor on a wreck has a will which is obstructed. One of his ideas is that of his sore hands, of the nameless exhaustion of his whole frame which the act of further pumping involves, and of the deliciousness of sinking into sleep. The other is that of the hungry sea ingulfing him. " Rather the aching toil! " he says; and it becomes reality then, in spite of the inhibiting influence of the relatively luxurious sensations which he gets from lying still. But exactly similar in form would be his consent to lie and sleep. Often it is the thought of sleep and what leads to it which is the hard one to keep before the mind. If a patient afflicted with insomnia can only control the whirling chase of his thoughts so far as to imagine one letter after another of a verse of scripture or poetry spelt slowly and monotonously out, it is almost certain that here, too, the specific bodily effects will follow, and that sleep will come. The trouble is to keep the mind upon a train of objects naturally so insipid. *To sustain a representation, to think, is*, in short, the only moral act.

. . . *The terminus of the psychological process in volition, the point to which the will is directly applied, is always an idea.* There are at all times *some* ideas from which we shy away like frightened horses the moment we get a glimpse of their forbidden profile upon the threshold of our thought.[1]

When we thus " shy away " and refuse to face disagreeable facts James does not call the act a " self-deception." As he describes it it is more like a self-blinding, a hiding from oneself, a voluntary acquiescence in inattention. We put out of sight the objects on our desk that would remind us of what we ought to do. We turn in the other direction, he says; we perform random acts. We snatch

at any and every passing pretext, no matter how trivial or external, to escape from the odiousness of the matter in hand. I know a person,

---

[1] William James, *The Principles of Psychology* (New York: Henry Holt & Co., 1890), Vol. II, p. 565.

for example, who will poke the fire, set chairs straight, pick dust-specks from the floor, arrange his table, snatch up the newspaper, take down any book which catches the eye, trim his nails, waste the morning *anyhow*, in short, and all without premeditation,—simply because the only thing he ought to attend to is the preparation of a noonday lecture in formal logic which he detests. Anything but *that!* [1]

Some of the more familiar dodges in the practice of fooling ourselves are:

(1) Pleading necessity, the favorite moral alibi.
(2) Procrastination.
(3) Exception making.
(4) Defending our privileges.
(5) Sheep-mindedness.
(6) Selfishness.
(7) Pretense of unselfishness.
(8) Autocracy unavowed.
(9) Liberalistic slovenliness.
(10) The attempt to get something for nothing.
(11) The appeal to " self-preservation " as a right.

1. THE MORAL ALIBI

Spherical billiard balls are not virtuous or vicious. They go where they are sent, and if they go wrong the fault is the table's or the billiard player's, not theirs. When we try to make up our minds on a question of right or wrong, we should first clear the ground by ruling out the chance that the act in question is, like the roll of a billiard ball, neither right nor wrong. It may be a non-moral occurrence, like the behavior of rocks, trees, birds, and billiard balls.

Are there many " billiard-ball situations " in human lives? The novelists and the diplomatists like to tell us so. Heroes yield to " ungovernable passion," to " irre-

[1] William James, *loc cit.*, Vol. I, p. 421.

sistible impulse," to an "uncontrollable urge." They cannot choose. They are driven like the billiard ball. Necessity, not freedom, is exhibited in them. At any rate it is convenient to say so. If one of these "urges" led a man to murder and so to a court-room, he used to plead that "temporary insanity" was the diagnosis. Medical authority now backs no such plea, provided, as can usually be shown, the accused has shown no convincing sign of insanity before or after the murder. "Temporary insanity" is merely a plausible excuse.

If we are really convinced that the culprit could not help himself and therefore was not responsible for his actions, we do not blame him, nor ask ethical questions about him. To the billiard ball the stroke of the cue is irresistible, uncontrollable, ungovernable, etc. The balls roll along under necessity. But what is necessity?

Genuine necessity is of two kinds, physical [1] and logical. A man falling out of a window, a man drugged, a man insane is under physical necessity. What he thinks or feels at that moment makes no difference in the result. His motions register physical, chemical, or biological activities outside his control. A sneeze may be really necessary. One may strive with all one's force and all one's ingenuity to hold it back; yet in spite of all it may burst forth. The compulsion is partly external (the irritant), partly internal (the sensitive nose); but in both situations it is genuinely irresistible. When we speak of "necessity," then, in the physical sense, we register the belief that our endeavor plays no part in modifying the action of physical, chemical, or physiological processes on our organism or in it.

---

[1] I use "physical" to include chemical necessity and the hybrids, physiological and psychological necessity, all that we know about which is their physics or their chemistry.

The other type, logical necessity, is equally but differently compelling. When you walk north you are compelled to quell for the time your southgoing tendencies.

Persons hard up for an excuse often produce what is supposed to be a third kind of "necessity." "She asked me what I thought of her singing; I simply had to lie and say I liked it." Was the lie physical necessity? Were the liar's vocal cords excited by electrical stimulation so that they and not he produced the falsehood? Obviously not. Was it a logical necessity, such that silence or veracity would have been a self-contradiction? No. Then what sort of necessity was it? It was not necessity at all. It was a plausible excuse, the commonest of all the excuses hit on by modern featherless bipeds in search of one. It is the usual excuse of quarreling children, of the mothers of delinquent boys, of heroes in novels, and of diplomats at the onset of war.

You come upon some youngsters in a quarrel. You ask what's the matter. You are told: "It wasn't my fault. Charlie made me do it. I couldn't help it." You question the mother of a boy caught stealing. "Oh yes, he is a good boy; but he got in with a bad gang and they pulled him into it. He never would have done anything like that of himself." In the war of 1914–1918 not one of the main contestants entered the conflict freely.[1] All were compelled to enter it, or so, at least, their spokesmen declared. They did not want to go to war but they had no choice. Believe it who can!

At present the favorite excuse for a man or a nation under suspicion is: necessity. We claim it as an alibi when we feel public disapproval hovering near us. Public opinion is now more sensitive than once it was, especially

[1] See Appendix C.

about war. I do not remember that any one took the trouble to justify any of the wars of medieval or classical history as " necessary." Even in the last century public opinion against war was so feeble that Napoleon did not usually excuse himself on grounds of necessity when he was ready to make war on some one. Necessity as the reason for entering a war is a modern excuse. The phrase, " a necessary lie," is also of modern manufacture, I think.

Frustration, the negative side of necessity, often appears in our stereotyped answers to invitations, as when we " regret that we cannot accept," that is, are prevented from accepting, the kindly offered hospitality. In less obviously formal usage the same phrases occur in declarations of war.

For ethics it makes no difference whether a person is held back by forces outside his control, or pushed on by them. In either case he is helpless and so neither right nor wrong. It is not his desires that bear fruit, good or bad. If we have been trying to estimate in ourselves or in others the rightness or wrongness of an act, we give up the attempt as soon as genuine necessity or frustration appears. But warned, as any sensible person is, that the plea of necessity or frustration is usually false, we seldom accept it without scrutiny.

We are on our guard to some extent against taking credit when good luck has landed us in clover. But there is more temptation to boast of our free and personal achievement when we are successful than when things go wrong. We are apt, as Professor R. B. Perry and others have pointed out, to believe in the freedom of our personal initiative when we succeed, and to talk as if we were the victims of fate when we fail. A friend of mine who played the cornet and was an enthusiastic member of an amateur " brass

band," often joined the rest of this friendly group in
" serenading " about the streets of his native town until
the small hours of the morning. After one such adventure
he found himself about daybreak near the office of the
railroad company where he was employed as district superintendent of freight and passenger traffic. As he thought
it too late to go to bed, he went up to his office, opened
his desk, and sat down, about four in the morning, to work.
By an extraordinary piece of luck he was discovered there
by the energetic president of the railroad who happened
to be in town on a tour of inspection, and happened also
to be an early riser. He was so much impressed to find my
friend at work that he shortly afterward gave him pro-
motion.

In a case like this a man is obviously no more responsible
for his good fortune than Hamlet was for his ill-fortune in
being born the son of Claudius and Gertrude. Necessity
is called good luck when it leads to happy issues. We do
not naturally think of the physical forces, the utterly un-
connected group of events which led to the fortunate
crossing of a serenader's and a railroad president's paths.
Yet it is true that my friend was forced into his good luck
by a combination of events, as irrelevant to his will, as if
he had been struck by lightning.

Habitual actions become in time almost as automatic
as the sleepwalker's or the maniac's. By processes nearly
as unconscious as winking, the house-key comes out of
your pocket as your house-door comes in sight. The key
may emerge even when you approach a stranger's door
that looks like yours. No reason, good or bad, no choice
or control, appears in so deeply ingrained a habit. The
action has slipped down into " nature " and there is in-
nervated without will or choice.

When such habits lead to disastrous results, when a habit of daydreaming leads to a smash-up, in a motor car or in *Lord Jim's* career, we naturally suspect that, farther up the road, there was a way to control the events which built the habit. A man may honestly plead that when he drove his car head-on into another, he was so sleepy that he had no idea where he was going. At that moment he was " beyond good and evil." But a few hours earlier he was as responsible as the rest of us, and could have avoided the attempt to drive his car when he knew that he was dangerously short of sleep.

The form of " necessity," which appears in habit is like a tool in one's hand. The hammer, not the hand, strikes the nailhead or shivers the window-pane. But the hand uses the hammer as we use (or permit) a habit for useful or dangerous purposes. One step away from the frontier, human desires are still active. They swing the hammer or the habit like a tool.

Error is unconscious deception, not by self but by circumstances. Proof of ignorance or error, like proof of necessity, wipes clean the ethical slate and leaves no right or wrong action behind. If a child " knows no better " we do not blame him. He may torture other children, quite ignorant of what he is doing. Forces outside his control have led to his ignorance and through this to his action. Yet not every one finds it easy to see the difference between innocent error and willful wrongdoing, because we use the word " error " both for mistakes in arithmetic or typesetting and for acts done when we know better. One does not ordinarily make a false addition on purpose. Error, not malice is the diagnosis. On the other hand, when we procrastinate there is no error about it. We are not idiots and understand well enough the nonsense that we address as an excuse to ourselves or to others.

This distinction is clear enough when we stop to notice it; but we often permit equivocal words such as " mistake," " wrong," or " error " to blur it. I was once disastrously in error about a diagnosis in the case of a medical friend of mine. At the end of my examination I was in doubt; but the weight of evidence seemed to point to pulmonary tuberculosis. He asked me what I thought and I told him. A week later I met him in the street apparently quite well and boiling with indignation. " Why did you tell me such a thundering lie? You said I had tuberculosis when I didn't have it. You scared me half to death!"

My friend the doctor did not use the short and ugly word for all his own mistakes in diagnosis. He knew that he could only do his best, refuse to be careless, act with the best light he could find, and, now and again, make mistakes despite his best efforts. This seems too clear to need a moment of thought or a page of discussion. Yet when Oedipus married an unknown woman who turned out to be his mother, those very intelligent people the Greeks saw not only error but crime in the tragic horror of his marriage. Errors, even when purely innocent, often lead to so much disgust, rage, or grief that these emotions blur our vision. Like my friend the indignant physician, we pounce on a hapless man's blunder as if it were an outrage, though when we cool down we know that he could not help it.

Sometimes this confusion of error with wrongdoing is due to a half-suppressed suspicion that the wrongly added column of figures, the mistaken diagnosis, the tragic incestuous marriage, was the result not indeed of intention, but of a *guilty inattention*, carelessness or recklessness, and so was at bottom culpable. What the law calls " negligent mistake " is within the field of ethics, even though it is called a mistake. I suspect that my medical friend who did not have tuberculosis was indignant because he fancied that I could have avoided my annoying blunder if I had taken proper pains as I used my stethoscope. Well, if so, I did wrong and was not merely in unavoidable error.[1] A person who fails to meet his engagements because he is careless is inside, not outside, the field of ethics. No plea of unavoidable error excuses him. He is closely akin to the reckless man of whom I have something to say in Chapter XVII.

I take it, then, that our most plausible excuse for our misdeeds is the plea that we were victims of necessity, frustration, unconscious habit, or innocent error. Any of these excuses might be true. Only the person who offers them falsely can be sure of the fraud. No one else can look into his mind and accuse him on the basis of certain evidence. But we know ourselves better. My contention is that until we have grown very old in the art of self-deceit we know very well when we fool ourselves and when we do not. In time we become so completely self-blinded that we can no longer recognize even ourselves. We can punch our own heads and really believe that some one else did it. We no longer recognize the twitch of our own muscles or the fraud in our own ideas. But this takes time. In the earlier stages of it we can catch ourselves in the act, and be as sure of it as we are of our feelings and our sensations.[2]

2. NOT JUST NOW

I think almost every reader can recognize in himself some of the following features of procrastination. The resistance to getting ourselves started on a new course is due

---

[1] The subject of negligence is so subtle and complex that I shall go into it further in Chapter XVII.

[2] In this belief I am obviously at issue with most writers of the Freudian school.

to an inertia which is as definite in the nervous system of man as it is in a railroad train. It takes more power to start a heavy train or a new task than to keep it going. This fact helps to explain procrastination. But there is another element in it. To start is difficult; but it is especially so if one has to begin something that is disagreeable or irksome even after it is in motion.

The psychical expression of the difficulty in starting an unwelcome job is the effort to persuade oneself that " some other time will do " as well as the present. We try ingeniously to persuade ourselves that the job does not need to be done just now. Here is a theme to be written, a bill or a visit to be paid; but, we say, some other time will do as well. Now we don't feel like it. Besides we have other things on hand. It is inconvenient to break away from them. Probably also we are tired, especially when we think of doing that bothersome job. " I eats well and sleeps well," said a private to the company doctor, " but when I sees a job of work I'm all of a tremble."

One who hates to take exercise will procrastinate about moving. One who hates to keep still will put off the moment of settling down. Those who hate to write letters succeed in forgetting them. But to some facile letter-writers it is hard to refrain from writing letters when less inviting tasks are in order. New efforts and efforts without immediate reward we tend to put off.

The evidence of one's procrastination accumulates in bills unpaid, drawers not cleared up, soiled clothes not sent to the wash. To pitch them into a closet and shut the door is the physical parallel to what one does with the ideas which remind us of our neglect. With a twitch of attention we pull down the shades of consciousness, turn off the lights, and so after a little we get relief.

Almost every one procrastinates about something and

on some occasions. If my description of the mental state is wrong, the reader can correct it, for he knows all about it. The amount that one "rationalizes" varies with the glibness or dumbness of one's temperament, and with the presence or absence of a critic. Self-defenses are extemporized when they are needed to repel adversaries inside us or outside us. But I think the element of self-deception is almost always there when one procrastinates. For one does not refuse the disagreeable job once for all. It is not definitely repudiated; it is accepted as a proper claim, some time,—only not just now. When I am in any doubt about whether such a plea is true I ask myself, "Can you name another time that will really be any better than this? If so mark it down in black and white. Let some one else know about it, and if possible, remind you of it when the time comes." If I cannot name such a right time I diagnose the case as self-deception and stand self-condemned to immediate performance. It appears that I am for the law in general but against its enforcement at any specific instant. To make this plausible and so to get relief from the nagging of conscience, I procrastinate.

The plea of the procrastinator always might be true. There *are* times and seasons for everything. When one is on the point of writing and posting an important letter on the spur of anger, all the procrastinator's arguments are true. Then it is really better to wait till another time. One means still to write that letter of protest, of criticism or accusation. But one should cool off first. There is really no hurry.

3. JUST THIS TIME

A third common form of self-deceit is the habitual appeal to exceptions and emergencies. Procrastination says: "*Not just* at this time." The opposite wriggle of self-excuse says: "*Just* this time." Ordinarily one does not cut across the grass because one does not wish to see a path worn there. "But just this one hasty dash won't establish a path. I am late and must save time. There's no great harm in it just for once. Every rule has its exceptions. Indeed exceptions prove the rule." In general we do not believe in lies, but now and then, in a tight place, one has to make an exception. Usually laws should be obeyed, in spirit if not always in letter. This time, however, a slight violation is not serious. As a general principle one does not countenance false impersonation. It is too much like forgery. But just this time, as a favor to a friend, it is all right to sit in his seat in the lecture room so that the monitor may mark him present. He really can't afford a cut.

Such arguments are entirely respectable. Rules do have exceptions, and laws should be obeyed in spirit but not always literally. The question is, are we really facing *now* a good reason for making an exception? Are we ready to see every one else do the same when he feels as we do now? Granted that emergencies demand exceptional behavior, it still is true that some of us find too many of them. We are like the beggar who always needs your money to meet a special crisis. He must get to the next town where his people are. He must have one square meal so that he will be strong enough to go to work. This dime, like all the loans that spendthrifts ask of us, is for quite temporary and extraordinary needs. Next week, as in all previous weeks, he will have plenty of money and can easily repay. In time the petitioner almost becomes the person he has pretended to be. He comes veritably to believe that he is perpetually in hard luck. From that moment on there is no more self-deceit about his plea. He has made himself believe that he actually will be able to repay next week.

Self-deception is all the easier when we can voice it in a stock phrase inherited from past generations of self-deceivers. Then it is amazing what nonsense we manage to cling to in our extremity. We say for instance that " Exceptions prove the rule." Of course they do not and never did. It is in spite of exceptions, not because of them, that any rule survives. One might as well say that gunshot wounds improve health, or that a rainy day increases drought. That such stuff should be asserted as plausible shows how gullible we can make ourselves when we try, and adds to the evidence that we are self-betrayed, not ordinary liars nor victims of accidental error.

William James has shown that this particular form of self-deceit is especially pernicious when we are trying to change a habit. " Never suffer an exception to occur," he says, " till the new habit is securely rooted in your life." This is to some extent a counsel of irrationality, but it is a shrewd one, because something tougher and more obstinate, blinder and less considerate than reason is what we need just here. Reason tells us that an exception, a single lapse, is a little thing. Yes, it is as slight as the muscular twitch that lets fall " a ball of string which one is carefully winding up; and undoes more than a great many turns will wind again." . . . One may excuse himself " for every fresh dereliction by saying, ' I won't count it this time.' . . . But down among his nerve-cells and fibers the molecules are counting it. . . . Nothing is wiped out. Of course, this has its good side as well as its bad one. As we become . . . drunkards by so many separate drinks, so we become saints in the moral, and authorities and experts in the practical and scientific spheres, by so many separate acts and hours of work. . . . Continuity of training is the great means of making the nervous system act infallibly right. . . . Failure at first is apt to dampen the energy of all future attempts, whereas experience of success nerves one to future vigor." [1]

4. WHATEVER ADVANTAGES I HAVE I OUGHT TO HAVE

" I have power and privilege. Therefore I ought to have them. They are my rights." This is a favorite self-concealed assertion. Boards, committees, commissions seldom abolish themselves even when it is obvious to an outsider that they no longer have any good reason to exist. They have the power to go on existing. They have authority to function; therefore they persuade themselves that they are of use. By a similar fixation of our attention it is easy to persuade ourselves that if, in the distribution of this world's goods, we have an unusually large share, it ought to stay with us and should not be taken or given away. To regard ourselves as trustees for the community is a comfortable and therefore a dangerous belief.

The propertied man finds it easy to believe in private property. The heir to property is easily convinced that inheritance is a good thing. It is natural for a doctor to think well of medical authority, for generals and admirals to approve of large armaments, for good athletes to contend that athletics should not be interfered with by college authorities, for business men to fear encroachments by the State and therefore to assert that they are wrong in principle. Those near the head of a queue at a ticketseller's window think well of the custom of forming such a queue. Those at the other end are inclined to be dubious about it.

It is so comfortable to have power, to enjoy easy leadership, wealth, and prominence, that every one who enjoys these privileges tends to think that he is the right man in

[1] William James, *Talks to Teachers on Psychology* (New York: Henry Holt & Co., 1899), pp. 68 ff.

the right place. He is inclined to be a conservative, to believe in strong government, in law and order. He distrusts agitators. Even the opinions that he holds seem to him right partly because he holds them and does not want to lose them. With this danger in mind it is clearly the duty of every one who wants the truth and hates self-deceit, to suspect his right to enjoy any privilege, to weigh the question skeptically when he sees his own comfort and power in one scale of the balance, and somebody else's want in the other. We try to prevent judges and legislators from settling questions in which they have a pecuniary interest to decide in one way, and will get no profit if they come to an opposite conclusion. We do this not always because we suspect deliberate corruption in these officials but because we know that it is very easy for them to be confused and to confuse themselves, when self-interest is strongly on one side of the question before them.

We cannot avoid the need to decide on some matters which we know are prone to lead us into self-deceit. But we can mark them as we do all cases of "necessity," postponement, and exception-making, with the label, "Ancient Pitfall of Self-Deceit."

5. CONVINCING OURSELVES THAT WE ARE NOBODY

Our *sheep-mindedness* leads us into a fifth type of obfuscation. In our wits as in our muscles we are creatures of "the herd." In terror of isolation, in dread of ridicule, we merge ourselves in the crowd. We, especially the 1933 model of the American people, like to believe that we are independent, stand on our own feet, and make up our own minds. Yet in reality our American tendency to imitate each other, our fear of seeming queer, our terror of being laughed at are notorious.

I recall a day not very long ago when a club of medical

professors lined up before a microscope. One of them was to demonstrate a rare specimen, a quartan malarial parasite caught in the moment of dividing into a new generation. He found the field, focussed the microscope, and went off for a moment to find another specimen. We formed a queue and filed up one by one to study the parasite. As I waited near the tail of the line I was struck by the silence of those at the head of it. No one made any comment. No one seemed surprised or even intelligently interested. When it came to the turn of the man next ahead of me in the line, he put his eye to the microscope, refocussed the lens, stopped to wipe his eyeglasses, looked again, grunted, paused. Finally he straightened up and called to the demonstrator, "Smith! Won't you come over here and show me this beast? I can't see anything here."

Smith came up hastily, looked through the instrument, and burst into a loud laugh. "Why there's nothing there! The specimen must have got moved." And he began to hunt through the preparation to find again the field which contained the parasite. As he did so I glanced at the other men who had already "seen" the parasite and passed on. Some were heartily laughing and confessing to each other that they too had seen nothing but hadn't dared to say so; some looked rather confused and blank; a few were quite easy and unembarrassed. I suppose no one will ever know at what point in the line of wise professors the specimen became displaced so that there was nothing there to see. Perhaps none of them saw anything. But my impression is that the first three or four really saw the parasite and that, out of the remaining eight or nine, several thought they saw and did not, while two or three knew that they did not see anything but were ashamed to confess this to their brother professors. At this early period of the club's existence we were much in awe of one another and far less willing than at a later period to confess how little we knew. After some one had started the fashion of unashamed ignorance on special points, it became easy to join in. But before we had discovered that it was respectable in our group to admit our ignorance and even to doubt the omniscience of the others, we were cautious about saying anything that might show how little we knew. We sought the shadow, we colored ourselves protectively, so that no peculiar belief or ignorance might be recognized in us.

Not all of this conformity was self-deception. In part it was deliberate self-concealment. But I am confident that in the early meetings of this club some of us were trying to persuade ourselves that we saw, heard, or felt all that the others said they did, while in reality we saw, heard, and felt nothing at all. In those whom we call quacks, hypocrites, charlatans, I believe that ordinary lying passes through the stage of self-deception into involuntary error. I do not think I have ever known a genuine hypocrite, one who systematically and steadily pretended to possess virtue which he knew he lacked. Dickens' *Pecksniff* and *Stiggins* are glorious but impossibly consistent fakes. More human is the half-light somewhere between believing and not believing; it is here that many of us put up our bluffs. But in the beginning this half-light was not inevitable. We grope about in it because we have first gone indoors and pulled down the shades, for fear of what we might see if we exposed our minds to the full light of fact. At the outset we were not the unfortunate victims of defective sight. We have pushed ourselves into dark corners because we have been trying to hide from ourselves.

The classic example of sheep-minded self-deception is Hans Christian Andersen's story of "The Emperor's New Clothes," which I shall try to summarize.

The Emperor was so fond of new clothes that he spent all his money on them. One day two swindlers came to his palace and said that they could weave the most beautiful stuffs imaginable, which had moreover the peculiar and valuable quality of being invisible to every person who was not fit for the office he held, or who was impossibly stupid.

"These must be splendid clothes," thought the Emperor. "By wearing them I shall be able to discover the unfit and to distinguish the wise men from the fools."

So he gave the swindlers a heap of money in advance. They put up their looms and pretended to weave. In reality they had nothing whatever in their shuttles. Those who came to see how they were getting on saw nothing, but not daring to admit to themselves that they were stupid or useless, they pretended to see beautiful cloth growing up on the loom. They even praised it extravagantly. Like the swindlers they named the colors and described the pattern so vividly that some of the onlookers almost thought they saw it.

The Emperor himself and his officials when they visited the looms were astounded, terrified, but first for self-protection and perhaps later in self-deception, they praised the new cloth like the rest. Then the swindlers pretended to take the finished cloth off the looms, to cut it out in the air with a huge pair of shears, and to stitch it with needles that had no thread in them. When they had finished, the Emperor took off his clothes and the swindlers pretended to put the new clothes on him, to show their effect in the mirror, and to admire their fit. Then the chamberlains who were to carry the train of the robe stooped, pretended to lift it from the ground with both hands, and walked along behind the Emperor with their hands in the air. They dared not let it appear that they could see nothing. And everybody in the streets exclaimed, "How beautiful the Emperor's new clothes are!" . . .

"*But he has nothing on!*" said a little child. "Oh, listen to the innocent," said its father. Then one person whispered to the other what the child had said. The crowd began to chatter

"He has nothing on!" at last cried all the people. But the Emperor held himself stiffer than ever, and the chamberlains held up the invisible train.

This story was written before the facts of hypnotism, mob-suggestion, and auto-suggestion, had come into general notice. Andersen may have meant his tale to illustrate nothing but pure fraud and cowardly lying. But in my belief many in the crowd persuaded themselves that the clothes must be really there and a few actually saw them. In the end they saw what they wanted to see and what they thought everybody else saw. Not all of them were consciously pretending to see what they knew was not there. Nor was it for many a pure hallucination, like the black snakes, beetles, and elephants that the sufferer from *delirium tremens* sees, not because he wants to see them but because he cannot escape them. He is terrified because he sees them. Some of my colleagues in the medical professors' club were alarmed because they did *not* at first make out the malarial parasite. They were frightened into a half-believed vision.

Sheep-minded self-deceit is neither conscious fraud nor helpless hallucination. It is something intermediate. It is like the self-suppression by which we acquiesce in fashions of dress which for a brief instant we (almost) know to be hideous. There is a moment's glimpse of truth. But we cannot muster the courage to confess it. We pass through the stages of " guessing it's all right," to rather liking it, to thinking it is very smart, indeed beautiful. It will not do to think otherwise. By the same sophistication we discovered in 1848 that it was the " manifest destiny " of the United States to gobble up Texas and New Mexico. So doctors have decided that fee-splitting is inevitable. So people have now ascertained that it is all right for young girls to get drunk now and then. (For babies, even girl babies, it is still wrong.)

If the clear light could be turned on we should know better. Then we might " become honest overnight," as a Boston trustee complained that his friends had, when they objected to his false oath about the estate of a client.

But by self-deceit the light is turned so low that it is possible to think one sees as much as one wants to see and no more.

In the next chapter I shall present further examples of the ways in which the psychic poison of self-concealment is secreted in our daily lives.

Chapter XVI

OTHER DEVICES OF SELF–DECEIT

1. PRETENDING THAT ONE CANNOT SEE

Selfishness is not the same trait as innocent narrow-mindedness or deficient interest in others. It is not mere ignorance or defect. A person who is deaf is not to be blamed if he speaks loudly in a library reading-room or in a church. He does not know that he is annoying others. He stops as soon as he is warned of it. A surgeon with blood from his last operation still on his coat may walk innocently through the waiting-room of a hospital where " new " patients are waiting their turn. He scatters horror among them, not because he is careless of their feelings but because he is unaware that they are seeing the blood on his coat. It is not selfish of me to let a man die alone and unaided in the attic of the house next mine provided I have no inkling of his existence, as in a great city is often enough the case. In all these cases, ignorance, not selfishness, is the correct diagnosis.

Selfishness is ignoring another's need as if I did not know its existence, when in fact I do. Here in my corner of the trolley car waiting to start, I sit huddled up behind my evening paper. As ladies come in and stand in the aisle not far off, I hold my newspaper higher and spread it more widely so that I remain quite unaware whether any of them are standing opposite me. Should I lower the newspaper and discover that a lady is standing close in front of me I should probably be shamed into giving her my seat. Her tired, drooping figure and the glances of others as I should then meet them, would reënforce my belief that able-bodied men should *ordinarily* give up their seats to tired women standing in a trolley car. But I dread the bother of this enlightenment. So I snuggle down behind my paper and see nothing. My selfishness is a voluntary limitation of my field of moral vision.

Without selfishness, our awareness of others' lives is often inevitably blurred by distance and by time, by our ignorance and unappreciativeness, by their inability to get into communication with us, and by our limitations of energy or of resource. Multitudes of needy men must remain for us utterly unknown or known only as statistical units or passing faces in a crowded street. An accident, a heroic deed, a terrible crime, may bring some unknown man into our newspaper consciousness for an hour or two before we turn, rightly enough, to the affairs that more directly concern us. Most members of the human race concern us hardly more than the moles under ground or the trees in an equatorial forest. Doubtless, we say, they have their part in the world's economy; but they are none of our business. We must keep most of our attention on the matters for which we are chiefly responsible.

Our invincible ignorance then, and the superior claim of our own affairs upon our attention, inevitably shut our minds to most of the earth's inhabitants, most of those in our own country, most of those even in our own neighborhood. Admittedly we have close economic relations and important political dealings with people in distant parts of the earth. "Because fashionable women in Paris, London, and New York have cried to one another, 'My dear, you can't possibly wear that,' and less fashionable women have repeated it after them, machines are lying idle and chimneys have stopped smoking in Lancashire." But most of these relations are quite unconscious and probably should remain so to the majority of us, though they may influence our vote in a presidential election. All this shows our inevitable narrowness, not our selfishness.

But a part of our ignorance of other people's lives is of a different character. Some of it is as selfish as the ignorance of the trolley passenger behind his newspaper. It has been said that monkeys do not talk because they are afraid that if they did they would be made to work. Men certainly blind themselves to knowledge which they suspect would compel hard thinking. Some of our ignorance is assumed because knowledge would cost too much. We know that the people whom we meet are just as real as we are and that if we followed that knowledge up to what it implies, we could not treat them selfishly. Their pain would hurt us and we should be led to take some trouble about it. Therefore we keep ourselves so busy that we do not notice them.

> The conductor on the railway train when I travel is for me just the being who takes my ticket, the official to whom I can appeal for certain advice or help if I need it. That this conductor has an inner life, like mine, this I am apt never to realize at all. He has to excite my pity or some other special human interest in me ere I shall even begin to try to think of him as really like me. On the whole, he is for me . . . an automaton. . . . Occasionally I do realize him in another way, but how? I note . . . that he is courteous or surly, and I like or dislike him accordingly. Now courtesy and discourtesy are qualities that belong not to automata at all. Hence I must somehow recognize him in this case as conscious. But what aspect of his consciousness do I consider? Not the inner aspect of it . . . but still the outer aspect of his conscious life, as a power affecting me. . . . It seldom occurs to me to realize how he feels. . . .
>
> The butcher, the newsboy, the servant,—are they not for us industrious or lazy, honest or deceitful, polite or uncivil, useful or useless people, rather than self-conscious people? Is any one of these alive for me in the full sense,—sentient, emotional . . . like myself, as my own son, or my own mother or my wife. . . ? Is it not rather the kind

of behavior of these beings *towards me* that I realize? . . . They are
all good fellows or bad fellows, good-humored or surly, hateful or admirable. They may appear even sublime or ideal beings, as a Caesar
might to a student of history. Yet their inner life need not therefore
be realized. They remain . . . ways of acting, dispositions, wonder-
ful examples of energy. They are still seen from without. Not their
inner, volitional nature is realized, but their . . . outward activity;
not what they are for themselves, but what they are for others.[1]

Selfishness rests upon a self-illusion like the dwarfing of
perspective. A man on the horizon is seen as a mere dot.
He is "very far off," we say, meaning very far off from
that center of the world, myself. But we do not doubt
that he is in fact as tall, as heavy, as vigorous and important as ourselves. He looks like a speck of dust; but
we are not deceived. We realize well enough that this is
an illusion like the apparent convergence of railway rails
when we stand between them and look along the road-
bed. We do not fear that our railway coach will run off the
track because of a real convergence of these rails. We
know that our senses record the facts wrongly.

But in the moral field it is our selfishness that creates
the illusions of psychic perspective; we take care to have
only a "head knowledge" that other people's interests,
desires, feelings, rights are as important as our own. Yet
we do not really think them born to be our slaves. Aristotle apparently thought so and certainly wrote so. For
him slaves were men born with a "slave nature," a slave
mind, and were meant therefore to be treated as slaves,—
they and their descendants forever. But we know better.

Why are we apparently so much more gullible in the
moral than in the physical perspective? It is not because
the situation is complex or subtle. Take the illustration

---

[1] Josiah Royce, *The Religious Aspect of Philosophy* (Boston: Houghton Mifflin Co.,
1887), p. 149.

already used. There is nothing difficult about seeing the women who enter a trolley car when you, a male, are seated in it. To get a correct view of the facts you need no special education or abstruse calculation. In fact you had to hold the newspaper sheet up before your face to prevent your seeing them. Yet men who are keen, intelligent, shrewd on most matters will do and say the most absurd things when selfishness enters as an element in their judgments. They will declare with Aristotle and our own Southern States before the Civil War, that slavery is an institution created by nature itself, or that opium is good for the health of Orientals. They are deceived because they want to be deceived. In other words, they are self-deceived. A confederate within the city has opened the gates to the invading error.

This is not the only type of selfishness, though I believe it is much the commonest among "educated" people. The smoke screen of words, "rationalizations," explanations, and excuses, is emitted most copiously by those for whom talking is easy. I have known few who do not try to dress up their selfishness in respectable guise. But now and then one meets an "honest hog" who has no illusions and seeks his food whole-heartedly. He knows that others have rights, but he does not care. He chooses to act as if they did not. This is the anaesthetic type of selfishness. When such a man robs a bank he does not elaborate explanations about getting even with those who have already robbed society, or about his poor wife and children who need the money which rich bank depositors will never miss. If he wants to get drunk he does not feel the need to quote John Stuart Mill's *Essay on Liberty*, or to prove that beer is a valuable food recommended by many doctors. If he wants to hold the end seat in an open trolley car and oblige all who get in or out to climb over him, he does not think it necessary to explain that he is getting out very soon. He simply holds his place.

But this is not a popular course of behavior. It rouses antagonism; it piles up obstructions, which in time may bring the " honest " bandit to a standstill. He is forced to allay the irritation or to circumvent the opposition which he has aroused. In order to get on he must become respectable. Then he tries to elaborate good reasons, or at any rate plausible reasons, for disregarding others' rights. But if these reasons are plausible enough to deceive the public they are almost certain to exert some force upon the man who elaborates and employs them. In etherizing his fellows he inhales so much ether himself that in the end he is almost unconscious of his own sophistries. In any case the best way to make others believe them is to believe them oneself.

Medical excuses for selfishness are especially plausible. J. B. Priestley's *Mrs. Tarvin*,[1] wife of the boarding-school master, has *crème caramel* and cream for dessert. The boys are given stewed prunes, old and withered. She declares that she is herself very fond of these prunes but is not allowed by her doctor to eat them. Her male equivalent whom we all know is too lazy after dinner to help wash the dishes or to carry up the coal. How easily he persuades himself that he is physically not well enough to undertake these jobs at the present time. In actual fact the thought of doing them does make him feel seedy. So much is really true. Given a little help from the credulity of selfishness, it is easy to take the next step in the argument: When I think of these jobs I feel almost sick. But no one should force himself to heavy work when he is sick. Therefore I ought not to move off this sofa. Q.E.D.

The chief flaws in this argument are, first, that on pre-

[1] In *The Good Companions* (New York and London: Harper & Bros. 1929).

vious evenings when I felt exactly as I do now, I have nevertheless carried up the coal and washed the dishes and felt if anything a little better after these exertions than before. The next absurdity in the argument is that my daughter, who is a good deal more delicate than I am, will have to do these chores if I do not. Any arguments on the score of health apply more strongly to her than to me. But the final and all-inclusive argument against me is that when I face the facts I know perfectly well that what I am saying is bunk. In the case of any one else in my place I should jeer or get indignant. Is my place in any way peculiar, exceptional? No, but it feels so, because I want to feel it so.

2. " MY POOR WIFE AND FAMILY "

Not quite so common as selfish self-deceit is *the pretense of unselfishness*. To marry and raise a family multiplies our " temptations to rightdoing " [1] but also increases our momentum toward the habit of pretending to be incapacitated for ordinary duties by our duties to our family. It is supposedly harder for a married man to make any change for good in his way of living. The father of a family nourishes expectations that he can be depended on to furnish money for a certain scale of living, to come home at a certain hour, to take certain holidays, and enjoy evening recreations with the family. Sometimes these ties tend to keep him steady and to raise his standards. They are also and less obviously a temptation to corporate, respectable selfishness. If business slumps and earnings fall, luxuries and recreations ought to be cut down. But *paterfamilias* is naturally fond of his comforts and does not want to give them up. When he thinks of his family and their

[1] Ella Lyman Cabot, *Temptations to Rightdoing* (Boston: Houghton Mifflin Co., 1929).

deprivation he can easily persuade himself that they, and he, ought not to lower their " standard of living." It is disgraceful to lower any standard. So it is incumbent on him to find some more money in other ways, by " playing the stock market," by loans, by installment buying, by letting his bills run on, or by some of the less obvious methods of stealing called embezzlement.

Here laziness veiled by the cloak of family duty achieves a measure of self-respect sufficient to carry on with. The family is not the only group in which one can hide one's sloth so successfully as to deceive even oneself. Duty to one's stockholders, loyalty to one's profession, have a similar usefulness as disguises. Of course one has a duty to family, to stockholders, and to one's profession. Every word of the pretended altruist might be spoken by a true altruist. No outsider has a right to final judgment in such matters. Only the man himself can tell when the plea of necessity, of postponement, of " just this time," of rightful privilege, of proper conformity to others' ways, of consideration for others' rights is true, and when it is false.

3. AUTOCRACY UNAVOWED

Absolutism was never less popular than now. Yet it is as convenient for the autocrat as it ever was. Hence in our time there have grown up a number of devices to disguise it. Some of them are so successful that after a little practice one can fool oneself with them. " The rule of my labor policy," says the hard-boiled employer, " is always to do what is fair. I pay fair wages, hire and fire justly, am open and square in all my dealings with my employees."

What more could one ask? It sounds perfect. But essential words are dropped out: " To do what is fair "? Yes;

but after these words the speaker semi-consciously adds several more which change the tune entirely. " My rule is to do what is fair " (as I see it and without consulting the employees). " I pay " (what I consider) " fair wages." " I hire and fire justly " (according to my ideas of justice). If this employer had the habit of meeting his men in joint conferences and deciding with them the policies of hiring, laying off, or discharging men, of shop discipline, shop conditions, wages, and hours of work, he would speak not of " my " labor policy but of " our " labor policy. He would not say " what is fair " but " what seems fair to all concerned." His autocracy is still active, but it is so well concealed that it deceives him too.

" The labor spies in my factory can't do any harm to any employee who is behaving himself. If they are not hatching a plot against us they need not fear the detective, or any one else who tries to investigate their behavior." But the labor spy is not looking only or chiefly for wrongdoing, for sabotage, theft, or carelessness. He is looking for the leaders of labor union sentiment, the leaders of future strikes, whom their employer wishes to get rid of. Hence the sentence quoted above should read: " The labor spies in my factory can't harm employees who behave themselves well *according to my standards of good behavior.*" The spy is harmless to those who have no ideas of their own, who are contented, docile, and not ambitious to improve their condition. It is the agitators, that is the labor union leaders, who have to be weeded out secretly through spies, because no employer can acknowledge the intention to discharge them because of their views on labor questions. That is contrary to law in most places, and enrages public opinion everywhere.

" If the truth will help a person, even though it hurts him at the time, I tell the truth. But I should never hesitate to lie for another's good." Who decides, in this case, whether the truth is going to hurt permanently or to help permanently? The speaker himself settles this. He is a benevolent autocrat, but still an autocrat, unavowed. For he does not consult the person most concerned, the person whose weal or woe is to be affected by knowing the facts or by having them concealed from him. The benevolent liar does not say in advance, " Would you think it wise for me to tell you the truth about matters of this sort, or would you prefer to have me lie to you? " That would not work. It would usually bring an explosion of wrath. So he chooses the quiet, unobtrusively autocratic policy.

When we hear in college circles or in business groups that certain things should be done " quietly, unobtrusively, without making any fuss about it," we come to expect that something autocratic is about to be put through. Business men hated Theodore Roosevelt's noisy way of putting economic questions before the public in picturesque phrases. He made autocracy a little more difficult for the financial magnates of his time.

Perhaps such autocracy may work well. I am not discussing that question. Sometimes, I believe, it works so well that in the end it deceives the autocrat himself. His rule of life then should read, " If (I consider that) the truth will help, I tell it. I will lie for (what I consider is going to be) the good of another. But I won't consult him." Say these things and every one rebels. Act them and many applaud you. Benevolent medical lies, told to spare the patient's feelings and so to conserve his strength, are the commonest form of unavowed despotism known to me. But they seem to me self-deceptions because they can, I think, usually be shown up by the following questions:

" Doctor, would you think it right to act contrary to your patient's wishes without consulting him? "

" Certainly not, if he is sane."

" Are you quite sure that he desires you to deceive him about his condition or about his treatment,—for his own good, of course? "

" I am pretty sure that he doesn't want to know the truth and anyway I know that it is bad for him."

" How can you be sure that he does not want the truth even if it is bad for him? In any case why not let him have some say about his own affairs? Is it not tyranny to refuse to consult a person's wishes before you act for him in a matter that is peculiarly his own concern? Benevolent tyranny, but still outrageous."

War departments give out in war " as much of the truth as the public can stand "; that is, as much of the truth as (the war department in its wisdom decides that) the public can stand. Would the public agree in these decisions? Who can say; the public is not consulted. The war department exercises (what it considers to be) a benevolent and beneficial autocracy. Should not the public be asked at the outset of the war how much it wants the war department to deceive it? The war department is careful not to face this question.

In these examples I am not harping on the obvious fact that any one's conscientious judgment may be mistaken. I am not calling for modesty nor attacking conceit. I am attacking the habit of soft-pedaling the utterances of one's own thoughts when one has decided benevolently to settle other people's affairs without consulting them. Autocracy is so unpopular a practice in this country that few will attempt it with their eyes fully open. It will not bear the light, even the light of one's own clear awareness. Hence one pushes it out into the shadows.

4. MODERATION IN ALL THINGS

We deceive ourselves by *sloppy thinking disguised as liberalism*. Liberalism is an excellent guaranty of respectability in the intellectual field. It is the opposite of dogmatism. The liberal preserves an open mind. He is free, because no settled opinion binds him to its service forever. He expects change and hopes for progress in morals, politics, religion, art, and all other human achievements. Most of us would agree that we need this sort of freedom in our mental habits. But freedom of any kind can easily degenerate into license. Liberalism is apt to soften down into muddy thinking, especially when it is snatched up in hot haste to repel an attack. Because dogmatism is apt to ossify certain of our opinions, liberalism is invoked to defend misty vagueness. "Never go to extremes," says the liberalistic slumper. "Be moderate in all things." (At this point he is apt to invoke the authority of some Greek mottoes.) "Extremists and fanatics are a curse to every one, including themselves. We should always be tolerant, broadminded, ready to see the exceptions to all rules and the objections to all theories. We easily get too much of a good thing no matter how good it is. There are no absolute truths. Everything is relative."

Excellent advice for certain people and at certain times. It all depends on who invokes it and when. I have heard it invoked in defense of mere muddle, by some one who wants to be let off easily from the task of clear thought. He wants moderation shown to *him*, not "in all things" or to all persons. For if one presses the point that "moderation in all things" is rather a large order, it is soon admitted. Suppose we say, "Be moderate in your murders. Don't go to extremes when you forge. As a rule, to kidnap children is not wise. But of course there are exceptions to all rules.   The hit-and-run trick when your automobile has just killed an old lady is usually an extreme procedure.   But one must not be narrow or dogmatic about it.   No one should be fanatical in his condemnation of the citizen who sets fire to his own house in order to get the insurance.   One should always be tolerant.   Perhaps the gentleman sincerely believed that his insurance company needed to be bled.   To abstain from beating one's wife is a good thing, but one can get too much of a good thing."

No one wants moderation in all things, but only in some things.   Going to extremes is an excellent move, provided we choose our extremes wisely: for example, extremes of accuracy in bookkeeping or in piano playing.   Have we any objection to extreme exactness in the dosage of powerful medicines or in the starting and arrival of trains on time?   Do we prefer only moderate safety in the structure of large buildings?   Few will plead for moderation in the number of times a man treasonably sells his country to the enemy in time of war.   Extremes of abstention or of performance are what average public opinion requires in many cases.

Why then do we pervert the solid, sensible doctrine of liberalism into a slovenly plea for lax standards?   Because we want to be let off easily this time.   It sounds piggish to ask exemption only for ourselves.   So we universalize the plea with the aid of pseudo-liberal mottoes.   What we want is a rule that applies to others when we need their efficiency, but not to ourselves when we want the leeway to be careless.   "A man," says G. K. Chesterton, "may throw himself into a hammock in a fit of divine carelessness.   But he is glad that the hammock-maker didn't make the hammock in a fit of divine carelessness."

Another self-deceiving dodge which, in pseudo-liberal

moods, we often try, is to discredit " theory." " Yes," we
say, " your idea (or ideal) is all right in theory but in
practice it doesn't work." " It is proper enough to work
out theoretically how a thing ought to be. But when
you come right down to brass tacks theories are not much
good." Such phrases are especially popular among Americans and Englishmen who believe themselves, rightly
enough, to be strong on practical matters, experts at the
application of knowledge to business, medicine, and engineering. But to discredit " theory " is also a convenient excuse when we wish to dodge the labor of clear
thinking which many " Anglo-Saxons " hate.

If we consider for a moment what " theory " means it
will appear that our good-humored contempt for it is
often a form of self-deception and not a counsel of shrewd
practicality. The working-drawings made by the architect and used by the housebuilder to guide construction
are pure theory. The actual house is built in accordance
with them. That is practice. A theory states some one's
plan of action or some one's plan for interpreting facts.
The atomic and electronic theory states, in formulae and
symbols, the plan which students of physics now believe
best interprets the facts. If it does not fit the facts it is a
bad theory and should be changed. It cannot be a good
theory unless it is practical. The architect's plan of a
house is a theory of what he, or the owner, intends. When
they come to practise this theory by building the house,
they may find that they have left out the back stairs or
the bedroom closets. Then it was a bad theory; the facts
have revealed its imperfections. It would have been a
good theory only if, when put in practice, it had been
shown to fit the intentions of the architect or owner. No
one would be so stupid as to say, " The blue prints were
all right enough but in practice they didn't work." The

plan, or theory, was as good or as bad as its application showed it to be.

If this is true no one can sensibly say, " The idea that one should always keep one's promises is all right in theory but in practice it doesn't work." If it does not work it must be restated, modified, amended until it does. But if one hopes to postpone or to avoid the labor of clear thinking, and the sacrifices to which it may lead, it is easy to fool one's intellectual conscience by discrediting theory.

5. THE THIRST TO GET SOMETHING FOR NOTHING

Pasteur attacked the partisans of spontaneous generation in bacteria and other low forms of life, partly because he had experimental evidence against them, but partly also from his conviction that their belief was a lazy one, that is, one which justified men in making no effort to find a precursor of microscopic organisms. The " spontaneous variations " of the Darwinian theory were recognized, not as miraculous events but as labels for our ignorance. But spontaneous *generation* was not so labeled. Without extreme fancifulness we can describe the belief in spontaneous generation as a psychological cousin to our popular American desire to get something for nothing. No cause for the existence of life need be laboriously sought, because there isn't any. A fiat, a miracle, a vital activity has given us the new life for nothing. Another psychical relative of spontaneous generation is the " fallacy of ordering and forbidding " referred to in Chapter XIX. Under this popular fallacy a change in something as fixed as habit is expected merely because we forbid it. Like fiat money, the veto is thought to acquire value and weight merely because some one speaks.

These forms of lazy thinking succeed in fooling us the more readily because nature or chance does sometimes give us presents without any exertion of ours. This happens often enough to make some of us fancy that we can plan our lives that way. We get air to breathe, wind to sail by, water-power to generate energy, we get natural beauty, parental love, glorious music with so little exertion that it is no great exaggeration to say that the best in life comes to us without effort. Only by experiment we find out what we can get for nothing and what we cannot. The essence of self-deceit in this matter is in continuing to believe that we can get for nothing the particular things that experience has shown us we must work for. Gambling, alcohol, and drugs are the most popular means to fool ourselves into the belief that we have got something valuable without the trouble of working for it. " Alcohol furnishes the means to get relief from the full consciousness of responsibilities in life." [1] There are few if any so handy tools of self-deceit, for a drug gives us just the sort of glamorous half-light in which we can believe what it is most comfortable to believe. Not only sorrows but responsibilities, difficulties, self-distrust, and self-reproach are drowned.

6. THE DUTY TO SURVIVE AT ALL COSTS

The supposed law of self-preservation is at times a convenient tool for self-deceit. After a hideous prison fire [2] which burned over three hundred convicts to death, the newspaper accounts suggested that some of the wardens were not anxious to risk their own lives even to save three hundred convicts from roasting to death in iron cages. The evidence is not clear and I make no assertion of fact. But supposing this interpretation to be true, some one

[1] A. W. Stearns, M.D., *The Personality of Criminals* (Boston: Beacon Press, 1931), p. 35.
[2] At Columbus, Ohio, April 21, 1930.

might point out that after all such a warden would only be obeying nature's first and grandest law, the law of self-preservation. Biologists have pointed out that it is in virtue of obedience to this law that we have survived upon our crowded and uncomfortable planet. The fittest, that is the strongest and shrewdest, survive in the struggle for food because they have made self-preservation their god.

Further down the scale of life we see the same law in the unconscious self-maintenance of our bodily tissues. Cells and organs survive because they are incessantly seeking their own self-preservation.[1] Higher up, among the human race, economic progress, on which, we are told, all other progress depends, is said to result from the same incessant struggle for self-preservation. Unselfishness is a luxury. To earn a living, to maintain existence each must seek to preserve his own life by adaptation to his environment in more and more civilized and intelligent ways. It is a law of nature and we cannot often break the law even if we wish. A similar contention is often maintained in ethical discussions. How can any one be blamed for selfishness? Isn't every one selfish at bottom? Doesn't every one carry out his own will and seek his own satisfaction even in so-called " altruistic " actions?

I add to my list of popular self-deceptions this argument that " self-preservation is a universal law of nature," because I think we possess but choose to forget the abundant evidence that it is not true. Almost every newspaper gives us instances of heroism which contradict it. The physician who fights an epidemic is not working for self-preservation. Two of my medical acquaintances have died in epidemics, one of typhus, one of yellow fever,

---

[1] Walter B. Cannon, *The Wisdom of the Body* (New York: W. W. Norton, Inc., 1932), *passim*.

into which they went, not to attend patients, but to study the bacteria of these diseases. These deaths, one can say, further race-preservation if not self-preservation. The human race, through its bacteriologists, is fighting to save its existence from the inroads of barbaric germs. But is this a fair account of what happened? Few, I think, of those who risk their lives in epidemics either as practitioners or as bacteriologists are working to save the human race from extermination. They know that the mortality from typhus and yellow fever is low. They are working partly to earn an honest living, but chiefly because they are interested in the study of disease. The preservation of their own lives or of human life is a negligible factor in their motives.

Those who use the argument of self-preservation know well enough that war has not yet been abolished and that no one goes to war for his health or to preserve the human race. We go because others go, because we cannot get out of it, for excitement and adventure, for the dictatorship of the proletariat, to defend our nation, or because we believe our cause is just,—for every sort of reason except self-preservation.

All this is mere commonplace. Every one knows it. Yet knowing it we still strangely turn away from it and argue that self-preservation is a universal and authoritative law of life, human and non-human. If self-deception and a desire to defend one's somewhat indefensible behavior are not the reasons for this paradoxical lapse of memory, I cannot explain it.

Summary. Instead of describing any further types of self-deception, I shall quote from the seventh book of Victor Hugo's *Les Misérables* a passage in which he skillfully weaves most of the devil's favorite arguments into the

soliloquy of his hero.   Jean Valjean, for a petty and excusable theft, has been condemned to years of imprisonment as a galley slave.   He escapes, takes up life again
under an assumed name in a new town, prospers, becomes
the leader of its industries, and finally its mayor.   Another
man, Champmathieu, is mistaken for him and is therefore
accused and about to be tried for Valjean's theft.   Champmathieu has in fact also stolen, but it is not for this theft
but for Jean Valjean's old " crime " that he is now held.

Never had the two motives which governed the unhappy man entered upon so serious a struggle.   His first thought was to go forth, to
denounce himself, to take Champmathieu out of prison, and take his
place.   This was sharp and painful, like an incision in the flesh; but
it passed away, and he said to himself, " We shall see."   He repressed
this first generous impulse; he shrank from such heroism.

(1)[1] In the presence of such a terrible juncture he was carried away
by the instinct of self-preservation.   He hastily collected his ideas and
recovered his calmness as a gladiator picks up his buckler.   He distinctly saw in the darkness an unknown man, a stranger, whom destiny
mistook for him and thrust into the gulf in his place. . . .   He had
only to let things take their course. . . .   He confessed to himself that
his place in the galleys was empty, but he said to himself that he now
had a substitute; a man of the name of Champmathieu had this " ill
luck "; and that in future, being himself at the galleys in the person
of this Champmathieu, he would have nothing more to fear, provided
he did not prevent justice from laying over the head of Champmathieu
the stone of infamy which, like the tombstone, falls once and is never
raised again.

(2) " And all this has taken place without my interference.   After
all, if some people are unhappy, it is no fault of mine.   Providence has
done it all, and apparently decrees it.   Have I the right to meddle with
the arrangements of Providence?   Who am I to interfere?   It does not
concern me.   I have attained the goal to which I have aspired for so
many years—security.   It is heaven's will.   I cannot run counter to
heaven's will.

[1] This and the succeeding six numbers are not in Victor Hugo's text but refer
to the types of self-deceit listed at the end of the quotation and to the movements
of his revolt against it.

" And why has heaven decreed it? That I may continue what I have begun; that I may do good; that I may one day be a grand and encouraging example; that it may be said that there is, after all, a little happiness attaching to the penance I have undergone, to that virtue to which I have returned.

" It is settled. I will let matters take their course, and leave the decision to heaven." . . .

(3) [Then, with a sudden shift of his mood he saw that] to allow this mistake of destiny and of men to be accomplished, not to prevent it, to lend himself to it by his silence . . . was the last stage of hateful hypocrisy; it was a low, cowardly, cunning, abject, hideous crime. Was it for so paltry a thing that he had done all that he had done? Had he not another object, which was the great and true one—to save, not his person, but his soul; to become once again honest and good; to close the door upon his past?

If he gave himself up, freed this man who was suffering from so grievous an error, resumed his name, became from a sense of duty the convict Jean Valjean—that would be really completing his resurrection.

Therefore he must go to Arras, deliver the false Jean Valjean and accuse himself, the true one. He could see, as though they moved before him in tangible form, the two ideas which had hitherto been the double rule of his life—to hide his name and sanctify his life. For the first time they seemed to him absolutely distinct. He recognized that one of these ideas was necessarily good, while the other might become bad.

At another moment the idea occurred to him that when he had given himself up to the law, the heroism of his deed, his honest life for the last seven years, and the good he had done in the town might perhaps be taken into consideration so that he would be pardoned.

If he let matters take their course and remained at M—— his good name, good deeds, the deference and respect paid to him, his charity, wealth, popularity, and virtue would be tainted by a crime; while if he accomplished his sacrifice he might allow a heavenly idea to perish in the galleys, the stake, the chain, the green cap, the unremitting toil, the pitiless shame.

He must choose either outward virtue and inward abomination, or holiness within and infamy without.

(4) " But hitherto I have thought of myself only, consulted only my own convenience, whether it suits me to be silent or to denounce myself. All this is egotism, under different shapes, 'tis true, but still

egotism. Suppose I were to think a little about others. It is the first duty of a Christian to think of his neighbor. Leaving myself out of the question, what will become of all this? Here are a town, factories, a trade, working people, men, women, old grandfathers, children, and poor people. I have created all this. I keep them alive. Before I came here there was nothing of all this. When I am gone, its soul will be gone, all will die. This will happen if I give myself up. If I do not . . .

(5) " Well, this man will go to the galleys, it is true, but hang it all, he has stolen. I may say to myself that he has not stolen, but in fact he has done so. I remain here, and continue my operations. In ten years I shall have gained ten millions. I scatter them over the country. I keep nothing for myself. I am not doing this for myself. The general prosperity is increased, wretchedness disappears, and with it debauchery, prostitution, robbery, murder, all the vices, all the crimes.

(6) " Why, I was absurd when I talked of giving myself up, because it pleases me to play the grand and the generous. It is pure melodrama after all. I only thought of myself, myself alone, and in order to save from a perhaps exaggerated though substantially just punishment a stranger, a thief, and an apparent scoundrel—a whole country must perish, a poor woman die in the hospital, and a poor child starve in the street, like dogs. These are fine scruples which save the guilty and sacrifice the innocent, which save an old vagabond who has not many years to live, and who will be no more unhappy at the galleys than in his hovel, and destroy an entire population, mothers, wives, and children.

(7) " Let us put things at the worst. Suppose I commit a bad action in this, and that my conscience reproach me with it some day; there will be devotion and virtue in accepting, for the good of my neighbor, these reproaches of conscience which weigh only on me, this bad action, which compromises only my own soul.

" I will let matters take their course; no more vacillation or backsliding. It is for the interest of all, not of myself. If any one else happens to be ' Jean Valjean ' at this moment, he must look out for himself . . . , it does not concern me.

[He then proceeds to do exactly the opposite. He goes to Arras, appears at Champmathieu's trial and raises his voice:] " Gentlemen of the jury, acquit the prisoner. Judge, arrest me. He is not the man you seek—I am Jean Valjean. . . . I thank you, sir, but I am not mad.

. . . You were on the point of committing a great error. Set that man at liberty. I hid myself under another name, I became rich, I became Mayor. I wished to return to the society of honest men; but it seems that this is impossible."

With masterly ingenuity Victor Hugo mobilizes in this soliloquy most of humanity's well-worn devices for self-excuse.

(1) Self-preservation is nature's first law. In the battle of life, in the struggle for existence, I am like a gladiator facing necessary peril. I snatch up my shield and fight for my life. (No. 11 below.)

(2) This questionable act (my silence while another man is condemned for my crime) is really no fault and no business of mine. It is the silent working of cause and effect. It is the will of heaven. It would be madness for me to interfere. (No. 1 below.)

(3) In any case the matter is already settled by luck, his ill luck. I cannot interfere. I am helpless. Champmathieu must take what has come to him. (No. 1 below.)

(4) I am bound to consider the greatest good of the greatest number. Heaven (or chance) has preserved me in order that I may continue important work for others' good and in order that my rise from obscurity to great public service may be an inspiring example to others. In ten years I can regenerate society, abolish poverty, vice, and crime. (No. 7 below.)

(5) If I remain silent another man will, it is true, be sentenced to the galleys in my place. But then, hang it, he has stolen, and his punishment, though exaggerated, will be substantially just. (Two wrongs make a right. A twelfth form of self-deceit not listed.)

(6) To give myself up to justice would be hypocrisy, playing to the gallery, melodrama. (No. 8 below.)

(7) After all, it is selfish to consider the good of my own

soul. Instead of thinking about my own honor and goodness, I should focus attention on the tangible good results
that will follow if I do this so-called "wrong" act.
(No. 8 below.)

Chapters XV and XVI exemplify, in eleven forms, the
root principle of self-deceit, that *the comfortable is the true.*

(1) As victims of *necessity* (compulsion, frustration,
blind habit, or innocent error) we are excused from reform
and shielded from blame. It is pleasant to believe that we
could not help ourselves; therefore it is true.

(2) *Procrastination* saves the pain of present effort;
therefore "some other time" is a plausible excuse.

(3) By *making an exception* we can violate agreements
comfortably; they are put in parentheses and so ignored
"just this time."

(4) *Self-protection in our privileges* secures our ease.
Therefore, by the legerdemain of self-deceit, they are justly
ours. "They are ours, held in trust for society."

(5) *Sheep-mindedness* is plausible because it is easy to
move with the crowd and hard to stand alone. Besides,
"everybody's doing it."

(6) *Selfishness* is more comfortable than the shame or
the effort that would follow recognition of others' needs.
We refuse to see them because we are "minding our own
business."

(7) *Pretense of unselfishness* dilutes the reproach of conscience and of the public, and so makes it more convenient
to be selfish for "my poor wife and children."

(8) *Autocracy unavowed* disarms criticism and so preserves our peace of mind when we wish to settle other
people's affairs without consulting them. "People can't
stand the truth," we say. "I shall have to lie to them."

(9) *Pseudo-liberalistic slovenliness*, with the motto of

" moderation in all things," gives us the pleasure of being moderately lazy in thought and in action.

(10) *The hope to get something for nothing* creates many means to fool ourselves.   Gambling and alcohol are two of the commonest.

(11) The excuse that *self-preservation is a natural and therefore universal law of life* frees us from the disagreeable necessity of risking our lives in a good cause.

CHAPTER XVII

RECKLESSNESS

In the forms described in the last two chapters the self-deceiving impulse is a reckoning, not a reckless impulse. It palavers, sophisticates, "rationalizes." It gets its will, the will to be comfortable, not by force but by fraud, not in ruthless and barbaric directness, but by insinuation, wriggling, and a cloud of words. It is a result of perverted civilization. It is the talker's impulse. In contrast with this comes the sudden, silent, and ruthless impulse of recklessness, which gets comfort by refusing to "reck," to reckon or consider consequences. Recklessness perverts the elemental in us. It is intentionally harebrained. It is deliberate barbarism. But in fact the savage is not reckless. The feeble-minded are rarely antinomians. They avoid risks if they can. They do not jump into them with a defiant gesture.

1. THE RECKLESS DO IN FACT RECKON

Recklessness, like all self-deception, is a paradox and a pretense. It is an old friend in daily life, but when we try to think it out it seems impossible. For when the reckless man declares that he doesn't care, he proves that he does care. He knows the restraint that he ignores. He turns his head away, but he knows what he disregards. Here he differs from unconscious streamroller directness, and from the brutality of the savage. I know very little about savages. The nearest that I come to knowledge of them is in the feeble-minded. Certain types of them com-

bine stupidity with callous indifference to others.   They
are like Chesterton's description of the idiotic Norsemen
invading England:

> They only saw with heavy eyes
> And broke with heavy hands.[1]

The reckless man's eyes are not actually so heavy.   But
he acts as if they were.   He strikes as if he did not see what
he is hitting.   He does not argue.   But his head is over his
shoulder.   He glances backward as he walks forward.   The
reckless motorist, for example, has a " gey guess " that he
may hit something; but he does not care, because it is
easier not to care.   The reckless gambler sees the chances
and takes them.   The aborigine takes them without seeing
them as chances.

2. THEY BREAK PLEDGES

If we grant, then, that reckless people face the chances,
accept the challenges of fate, and choose the risks involved,
what business has any one to object?   Every one has to
take some risks.   We cannot take " our walks abroad in
tin shoes, and subsist wholly upon tepid milk," like R. L.
Stevenson's valetudinarian.   " To be overwise is to ossify;
and the scruple-monger ends by standing stockstill."   He
" who reckons his life as a thing to be dashingly used and
cheerfully hazarded, makes a very different acquaintance
of the world, keeps all his pulses going true and fast, and
gathers impetus as he runs. . . . The serviceable men of
every nation . . . pass flyingly over all the stumbling-
blocks of prudence. . . . Who would find heart enough
to begin to live, if he dallied with the consideration of
death? . . . It is better to lose health like a spendthrift
than to waste it like a miser. . . . Does not life go down

[1] G. K. Chesterton, *Ballad of the White Horse.*

with a better grace, foaming in full body over a precipice, than miserably straggling to an end in sandy deltas? " [1] Surely!

But this is not a description of recklessness. It is a paean to courage. Where is the difference? Not in the quantity or quality of the risk. *It is in the breaking of promises by the reckless.* If he takes his risks but is no traitor to his own engagements, with himself and with others, he is not reckless but brave. The venturesome man risks time, money, health, perhaps life; but he ventures them only so far as his promises, silent or spoken, permit. Careless of risk? Perhaps. Careless of pledges? No.

The gambler who recklessly stakes the money on which his wife and children subsist, may be brave enough in risking his own comfort; but he is merely a blackguard when he risks their necessities without their consent. The heedless college loafer usually breaks implied promises, sometimes to parents whose money he is wasting, sometimes to a girl who has a right to expect construction instead of destruction in her partner's college years. Most often, perhaps, he breaks a promise made to himself, that he will amount to something. Imagine that he had made no such promises. He would then be no more to blame than a hippopotamus. We might pity his idiocy, but if he knew no better and had never embodied any such knowledge in understandings with himself or others, we could not look to him for intelligent action.

Among criminals we distinguish the violent impulsive types from the sneak-thieves, pickpockets, and blackmailers. So in ethics, the reckless smashing of promises, to oneself or others, is different from the smooth, voluble evasions by which the self-wheedler soothes his conscience

[1] R. L. Stevenson, *Virginibus Puerisque and Other Papers* (London: Chatto & Windus, 1916), "Aes Triplex," pp. 110–113.

while he escapes his responsibilities. Nevertheless both methods accomplish the same result. Both cut the bonds that hold personality together. Both contradict their own acts by further acts. One does it swiftly, charging like a bull through the structures of his neighbor's life and of his own. The other does it secretly, with subtle acids which eat out his vitality like a disease.

No onlooker can judge us to be self-deceitful or reckless with any degree of certainty that he is right. Either we are self-condemned or we are (morally) innocent. But when I write "self-condemned" I assume that no judgment, even self-judgment, is final, because the human soul, like the human body, has indefinitely great powers to heal itself, apparently endless reserves of power to pull itself out of the mud and start afresh. I suppose it is in part our dangerous confidence in this body of reserve strength that makes us put off our day of reckoning with ourselves.

3. THEY GAMBLE. WHY NOT?

A reckless person is one who *treacherously* risks his own or others' lives. He is essentially a gambler. Let us look at him from this point of view. The gambling instinct is rooted so deep in us that we hesitate to condemn it root and branch. Yet no one wants to be called a gambler. To most people mild occasional gambling, like white lies, seems permissible, perhaps salutary. It is confused with the legitimate risks which are assumed by every pedestrian, every householder, every investor. Their legitimacy consists in the fact that they violate no agreement and that they are elements in the accomplishment of something admittedly worth while. If we are to live and not merely to exist, we must take risks. The more desirable the end, the more it is right to risk for it, when we know no safer path. Moreover, legitimate risks are mostly minor risks, not fatal to life, honor, or fortune even if worst comes to worst.

To marry is undeniably to take a great risk of unhappiness in personal relations, of sorrow for intimacies cut off by death, of humiliation from our own or others' failures. One can diminish these risks by prudence and determination. Nevertheless they remain formidable. But it is hard to be patient with one who shrinks from marriage merely because of its risks. Most of those who have faced these chances and suffered from them are glad of it and would accept them again if they had their lives to live over. The chances of getting in marriage a large part of what we most need in our term on this planet are so great that its risks are well worth taking.

Marriage is risky but need not be a gamble, because any one can reduce its risks by intelligence and effort; also because we can learn from it, and usually gain much joy from it, whatever comes. In gambling the chance of loss is at least as great as the chance of gain. Success is not dependent on intelligence and effort. So far as brains come into the venture, the gambling element goes out, and it becomes a matter of skill. An "inevitable gamble" is a risk, not a gamble. A woman who marries with the strong hope of bearing a son faces a situation governed at present by pure chance. If she has a child her chances of happiness in a son, or of disappointment in a daughter, are nearly balanced (about 105 to 100 in the United States), and there is nothing that she can do about it. It is a matter of "chance" whether we are born male or female. If we are looking for good weather on the holiday, physical forces, not our efforts, decide. In such matters we are slaves of chance. But the best of life is not chance-ridden. What we prize most in civilization stands for the conquest of chance. (Agriculture, manufacturing, science, art, scholarship, health, law, politics, friendship have grown up through the use of that intelligence which the gambler surrenders. In his capitulation to chance he betrays civilization. He could not take the train nor find the passage to the gambling table unless civilization had given him the intelligence which he treacherously surrenders when he begins to play.[1]

The more obvious evils of gambling, such as loss of money, time and temper, the breaking of engagements, the involvement of others in the ruin that ultimately catches more than ninety per cent. of gamblers and speculators,[2] are subordinate to their central vice, the voluntary surrender of intelligent choice, because that betrayal poisons the gambler even while he wins. The other evils he may escape for a time, but he never escapes the deterioration of his morale which his self-stultification produces just as fast when he wins; perhaps faster, because the successful gambler is led in deeper, while the losing gambler may be scared out.

Of course we do not abolish intelligent choice every time that we give over some of our power to forces outside our control. To board a train, to eat an apple is to surrender considerable areas of ourselves to forces that we cannot suddenly stop. But we use them for our own ends. " Chance " means the random events outside our control, the fall of unloaded dice or of well-shuffled cards. Civiliza-

---

[1] Does this mean that courage must decline as civilization advances? The need for courage would be eliminated by our safety devices if new risks were not simultaneously evolved by our " progress." But if progress involves novelty, it will always bring fresh hazards and so the need for courage will remain. Experiments and explorations with risk that calls for fortitude will always be possible.

[2] According to an investigation made by Professor Arthur S. Dewing of Harvard, speculation on the stock exchanges of New York and Boston brings consistent gain to about two per cent. of those who try it. Between four and five per cent. drop out without loss; considerably over ninety per cent. end with losses.

tion advances only as fast as we control for rational ends the same blind forces to which in gambling we yield ourselves.

Yet it is sometimes a duty to decide important questions by chance. When a conscription law was adopted by the United States government in 1917, it exempted from military service certain classes, such as those physically or mentally unfit, those above a certain age, and the " key men " particularly needed to carry on important work. So far we used intelligent power of choice. But there remained more men than were needed or could be equipped at once. Who should have the privilege or the burden of going to war first? Under a conscription system no better way to settle this has yet been devised than "tossing up" or its equivalent. Honestly and intelligently carried out, this gives each an equal chance to go or to stay. Favoritism is avoided. Complaints are unjustified. It is not only a permissible system; it is, thus far, the duty of the government to choose by chance, because it is the best system in sight.

If war is abolished, as it should be, the need to use chance in obtaining adults for jury duty or for other civic services will remain. Tickets for college football games are now assigned to graduates and undergraduates by lot, after certain privileged groups have been provided for; and though this system does not gain all the ends for which it was devised, it remains more satisfactory than any other yet suggested. It is better, for instance, than the system of " first come, first served," which in some other fields works tolerably well.

Chance still governs our lives in the many regions where civilization has found no way to apply intelligent control. The amateur farmer, fisherman, prospector, the greenhorn in billiards, baseball, or dancing can predict but few of his results. We try to control or abolish this dominion of the unforeseen. But there are limits even to our desire for

intelligent control. A wife needs to know in a general
way what behavior she can count on from her husband
and from her children. She needs to know what she can
spend and how many are coming to dinner. But she does
not desire the power to predict every word that will be
spoken, every joke that will be made at the dinner table.

4. WHEN WE NEED SURPRISE

If the unpredictable is often a curse, why is it a blessing
in conversation? Because new ideas are what we are looking for there,—notions not utterly strange and outlandish,
but familiar enough to be understood and not familiar
enough to be stale. We want variations within the range
of this familiar art, as we do in the other arts. When we
buy a picture of a landscape we want it to be recognizable
as a landscape. We do not want to be in doubt whether it
is a landscape or a portrait. But we hope to find in it some
beauty not cloyed by familiarity, some individual way of
seeing the outdoor world. We want to be surprised.

An artillerist does not want to be surprised by the
course of his shell after he fires it. He succeeds when it
goes as he expected. But conversation is a failure if its
phrases go just as we expected. We hope for novelties; we
expect the unexpected. We do not desire to control the
whole situation; for if we do there is no zest to it and
nothing gained out of it. Even in competitive games we
want our opponent to provide unforeseen situations to
test our skill. Such a zest, I suppose, is what the gambler
craves, along with the easy acquisition of wealth. We all
crave stimulus, novelty, surprise. We soon deteriorate
without them. When have we a right to them? When they
lead to growth, through refreshment, amusement, adventure, through new construction on the basis laid in past
experience, through gain that is no one else's loss, through

the pleasure of using our brains and other people's brains in complex teamwork. Of these prizes, how many does the gambler get? A little refreshment, perhaps, soon wiped out by fatigue. A bit of adventure surely. That is all.

He expects the unexpected, not in order to stimulate his imagination but to give him the reward of work without the labor of it, and to distract him from his losses. He wants novelty, not because it is new but because he hopes it may give him profit without exertion. The old suits him better than the new when luck is running his way. He does not want surprise for its vistas of new zest in life, but only to relieve the monotony of loss.

No one ought to crave endless novelty, unlimited surprise, the perpetual stimulus of the unexpected. We need time for digesting the new experiences that dart by us. We get stodgy or nauseated if mental food pours in faster than we can assimilate it. Or we let it run through us in a stream of undigested impressions, each stimulating, none retained. The gambler's wheel, the rattling dice are the types of change where nothing abides. It is fashionable nowadays to deride the " static " and to applaud what is " dynamic." But it is worth noticing that nothing can change in any respect unless it remains identical in some other. A tune manifests changes in pitch only so long as it continues unchangeably to manifest pitch. When it changes into noise it does not change in pitch but combines various pitches, as a pudding combines various ingredients. Still it remains sound through the change from tune to noise.

A profitable or unprofitable change can take place in a human being only so long as he remains recognizably himself and retains his identity amid his changes. The profitable and pleasant stimulus of novelty in conversation and in other arts implies a core of personal identity that can take in or reject new ideas without being overwhelmed by them. To a mind as to a nation, new immigrants may come so fast as to swamp or confuse it. It is easy to be dazzled by stimulating sensations, befuddled by new ideas.

The gambler's itch for excitement differs from our rightful expectation of something incalculable in the fortunes of every good talk, because in such talk we have, prepared by labor and education, a soil where chance can stimulate the growth that we desire and need. We do not want pure novelty nor endless novelty. We want such and as much as will develop or refresh what intelligent control has built up. "Chance," not only "favors the prepared mind," as Pasteur said, but it curses a mind avid for shocks and void of the power to turn chance into opportunity.

Recklessness means taking chances that we have no right to take because they stunt growth, because the agreements of our previous lives have committed us against them, instead of preparing us to use them fruitfully. It is surrender of control for no reason better than the self-blinded impulse to smash things, to forget one's troubles, to let out one's strength, to escape one's entangling past, to do as one wants when one wants it, no matter what happens. The trouble with recklessness is that what happens *does* matter and we know it.

Recklessness is so nonsensical that, naturally, we can give only causes for it, not reasons. It has been led up to or caused by previous lapses of the same kind, by particularly irritating circumstances, depressing weather, poor health, inherited instability. But these events impinge on many people who do not recklessly blow up their own and others' plans. Unless we have bowed to the irrational dogma of determinism we shall not say that only causes, not conscious reasons, are effective in this world. Sane people are reckless because they do not choose to be otherwise, not because they are enslaved by physical or psychic causes. Such slaves are common enough—the epileptic, the insane, the patient with *delirium tremens;* but they are not reckless in the ethical sense. They explode.

5. THE SPORTING SPIRIT

Yet something a good deal like recklessness is precious to us all, something that L. P. Jacks [1] calls the " sporting spirit," that Emerson called " genius," or " instinct." Something like an artist's intuition is central in the best ventures of our lives. When we come nearest to heroism or to originality, we are not far from recklessness. The flash of inspiration at a crucial moment in politics, in marriage complications, in a baseball match, lights swift action without consciousness of restraints, duties, scruples. That sounds like recklessness. The essential differences are in what leads up to it and in its choice between alternatives. The inspired impulse of a veteran ball-player rests on a foundation of enormous labor in the learning of his trade, and probably on many reasoned discussions of somewhat similar situations. A schoolboy might have an impulse which feels similar, yet is foolish in its origin and disastrous in its results.

At the moment of an inspired political move, alternatives may not be consciously balanced, but they are unconsciously or half-consciously excluded. Vision surveys and rejects in a flash the " impossible " choices. But one who simply jumps at a conclusion has made no choice. He might as well have jumped at many another.

Our respect for the " sporting spirit " which takes great risks, does unexpected things, is ready for sacrifice, acts on swift impulses, and enjoys it all, springs from its

[1] L. P. Jacks, *Legends of Smokeover* (New York: G. H. Doran Co., n.d.).

illuminating and contagious warmth and from our deep-rooted impression that, at its best, human life is spontaneous and free, not a " grunting resistance " to one's native devils.[1] Recklessness does not gruntingly resist. Neither does genius. But the reckless man yields to a primary spontaneity, permits an explosion; genius issues in a secondary spontaneity, built up by long labor and rich experience. That is what we want. Nothing less has in it the " sporting spirit " that is so much more vision than sport. I shall go on with this topic in the chapter on Supermorality.

Now I want to get back from the heroism that often looks like recklessness to the self-deceit that in recklessness may simulate heroism, or at any rate courage. The central characteristic of our reckless acts is conscious self-contradiction. We act as if we did not care, when in reality we know that we do. We snuff out our consciousness of the right more swiftly than the palavering sophist. But we accomplish the same suicide and for the same reason,— to avoid the pain of facing the truth which we know is there awaiting us.

We need to grow. It is the hunger of our life. But it hurts to grow, or we think it will. Hence we turn away from the painful light to comfortable darkness, swiftly in our reckless moods, gradually when we feel the need to give excuses to ourselves and to others. By either road we hope to remain in comfort, but in fact we amputate a member of the society which makes up our character.

In view of the illustrative material piled up in this and in the two previous chapters, it is time now to analyze as well as I can the structure of this very odd and characteristic human habit—self-deceit.

[1] R. W. Emerson, " Spiritual Laws," *Essays, First Series*.

Chapter XVIII

ANALYSIS OF SELF–DECEIT

The illustrations of the last three chapters should make obvious the habit that I am talking about. It receives many names. I am not certain that self-deceit is the best one. It could be called self-concealment, self-blinding, self-confusion, the attempt to excuse oneself, to dodge oneself, or to escape oneself. Popularly it is just now often called " *rationalization* " which is a poor word used as the opposite both of its old philosophic meaning and of its modern industrial meaning. It is also called fooling oneself, " kidding oneself," or even " bunk." It used to be called *sophistry* or making the worse reason appear the better. I am not much interested in the name. The familiar fact any one can verify in his own experience.

1. IT STARTS IN FEAR

I have distinguished two types of self-deceit:

(a) The " palavering " type. (Chapters XV and XVI.)

(b) The reckless or anaesthetic type. (Chapter XVII.) Both begin with an uncomfortable emotion: fear, shame, or impatience. Both go on to self-defense. Then the types diverge. (a) The palavering type concentrates attention on a false but comforting picture of the situation ("I couldn't help it," "I needn't do it now," "This time won't count "). (b) The reckless type suppresses thought by immediate action. Thus by focussed attention or by thoughtless action we force out of consciousness the painful facts and ideas, and so in the end achieve self-deceit.

In the beginning we know well enough what we are about. In the end we have evolved a blind spot. By either road we achieve peace of mind, or at least relief, either by shutting ourselves into a single idea or by rushing out.

In both acts we fear reality because it bids us grow. We are asked to stretch our minds, to take in new facts, to fit new situations to our needs, to maintain ourselves by changing. This hurts; at any rate we fear that it will. So our natural thriftiness of mental effort inclines us to economize not only when we can do so without missing our aim, but even when economy is disastrous. Even the restless, reckless, careless type of self-deceiver seeks rest from the effort of stretching his brain to take in self-accusing ideas. He " plunges " to escape them.

Comfort, then, through self-blinding thought or through self-blinding action, is the goal of the self-deceiver. Whatever it is unpleasant to believe he does not face.

2. THEN IT TURNS OFF THE LIGHT SO AS TO HIDE

A characteristic mark of self-deceit is a restriction of the field of consciousness.[1] As a photographer focusses on the spot of interest and expects the margins of his field to blur, so our self-deceiving impulse focusses energy in one thought or in a thought-quenching action. The rest of the mind is a blur. The act of focussing is voluntary, with comfort as the goal. Self-deceit is a by-product, not desired.

This voluntary restriction of our mental field sounds like cutting off a limb. Why should we thus murder truth? Is it not obvious that we *always* need as much light as we can get? On the contrary, every voluntary act, because it gives attention to the road ahead of us, to a fact or to a fiction, shuts our mind away from something

---

[1] See Pierre Janet, *The Major Symptoms of Hysteria* (New York: The Macmillan Co., 1907), and *Névroses et Idées Fixes* (Paris: E. Flammarion, 1898).

else. When we concentrate on a book, or on a ship seen through a field glass, when we sympathetically put ourselves in another's place, when we throw ourselves into a card game or work ourselves into a passion, when we lose ourselves in drama or in drink, we narrow the field of attention. One experience is brightly illuminated; competing areas are shut off. Any one who is " all there," who is wholly " in it," turns attention like a spotlight on one thing and off everything else. The only alternative is to be perpetually mooning about with one's mind diffused thinly over everything in sight.

But there is one essential difference between self-deceit and focussed attention. Self-deceit denies what it excludes. Studious or dramatic concentration does not. We deny no truth when we focus attention on a microscope, a telescope, or a mathematical problem.

3. SO WE FIND EASE

Self-deceit of the " palavering " type is obviously a form of laziness, though it spends energy in elaborate excuses. Recklessness seems at first to be the opposite. The reckless squanderer of time and money, the reckless liar, the reckless aviator or speculator, seems active, not lazy. His energy explodes in imprudent action. Is this a correct account? If so he is neither right nor wrong. He is a piece of nature, dangerous to himself and to others. We may restrain him if we can, but we see nothing ethically wrong about him. He does not violate his own standards.

But another sort of rebel says, " I know it is wrong," or " It may be wrong," " but I don't care. I am going to do it anyway." He is not lazy about action; only about thought. If he takes a good look at the reasonable action he will start the painful labor of thinking. Sudden reckless action frees him from this, but not until he has reckoned enough to see his pet aversion and to shut his eyes to it. We say that we do not care, but we do. We deny any "reck," that is, any awareness of a previous agreement which the reckless act will break. But all the time we know that it is not so. We brutally disregard our own promises. But to disregard them is to look away from them, which implies awareness that they are here. We ignore them but we are not ignorant of them. We turn away from them because it is unpleasant to feel their image on the mental retina.

The person who thus follows the path of least resistance is mentally lazy. There is less self-consciousness, less ingenious argument, than in the palavering form of self-deceit. Yet the sloth and the self-contradiction are the same in both. "Fatigue," says Professor Whitehead,[1] "is the antithesis of reason. It is the defeat of reason in its primitive character of reaching after the upward trend. . . . If we survey the universe of nature, mere static survival seems to be the general rule, accompanied by a slow decay. The instances of the upward trend are represented by a sprinkling of exceptional cases." When the desire for ease and the consequent economy of mental effort lead us through palavering or through recklessness to self-deceit, we follow this trend to "mere static survival accompanied by slow decay." By sophistry or by recklessness we try to step from the human toward the subhuman world where things follow in the line of least resistance. By force or fraud, with violence or by palaver, we make a fraudulent contract with ourselves, with the certainty of being cheated.

The mischief of it is that by dodging, silencing, ignor-

[1] A. N. Whitehead, *The Function of Reason* (Princeton University Press, 1929), pp. 18 and 23.

ing, confusing himself, a person ceases in time to know where he is. Yet unless he knows where he is he cannot take the next step toward any goal, good, bad, or indifferent. Unless he knows where he is, his next step may be away from his desired end. The result is a sense of insecurity, a chronic fear that he has no self and no goal, and that other men are hostile because they are probably liars too.

4. IT CONSCIOUSLY MAKES US UNCONSCIOUS OF ITSELF

It is customary among those influenced by the psychoanalysts to say that self-deceit is usually subconscious or unconscious. If we were clearly conscious of the process, how could we be deceived? I have tried to show that it is only at the beginning of the fraud that we know what we are doing. Later, self-deceit becomes conviction because the process which landed us there is forgotten. But if the process were unconscious throughout it would be like a mistake in arithmetic,—an error, not a wrongdoing. One of the contentions of the psychoanalysts is that unconscious error and wrongdoing are the same thing. This is plausible so long as we merely watch the mental processes of other people. But any one who takes the trouble to watch himself knows that self-deceit is as different from arithmetical error as desire is from aversion. We know the difference simply by observing what goes on within us. All science rests on similar intuitions of inner or outer sense.

Sometimes we are deceived against our will; we mistake a ringing in our ears for a singing insect. Sometimes we are deceived because we do not wish to face what we know, at the outset, to be the facts. Any one can remember instances of both kinds in his own experience. No one can be as sure of them in any one else. The difference between error and self-deceit can only be inferred in others. It is directly perceived in ourselves. If there is any one who has never seen himself pleading " necessity " when he knows it is an excuse, who has never watched himself procrastinate, quibble, sophisticate, throw dust in his own eyes as well as in other people's, then these chapters have no meaning for him.

5. IT IS THE TECHNIQUE OF ALL INTENTIONAL WRONGDOING

Can all forms of moral evil be explained as self-deceit? Does it account for our meanness, our cowardice, our licentiousness, our cruelty, and all the other familiar vices of man? Only if we first rule out many actions often assumed to be morally evil. Many of the most dangerous, destructive, and socially intolerable of vices are not *moral* evil at all. A considerable fraction of criminal and vicious behavior in men is, I believe, just as innocent as if they were beasts of prey. No one calls the tiger cruel or the coyote mean, because they know no better. Subtract the cases of antisocial but innocent behavior and we have left the actions done when a person knows better and is aware that he is doing wrong. By what process can the alternative right action be suppressed so that it does not become effective in our muscles? If it is merely forgotten, we cannot blame the forgetful mortal. We are all forgetful. It is only for the matters that we *intentionally* forget that we can be judged morally, and intentional forgetfulness is another phrase for self-deceit.

Can we say that the desire for the bad action wins out in its struggle with the better desires and simply displaces them? But still we must ask: does the individual's conscious choice come in between the contestants? If he can help himself and knows that the act is contrary to his own agreements and needs, by what process does he deprive these of their authority over him? I can imagine none except the soft-pedaling process which I have described as self-deceit.

But this logic and this appeal to imagination would not be convincing to me if I knew any instance of conscious wrongdoing that did not bear the earmarks of self-deceit. Watching my own and others' bad behavior has yielded me no case in which I was confident that a moral wrong was done yet found no self-deceit. When people are cowardly and not merely panic-stricken they interpose a " rationalization " between the act and their conscience. When people are sensual in their behavior to the opposite sex they try to persuade themselves that it is all right when they know it is not, or else they genuinely believe themselves to be doing right and feel no shame in the matter; in which case we have no proof that they violated their own standard or committed any moral wrong. It is because morals, as I conceive it, must be the application of one's own standard to oneself that self-deception seems to me to play so enormous a part.

Take it from the side of shame for one's actions. If a person feels no shame for a supposedly bad action, I see no good reason to call it a violation of his own code. If he does not violate his own code he knows no better than to act as he does, and if he knows no better he does no moral wrong,—though he may be socially impossible. If on the other hand, he *is* ashamed of himself, I can explain that shame only by supposing that he recognizes himself to have acted *as if* he knew no better when in fact he did know better, and that paradox I can explain only as self-deception. What else could keep the better action from taking place when it represents our desires as well as agreements?

In the first six chapters of this book I wrote what I believe about the meaning of moral good; in the last three I have said my say as to the meaning of moral evil. In the next three chapters I hope to show what use can be made of clear ideas about right and wrong when we mobilize good sense against the practical difficulty of putting them into effect.

C. IMPLEMENTATION

CHAPTER XIX

THE NEED OF TEETH IN ETHICAL LAWS: THE WEAKNESS OF ORDERING AND FORBIDDING: REWARDING AND PUNISHING

Much that used to be called goodness has rightly fallen into disrepute because it is inefficient. It has no well-organized department of ways and means. The right is seen as an ideal, but no one proceeds to organize it.

1. DIAGNOSIS SHOULD LEAD ON TO TREATMENT

Ethical theory is an attempt to orient ourselves in the business of asking and answering questions about right and wrong, what these words mean, and when to apply them. We study ethics first to organize our plans for the journey which we are undertaking. Having straightened out, in some measure, this set of problems about the journey, it seems to me only common sense to step on to *the implementation of ethics*. We have decided that we ought to have world peace. Well, how shall we get it? By what diplomatic skill, economic reorganization, linguistic and cultural education shall we make it worth while to have conceived the ethical ideal of world peace?

Yet in the study of ethics it is often assumed that ethical insight can be profitably attained without its issuing in increased ethical strength. By a similar fallacy the psychiatrists attached to juvenile courts have allowed themselves to be used as diagnosticians only. Treatment has been handed over to social-workers, to foster parents, or to those in charge of reform schools, and so treatment has been largely a failure thus far. But, as I see it, ethical diagnosis, like physical diagnosis, has a practical end. We need to know what to do next and then to plan the next move. Diagnosis is never properly an end in itself, though absent-minded physicians often seem to think so. It is an early stage in a journey that includes treatment. For diagnosis itself often has results on the patients, and treatment leads to revised diagnosis.

Moreover a diagnosis, physical, ethical, or psychological, is not known to be worth the time it has cost until we have undertaken the treatment to which it points. It is a rough map for a journey of prediction and control, but it cannot foresee the whole journey at the start. It only marks out the trail for one stage. After this stage has been covered, the diagnostic part must be revised, in view of the new knowledge attained by the last day's journey.

I can best illustrate this idea in the simpler field of physical diagnosis. A child with cough and pain in the chest is found on stethoscopic examination to have bubbling sounds in some of his bronchial tubes. His temperature and pulse are found to be above normal. X-ray films are normal. His sputum contains no germ of significance. Nothing else is found wrong with him. In view of these facts the diagnosis is bronchitis. But this is not enough. There are many kinds of bronchitis. The more correct diagnosis is: bronchitis, type so far unknown. The rest of the diagnosis can best be cleared up by observation, which means treating the sufferer as if the true diagnosis were simple bronchitis, that is, a bronchitis of unknown cause which will disappear after about a week in bed and without drugs. The results of such treatment will develop the further significance of the original, partial diagnosis.

Suppose the disease does not clear up in a week. The fever continues and the patient begins to have chills. A second X-ray picture shows that a large air tube is plugged, but does not show what plugs it. Looking down the windpipe through a bronchoscope, we see in one of the tubes a peanut shell. In view of this we recognize that the original diagnosis, bronchitis, was not untrue but partial. The part left out of it, the peanut shell, was the most important. The significant diagnosis, significant because it guides action helpfully, is now: peanut shell in the bronchus. There is also some bronchitis from irritation of the tubes near the peanut shell. But this inflammation will disappear when the bronchoscopist's forceps grasps the peanut shell and cautiously draws it out without breaking it or leaving fragments behind.

Many an ethical diagnosis stops with a single word, such as " laziness " or " dishonesty," or with psychological terms which state the same facts in Greek, or with college-office terms such as " unsatisfactory record." The significant context around these facts is what we need to know. Sometimes it can be found merely by asking the victim more questions. But there is a limit to this. Sometimes the diagnostic process, including the diagnostician himself, makes the disease worse.[1] Giving one's troubles a name sometimes seriously aggravates them. In 1918 the timidity of certain soldiers at the front was greatly aggravated when some of its minor results (rapid heart, sweating), led us to use a medical phrase, " effort syndrome." The soldier soon construed this as a form of heart disease. When this idea dawned on him he began to be much worse. In this instance the diagnosis turned out to be a harmful form of treatment. The essential nature of the trouble was revealed only by the bad results attained by treating it like a disease when we should have treated

[1] J. S. Mill's diagnosis of himself in his relations to the universe made him sick. Marriage nearly cured him.

it like a blundering diagnosis. Sent to the rear, out of danger and kept at rest, in good hygienic surroundings and under medical supervision, most of the men got worse. Kept at the front many of them soon recovered.

In ethics as in medicine, it seems to me foolish to end with diagnosis. We should study not only ethical diagnosis but the useful methods to use the diagnosis itself as a step toward a more satisfactory organization of a person's life. We need implements to hold other tools, as an auger holds a bit.

Ethical implementation is an endless topic. The examples presently to be given under (a) praise and blame (see below), (b) automatic brakes and tractors (Chapter XX), and (c) clearing the decks for action (Chapter XXI), are only the leading items in a list that might include hygiene, applied economics, manners, eloquence, tact, imagination, and almost any other valuable human trait. These are useful means to the ethical ends that most of us desire. Practical skills, physical, economic, intellectual, cultural, represent for ethics a set of valuable tools for future work. The disciplines necessary to master these skills, the friendships which give us glimpses of characteristics which we lack,—these are branches of the inclusive ethical need to find out the next stage in our growth and to attain it. In this and the next two chapters I shall first look over certain points about habit and then discuss the quack remedies familiarly known as *ordering* and *forbidding*.

2. THE TOUGHNESS OF HABIT

In the foreground of any one who looks about him for the implements through which ethical ideals must be realized, lies a storehouse of habits, good and bad. No one who desires to control the territory assigned to his care, his own body and mind, can long ignore the fact that he

lives mostly by his habits. In the development of our
bodies, nature found out aeons ago that habits are convenient ways in which to organize our energies so that
bunches of ideas or motions can start, stop, and play out
their little games without conscious attention to the details. Habits of dressing, walking, eating, talking, working set us free to plan new work. They save energy and
time. Hence they are a large subdivision of the department
of ethical ways and means.

No one needs to be taught how to hold on to a habit
once acquired. That takes care of itself and often of us
too. But the technique for accomplishing what we desire (and think we need) is especially assisted by any device
that helps us to form new habits or to break old ones.
Old habits offer amazingly stubborn resistance to change.
Whatever we can do to break down this resistance may
help us to go in the direction that we prefer. It may also
help us to deteriorate. Habits stiffen us to resist any change,
for better or for worse. Hence whatever helps us to alter
our habits involves the risk of changing them for the
worse as well as for the better. To enter college from a
small rural community where habits, good and bad, are
more uniform and more fixed than in the city, is to shift
oneself into a position where it is easier to grow up, but
also easier to disintegrate. There are more opportunities;
there are also more diseases. There is a greater variety of
diet, physical and intellectual; more chance for development; also more chance of moral indigestion, obesity, bewilderment, and vice.

Only a deep instinct for finding one's way can steer a
man into the sort of education and the sort of company
which will draw out his particular powers of growth
without pulling him to pieces. In a crowd of new acquaintances, in a new city, in a new school or college, a

" good groper " feels his way into companionship with a set of people whose brains move fast enough to stimulate his interests but not fast enough to confuse him. He will then form new habits fast enough to keep him from stagnation but not so fast as to break him up.

Some points about the formation, control, and break-up of habits are discussed more in detail in Chapter XXI. But I want to emphasize at the outset my belief that the inefficiency of a large fraction of our efforts at moral training, " character building," civic reform, and the like is due to our failure to realize (a) the toughness of the structure of habits built into our bodies and minds, and (b) the large proportion of our daily behavior that is governed not by our intelligent choices but by these chains of habit which run along from feeling and thought to act, and from act to thought and feeling, in grooves almost as fixed as the law by which water runs down hill.

Against the strength of old habits, our naked wishes to do otherwise are about as effective as a peashooter against an armored battleship. How little we seem to realize this is shown by the popularity of the familiar *fiats* which we launch against our fellow beings or against ourselves in the hope of molding behavior to our will.

3. ORDERING AND FORBIDDING

It seems to be tacitly assumed in most books on ethics that when we are clear about what we ought to do, all we have to do is to order ourselves to do it, and to forbid ourselves to do what interferes with it. We can, it is supposed, reform ourselves simply by making up our minds that we ought to do so. When we issue the word of command, our hitherto disobedient habits will disappear.

But does experience confirm this? Do children, pupils, employees always obey? When does a simple word of command control them? In a recent book by Professor Sheffield [1] the chapter on " Ordering and Forbidding " focusses attention on this problem. If the " order " given us is quite in line with our current habits, it will probably be obeyed so easily that it need hardly be called by so violent a name. A hint or a suggestion will do. But if it is contrary to our wishes or against the grain of wont, something more than a fiat is needed if any change of behavior is to result. For the self which receives the simple *word* of command is itself a whole *book* of previous commands, fixed in its habits and bents. The fiat is like one man attacking an army, each member as well armed and as ardent as he.

To be effective an " order " must either go with the current of wishes in whoever receives it, or it must somehow manage to gather a force as great as what it opposes. To an habitual worker the order to work is superfluous. To an habitual loafer it is mere wind, unless backed by authority that he fears, respects, or loves. A leader differs from those who merely issue orders and vetoes, because he controls currents of effective energy which he also obeys himself. Currents of fear, of affection, or of intelligence run through him to those whom he leads, and it is these currents which give force to his words. He touches a button and completes a circuit. The labor of building that circuit came earlier. But if he orders or vetoes *in vacuo*, and without the previous labor of building up the circuit, nothing happens, even when the command is given by himself to himself.

When a contented working force is accustomed to be on the job from eight to five with an hour off at noon, a whistle is all that is needed to synchronize their comings and goings. No order is needed. When an individual has trained

---

[1] A. D. Sheffield, *Some Principles of Social Thinking* (New York: The Inquiry, 1930).

himself to raise his hat on meeting ladies of his acquaintance, he has no need to cudgel his reluctant will. The sight of the lady sets off the action. In such cases a train is laid. One has only to touch it off.

But sudden, arbitrary, or unpleasant orders to persons unprepared by any training process, can only secure obedience by some extraordinary accident. Successful ordering, as Professor Sheffield says, is prepared for by previous legislation (or I should say, agreement) concurred in by those concerned. In this "legislation" the trains and circuits are prepared, the educational and persuasive efforts are expended so as to give us a basis for subsequent commands. From the end of a lever sufficiently long Archimedes could command the world. Powerful psychic or ethical leverage is secured by some process of education and agreement. Without this, irritation is the only predictable effect of an order.

When we expect a person's behavior to be controlled in education or in industry, merely by the fiat of an order, we cherish a belief in magic that has been expelled from the rest of our lives. A good idea weighing a pound is supposed to lift a ton of opposing inertia without any lever to multiply the idea's effectiveness. Only levitation or some other magic could do it.

When we hope thus magically to make people do or forbear something against their wishes and habits, we may use effectively for a time the fear of punishment. "*Make* him obey or fire him," is a formula which dispenses with the slow process of building up agreements for effective leadership. But those who obey solely or chiefly because of fear, need a ruinously expensive amount of watching, because they are tempted to use their ingenuity in "getting by." A log to which we apply force is passive, and with tools and skill we can mold it as we

wish. But the active human wills which we may rule by
fear or force for the moment, soon come to rule us, because when combined against any ruler they can exert a
force that he cannot match. Among interests opposed to
him, the ruler is nowhere.

The most successful orders are preceded by an educational
process which makes the need for them clear to all. As he
nears the float the coxswain of an eight-oared boat has
only to tell his crew when to stop rowing. He indicates
the facts; the crew's own awareness of them does the rest.
But if orders seem to issue not from the need of a situation
but merely from a man's mouth, they are no stronger than
the faith of those who receive them. They may believe
that the leader knows the need though he has no time
now to explain it. In that faith they may obey him. In
emergencies, or in very complex or technical matters, one
often obeys, by reason of one's faith in the leader or the
expert. At other times intelligent obedience presupposes
intelligent coöperation.

In industry, effective orders should come through a
leader from the " law of the situation " [1] itself, that is,
from the wills of those who have learned to wish it carried out because they are already interested in the goods,
services, enjoyments, which it furnishes. The strength
of the order is ultimately the consent of their own wills
directed to achieve results which they think worth while.

Forbidding, if successful, brings home to another person the fact that his own needs, that is his own well-
considered interests, are against the forbidden course.
The coxswain can see where the boat is going. The oarsmen cannot. But their wills are fixed and agreed on one
point. They do not want to run into the float as they
approach it. The coxswain's order to stop rowing when

[1] A. D. Sheffield, *loc. cit.*

he thinks they have momentum enough to get there, calls into action the power of their own desires. He forbids them to row any more, just as they would forbid themselves if they could see ahead. He is their eyes. They are his arms and legs. Their common need is expressed now by the oarsmen's pull, now by the coxswain's voice.

Orders are well received when they do not seem arbitrary, autocratic, foolish, or unjust to those who hear them. These disqualifications may become active and lead to disobedience because of the belief that there is no good reason behind the word of command. If there were, the commander would himself be obeying it and so he would not be or seem autocratic. A reasonable order is not arbitrary because the leader does not himself choose it. He himself obeys and articulates for others *an order from the facts of the situation* which cannot be foolish or unjust. They are facts for all if they are facts at all.

The efficient leader, teacher, judge, general, orchestral conductor, captain of industry is one who interprets and passes along facts to others. His power to influence, direct, or determine action comes from the truth for which he stands. His business is to make that truth seen, then to stand aside and let it work.

All this is clear when we think of commands or vetoes addressed by one person to others. They have the force of whatever already dominant desire they can evoke. They have no force of one will over others. Is it any different when we order or forbid ourselves? Such imperatives press a button. Are there any wires and batteries behind it? Categorically we may " call spirits from the vasty deep " of our own character. " But will they come? " It is often easy to make up one's mind upon a course of action radically different from that which we have traveled hitherto; but when the glow of decision dies out the old habits reassert themselves. What effective forces can the new decision call to back it up? Mere decision, mere will pushing against old habit? Such will is as powerless as a child who leans against a hundred-ton locomotive and tries to push it along the track. If he knew enough he might get coal and water into it and might turn their power through the great machine to set it in motion. Then he would release dormant energies vastly greater than his own, and through one will-less energy he would control another.

4. PRAISE AND BLAME

I have tried to show that a moral alibi is the favorite defense of the quarreling child, of the belligerent nation, of the erotic hero. "You cannot blame me. I was not there. I was outside the jurisdiction of ethics; I was under compulsion and couldn't help myself. Irresistible force tied my hands, or propelled me like a projectile." To the dispassionate observer most of these excuses are transparently false. Genuine necessity, real frustration are rarely found where we are asked to look for them. What we find is a screen to ward off blame, because our generation is very sensitive to it. I doubt if there has been another epoch in history when people the world over were so sensitive to the moral judgments of their fellows. This is strange, for it is also characteristic of our time to hate the censorious, to preach charity in judgment, and even to suggest a moratorium on all moral judgments. We are doubtful whether any one should be blamed for anything. For blame, we say, often leads to punishment, or is itself a penalty, and we have begun to doubt whether such correction ever corrects. Few of us, I fancy, who look back on the punishments we received in childhood are confident that we are any the better for them. We are even less sure that it is wise to inflict similar discipline on our own children.

But blame is chastisement which we dread because we sanction it. Even national governments, least ethical perhaps of human agencies, are somewhat afraid of international blame, and to fear it implies that we grant it some legitimacy. Here is a paradox. We doubt whether blame is of any value. We deprecate censorship and even moral judgments. In rebellious moods we view moral judgments not merely as unfair or disagreeable, but as meaningless. Yet when blame or moral censure is directed against ourselves we dispute it with earnestness. Why?

We do not wince under attack that we regard as meaningless. We are quite unconcerned when people call us heretics, because we no longer consider heresy of importance. Moral blame, too, we may consider in general insignificant; yet it becomes terribly significant when directed against ourselves. The criminal, we say, is sinned against, not a sinner. Do not blame him. He could not be other than he is. All his acts are caused by the nervous mechanism which he inherited, or by the environment in which we have permitted him to grow up. He has, we say, no free will. But we do not abdicate our own free will when we are praised. Then we seldom deny our responsibility, though we often plead our helplessness and therefore our innocence when people blame us. We blame them for blaming us. We may be determinists. Yet we want credit for our honorable attempts.

The same paradox emerges when we notice that our age, though doubtful about punishment and about blame, is ready enough to praise. The criminal's bad qualities, we say, are not really bad because he cannot do otherwise. But his good points we gladly acknowledge, and we do not expunge them by saying that he could not help them.

We point to his fine struggle to be decent, to his redeeming fair-mindedness, to his admirable courage in tight places. Moral censoriousness, indeed, we despise, for it implies a consciousness of our superior virtue. But we see nothing conceited or supercilious in our readiness to impute good, to give every man his due, to recognize strength even in the weak.

This is illogical. If our praise is meaningful, our blame cannot be meaningless. If favorable judgments are reasonable, unfavorable comments must have an equal right to exist. If men are free to do right against the resistance of their own cowardice and laziness, and if our admiration rightly goes to the winners of a hard fight, then these same men must also be free when they take the other turn of the road.

5. BLAME AND THE SENSE OF INFERIORITY

The judgment of right or wrong is one thing. The prompt *expression* of this judgment to the person most concerned is quite another. It cannot be sensible to make all judgments positive and none negative. But I think it is sensible to express many judgments of praise and few of blame. Judgments should be matters of impersonal fact and logic. But the expression of judgments calls for careful study of those to whom we express them. Most of us have noticed that when we have done something that we ourselves know perfectly well is wrong, something in violation of our own understandings with ourselves and with other people, we are *down*. Our self-respect is at a low ebb. We are sick in mind and often in body too. When we are in this state, another's condemnation, even if expressed without rancor or self-righteousness, usually depresses still further our scanty supply of hope. The remaining rags of our self-confidence with which we try to cover our nakedness are precious. Without a minimum of self-respect we can hardly think straight, scarcely form a plan, barely pull our energies together for action.

The sense of incapacity, or, as it is now fashionable to call it, the " inferiority complex," of which almost every one has a share, is increased by blame. A valuable service has been done by the psychologists who have popularized these facts. They have focussed attention on the vital importance of self-respect, not merely for ethics but for the very existence of our mental energies and even of bodily health. I do not know that a man can die solely from a sense of inferiority. But I think it probable that he can come dreadfully near death. I am certain that his sleep, his digestion and nutrition, the daily repair of the tissues which he burns up just by living, and still faster by criminal living, can be seriously impaired. Under these conditions, to blame any one is to strike him when he is down.

Body and mind are hardly distinguishable at this point. To be " low in one's mind " is certainly to be low in those essential vital energies without which we can do nothing of any importance. When we face blame, or any other attack which threatens to abolish our already depleted stock of the central fuel which sustains our powers, we no longer stop to judge ourselves at all. We fight for our lives, as we would fight for breath if some one took us by the throat. We admit nothing. We justify everything. Our conscience is clear. Desperation, not judgment, speaks. We cannot afford at this point even to blame ourselves, far less to admit that others are right in blaming us.

Later perhaps, when we have accumulated a balance of self-respect in our mental savings bank, we can blame ourselves, and so start reconstruction. Show us that we have good stuff in us, persuade us that we are all right at bottom, point out that it is from our usually straight course that we have temporarily swerved, and we can admit, perhaps correct, the deviation. But the impression received by the subject of unmitigated blame for a single act is that he always has been and always will be a failure. If that were true, if he were a total failure, of course he could not even bestir himself to do differently. He would have neither fulcrum nor lever to lift with. He would be in a hopeless plight and that is where blame tends to land him.

" Aren't you ashamed of yourself? " asks the indignant parent, and if his child is neither a cowed weakling nor a callous " roughneck " he usually defends his scanty self-respect by vigorous denial. For he knows that no one ever ought to be ashamed of *himself*, that is, of his whole personality. It is of particular deeds, separable from himself, that he ought to be ashamed. To ask a person to be ashamed of himself is like calling him a liar because you have caught him in a single lie. The average man who will admit an occasional lie rightly rebels if he is called a liar. That seems to incriminate his whole character, and to mortgage his future. Before he can admit that he has been wrong even in this special instance, he must have his feet well planted on solid ground. Then, like one who has just escaped drowning, he can look back perhaps with a shudder at the danger he has been in.

When I hear a parent insist that the misbehaving child must " say that he is sorry " before he can be restored to grace, I hope with all my heart that the culprit will not give in. If he does, the confession will probably be a lie told to get him out of trouble or to get rid of his tormentor. Even such a lie would do him, I believe, less harm than the groveling disheartenment into which an admission of the truth would plunge him. This moral bankruptcy is especially a danger when the confession is public, when the whole family and perhaps even strangers are looking on. I recall the bravado of a small boy who, as he was hurrying through the parlor where his mother had guests, brushed against a large vase of flowers and upset it. The vase was smashed and water poured across the floor. I think the boy really felt quite shaken. But what he loudly shouted was: "I'm glad I did it!" Knowing him well, I am confident that he was in fact very sorry. But in defense of his threatened self-respect he hastily assumed a mask of bravado under cover of which he began to pick up the pieces of broken glass, to sop up the floor, and to make himself as useful as he could. His wise mother demanded of him no confession of wrong. There was no need of it.

Such a confession some of us expected Germany to make before the waiting family of nations when she was defeated in 1918. We looked for her to acknowledge her guilt. We made her say as much in her signature to the treaty of Versailles.[1] But I am convinced that even if Germany had been as much to blame as that treaty represents her to be, she could not with any self-respect have admitted it. To ask a nation to give up its self-respect is to attempt a crime; for its self-respect is its soul.

In view of this I believe that our generation is right in rejecting the type of morality which consists chiefly in blaming ourselves or other people. Clear moral distinctions are, I think, unescapable. The procrastinator knows that he is procrastinating, and the debtor that he still owes the debt, though they may try to bluff it off and to escape their obligations. But the emotion of shame is a very different matter. I believe it is useful to those who are not likely to lose their good opinion of themselves under any conditions, useful for the self-confident and the

[1] See Introduction, p. 2.

aggressive, useful to those who have many friends and an excellent reputation. But in the diffident, the discouraged, in any one who feels himself for the moment down and out, shame is a corroding acid, rightly rejected by the self-defending instincts of the organism.

The more worthless we feel, the nearer we approach a barrier of true necessity, physical and logical, that makes shame impossible. A man must see worth in one part of himself before " he " (that part) can condemn " himself " (the other part). Without a sense of worth there is no psychical energy free to express itself in shame.

6. SELF-BLAME AND SELF-DIRECTION

The main use of ethics, that is, of thinking clearly about the meaning, the distinctions, and the types of right and wrong, is in prevention and in education. I doubt whether a sense of shame has much value here. A man should look before he leaps. He should make sure that he wants to take the risk, and that he has measured the jump. But while he is leaping he should expend no energy in looking. And if he has leaped and failed, he must pull himself out of the mud before he can afford the strength to curse himself.

Our generation doubts the value of censorious emotion without nascent action to better bad business. Hence we doubt the value and even the meaning of blame and shame. We have been brought up, perhaps, by those who judged too much from the evidence of emotion and who were too glad to see us flush and cry, because that was evidence that we were thoroughly ashamed of ourselves. I think effort at reform can begin without any obvious emotion of shame, and may be held back, not assisted, by blaming people, unless the depressing emotions roused by this blame can be more than counterbalanced by encouragement.   If we hope to bring any one to see that he has acted wrongly, we must set out in a spirit of confidence if not of affection.   When the culprit's self-respect has been thus reënforced, and when the fear of a censorious or self-righteous judgment has been dispelled, we may succeed in showing him that he is off his own track.

This is our object, because it remains as true as ever it was that unless a person locates the root of a misdeed in himself, which is the essence of blame, and unless he sees that what he has done could and should have been prevented by his own efforts, because it was contrary to his own permanent needs, he will not find the energy to do differently in future.   If he calls it a mistake, a slip, a social solecism, a breach of conventions, a fault of taste, he is placing its cause, and therefore its future prevention, outside his own control.   Then he is more than likely to do the same thing again.

The best evidence that a person has blamed himself and that this has value, is not an outburst of emotional remorse but a bit of new planning to prevent the same thing from happening again.   If he thinks himself helpless or impeccable he will do nothing.   We do not blame ourselves for forgetting the faces of those whom we meet in a crowded street; so we take no steps to prevent similar lapses in the future.   We know well enough that we are powerless to prevent them.   But when we locate the cause of our misdoing in the controllable parts of ourselves and not in urges or circumstances beyond our power, then we have made a diagnosis that can set machinery in motion to prevent similar wrong in future.   We may begin to educate ourselves.

Intelligent diagnosis and sensible measures to prevent recurrence are the objectives of blame for wrongdoing. The emotional side of it has value chiefly when it is a stimulus to clear self-diagnosis and to efficient treatment. When we deprecate blame it is because we expect from it no better shaping of the future, but only resentment, humiliation, or perhaps the perverted luxury of confession and emotional self-reproach. Some people are so eager to be the center of interest that they will lap up our reproaches and add new ones themselves. But if no change in behavior follows it is pretty certain that nothing but an emotional debauch has occurred.

On the other hand only those who can blame themselves, and so under favorable conditions can admit the justice of others' blame, will plan efficiently to avoid a recurrence of the misdeed.

At last I said [to the forger], " You have told me what you did before you concluded to reform. I am curious to know how, in those days, you looked at things. Was there anything which you wouldn't have done, not because you were afraid of the law, but because you felt it would be wrong? "

" Yes," he said, " there is one thing I never would do, because it always seemed low down. I never would steal."

It was evident that further discussion would be unprofitable without definition of terms. I found that by stealing he meant petty larceny, which he abhorred. In our condemnation of the sneak thief and the pickpocket we were on common ground. His feeling of reprobation was, if anything, more intense than that which I felt at the time. He alluded to the umbrellas and other portable articles which he had noticed in the hallway. Any one who would take advantage of an unsuspecting householder by purloining such things was a degenerate. He had no dealings with such moral imbeciles.

It seemed to me that I might press the analogy which instantly occurred to me between " stealing " and forgery.

" Do they not," I said, " seem to you to amount to very much the same thing? "

I had struck a wrong note. Analogies are ticklish things to handle, for things which are alike in certain respects are apt to be quite different in other respects. His mind was intent on the differences. The sneak thief, he told me, is a vulgar fellow of no education. The forger

and the check-raiser are experts. They are playing a game. Their wits
are pitted against the wits of the men who are paid high salaries for
detecting them. They belong to quite different spheres.[1]

This story shows, among other things, that until a
man blames himself, his admission of what society calls
a crime, forgery for instance, does not advance him an
inch towards reform. As truly as education is self-educa-
tion, reform is self-reform. It must start, therefore, with
a perception that his "form," that is his habit, is not
what he desires it to be. The emotional side of this perception is self-blame, which is, I believe, as essential an
ingredient in a decent life as any one ever thought it. Self-
blame we need if we are to grow, and growth we need if
we are to live. But the expression of blame *by other people*
generally checks the vitally important growth of self-
blame on the vitally necessary basis of self-respect. That
we see better, I think, than our grandfathers did.

7. THE VALUE OF PRAISE

Though I touched on the subject of praise at the beginning of this chapter I said nothing of it as part of the ar-
mamentarium of ethics. Like blame it is used a good deal
more with children than with adults. In the form of
approval and encouragement no one doubts its value, I
take it, in the education of timid, self-distrustful children,
especially if there is a background of contrast with reti-
cence or disapproval. Children praised for everything
are sure to be praised for some act that does not deserve it
and so are apt to be spoiled. Discriminating praise which
dwells on the good piece of work rather than on the child
himself is a valuable aid to his judgment of himself.

This is just as true of praise given to adults. It is a

[1] S. M. Crothers, *The Pardoner's Wallet*, " As He Sees Himself " (Boston: Houghton Mifflin Co., 1911), pp. 223–225.

valuable guide if we learn to recognize those whose praise is discriminating. Thence it merges into public approval such as is shown in the demand for our goods when they please the public. The distinction between earning praise or approval by giving people what they want, and earning less approval or even none at all by giving people what they need, has been already touched on. Every public speaker gets to know how to please an audience, and faces thereafter the temptation to please them by claptrap and demagogic methods. One of the best and most conscientious speakers that I have known makes it a rule to say in the course of each address something that he thinks may not please his hearers or may displease them. A speech that pleases everybody from start to finish is apt, he says, to contain something said for effect and with the intention to flatter.

Flattery is sometimes confounded with praise. The distinction is in the fact that most if not all flattery is insincere and done with the object of hoodwinking him who hears it. From just and discriminating praise it is as different as food from poison. A considerable portion of our fellow beings deserve and need a great deal more appreciation than they get. It helps them to judge their own actions objectively. Flattery deceives and misleads.

8. PUNISHMENT

Something should be said here of punishment as one of the tools of ethical engineering. We think of it chiefly in relation to children and to criminals. The non-criminal adult does not get much of it if he has no one to scold or to nag at him. In children it is considered part of the formation of good habits, and is to be judged by its results and by the quality of the habits formed. In my observation, the older the child the less often is punishment effective. It is apt to hurt the relation between child and parent in ways that do more harm than punishment could possibly do good.

In criminals it is rarely valuable, usually ineffective or harmful.[1] When it is of value it is because the offender uses his term of imprisonment to get into better health, to make up deficiencies in elementary education, or in rare cases to face his own blunders and to make better plans. In prisons and reformatories, education is beginning to be substituted for punishment. It could hardly be less effective, and we may hope that it will turn out vastly better. But no one can yet foretell the result of the new experiments.[2]

Punishment is something quite different from the effect of meeting the disagreeable consequences which duly follow a misdirected action. If we come to vote after the polls are closed, or turn up on the wrong day for a college examination, we suffer the consequences. But nobody accuses us or directs a penalty at us. We face the result of our own blunders and not infrequently profit by it. We learn by such mistakes as we do in many processes of trial and error. The absence of an accuser, of blame, and of the human machinery of censorious or punitive action makes us more apt to pay serious attention to what has happened, and to bend our habits in accord with its lesson.

Reward, like punishment, is clearly of benefit in the foundation of desirable habits in children. Whether it has value in adults is not, I think, yet clear. I refer, of course, not to the "rewards" which are more properly

[1] See Sheldon Glueck and Eleanor T. Glueck, *500 Criminal Careers* (New York: A. A. Knopf, 1930).

[2] See the *Superintendent's Report* (Commonwealth of Massachusetts, Department of Correction) of the State Prison Colony at Norfolk, October 1, 1930, and *The New Prison at Norfolk, Mass.*, a pamphlet dated November, 1930.

consequences of efficient action, but to special prizes offered in addition to the success of the action itself.

Any value that there is in rewards and punishments is much more apt to come to us if we are not preoccupied by internal conflicts which distract our attention from the obstacles in our path and prevent us from steering better after we have run into them. In the next two chapters I shall say something first of devices for getting ourselves started and for bringing ourselves to a halt when " pure will" proves ineffectual, and then of these internal conflicts whereby our minds are cluttered up like the decks of a ship whose deck load obstructs the work of her sailors.

Chapter XX

ETHICAL BRAKES AND TRACTORS

Ethical action springs, not from thought nor from "will" alone, but from the blending of the two in rational desire. No one does anything until his muscles are set in action; and this does not happen by "pure will" unless we have a habit to fire off. "Pure will" in a new situation is like the pertinacious energy which jams the wrong key again and again, harder and harder, into the keyhole. There is no lack of "will" here. We need more brains. Our stupid push is like the "repetition of impossibilities" which we see when we test the feeble-minded in mechanical tasks. On the other hand, pure thought, brains alone, gives us only good intentions. The intention, if it is to be fruitful, will hunt up the tools needed to carry it out. Then it will find some existing desire and gear it to the good intention. The energy of desire and the gearing, which intelligence provides, are equally necessary.

Natural forces are as essential to the conscientious man as to the bridge builder who uses the cohesion of his materials or to the doctor who uses the energies of food, water, air, and medicines to get his ends. In ethics we use not only these energies, but the forces of human desire, which are also "natural" in that they are not the product of will but emerge spontaneously when we set the stage for them. We harness the force of some available desire, then, so that it will pull us on despite our resistance. Our moral freedom goes as far as the intelligence which harnesses available forces and circumvents obstacles to our will.

The harness which a sincere good will methodically puts upon itself is made up of such parts as:
1. Mechanical devices.
2. Trains of association.
3. Commitment to interests or to persons.
In well-organized human lives, the third of these includes the second, and the second includes the first.

It is convenient to divide our tools into the *tractors* and the *brakes*, that is into devices which start us or keep us agoing, and contrivances which check our motion. We often find that we cannot start ourselves at the right moment. We are forgetful, sleepy, inert. We cannot " make ourselves " do what we want and know we ought to do. Or when we are in motion we cannot stop ourselves at the right moment. But we can imitate the employer who says, " No, I can't write advertisements, feel the public pulse, or keep my workmen in good humor, but I can hire those who will." We can enlist natural forces on our side. We can " hire " them.

1. MECHANICAL TRACTORS

The alarm clock is the most familiar example. The natural forces and mechanical devices used in clockwork can be geared overnight to an intelligent desire so as to circumvent our natural sleepiness next morning. It needs very little labor to set the clock. Overnight we spontaneously desire to do this, and it is set. Then by our free act forces have been set in motion which will compel our obedience in a moment of rebellion. Forces set to work in the alarm clock pull us out of sleep, not at the hour when we might freely desire to get up but when our drowsy wrath still protests.

Some of us have learned, however, that though the clock

wakes us, it does not get us out of bed. Almost automatically our sleepy hand reaches out and quenches the offending noise by turning off the alarm. The same hand that wound and set it the night before, in order to checkmate sleepiness, now obeys sleepiness and checkmates the desire of the night before. Some of us can do this treacherous act so swiftly and forget it so completely that when we wake at 10:30 and find the alarm turned off we cannot recall the clutch by which we defeated our own better will. We are genuinely astonished to find that we have overslept. We glare at the clock in indignation only to find in it the proof of our self-contradictory act. For we can still remember that last evening we set the alarm for 7:30, and now the clock hands point a quarter circle away from that. No one else can have turned the alarm off.

After such an experience we have to devise means to defeat the treachery of our own self-defeating hand. We wind and set the clock as before; but this time we put it not by the bedside but on the table in the middle of the room. It is still near enough to break sleep when it goes off. But now when it wakes us, we cannot stop its noise without getting up to do so, and once up it seems hardly worth while to crawl back into bed. Here, then, we have worked out, by trial and error, an effective device which gears tonight's sensible will to tomorrow's rebellious muscles by means of a clock-mechanism. Thus an " act in hour of insight willed may be through hours of gloom fulfilled." The unknown machinery connecting will and muscles inside our bodies is supplemented by man-made machinery outside us.

Other examples of external aids used to make desire effective are: staring at a light to consummate a sneeze, tickling the throat to start vomiting, arranging automatic block-signals in a railroad system so as to stimulate the engineer's mind at the right moment. Some people snore only when they lie upon the back. If one belongs to this class, a spool sewn into the back of one's pyjamas will stop the snoring by interrupting sleep at the right moment, or prevent the snoring by leading us half unconsciously to avoid the painful position.

I know an executive who hates to write letters and hates still more to dictate them. But he can usually muster strength to push a button on his writing-desk. His secretary enters with an expectant look. Once she is before him he would feel too foolish if he sent her away again. The letters are still before him on the desk, and to lift one and look at it is almost an automatic act when his secretary's open notebook, poised pencil, and inquiring expression confront him. Once he has looked at a letter, words of answer begin to suggest themselves. After that, nothing is needed but to sign the letters, which is almost enjoyable when the group of neatly typed sheets is put before him. Many a man discovers that even in lazy moments he has the strength of mind to push a button which he knows will start a train of events each of which calls up the next one by associations almost as automatic as the movements of one's feet on the first, second, third, and later rungs of a ladder. Each item springs the next, as the mechanism of a coiled watch-spring pushes a wheel and that another wheel, and so on up to the moving hands on the watch face.

A friend of mine is fond of taking a hot bath. But the trouble with this, he says, is that once in the bath he cannot summon the will power to get out again into the cold air, and so is apt to waste half an hour in the tub. But one day he discovered that, without lifting any part of his body into the chilly air, he can kick out the drainage-stopper with his big toe. Once the stopper is out he cannot replace it with his toes or without raising himself from the warm water. So, inevitably, the water drains away. He has enough will power to give a kick of his toe. That starts a train of events which runs on to the desired end.

Signing one's name on a check is far easier, entails far less consciousness of painful deprivation, than paying out cash. When charitable societies beg for money they get it far more easily from those who can give merely by signing a check, the rest of which has been filled in by a secretary, than if the donor has to take the greenbacks out of his pocket and painfully separate himself from them. When he signs the check he does not vividly realize his loss. That will come to him later, but he need not face it now. So his healthy unimaginativeness can be enlisted on the side of his languid generosity.

As we set in motion a desirable but difficult train of events by signing a check, so we can achieve similar success by signing a contract. "One summer," writes a college student, "I did not wish to spend the time idly with my family, so I signed a contract to work all summer with an engineering firm. It was easy to sign the contract, but the tractional force of that signed agreement kept me at work all summer, although the conditions were decidedly unpleasant."

2. AUTOMATIC BRAKES

A somnambulistic patient told me that he had found his nocturnal ramblings apt to lead him into embarrassing or dangerous situations. To check himself he arranged two rocking-chairs back to back at the side of his bed, so that when he got up, his shins would strike the sharp protruding rockers of one chair or of the other, and cause pain which wakened him effectually.

Whoever invented the bell which rings in a typewriting

mechanism when the typist approaches the end of a line, followed the somnambulist's principle. A mechanical stimulus is arranged to arouse attention when we need it. By a similar chain of events a trolley car or an elevator so arranged that the operator cannot start it until all the doors are closed, automatically checks human forgetfulness and carelessness.

A nail-biter of my acquaintance decided to cure himself of the habit by wearing gloves at all times. It would of course have been quite possible for him to take off his gloves and get at his nails. But to do this would be a conscious, deliberate act. His nail-biting was a semiconscious habit and did not occur when anything roused him to full cerebration. So the gloves proved an effectual check. By a similar plan a wise lady tied her own hands to the sides of her pyjamas when she found that a troublesome inflammation of her eyelids was kept from healing because she rubbed them with her fingers during sleep.

College students, like many of their elders, have trouble in keeping down their expenditures. One such easy spender found it effective to keep almost all her money in a bank at some distance from the college buildings. When she was tempted to unwise spending, the prospect of having to go down to the bank, make out a slip, and stand in line with it before the paying teller's window was enough to discourage her. "When I need to cut down on cigarettes," wrote a student of my acquaintance, "I buy loose tobacco and make myself roll them. It is so much bother for me to make a cigarette, especially in a wind, that I smoke many fewer in this way than if I buy them ready made."

3. STARTING OR BRAKING TRAINS OF MENTAL ASSOCIATION

There is no sharp distinction between this class of tricks and the more mechanical devices just exemplified.

In both, the environment is called in as an ally to rouse us or to quiet us according to the need of the moment. But in the examples which follow, the machinery is more psychological, less external.

(a) *Tractive links.* " I cannot study in my room. There is too much going on there. But at Widener " (the college library), " where it is quiet and every one else is at work, I quite easily fall in line. The only difficulty is to get myself there in the first place."

On the same principle many obese, diabetic, or alcoholic patients go every year or two to a " Hot Springs " or a " Kur-ort " where they are supposed to be cured by drinking and bathing in expensive mineral waters. Why shouldn't they drink and bathe in the same waters at home? It can all be arranged and at far less expense. But in point of fact it is not the mineral waters but the " water wagon," the diet, the regular exercise, and the long hours of sleep that cure the patient at the " Hot Springs." At home he could put the same mineral constituents into his bath and into his drinking water, but they would not keep him to the strict diet, take his regular exercise for him, nor hold him away from alcoholic drinks. The environment of the " cure," where every one is under the same restrictions and follows the same well-planned routine through every hour of the day, is an essential part of it. It is an expensive remedy, but it works. By a single initial decision to take the " cure," one is bound into a harness of engagements which pull our wills along when they would otherwise flag.

To engage a business office and to fix one's office-hours is to harness one's vagrant willfulness until a chain of habit is formed. It needs only a few strokes of the pen to engage the office and to fix the hours. Thereafter one is drawn along and kept at work by something more substantial than one's own invisible, inaudible, indefinite will. There is rent to pay. The expectations of other people are aroused. The office machinery is around us, a visible symbol of the will to work. Once in the desk chair, the signs of yesterday's plans, of today's engagements, and of tomorrow's payments coming due, conspire to arouse our latent desire to work and our zest of it. Partners, assistants, clerks are on hand. They must be dealt with, kept busy, satisfied. In the current of their activities our own are aroused.

To sign up for a course of study in college takes but an instant, but that trifling act, that fiat of one's common sense, starts in motion a train of engagements, expectations, requirements that pull one along despite the resistance of natural laziness. I have known men to sign up for a course that they knew would be unpleasantly hard, recognizing that once in it they would be stimulated by its requirements to do far more work than they had been used to. They could start the machinery in motion. College traction would do the rest.

Shy men who fear to speak up in a college class have been known to arrange with the instructor to call upon them regularly and frequently. Some of their fellow students are irrepressible. No instructor needs to call on them. His chief difficulty is to keep them from talking too much. But Mr. Blushful will not open his lips in class from September to June unless the instructor unlocks them with a question. Yet he is thankful to any one who will set in motion his embarrassed muscles. In the intellectual tennis of the classroom such a student can never manage to serve the ball. But if some one else will serve, he can return it. Finally after sufficient practice in returning, he can go back to the service line, and toss up the ball himself.

Some bashful men have nevertheless enough strength

of mind to join a club or a social group. I knew one such unfortunate who often made himself accept the invitation to a party, but when he reached the door at the appointed hour could not always push himself up the steps to ring the bell. He would walk past the house several times before he could gather determination enough to press the electric button. Once that crisis was past he could not escape and in the end he generally enjoyed the party.

It often seems to me that the chief reason for taking music lessons is not the technical instruction nor the aesthetic insights given by the teacher, but the compulsion exerted over our laziness by the fact that every week we have to exhibit some degree of proficiency before a teacher. We have paid down the money. It is too absurd to get nothing in return for it, too humiliating to face the teacher with nothing accomplished since the last lesson. The traction of a chain of spaced lessons pulls us on like a moving treadmill. Once we are on it we must do something to keep up with it. The latent forces which we thus mobilize, are our own desire to get something for our money and our impulse to maintain self-respect. The machinery of the music lessons sets these forces at work to supplement our own naturally feeble inclinations to practise. Were that strong enough alone, the lessons would hardly be needed.

(b) *Brakes*. Thirty years ago a friend of mine, Nymphas C. Hanks, was blown up in a dynamite explosion which left him blind, and took off both his hands at the wrists. Nearly a hundred bits of copper from the dynamite cartridges were buried in his face and body, and had to be extracted one at a time. To relieve the nagging pain following these operations and the depression of facing life without eyes or hands, he began to take morphine, and in the course of the next two years, though he struggled hard to earn a living by peddling and storekeeping, he became a morphine habitué. This state still seemed to him the lesser of two evils, until one day, out on the Idaho line, he reached a point of confusion which he thought meant insanity. "I'd think something and then I'd say something different." This nerved him to a decision and like the other heroes of my tales he got aboard a train. But this was not a train of events, circumstances, or mental associations. It was a railway train and it took him back to the hospital where he was first operated on after the dynamite explosion and where he had first been given morphine for his pain. The doctor in charge was an old friend of his. "Doctor," he said, "I've quit morphine." The doctor laughed. "No," said Hanks, "this ain't no funny business. I want you to give me the best nurse you have and the best room you have, and let me fight it out in there. But whatever I do or say don't give me any more morphine."

"But you may die," said the doctor.

"All right then, I'll die. I don't want to go on the way I'm going, whatever happens. But whether I live or die don't you give me any more morphine."

It was agreed to. For a week Hanks went through the usual agony of "withdrawal pains"; but he came out cured, and has now earned his living for nearly thirty years without going back to morphine. The point I want to bring out is that by his decision "out on the Idaho line," he put in operation first a train of events and finally a system of brakes which checked effectually the plunge of his craving for morphine. He could not have broken the habit by "sheer will." Few men have ever done that; he had already tried it and failed. But he had sufficient free strength left to get aboard a train running to his old hospital and there to get aboard a train of treatment and restraint that would carry him to his destination against his own will, in spite of his own frantic pleas for the morphine which he was now locked up to escape. It was his own will that enlisted the help of a nurse and a doctor, and through them the service of physical and chemical weapons against his own enslavement.

Father George P. O'Conor of Boston has told me that in his opinion the strongest force of the Roman Catholic confessional is not in the cure but in the prevention of bad behavior. His parishioners know that they will have to face the confessional at the end of the week. That knowledge acts as a check upon misdemeanor. They have accepted the system. They have bound themselves to the practice of weekly confession. That once agreed to, any temptation to improper action meets in their own minds the thought that if this deed is done it will have to be confessed at the end of the week. The Church's disapproval is certain. It begins to act before it is spoken, before the act is committed, and so prevents it.

As a check on our own uncontrolled behavior we can take advantage of the humiliating psychological fact that what is out of sight is out of mind. The reformed drunkard avoids the streets where saloons or speakeasies beckon. At a distance he can forget them and keep away. Within a certain radius he is pulled into them as he would go down a greased slide. For one person it is liquor that he has to run away from or to keep at a distance. For another it is the shop windows or the candy shops which tempt her to spend too freely. Or it may be the periodical room in Widener Library, or the blue-book of a neighbor sitting too near one during an examination. He must sit farther off. Or perhaps the cards in our neighbor's hand are held temptingly low. Won't he be good enough to hold his hand up? Otherwise one really cannot help seeing the cards. If one is usually cross at breakfast time one plans to breakfast alone. If a political heretic rouses one's temper to fury one gets out of the room before his eloquence is well started.

The "saloon" that I have long had to avoid is the Boston Athenaeum Library. The books are so various, so new, so interesting, and so temptingly displayed, the nooks and corners are so quiet, and the chairs are so comfortable, that I have found myself again and again staying on there till I broke engagements and upset plans. I have kept away from there now for a good many years. Some men know well enough that there are women whom they have to avoid or even at a pinch to run away from. It is quite inglorious but quite necessary if honor is to be preserved. The great need is to recognize the moment for such inglorious flight and to distinguish it clearly from the more fortunate hours when one can stand one's ground and carry on respectably.

4. COMMITMENT TO INTERESTS OR TO PERSONS

(a) *Tractors*.   Emerson suggested a valuable though expensive method of transportation: "Hitch your wagon to a star." He recognized that we cannot ourselves supply the energy, physical or moral, that we need. We must enlist the moral forces of the universe, as we harness steam, gasoline, electricity, water-power to our plans.   But Emerson was thinking not of convenient little devices like those that I have been listing. His rule would come to something like this: "Accept a responsible position and live up to it." That will pull you along where you wish to go. It will also put on the brakes when you need to stop. Most adults do not live in a perpetual battle against their own temptations. They are carried along by their interests, their professions, and their affections.

There is no clear line of division between the influences of one's job, one's family, one's religion, and the force of such a system as the Catholic confessional. In these pages I am trying to extend and to deepen the effect of mechanical devices and psychological associations like those already described. As we grow up and settle down, such fragmentary and temporary helps should be organized under a plan of life which is our tractor with four-wheel brakes.

Intermediate between the most universal plans and the most particular devices are the *insurance systems* against death, fire, unemployment, sickness, and other misfortunes. These make use of the fact that in one of our more rational moments it requires comparatively little self-control to take out an insurance policy. Once that is agreed to, however, our deficient foresight, our scanty capacity to save money for emergencies, and also our more rational desire not to be interrupted at all seasons by the need for renewed will-fiats of saving,—all these are provided for. We are reminded automatically when the times for payments arrive. The insurance company wakes us periodically when the time comes. Between times we can sleep in peace without worry, without struggle of conscience, and without fear of insufficiency in our provision. The company makes the calculation for us and charges us for its trouble. We are left free for occupations and enjoyments which we think better worth while. All this valuable machinery is set in motion by insurance payments which we can make almost without waking up, that is, without being distracted from our favorite interests.

When a student goes to college he hitches his wagon not exactly to a star but to a system even more inclusive than insurance. At the outset it is his free act presumably, and throughout his college course he is perfectly free to

go to the devil or to carry on love affairs, business projects, or summer travels in foreign countries, without any
interference by the college. Nevertheless he has put himself within the magnetic field of the college. Its pull tends
to systematize his life and to diminish the bad effects of
his lapses, explosions, and centrifugal urges.

Of course the system is by no means a sure cure. College courses, college rules, college friendships, college
amusements may pull a youth in so many different directions that he is utterly bewildered or spins round in one
spot. Nevertheless college life does reënforce any tendencies toward orderly growth that a student may possess.
A group of people are going in his direction. It is easier
to go with them than to go it alone. Some of them may
be stimulating as well as irritating or distracting. Their
various influences may reënforce instead of neutralizing
one another. A dormant but native tendency to form sys-
tematic habits may be roused by the force of performing
daily a certain minimum of college work. So a college,
like a profession, like marriage, like religion, may hold
us in line (brakes), and still more probably, may dangle
in front of us a bait, intellectual, moral, or aesthetic,
which draws us on.

It is a commonplace that many people are greatly improved by marriage. Delinquents are sometimes thus
straightened out. Bad manners and bad tempers are improved, scattered energies are focussed. Granted that any
woman who marries a man in order to reform him is
courting disaster, it remains true that a marriage entered
without any special thought of reformation does sometimes change a person who before seemed unchangeable.
As in college, so in marriage, it is often the unforeseen,
the chance elements that lead people to be born again.
The death of a favorite child, the influences of the " in-

laws," the attempt to guide children, influences quite unforeseen and undesired when a couple take each other for better, for worse, are sometimes potent reformers. I suppose no one should seek a college, a religion, a profession, or a wife merely to pull himself out of the mud. But if one of these great adventures is undertaken for its own sake, it often gives us far more than we knew enough to expect.

The League of Nations and even the Kellogg-Briand pact for the outlawry of war are, I think, tractors (though not yet powerful ones) toward more decent international behavior. Any nation can pull out of the agreement. Yet despite the fact that we can rebel when constraints feel irksome, college work, professional work, marriage and the League lick some of us into shape.

The usefulness of the League of Nations rests on a fundamental fact which helps many other kinds of human association: namely, that we are not all of us weak in the same way and at the same time. We do not all go lame, get blind, or have our tantrums at the same moment. Generally there are enough well people to look after the sick. It is true that mob action, a simultaneous tantrum of the whole group, may grip us at any moment, and when it gets hold of us we behave even worse together than we should separately. But there is reason to believe that organically federated units, like the nations in the League, are less subject to the contagion of mob hysteria than if they simply inhabit the earth side by side.

For most of us, I conclude, *other human beings are the most powerful tractors that we can find*. Many of us sincerely believe that it is our families and our friends who are responsible for any success we attain in the business of decent living. I know but one force that can exalt us still more. When religion is centered in a personal relation which surpasses even friendship in intimacy, and is not subject to its separations, its misunderstandings, and its misleadings, we reach, as in Christianity, the mightiest star to which our wagon can be hitched and to which it can be rehitched as often as it comes loose. Even religion grows up, in most of us, I take it, through the influence of other people, living or dead. Directly or indirectly they are our salvation.

(b) *Brakes.* I met, at my dentist's years ago, a college student who explained to me, while we waited our turn, the system by which he had so far prevented himself from going to seed. He had arranged with our dentist to notify him at regular intervals of a dental appointment made and to be paid for whether he kept it or not. Thus he circumvented his natural tendency to neglect his teeth. His barber was directed to notify him once in six weeks that his hair needed cutting and that he, the barber, was coming to cut it that afternoon at 5:30. Being too shy to speak up in class, yet quite aware that he needed to take an active part in college exercises, he had arranged with three of his instructors to call on him regularly and frequently in class. Having noticed that eagerness for letters from his fiancée made him run back to his room too frequently during the mornings, he had arranged with her to post her letters only on Tuesday and Friday evenings so that he could look for them only by the morning post on Wednesdays and Saturdays.

Though we may think these brakes rather too mechanical, most of us have managed to acquire, without express stipulation, a friend or two who can be counted on to be annoyed when we exaggerate or twist the truth, and whose annoyance is certain to be vocal. We have voted for a mayor who has appointed a police commissioner whose motor policemen can be relied upon to check us at crossings where our ordinary impatience would lead us to take dangerous chances. We may even have acquired quite innocently an English butler like my uncle's. In this butler's decorous presence, it is quite impossible for my uncle to be snappish to the children at meals. I take it that such experiences are common enough to be commonplace. Dentists, barbers, policemen, butlers, college teachers, candid friends put the brakes on our tendencies to slide down hill. If such brakemen do not spring to the task spontaneously or as a part of their usual duties, they can be procured. It is our business to procure them.

5. DOES SUCH APPARATUS DEMORALIZE US?

Is the use of such brakes and tractors humiliating or perhaps weakening? No. It is about as sensible to despise such devices as it is to say that we will use no tools. We cannot get on without them, if we are to lift ourselves above the animals. We use a hammer or an axe to accomplish for us, under our direction, what we could not do by sheer will. Doubtless we lose something in accepting such help. The man who can make a fire without matches, by friction alone or with a flint and steel, possesses a fine piece of skill. Most of us have lost it if we ever had it. But the possessor of a box of matches gains more than he loses. He gains time in which to acquire other sorts of skill, skill in thought, in getting on with other people, in creative work.

Despite these arguments I hope that some one who has read thus far is now indignantly protesting that this is no way to manage one's life. Are we to be forever children, needing nurses to blow our noses and put on our mittens? Shall we ever learn self-control if we are perpetually managed by our machines, our mental associations, and our fellow creatures? Do not our wills atrophy like our muscles

if we support them at every turn with mechanical contrivances?

But I ask in return, "Are these contrivances any more
mechanical than the shelters we build to keep warm, the
clothes we wear, or the food and sleep on which we admittedly depend?" Perhaps we should be tougher if we
could get along without clothes and shelter, but we should
then certainly expend in keeping ourselves alive a quantity
of heat-making energy that could otherwise be put to more
interesting use. We use mechanisms whenever we walk
or talk. The mechanical contrivances in our habit-systems
pull us along and put the brakes on us in a way that any
one can regard as humiliating and disgraceful if he chooses.
The crucial question is, Do we use these implements to
set us free? Do we gear up devices of memory and habit
for moral reënforcement and for intellectual stimulation?
Does college, marriage, occupation enfranchise as well as
harness us? Do they release a few ergs of creative power
in us? Neither mechanical aids to self-control nor stark
unaided self-control discovers anything new, makes anything beautiful, original, or amusing. But I submit that
a person most of whose energy goes into keeping himself
warmed, fed, and safe from enemies is thereby made less
likely to accumulate spare energy for his own individual
interests.

The items of this chapter can be hooted at as nothing
but a collection of tools to weaken, block, trick, drug, or
circumvent our weak wills. It is perfectly true. But every
time we use a clock, a catalogue, a dictionary, or a yard-
stick, every time we put on a pair of boots or eat with a
spoon, we bow to the dominion of tools. Self-maintenance,
self-support, independence are impaired by every convenience in civilization. The dictionary and the card-
catalogue certainly save labor. But so, we may be told,

do the bread-line and the dole and every pauperizing device yet invented. It is no defense to say that a contrivance saves time and labor unless we can show that because of the economy this labor and time will be more profitably employed. To be sick or to die also saves at least one person's labor. But rarely does a person grow more productive intellectually, morally, or aesthetically because of illness and approaching death. Therefore we hate and fight sickness.

Civilization and the familiar tools of improved living which this chapter has brought to mind cannot be defended because they make us independent or self-supporting in any but a very superficial sense. They lead us from a dependence that enslaves thought, debases enjoyment, and diminishes creative power, to a dependence that, we hope, gives more scope to individual initiative, original endeavor, and free constructiveness, in more people for more hours per year.

Not independence of nature but control of nature for our best human purposes is the hope of civilization and of all the "automatic brakes and tractors" which I have been describing. We do not wish to get rid of force, coercion, or even of the control of one life by another. We hope to apply force where and when it serves ideals, and to apply it first of all to ourselves. We train, enslave, exploit our own muscles so that they no longer twitch, yield, tremble, or rebel when ordered to do our work. It is their rebellion, their physiological independence that makes us blunder in speech, write illegibly, or throw the ball into the bleachers.

To extend as well as to control the forces of our bodies is part of the task of civilizing them. To civilize them we have a right to treat them as we used to treat slaves, children, and "backward nations." Because we want to get all the work we can out of our muscles, we gear them up with tools, machinery, electric energy. The fisherman's fly-rod makes his arm longer, less visible, more delicate, as it drops a fly in a pool. The warning bell on a typewriter, the block-signal system in railroading, give a longer arm to memory as the fly-rod gives a longer arm to the fisherman. If a device extends the control of our wills over what opposes them, we have no reason to fear that we are becoming enslaved by it. Morphine controls pain for the time and so in acute disease it is a good tool. Thus used it increases our power to think, to build, and to enjoy. But in long illness morphine creates pain, quenches intelligence, warps desire. Therefore in chronic disease it is a bad tool.

If it appears that our large-scale-production machinery, our world-trade, our compulsory public school system, our automobiles and telephones narrow more horizons than they extend, distract more people than they educate, make us more and not less selfish, we shall know that we have got hold of the wrong tools. But we shall have no reason to doubt the value of *all* tools. We shall continue to extend the control of our muscles and our minds by any device that will make them better servants.

When people have counted up their resources for controlling the weak and wicked they have usually been planning to control, not themselves but some one else. The devices referred to in this chapter are planned for the use of those who wish to paddle their own canoes rather than to drift or to be towed. The same is true of the measures to be described in the next chapter.

Chapter XXI

CLEARING THE DECK FOR ACTION

When we have made up our minds about a course of action, we are eager to get into it. But our deck is often cluttered up with all sorts of luggage and rubbish. " Let's go," we say. But I have a nail in my shoe, a crick in my neck, an itch between my shoulders, a floating black spot before my right eye, and a dull ache in my conscience. Before we can start I must say goodbye to an unfortunate love affair, bury two ancient grudges, and overcome four kinds of shyness. Internal obstacles, physical distractions, mental preoccupations fill the foreground of consciousness. Sometimes they make it hard to get started; sometimes they discourage us from carrying on. If we are to deal with them energetically, we may well begin with:

1. INERTIA

When a man wants to "make himself" work, take exercise, add up his accounts or write to his parents, a large part of his difficulty is in overcoming simple inertia. Many of us have no self-starter. We do not move unless some one comes along and cranks us. Yet once in motion we go along well enough. It takes more energy to start a heavy engine or an inert human organism than to keep it going. Hence good sense should lead us to study the machinery for getting started.

We need (a) *sudden violence at the start*. We cannot quietly and gradually start a new habit, say of planning out the use of our time. If we are going to start and maintain it we must launch it "with as strong and decided an initiative as possible." Watch a freight handler pitching trunks into a baggage car. He does not slowly raise a trunk inch by inch from the ground. He snaps it up with a quick jerk. We can learn a similar knack of handling our own inertia. Slow beginnings prolong the agony of effort and may defeat it. We must rush at the job, pounce on it, jump into it. The new habit is more apt to get under way if we go at it noisily, suddenly, violently, ostentatiously, with punch and dash. Because there is inertia to be overcome, we need to throw all our strength against a single point of resistance and to increase our momentum through speed. Speed brushes aside hesitation, leaves no time for insidious doubt, quenches thought when thought antagonizes action. For it is by the "pale cast of thought" that resolves are "sicklied o'er . . . and enterprizes . . . lose the name of action." Reasoning is fatal at the moment when we need to snap into action. Just then thought is a vice and thoughtlessness a virtue. We need more blood in our muscles; for the time this blood must leave our brains. Then cerebral anemia stills the grumbling of our laziness. Emotion, not thought, is what we need to get us started, because emotion raises the psychical temperature, softens down the rigid structures of old habit, releases energy. To clench our fists and jump into our task, to "get mad over it," to run into it as if the devil was after us, all this theatrical ostentation helps to kindle emotional power and to lift us over the hurdles. The tendency to be gentle, gradual, reasonable at such times is a temptation of the devil. It is like the morphinist's attempt to taper off on the daily dose of his drug, or like the hope to save a dog pain by cutting off his tail an inch at a time. Violence and suddenness, not gentleness, is the need.

William James phrased the idea of "pouncing" (sudden violence at the outset) in psychological language and with emphasis not so much on the suddenness as on the motion: "Seize the very first possible opportunity to act on every resolution you make and on every emotional prompting you may experience in the direction of the habits you aspire to gain. It is not in the moment of the forming but in the moment of their producing motor effects that resolves and aspirations communicate the new ' set ' to the brain." [1]

Why is *sudden* action called for? Because we must strike while the iron (that is the emotion) is hot. When it cools we are lost. The " iron " in this metaphor is the zest roused, for the minute but not permanently, by the clear perception of what we ought to do. Thought is powerless until it gets so energetic that it passes over into desire. A good intention opposed to an old habit is like a feather waved in the air to smash a fortress. Reason cannot get an act into motion if there is any considerable resistance of habit against it. It is in the face of such resistance that most moral contests arise.

While the iron is hot, while the duty is vividly seen, one must do something, literally without waiting a minute. Perhaps the whole battle may be won in that minute; usually we muster only enough energy to start a train of events which will do the work for us.

All this I have dealt with in the chapter on " Psychic Brakes and Tractors." Here I want only to make clear the principle that moral energy must be used when it is present, else it escapes in forgetfulness. While emotion is hot a binding act can easily be welded onto the future so as to fix our will in advance.

---

[1] William James, *The Principles of Psychology* (New York: Henry Holt & Co., 1890), Vol. I, p. 124.

(b) Another useful rule is: *Stop on a down-grade.* To control habit, some positive desire, not thought only or will only, must by hook or crook be found. "Accumulate all the possible circumstances which shall reinforce the right motives; put yourself assiduously in conditions that encourage the new way; make engagements incompatible with the old; take a public pledge if the case allows; . . . envelop your resolution with every aid you know." [1] In short: Stop your engine on a down-grade. Locomotive engineers know that if a heavy train comes to a standstill on a level or on an up-grade they may have trouble in starting again. They try to stop on falling ground so that the pull of gravitation will help when they are ready to start again. In most of our jobs there are up-grades and down-grades. Finding that we can take the up-grade more easily while we are well warmed up to our work and have accumulated momentum, we learn to push on without stopping until we come to a bit of " down-grade," that is, to a point in our work which will seem unusually inviting when we come to start it again after a pause. The same principle leads a writer of magazine serials to end his installment at a point where the reader's suspense is keen. He calculates that the pull of suspended curiosity, like the pull of gravitation, will start his readers on the new installment.

Some ingenuity is needed to pick out the " down-grades " in a piece of work and some energy is needed to stop there, for we do not feel like stopping just then. But most of us find by experiment that there is economy in this halt. In the end we get more done.

(c) It is possible to warm up the pale cast of thought into desire, and so into action. James has described in a famous passage a third self-starting device for lazy people.

[1] William James, *loc. cit.*, Vol. I, p. 123.

He designed a piece of mental machinery to pull us through the difficulty of getting up in the morning:

> We know what it is to get out of bed on a freezing morning in a room without a fire, and how the very vital principle within us protests against the ordeal. Probably most persons have lain on certain mornings for an hour at a time unable to brace themselves to the resolve. We think how late we shall be, how the duties of the day will suffer; we say, "I *must* get up, this is ignominious," etc.; but still the warm couch feels too delicious, the cold outside too cruel, and resolution faints away and postpones itself again just as it seemed on the verge of bursting the resistance and passing over into the decisive act. Now how do we *ever* get up under such circumstances? If I may generalize from my own experience, we more often than not get up without any struggle or decision at all. We suddenly find that we *have* got up. A fortunate lapse of consciousness occurs; we forget both the warmth and the cold; we fall into some revery connected with the day's life, in the course of which the idea flashes across us, "Hollo! I must lie here no longer"—an idea which at that lucky instant awakens no contradictory or paralyzing suggestions, and consequently produces immediately its appropriate motor effects. It was our acute consciousness of *both* the warmth and the cold during the period of struggle, which paralyzed our activity then and kept our idea of rising in the condition of *wish* and not of *will*. The moment these inhibitory ideas ceased, the original idea exerted its effects.[1]

The three self-starters so far suggested, then, are:—

(a) Pounce furiously on the needed act.

(b) Stop on a down-grade.

(c) Get attention focussed on your goal.

James's self-starter is a device to eliminate counter-attractions. Almost any idea will carry itself out provided there is no other idea pulling simultaneously in the opposite direction. The blind and deaf person easily concentrates his mind on his Braille types because the distractions of sight and sound do not touch him. To arrange things so that he is blind and deaf to all but the task before him is

[1] William James, *loc. cit.*, Vol. II, p. 524.

therefore a clue for every procrastinator. A quiet room for work, an eye-shade that serves the purpose of a horse's blinders, are familiar expedients. In the mind itself we can accomplish something like this by forming the habit of squashing intrusive ideas the instant they appear, nipping them in the bud before they have time to get large and strong. Have Luther's inkstand close to your right hand to throw at any intruding devil the instant his head appears. You can scare him even though your aim is imperfect; but speed is essential and reflection is, just then, a crime.

2. FEAR

Against the fear of pain, ridicule, failure, it is useful to recall that in a large proportion of cases the anticipation turns out to be worse than the fact. Most fears have two components: (a) the rational anticipation of future facts, and (b) the luxuriant improvisations of fancy. Half-sight, the glancing light of a consciousness that touches the object and swiftly leaves it again, is far more terrifying than full sight. The skittish horse shies away from what he only half sees in the road. When we turn his head so that he looks straight at it he is less frightened. So I have often tried to turn the thoughts of patients panic-stricken by the possibility that they might faint in church or in the street. When they are led to consider in full-colored detail the very worst that the experience might entail, they can laugh at their fears. The indefinite, the shapeless, the half-seen is what scares us most. Give it the full outline of reality and we rob it of its worst terrors.

Carrying the procedure a step further we may induce ourselves, or others, to face the reality not only in thought but in action: to step into cold water, to walk into the experience that we dread, with help at hand in case of need but without hesitation on the brink. Those who fear their own incapacity, ineptitude, and general inferiority often shrink not from a reality but from the creations of their own fancy. Most of us have seen this happen to others. When we are the victims of our own bogies we ought to remember what we have seen in others. We can draw out our own unconscious strength as accurately as the psychoanalyst draws out our unconscious weaknesses, and far more cheaply. The psychoanalyst is paid to make us recall what we had forgotten. Why not be our own analysts and talk it all out with ourselves?

3. FORGETFULNESS

Why do we forget? Freud's theory that we drop stitches usually because we (unconsciously) wish to drop them is, I think, one of the most ill-founded that he has thus far elaborated. There is more foundation for the idea that we differ greatly in native power to hold on to certain classes of our experiences. Yet when people say jauntily that they "have no memory," all that they mean is that they forget particular classes of facts. Even idiots remember the sound of the dinner-bell. To have no memory would be to have no character, no individual existence, and certainly no morals. No one can be either virtuous or vicious without forming habits of memory.

When we forget certain classes of facts such as telephone numbers, dates, or the names of our acquaintances, it is often because we have never taken much trouble not to drop a stitch twice in the *same* place. Every one drops a stitch now and then, but there are some stitches, our engagements for example, which it is of special importance not to forget. Memory then becomes a matter of ethics, and memory-devices a part of duty. A good manager is one who, finding by experience what he cannot do unaided, hires some one to do it for him; he calls to his aid the familiar devices for making memory work better. He gives up the idea of increasing memory in general and focuses attention on a few well-chosen devices which catch and hold certain slippery items.

Memory holds: (a) What we succeed in weaving into a durable tissue with other ideas logically related to it, or effectually hooked up by arbitrary association. (b) What we impress on our brains by putting muscle into it.

Most popular memory-devices depend on the first of these principles. No one forgets everything. Therefore if we can hitch the slippery item to some of those which ordinarily are *not* dropped from memory, it gets carried along with the rest. Most citizens still wear hats when they walk the streets of large cities. They forget to post letters but they do not forget their hats. Put the letters on the hat and they go out together. Such alliances are the stuff of memory. For the art (and duty) of memory, like the art (and duty) of thinking, is a process of *thickening*, that is of felting ideas into a tough fabric. Pick up one end of a well-knit fabric of ideas and you lift the whole of it.

Some items are hard to knit together. Proper names, for instance, are hard to recall because they are not assigned on the sound logical principle used by the Indians. If an Indian has a broken nose we call him Broken Nose. Then we do not forget his name because it is written across the middle of his face. But by one of the lapses of our civilization, Mr. Smith does no work in the local smithy, and the Browns are mostly light pink. They are not attached to their names either logically or psychologically. By logical attachment we remember a whole when we see a part of it. A keyhole logically implies a key and no one forgets to feel for his key when he approaches his house-door. But a key does not logically imply a pocket. It has just as much relation to the floor onto which it may have dropped out of a pocket, and it may still have continued this irregular relation to the floor, because no one perceived the desolation of the bereft pocket. Somehow a logical or psychological marriage of key to pocket must be arranged and made as nearly indissoluble as may be.

No matter how absurd the linkage is, it *may* work. But the less absurd it is, the more likely to last. A watch-pocket comes to be recognized as destined for a watch and so watches are less likely to be left at home than keys. A forgetful man of my acquaintance fastened his door-key to his watch-chain. Then the chain of memory-links was complete. He could remember to dress in the morning. To put on his clothes included putting on his waistcoat. Once that was on, its watch-pocket cried audibly for his watch and so for the chain to which his house-key was attached. So long as he could remember to dress in the morning he would be sure to have his door-key with him at night and would not have to ring his own door bell.

Much unnecessary annoyance is added to the lives of one's fellow actors in private theatricals if one does not know one's part at the date agreed upon for rehearsal. It is therefore a moral duty to learn one's part. Appreciation of this duty makes us search for ways and means to remember it. If one has read this book, or others which give the same hints, one knows that there are two valuable aids in the mnemonic tool-kit: logical (or psychological) clips, and mental elbow-grease. Try the latter first. Use your muscle on the part. Write it out in large bold script using colored pencils, one color for the cues and one for the text. The harder work you make of it, the more violent and extravagant your motions, the more numerous your recopyings, the sooner you will have obeyed the call of virtue: Learn your part.

The other tool of virtue, the logical clip, is applicable especially to a part in which the author used logical connections as he wrote it. Logical connective tissue is easier to find in Shakespeare, for instance, than it is in Browning. But with a little stretching one can usually find it in any drama that is worth learning. If there is rhyme the jingles call each other up in memory by psychological rather than logical linkage. The color associations (blue cues and scarlet text for instance) are useful for people with the visual type of memory. Those who remember by sound can join muscular with auditory memory by seeking out a secluded pasture and shouting their lines to the patient cows. Not many people will take so much trouble. Their fellow actors have to pay for their laziness.

Logical categories are a help to memory partly because they are a help to understanding. We divide things into classes and so conquer them in detail. It would be much harder to remember all the cards in the pack if they were all clubs or all diamonds. With a mass of new acquaintances, say historical events, before us to memorize, the first task is to group them by their neighborly characteristics. It is certainly useful, though somewhat arbitrary, to divide European history into ancient, medieval, and modern. When we have seen the chaotic mass of facts swept up into these three piles we begin to notice how Assyria, Egypt, and Greece differ from crusades, cathedrals, and charters, and what bonds hold each group together. Its members stick in memory because they stick to each other. Without classification they repel each other and memory repels them all.

It is hard for a beginner to remember the sequences of history because at the beginning all history seems alogical.

Any principle of understanding is a principle of memory. But no philosophy of history is yet generally accepted. Lacking this, it takes an expert to grasp the personality of an epoch or of a country, as we grasp the personality of a friend, by the logical or illogical linkages of character. The vaguely traced principle of the historic pendulum whereby we are supposed to swing from " tight government " (under Taft and Wilson), to " loose government " (under Harding and Coolidge), and then, sooner or later, back to a stiffer form again,—even this dubious principle aids memory because it has in it at least the semblance of a predictable order. But how long did the " strong " type of government last before it rolled sleepily over into the " freer " type? A decade, a generation, a century? The cyclical principle does not tell us. " Pure memory," not principle, must tell us that, and so we generally forget it.

Obviously the cure of forgetfulness cannot begin until we sincerely desire to be cured. But the sincerity of any desire for rescue is zero unless it sets us hunting for a *means* of cure. " Oh, I never could learn a part in a play," is a familiar remark, which usually means that the speaker is too lazy to take the means which other people take when they have parts to learn. The cure of forgetfulness begins when people are intelligent enough and interested enough to notice what it is that they forget, and what islands of durable memory stand out in the ocean of loss. Then they hasten to land forgettable items on one of these islands, and to fasten the items down by logical or psychological chains.

4. AVOIDABLE ILL HEALTH

Ethical tools for fulfilling our needs more swiftly, more economically, more certainly, include such devices as hygiene. Some people manage to get along with very little of it, just as an Indian, being extraordinarily strong, can get on with very few tools. But the lives of such people are often full of waste and misdirected energy. Hygiene, when it means the intelligent use of devices like diet, exercise, and rest, is a department of ethical ways and means, a part of due care. In other words, hygiene is a logically necessary consequence of vigor in our desires. When a man falls in love he begins to value his life more and usually to take better care of himself. His desires have become more intense and more certain of themselves. Hence they reach out more intelligently to ways and means. If you want to live and to succeed, hygiene is one of the useful means.

The weakness of hygiene appears when it is preached to people who have no strong desire to live and no idea what they want to do with their lives. For hygiene, like economics, is a hypothetical science. " If you want to banish gold, legislate for bimetallism." " If you want to get thin, take this diet." But perhaps you don't want to get thin or to banish gold. Then this command is fit for some one else, not for you. If you want to be always at your best, you must get your full allowance of sleep, when you have found by experiment what that allowance is. In case you do not care, or need, to be always at your best, you have no use for this particular tool of hygiene. For all tools are relative to special purposes and meaningless without them.

Good health depends considerably on knowing how the average hygiene applies to one's own organism. Each of us needs gradually to discover his own individual make-up, the garrets, cellars, closets, staircases, passageways of his own personality. One may get along very well without an inventory of the contents of one's own house, but an inventory of the contents of one's own personality, its resources and limitations, its tricks, leaks, loose screws, is essential. Some of the facts that one needs are not peculiar to oneself but common to many others, and are set down in textbooks of psychology and of hygiene.

" Ill health," said a wise friend of mine, " is often not a misfortune but a blunder." After putting aside the diseases, defects, and accidents which we cannot prevent, there are still a host of minor incapacities which hinder virtuous people from carrying their intentions into effect, incapacities that floor them today because yesterday they were too lazy or too habit-ridden to hunt up a way to avoid them. This headache, this incapacity to marshal our thoughts, this lapse of memory, this listlessness, this inability to concentrate, this depression, have you never had anything like it before? Is it not perfectly familiar and usually avoidable? Granted that health is to be sacrificed for any sufficient reason, the fact remains that many of us blunder into neglect of sleep or exercise, and eat and drink what we know quite well will upset us. We are prepared to take pains about what is important. We believe we are ready on occasion for heroic sacrifices. We have been known to meet an important challenge to fortitude or patience. But we stupidly succumb to seductions quite easy to resist, and for reasons no better than laziness or a disinclination to seem different from our neighbors.

The remedy is to act at the instant of our enlightenment. In the moment of insight, when we see clearly that it is imbecile to let important plans be spoiled by poor health, then and there we can tie our flaccid wills to some firm habit. In the flash of conviction, face to face with our own stupidity, we can use the energy of indignation to bind our future. We can make engagements which, once made, we are ashamed to break, engagements for exercise with a friend at an appointed hour, engagements that entail loss of money or of reputation if we break them. On this principle college men sometimes " go out " for some team or engage a paid teacher, knowing that in this sort of harness, vagrant impulses are controlled. The thought of the loss which a forfeit entails, the wrath of fellow team members, the waste of money, is often sufficient to keep a wavering purpose straight.

Depression, moodiness, blue spells are by no means always the result of blunders in hygiene. They look like unescapable misfortunes and, in the present state of medical ignorance, this is sometimes the truth. But there are also easily preventable " blues " for which common sense provides a remedy in reasonable care of health.

" I'm never any good before ten o'clock in the morning." Well, why not? Did you ever take the trouble to find out by experiment how many hours of sleep you need in order to leave you wide awake and refreshed at 7:30? Or, having found out, is there any sense in not going to bed earlier? How often we fool ourselves into treating the result of our own weaknesses as if it was a blight sent by unkind fortune!

Why does any one neglect hygiene? Aside from sheer ignorance, it is usually because one has only a languid interest in the business at hand. An arctic explorer does not neglect hygiene, because he is keen for his goal. His own maximum physical fitness is lighted up on the screen of his consciousness as part of the business in hand. But if one's interest in the day's work is torpid, why should one pay effective attention to the ways and means, one of which is good health? In slack moods we can fancy that we are not subject to the sordid limitations of the vulgar. And in truth we can " get by " the rules of health for a while just as we can go on drawing checks on an empty bank account. It takes time for the message " Account overdrawn " to reach us; but the fact is there and in time it catches up with us.

To be ignorant of what we might perfectly well know and certainly need to know is one of the common ways to put a ball and chain upon our own leg. Ignorance that the gun was loaded, ignorance of the adoption of daylight-saving time, ignorance that our application had to be in by the first day of the month,—such vacuities would be no one's fault if they were the first offense. But first offenders are hard to find. The same thing or something very like it has almost always happened to us before. The habit has grown up insensibly out of precursors that dwindle to a vanishing origin in ordinary carelessness. To realize this is one way to put teeth into the rules of ethics and of its servant, hygiene.

5. WORRY

" She can't do her work. She's all tired out with worry." But why has she never learned not to worry? Because she has regarded worry as respectable. To worry about *something* seems to many people a mark of proper sensibility. It is only the excess of it that they mildly reprehend. This state of things can be changed, I believe, by any one who will take the trouble to notice that worry always moves jerkily in a circle.[1] Our mind follows the dreaded future two or three steps and then begins at the same point, repeating the process over and over. Can there possibly be any sense in this, any advantage to any one?

[1] I have elaborated this point in *What Men Live By* (Boston: Houghton Mifflin Co., 1913).

I believe that all we need is to look at ourselves in the looking-glass, to catch ourselves in the act of treading this painful but absurd circle. It has no more value to any living being than wrong additions in arithmetic. No one adds wrongly on purpose. No more can one justify worry once he sees what it is. It is bad in moderation as well as in excess.

But can we escape it? Do we not need superhuman powers to escape it? No. For though no one supposes the medical profession to be made up of supermen, yet the vast majority of doctors have conquered the habit of worrying over their patients. They could not live otherwise; persistent worry would kill their efficiency. Worry is the real cause of most of the breakdowns for which overwork is blamed. Yet few doctors break down. Hence it seems fair to assume that most of them, like those whom I have questioned on the subject, have come to *realize that they needed* to get over worrying, and so have got over it.

When one faces the real nature of the worry-habit and sees how absurd and unnecessary it is, the battle against it is partly won. Complete victory is a growth in the power of concentration. Any one can learn to put an un-worrying train of ideas into his mind and hold it there by a grip as recognizable as the grip of a closed fist. Hard work does this for us in the daytime, practised concentration does it at night. But each must find out for himself what train of non-worrying ideas he can slip into his field of mental vision and hold there till he is asleep. With me it is a familiar road; with my cousin it is a problem in geometry. At first the worry shoots in again before we know it, but after we have kicked it out a certain number of times and firmly replaced the act of walking in imagination along the emotionally neutral path, we get peace.

6. EXPLOSIVENESS

Explosions of anger, jealousy, grief are familiar derailers of our chosen purposes. Some of us need first of all to get over a secret conviction that, like worry, they are a credit to their victim. I fancy this secret respect for explosions which, like storm or thunder, show power released, is less common today than it was in the last century. In any case the ground must be cleared of such superstitious respect for violence before we can begin to get rid of its mischief.

Next we inquire, " Who has been sitting on the safety-valve? " Outbreak follows thoughtless repression in most if not in all cases. Before a burst of wrath, a series of irritations, grudges, exasperations have been allowed to accumulate because no one took the trouble to dispose of them singly as they arose, or to prevent, by study, explanation, and readjustment, their recurrence. The same delay leading to a similar outburst has been allowed to happen again and again. Despite some fussing and fuming there has been no attempt to face the disagreeable task of coming to terms with causes of wrath. Grief bursts out in a passion because we have refused again and again to face the deeper sources of our pain.

The safety-valves of human economy do their work when we trust the powers of light rather than of concealment. To think out our troubles, to talk them out, to look into their causes and their meaning, implies trust in the power of intelligence to prevent their rending or corroding evil. The longer we put off the effort to talk out the causes of irritation or to think out the causes of discouragement, the more difficult it becomes to unravel the tangle. It grows more and more complicated, harder and harder to face.

Once it is thought out, talked out, exposed to the light and air of clear thought, machinery must be devised to prevent reaccumulation of the same dangerous explosives. Sometimes it is a tag-device or a warning-flag arranged to identify the dangerous intruder as soon as he appears. Knowing that we are apt to be cross when we are hungry, we can keep away from our fellows when we sight a hunger-tinged snappiness on our psychic horizon. Realizing that gloomy weather makes us take dark views of politics or marriage, we learn to pay no attention to our own cynicism at these times.

Sometimes explosion can be prevented by nothing more costly than a change of vocabulary. It enrages my grandfather to hear the word " socialism " pass my lips. But he is all in favor of public services for the public good. It is not always difficult to renounce one's affection for particular words provided the idea survives.

7. DAYDREAMING

Daydreaming often calls itself by more respectable names, and so escapes self-condemnation. One is sunk in deep thought, one is in a brown study, one is resting, one is getting ready for the next task, one is determined not to be forever at high pitch, one is musing on the precious past so that it shall not escape into oblivion. To see how much truth and how much bunk there is behind these phrases, ask the simple question, " Who is the hero, the conquering or suffering hero, of your meditations? " Do they ever wander far from the center of the lighted stage where our old friend Ego bows to universal applause?

I grant that in a daydream creative imagination *may* be at work. We may be dreaming about heaven or about a poem. We may be planning an invention, elaborating a musical theme, getting a fresh picture of the universe or of the Democratic Party. Who is *then* the hero? Why, there isn't any! Self is never more invisible than when imagination possesses it. The test-question reveals at once the difference between the self-aggrandizement of day-dreaming and the self-forgetfulness of active thought. Surely we need rest. But to be the hero of our daydreams consumes power instead of accumulating it. Strength is sapped, not generated, by these pleasant visions. Certainly it is worth while to store the values of past experience safe from the ravage of forgetfulness. But in daydreams the past is twisted out of all truth by the effortless victories of a telltale figure, oneself.

Once daydreaming is recognized for the sugary mess that it is, the remedy is seen to be the same as for most of our other blunders: Get into harness. Get into the activities of the world around us, and trust their economy to assign us a place, not at the center of the stage but wherever hard work wins opportunity.

Am I too dogmatic in this condemnation of daydreams? Are we always the hero, world-applauded, in them? No. Sometimes we are something worse still,—the victim mourned over with the maudlin tears of self-pity. When we were children we jeered at a " cry-baby " because we could see him and despise his tears. But when we pity ourselves in daydreams there is no outsider to jeer at us. We are free to weep for our unappreciated virtues and to call up the vision of sorrowing relatives discovering the dead body of their noble, silent, suffering boy. " Then they will know," we say. " Then they will realize what they have missed, how cruel and callous they have been."

No one can forgive himself such drivel if he catches himself at it. The daydream seems beautiful because it conceals us from ourselves. It allows Bottom to luxuriate in the flattery of Titania, his ass's head and long ears obvious to others but invisible to himself. Self-pity is self-adulation inverted. In other words it is the devil himself.

8. HALF-STIFLED REGRET OR REMORSE

Like a dull pain that pulls part of our attention inward when we need it all for the business of living, the sense of past blunders or sins benumbs us. Were we fully conscious of it we should be moved to atonement. It abides in the half-light where self-deceptions flourish. Like daydreaming it has chosen the wrong hero. The spotlight is not on the wrong done, the blunder committed. If it were, we could hardly help getting busy to do whatever can still be done to right the wrong, to correct the mistake, or to build defenses against its repetition. But when regret or remorse incapacitates us it is because we are staring at ourselves. Our own pain, not the harm that we have done, is in the focus of attention and we hold it there or stare at it under the same perverse attraction that sends the morbid tongue again and again to the sore spot in the mouth. First intellectual clarity and then vigorous action, are what we need to banish chronic regrets. It is the same treatment that cures daydreaming, worry, vacillation, and the rest of the ills born of half-consciousness and self-deceit.

9. MANAGEABLE DEPRESSION

Aside from recognizable mental disease, and ignoring for the moment congenital low spirits, we can distinguish avoidable or manageable fits of depression, lasting hours or days. Many people allow their lives to be blocked from time to time by such nightmares. Obvious blunders in hygiene are usually responsible, and the cure arrives when we are convinced that sensible care of our health is the only way to forget health. It is remarkable how foolish people are about this. They will use brains and sense about everything else, before they will condescend to do what they know they ought to do about their health. Then they wonder why they have no energy, why the sky seems so dark, why they cannot rise to the occasion. Gross illness they manage to avoid, but they are often worse off than if they did not, because from illness one often learns once for all how to steer one's hygiene without bothering about it. " Well " people, on the other hand, may be disabled for a good part of their lives because they never take the pains to understand and to master their minor ills.

But no study of physical hygiene avails to prevent the moods of depression, which occur because mental and emotional conflicts unsolved, perhaps insoluble, linger on half-conscious or less, often pushed aside and allowed to gather bitterness with time. This is not the place to say more of these tangles. They must be thought out and talked out so far as they can be. When neither poor hygiene nor mental-emotional snarls are at fault, the periodic or irregular waves of low spirits which upset or incapacitate many normal people are dealt with silently by the more skillful so that others do not discover them at all. People learn to burn their own smoke, to discount their own feelings, to realize that they will not last forever, and above all to make no important decisions while the dark mood lasts.

10. VACILLATION AND INATTENTION

When mind or body wanders from its own self-appointed task the lapse may show that the task itself is a mistake for us. If we are on the wrong tack or if there is reasonable doubt about this point, good sense bids us keep our weather eye peeled for another port. At such a time we ought to be in an experimental frame of mind.

Assuming that it is the time not to let our minds wander into a mood of experiment nor to balance various alternatives, but to concentrate attention on the chosen task, it is useful to have a test which tells us when we are wandering and when we are concentrating. Sometimes we seem unable to tell the difference between these two, or at any rate we act so. Then it is useful to precipitate the murky solution of our minds with questions: Are you measuring anything? Are you making a comparison? Are you asking a definite question that can have a definite answer? Do you know *why* you turned from your original project? Then there is nothing of vacillation in you. But did you turn your mind or did you *find it turned* by forces you know nothing about?

When we pull ourselves up sharply by such questions, it is a sign that the genius of attention, the spirit of order is at work in us. When we have reached this point we have already begun to be cured of our habit of wandering. We are not so sick as we feared.

But the prevention as well as the cure of inattention is on the program of many conscientious though disorderly minds. Voluntary attention or concentration is a habit which most of us know that we need to cultivate. We recognize that our minds are annoyingly prone to wander from the subject in hand, that "will power" is largely a matter of practice in concentration on one subject, and that success in study, business, or any matter requiring skill is largely the result of a solid, lasting grasp. How then, we ask, can we increase our powers of concentration? *By noticing and using such power as we already have.* People attend:

(a) To what interests them strongly (suspense, expectation, fear, hope, love).

(b) To what makes a strong impression on one or more senses.

(c) To whatever manages to maintain itself through relevant changes.

If we attend to any matter, a current of concern must already exist. Writers of newspaper headlines know that to catch the reader's attention they must tap his curiosity. Probably he possesses the perennial interests: in a fight (war, pugilism, riot, lawsuit, presidential election, athletic contest, collision of business interests); in a love story (in novels, drama, motion pictures); in a detective story or other "mystery"; in a well-known person; in a fire or any other disaster.

If one wants to increase attention to any matter, one must use one's brains to trace connections between that matter, say a lecture or the conversation of one's mother-in-law, and something that one is already interested in. Lecturers on economic theory appeal for the attention of their hearers by explaining at the outset that economics deals with the ways that men get their living. Almost any one is interested in getting his living, sooner or later. Some people, the economist goes on, get their living by farming, fishing, mining. These are outdoor pursuits with some adventure about them. Outdoor adventure interests most people. So if the economist can bind the definitions and the interweavings of capital, interest, rent, and profit to the risk and exhilaration of outdoor life and to the necessities of earning one's bread, he can rouse and hold attention.

Attention through the cultivation of interest, then, seems to depend on discovering how the subject that we need to attend to branches out of something that *already* interests us. Many people learn the details of their trade not from interest in the trade itself but because it is the means to a livelihood. So medical students learn anatomy not because it interests them, as it is usually taught, but because it is a necessary means to clinical work and finally to a degree in medicine. This pseudo-interest in something as a means to something else in which we already have a genuine interest is an inferior way to command attention. Not as a means to but as a branch of something that really interests him, comes the medical student's later work in the diagnosis of living people's ills. This he attends to easily and fruitfully because he likes it and likes the people. It is medical practice itself, scientific, personal, useful.

We assist voluntary attention by linking it with any potent spur to our involuntary attention, such as sound, color, or a vigorous sense impression. Children as they learn to read are lured into effort because some of the words are printed near a picture. As a small boy I was fascinated by Crùikshank's illustrations of Dickens' novels, and wanted to understand what they meant. This compelled me to spell out the words beneath, before, and after the pictures, until finally my investigations met in the middle, between pictures. Almost any one's attention is held by pictures, on a screen or in a book, by drawings, or even by diagrams on a blackboard. Merely to see the instructor pick up a piece of chalk as if he were going to draw may rouse a mild attention to what he is saying.

Another effective way to enlist voluntary attention in the service of memory and so of ethics, is to write whatever we wish to remember, for example a vocabulary, in large bright-colored letters and pin it up by one's dressing-table or wherever it will meet the eye many times a day. By this method advertisers lead us to attend to the foods, cigarettes, and stockings which they describe on the placards fixed in trolley cars.

William James and other psychologists have established

long ago the fact that we *cannot attend long to anything that does not change.* To hold attention on an idea or a visible spot on the wall we must go round it, think about it, turn it over in the mind. Otherwise we lapse into sleepiness or turn to something else. A monotonous voice and a steady point of light near the eye are among the best means of weakening attention and so of inducing sleep. We stay awake because we are stimulated by changes in what is around us or in what we think. A night watchman who has to hold his attention, and so himself, awake, keeps moving about or occupies himself with something that he can move.

11. LOSING ONE'S HEAD

In moments of hysterical excitement we make extravagant promises, forget binding engagements, put ourselves forward in fatuous conceit. Often this is more a physical than a psychical disaster. We lose our heads because we are exhausted, dazzled, or distracted with pain. We can do more to prevent such lapses by foresight and common sense than we can to stop them once they have occurred. For they have always happened to us before. There is no " first offense " in this field any more than there is in juvenile delinquency, in forgetfulness, or in bad temper. In the time between the second (or the fiftieth) offense and the following one, we can inquire, " Why do we lose our heads? " The answer is not often difficult. Usually it leads us back to some stupid neglect either of hygiene or of preparation for an " emergency " which we well know will emerge again. We lose our heads because we have not used them in foresighted rehearsal.

This chapter ends what I have to say on ethics proper and on the technique for applying its principles to the conduct of life. Ethics deals with what we do under a sense of obligation or in spite of it. But human action can rise higher than ethics. It can include not only beauty and skill, which are not relevant here, but something which I shall call *supermorality*, a devotion that goes beyond morality though in the same direction. My final chapter describes this.

D. SUPERMORALS

CHAPTER XXII

THE SUPERMORAL

Five classes of events happen in or to the human organism: (a) physical-chemical, (b) physiological, (c) habitual, (d) moral, and (e) supermoral. Each type merges into the others.

If a man drops from a yard-arm into the sea he is being acted upon by physical force. If his limbs jerk in epilepsy they are moved by physiological force, or perhaps ultimately by chemical energies. When he walks to business, enjoying the spring weather, his legs and arms move in an habitual rhythm, once learned with effort, now nearly unconscious, though still under a supervision which will usually interfere when anything goes wrong. When he leaves a piece of work that he is interested in and goes to vote, though he hates politics, he is doing a moral act. When he, a white man, volunteers to lead a negro regiment in our Civil War, against Southerners who are eager to show him how they despise such an act, it is heroic or supermoral action.

In this book I have described chiefly the fourth of these types, actions done with or against a sense of obligation which expresses itself in the making, keeping, and improving of agreements. In contrast with this, supermoral action is done, not from or against a sense of obligation but because of the love of some one or some thing. I mean here the " love " celebrated in Shelley's *Defense of Poetry:* " The great secret of morals is love; or a going out of our own nature, and an identification of ourselves with the beautiful which exists in thought, action or person, not our own."

No special talent or unusual endowment is implied in the supermoral acts called heroic. Valor needs no special brains or skill. It is common in people of quite ordinary intelligence. We recognize it most often in spectacular actions like the saving of life. But the same heroism lives unnoticed in the patience of those besieged by lingering disease or nagging relatives, or in courage like that of Richard P. Strong, who went to fight pneumonic plague in Manchuria when every one who could scramble out of that pest hole was leaving it at top speed.

Few knew of Strong's expedition; few have applauded it. There was nothing foolhardy in it. He took every known precaution in a methodical way. But despite all precautions he must have known that he faced a first-rate chance of death. He knew it still better when, on the pack-trail from Serbia to Albania during the Great War, he gave his only mosquito-net to a Red Cross volunteer who joined him uninvited but had forgotten to protect herself against malaria-carrying mosquitoes in one of the deadliest malarial districts in the world. Strong was bitten, caught the fever, and nearly died of it. Even if he had escaped the disease, his act would have been just as heroic, for he knew the chances he was taking to protect a blunderer to whom he was under no obligations.

I have known heroic humor in a dying man who joked to cheer up his heartbroken relatives, heroic eloquence in a wife defending the indefensible conduct of her husband, heroic foolishness in Don Quixote, heroic humility in Lear's love for Cordelia:

> When thou dost ask me blessing, I'll kneel down and ask of thee forgiveness.
> So we'll live and pray and sing and tell old tales and laugh at gilded butterflies.

Darwin's heroic persistence in bearing seasickness month after month for the sake of his studies in marine biology can be appreciated by all who have pitied themselves for a few days' nausea on an ocean voyage.

Heroism is born out of a love of some one, or, as with Pasteur, Darwin, and Richard Strong, of some thing, a love that reveals our central need, as I said in Chapter IV, and so stills the conflict of competing desires. Thus it leaps in the same direction that duty or obligation might demand, but further. The direction is essential; for, to mystics, enthusiasts, and to any of us in moments of excitement or self-delusion, it may seem lovely to do as we please! One man deserts his work-bench to save a fellow workman's life; another, to go on a spree. Both forsake ordinary morals, but in different directions. When a man settles down to support his wife and children he may be doing nearly what he was put into the world to do, and still more nearly when he leaves them to fight a forest fire. Some men desert their wives for a phrase like the second Mrs. Bertrand Russell's "right to be happy." [1] Almost any husband who wants to kick over the traces and leave his wife to do the pulling might welcome such a slogan. Some can persuade themselves that they are heroic deserters because public opinion is hostile to them,—until it forgets. In contrast with this bunkum, supermoral action includes keeping our promises, never excludes or contradicts it.

[1] Mrs. Bertrand Russell, *The Right to Be Happy* (Garden City Pub. Co., 1927).

2. ENTHUSIASM

Though heroism is the most familar, it is not the only sort of supermorality. We find it in a good string quartette, in an affectionate household, in a laboratory staff freshly started on a promising problem. Such enthusiasts meet their difficulties with appetite, and solve them with inspiration. There is a special beauty in such swift unnoticed feats because no one applauds them. No one thinks of morals or beauty when three members of a string quartette skip a bar to catch the impetuous fourth member, and wink at each other over the music stands. But it is supermoral teamwork. There can be supermorals in the quality of a smile, in the modulation of a voice, in what is left unsaid when water-pipes freeze and burst. There is supermorality in the invention of new tray decorations to please an invalid, in the sharing of favorite tools, stains, and ideas in a laboratory.

Creative art, like heroism, bursts out when the smoldering fires of life are blown to a blaze. The hero and the artist need something and love something more hotly than the rest of us. Their actions show it. But the last examples suggest that supermorality is the driving force, not only in the fineness of fine arts or the Herculean labor of polar expeditions, but oftener in the minor arts of living, where most of us find our only chance of creativity.

Suppose love gives us energy, not for an act of rescue nor for a work of art but for a fresh insight into the beauty of a human soul. We are at once abased and exalted, dwarfed in our contrast with the greatness before us, lifted by the chance to see it. Our impulse to answer, with some fit action, the challenge of supreme beauty is linked with the desire to be " all ear, all eye " so as to catch the miracle. Not only in first love, but whenever perfection crosses our path, in the play of children, in a hermit thrush's song, in the austere beauty of old age, in the joy of an athlete's dash, we are freer, more successful, more deeply honored than in our tamer moments, and so more eager to " play up " to the beauty before us.

If we can believe that such an experience as this is isolated in its own perfection, that it throws no light on the rest of the world, that it is as satisfactory in itself as anything that we shall ever know, then we are content to call it beauty or love and let it go at that. But, if its loveliness seems to remind us of something deeper than itself, if it stimulates us to believe that " the mind has a universal passport, is nowhere excluded or exclusible," so that " every thought-moment speaks and listens to the sum of created things," [1] then the words of Plato and of Jesus are validated by the experience, and we say that adoration is at the heart of it.[2]

Enthusiasm, scientific, philosophic, artistic, social, may spring up as suddenly as a hearty laugh. But in most instances it has been prepared for by labor. When people work hard and faithfully, they prepare the soil for discoveries which almost work themselves out when " their moment " arrives. Creation and discovery in their final stages seem inevitable. They are more or less than voluntary. In view of what has preceded them, they have to be thus and not otherwise. So creative artists have described their experience. After much labor the right phrase in a poem or a musical composition finally flashes into con-

[1] Basil de Selincourt, *Towards Peace* (Oxford Press, 1932), p. 3.

[2] Our central need as we conceive it is the direct call to supermorality. Desires are shrouded and needs revealed in the urge to heroism, creation, or adoration. In each of these our needs seem united into one supreme need of the whole personality, felt like a hunger for food, or a thirst for action. In Chapters V and VI I have called this supreme need " Growth."

sciousness without effort and almost without choice. Like the secondary spontaneity of trained muscles in athletics or in craftsmanship, the creative act grows out of trial and error. It rests on labor and practice, though in the end it rises above them.

In the laborious preparations for free creative work we are busy in clearing away the obstacles of our ignorance. We scarcely know our need at the start. We boggle, we get in our own way, we start off at cross purposes. Moreover, our way is blocked by our laziness, our preoccupation, our clumsy muscles, our prejudices. Still more we are encumbered by tricks, phrases, and conventional feelings caught from others. To clear away these obstacles so that the occasion itself may summon our responsive energies is the work of ethical preparation for freedom.

But though hard work leads up to them, love, admiration, adoration for things human or non-human, are in the end spontaneous. We do not feel them " on purpose." They are not obligatory, and if they fail us it is hypocrisy to go through their motions. Yet they are not outside the reach of effort; like heroism and creative art they grow in a soil prepared by work. We cannot " make " ourselves love anybody or anything any more than we can promise to make a greatly needed discovery in science. But we can take the path in that direction. Intimate understanding can often be attained by labor and pains. Then invention may blossom out of study and love out of deep acquaintance.

3. HOW DOES SUPERMORALITY DIFFER FROM PLAY?

Not at all, if we accept the liberal definition of Mr. Joseph Lee.[1] He provides room for heroism, creativity, and adoration on the canvas of his picture of play. Even

[1] Joseph Lee, *Play in Education* (New York: The Macmillan Co., 1915).

work is chiefly play, according to him. But to most of us, play is relaxation and recreation. It is less intense and less directly the ancestor of obligation than the fiery devotion which I call supermoral. Play is like supermorality because both are free of obligation, and issue directly from our strength. But play has not so much sense of need. One does not feel that one *must* play; one plays. In childhood, however, the distinction of play from supermorality is hard to maintain. About his fifth year it is a child's business to play. He is so beautifully united that the whole of him goes into each detached instant. His fragmentary acts have the originality of creative art. He escapes the cramp of habit. He has almost superhuman freshness and energy. Yet the rules of the game are clear to him, and he knows that they ought not to be broken. I think we have to say that the moral and the supermoral are so merged in children's play that we cannot clearly distinguish them.

Risk and the eagerness to take it are part of the impulse to supermoral action. There is adventure in art, love, and discovery, as there is in heroism. Some native ardor in us responds to this. Perhaps the pertinacity of the gambling fever, despite the manifest idiocy of it, is due to its measure of likeness to the spirit of adventure, itself blood brother to scientific exploration and to creative art. At any rate, something vital seems left out of any mortal devoid of adventurousness. Love is tame if the lover will take no chance of making a fool of himself in his devotion. To play safe in love is to lose it. For it is the unseen that we must greet with a cheer, and when we call, there may be no one there except to laugh.

Perhaps, then, the gambler has grasped the truth that we must play up to the universe with some spice of adventurousness if we are to get an answer in tune with our hopes. So far he is sound, and perhaps this fraction of sense in his folly makes his passion survive, though he will not see the difference between risking something on the certainty of his love and the pledge of his skill, and risking much, or little, on no certainty and no skill at all.

4. THE RELEASE OF STORED ENERGY

Morals are called out by our weakness, supermorals by our strength. Ethical action is performed against a resistance which is characteristic of the " moral " layer in us. Its tension is due to our unpaid debts. Our ignorance in a moment of ardor lets us in for much more than we expect. We undertake the responsibility of a family, a job, or a piece of research, keen for the new opportunity, but not for all its costs. We are glad of the excitement and novelty of the unknown, but ungirded for its sterner tests, in the choking jungles of the tropics, in the hateful disease of our best-beloved, in the wrong and disgrace of our children. We act in a world largely unexplored. When the road begins to climb we sense the weight of our packs as well as the zest of new experience. We do not see at once that the two are inseparable. Our ignorance makes it hard to stick to our path.

Or it is our weakness that baffles us. We have not got ourselves in hand; we are still too careless, selfish, and clumsy for the work. Hence another source of tedium in morals. At first we pull against our own curb and are sharply conscious of it. As we get more used to managing ourselves, we waste less effort. Difficult actions become habitual and hardly noticeable, though if we are still growing, new difficulties will appear meantime.

Morality is active in our struggle with weakness. The supermoral is an evidence of strength, stored ready for new tests.[1] The supermoral is the most vivid element in our life. Under its sway we feel more alive, more ourselves, and more intimate with our fellows. We are happy and successful. In the heroism of Garibaldi, in the statesmanship of Theodore Roosevelt, the scientific work of Strong, Michael Pupin, and John Muir, we feel the zest of hard work done with confidence and mastery.

In supermoral as in moral acts we obey the command of need, that is, of growth. But supermorality issues from a head of stored energy, and shoots straight towards its end. In such moments we have got what we want. There are no dissenting votes in us and no imperfections in the task. It is not a means to an end. It is the end itself. If all life could be like that, it would be heaven.

5. WHAT SUPPLIES THE ENERGY FOR THIS PREPARATORY LABOR?

Why do we work so hard to till poor soil? Because in an earlier experience we have known love to grow up without ardor at the outset. We have learned to be interested in a science or in a nation by laboring to understand it. So we are ready to try the experiment again. Moreover we want to express gratitude for beauty undeserved. We never earned Bach or Brahms, and to know this, creates a tension of answering impulses in us. We want to push on what they began, and so to thank them. By thanking merely in words and thoughts we promise to pay later in action. If we love them we keep their commandments by trying to pass on the torch they gave.

Thus morality, preparing us to be supermoral, emerges in response to supermoral gifts. Gratitude makes us want

---

[1] The habitual part of us is also in many cases a sign of stored strength become nearly unconscious; but habit consolidates old victories. It does not attack the new.

to live and to answer in the spirit of these gifts. It is from the unearned bounty of our environment that we get the sense of need from which morals and supermorals are born. The universe and its messages create us. We create in return a tiny fragment of it: the morality and then the supermorality that answer its call. Not under agreements with any human being were launched your best impulses. They came to you out of the blue, out of undeserved love, out of free curiosity. Agreements do not flower into supermoral action; but supermoral beauties, the devotion that was round us in childhood, the honor of heroes, loveliness in a face and a gesture, flashes of outdoor glory,—these are answered by the inchoate acts we call desires. Later they take shape in pledges given and received.

Sometimes we respond to a call from our inner environment rather than from outside us. The universe sends us messages not only through light, food, and sound, but through inherited promptings and through our ductless glands. When the best of these energies speak within us, we answer in a " joy without a cause."

> Oh, our manhood's prime vigor! No spirit feels waste,
> Not a muscle is stopped in its playing nor sinew unbraced.
> Oh, the wild joys of living! the leaping from rock up to rock,
> The strong rending of boughs from the fir-tree, the cool silver shock
> Of the plunge in a pool's living water. [1]

The freest and most creative part of us comes into action in delighted response to the messages that rain in upon the just and upon the unjust. They may seem like the reward of hard conscientious work. But even when we have betrayed every trust, the Hound of Heaven [2] pursues us.

[1] Robert Browning, *Saul*.
[2] Francis Thompson, *Poems* (New York: Charles Scribner's Sons, 1913), Vol. **I**, p. 107.

Our central need pushes us towards whole-hearted activity, in art, science, sacrifice, creative love, and religion. But this ardent energy is damped down most of the time by our laziness. We are too inert to draw from our surroundings the current of energy that can blow our embers into a blaze. We are repressed by our selfishness, and by our patchwork civilization. We hardly realize that, leashed in us all, is the passion for creation and discovery. We do not guess how hungry we are for fullness of human activity until we taste our own real food in Lindbergh's heroic dash across the Atlantic. In him the sick world acclaims a reassurance of its own primordial health, for he is one of us and sees nothing extraordinary in what he has done. Looking backwards from a vantage point such as Lindbergh gained for his contemporaries, we see how listless our lives have been. From what a base lethargy he roused us, and how long we have been asleep!

6. MORALS AND SUPERMORALS INTERPENETRATE

In August, 1921, I lived a week with an isolated sheep-ranching family at Cloverdale, California. With no servants but their own hands and minds, they faced the scorching summer of hard work and poverty like a game, and played it in high spirits. The men's hard outdoor labor was balanced by the women's drudgeries. But with jokes, artistry, and decoration they beautified the job. In sheep-herding, fence-repairing, cooking, dishwashing, they found a chance to express their mutual affection variously, unsentimentally, and with indubitable honesty. To act affection is more convincing than to speak it. Nothing but common work could have given them so good a medium in which to realize their devotion. It rose without gush or explosion, incessant, self-renewing, steadily self-increasing.

On this ranch, duty was perfused by free impulses of ingenuity, affection, and fun; drudgery was denatured by awareness of its reason and its end. No one could say that the work was not hard. Not one of those in it had freely chosen it. But they could not have named another way to give such free play to their affection and their good spirits. Done by any one of the group alone, even in manageable quantities, the work would have been a pure grind. Done together it was almost a lark, because together they made it a game, a river of jokes, and an enheartening proof of affection. Put the same family group together without the work, and they could not long have struck such fire from each other. It needed the chance suggestions of their ranching job to furnish such variety of stunts and jokes in which the whole family could join. Nothing else would have made them so content in a sense of accomplishment, or shown them to each other in such lasting attractiveness.

In the artistic and in the scientific conscience we see morality and supermorality entwined in another way. The ends are freely chosen; they are not matters of duty. But duty soon emerges. Honesty within the job, all the more quintessentially true because it cannot be gauged by others, sacrifice that looks for no applause, faithfulness that no one demands and that may produce no demonstrable results,—these and other " moralities " develop within the tasks of craftsmanship.

From each side the obligatory and the free invade each other, require each other, build on each other. Yet they are distinct, and may get separated for a time.

7. THE ULTIMATE DESIRE

When Weir of Hermiston [1] faced from the judge's bench his own son accused of doing murder in defense of a

[1] In R. L. Stevenson's last and best story.

woman's honor, he knew himself tied to impartial justice as the scientific investigator is tied to truth. He was bound to the truth wherever it might strike. He had surrendered himself to the necessity of reading off the verdict from the evidence, as the investigator of scientific truth surrenders his will to the verdict of the facts and follows them, for better, for worse, wherever they lead. His desire is a necessary desire. He cannot change it, and so long as he faces its demand he can only obey. When the swimmer commits himself to the sea at the cry of "Man overboard!" he has bound his will to whatever the venture brings. The attempt itself is worth while. He accepts the risk, as Thackeray did when he determined to write the truth about human nature as he knew it, whether it pleased the public or not.[1]

What is it that such a man desires when he commits himself to the mercy of fortune for the love of a mere abstraction: justice, truth, life? He desires to do and to endure whatever this abstraction demands. His ardor is as boundless as the sea. The more he gives the more he has. There is no measure to the decision. There is no respect of persons. The judge's verdict may hang his own son. No one inquires whether the man overboard is a genius or a waster.[2] Whoever wins or loses, the plunge for the right must be made.

All that is needed to create this determination in the stupidest or the meanest of us all is that he should fall in love with an abstraction so that he is hot to see justice done, to see truth prevail, to see life saved. Do many fall into this kind of love? Yes, many do, and all are hungry to, when the world puts its challenge up clearly to them.

---

[1] See preface to *Pendennis* quoted in Chapter IV, p. 104.
[2] Suggested by one of G. K. Chesterton's essays.

When that moment comes, any son of Adam knows that for this chance he has been waiting or pushing all his life. At last he is face to face with the Real Thing. Once we used to call this Real Thing the hunger and thirst after righteousness. That sounds priggish and self-righteous now. But the plain facts of human psychology are more inflexible than the fashions. The plain fact is that nothing is so deep in us as the passion for an opportunity that will bring the whole of us into action. Most of the time we are a dozen removes away from that. We dawdle along at a snail's pace. We peck and pull at a corner of our job. But when the chance comes to give all that is in us and to risk all for what we love, then we know that we have met our need, and that for this end we came into the world.

This submerged ardor I used to call the "Master Desire." But in fact it rarely masters us. We are not aware of any such hunger most of the time. It is rather the desire that alone has the power to master us when we are face to face with naked reality.

"I never hear the word escape," wrote Emily Dickinson, "without a quickened blood." Every one of us was made to act whole-heartedly for some minutes or hours before we die, and so, as we go edging forward, like an amoeba, now one bit of our hopes and now another, a sense of frustration grows up in us. Our divided mind hungers to escape into unanimity. Are we to be forever tongue-tied and speechless, forever packing our trunks but never starting, forever criticizing our twisted minds with a mind still twisted, forever selfishly trying to be less selfish? If we are used to calling the universe by its Christian name we can pull ourselves together and face Reality in prayer. But even prayer is imperfect because it needs to prove its sincerity in action. At our best we escape into a whole-hearted deed.

Ethical action is what we do while we are building up our chance to voice somewhere and sometime our thankfulness that we were born and reared on a planet that can show us such wonder, such beauty, such devotion.

APPENDICES

SOME UNSOLVED PROBLEMS OF ETHICS

1. WHAT DUTIES, IF ANY, HAVE WE TOWARD OTHER ANIMALS?

Most civilized communities have laws against "cruelty to animals" and a public sentiment that sustains these laws fairly well. "Cruelty" means the wanton or excessive infliction of pain on cows, pigs, horses, dogs, and other animals, or the neglect to feed and shelter those that we own. Excessive burdens for horses have also been prohibited. But the benevolence expressed in these regulations has narrow limits. We let cats suffer from hunger to a degree which we should think cruel if applied to horses. No one feeds rats and mice. Few have scruples against trapping them in painful ways or in encouraging cats or dogs to kill them. When we feed hens it is for our own profit. The feeding of other birds, except canaries, is uncommon. Usually we do it spasmodically and in order to bring them into convenient view. We have no idea of providing for their entire existence as we do for tame horses and cows.

We kill cows, calves, sheep, pigs, and poultry when we are ready to eat them. We kill cats when they are a nuisance, dogs when we think their lives are a burden to them, and horses when they are no longer useful. In most communities we allow the unlimited sacrifice of guinea pigs, rats, mice, rabbits, frogs, dogs, cats, and monkeys when they seem to be needed in scientific investigation or in teaching.

It is clear that, with the possible exception of dogs and horses, we treat all the "lower" animals as if they had no rights to be respected when they interfere with our comfort and convenience,—no rights save one, immunity from needless pain. We do not forbid people to thrash their horses or their dogs any more than we forbid parents and schoolmasters to thrash their boys. In both cases we ban cruel or excessive punishments.

So long as it was credible that while men have souls other animals have none, or so long as we believed that the other animals were created for our convenience, it was natural to go on using " domestic " animals as beasts of burden or as articles of diet. Today it is no longer easy in most civilized countries to believe that rabbits, ducks, and geese were created or evolved in order to become our servants, like the long-domesticated horses, sheep, and cows. Wolves, coyotes, rats, mice, flies, mosquitoes, lice and many other insects we regard not as servants but as pests. Such at least is the usual occidental view.

In India many people believe that the rest of the animal creation has as good a right to existence as men have, and that certain species, cows, elephants, are sacred. Not even in India, however, is this respect for animal life consistently carried out. For animals prey on crops, and crops are necessary for human existence. Gandhi confesses with sorrow that " all life in the flesh exists by some violence." He prays therefore for ultimate deliverance from the bondage of the flesh.[1] Meantime the best that he can do is to aim at the minimum of violence and injury to the monkeys and other pests which infest the crops at his school.

In this Gandhi does not differ from vegetarians and others who try to respect animal life; but he is franker and more truthful than many. We must defend ourselves against animal pests if we are to live. In the tropics they almost drive us out. In temperate zones their attacks are so intermittent that we can control them fairly well. In the arctic regions animal pests are scanty; but vegetation is also so scanty that the Esquimaux could not live without animal food and often subsist on practically nothing else.

Neither those who regard all animal life as sacred nor those who regard it as the legitimate prey or the predestined servant

[1] C. F. Andrews, *Mahatma Gandhi's Ideas* (New York: The Macmillan Co., 1930), p. 138.

of man, support their beliefs by convincing argument. But there are still greater difficulties in sight. Why should we regard animal life as so much more sacred than vegetable life? The usual answer is that animals can suffer and vegetables cannot. Certainly we see much clearer signs of suffering in dogs and horses than among the trees and plants. But there is a large group of animals too small to show us any suffering that they may feel. In the region of the very small, our mercy toward animals and toward vegetables depends on how much they bother us. We pay no attention to their sensitiveness, because we know little about it. How much the small vegetables or the small animals may suffer we do not know. A typhoid *bacillus* (vegetable) swimming rapidly about in beef bouillon certainly looks as if death would hurt him as much as it would hurt the *animal* parasite of malaria. Neither shows us any trace of a nervous system. But some plants are as sensitive to light and heat as we are. Some are obviously sensitive to touch. Why not to pain? They can bleed, droop, and die, like animals. How do we know that they cannot suffer?

We do not hesitate to exterminate animal parasites such as the organisms of malaria and African sleeping sickness. We give them no more consideration than the vegetable parasites (*bacilli*) of typhoid and tuberculosis. If the *trypanosoma* of African sleeping sickness were as easily visible as the louse we should probably be able to see it suffer. The truth seems to be that we kill small animals or vegetables without compunction simply because we do not see them wiggle or hear their cries. It is less unpleasant to kill a mosquito than to crush a caterpillar or a mouse. But are we any less cruel in one case than in the other? Aesthetic considerations weigh heavily with us. Most of us like birds and dislike rats. We condemn those who kill small birds and applaud those who kill rats. But I see no principle in these distinctions.

We treat the vegetables and the non-human animals as we do because we lack any clue to guide us as we are guided, intermittently, partially, in our relations to men. We think it stupid and brutal to use a man merely as a means. The fact is that he has ends of his own, as we have. This fact our action should respect. But we cannot get far into the consciousness of animals and plants because we cannot talk with them. We have no co-operation with them when we try to find out what is their part in the world's economy. We know what we want, and we think we know our needs. But we do not know much about what the other animals need. Certainly there is no evidence that they are built to be killed for food, or to be exterminated because they annoy us. Self-maintenance, self-defense, and the reproduction of their kind are among the most obvious trends in their behavior. Some of them undoubtedly can learn. Many of them can re-member. A few species love individual human beings, and will risk their lives for them.

The natural inference is, I think, that they too should not be used merely as means, as now we often use them. Some American Indians go through the form of asking the deer's permission and obtaining it (in a dramatic dance where men represent deer) before they kill them. This formal compunction we could carry further if we killed animals only in self-defense or for food when they are too old to enjoy living. In defense of our present habits the best that we can say is that if we did not kill animals they would die of cold, hunger, and disease or be killed by each other in ways probably more terrifying and more painful than ours. But if we left them alone they would have at any rate a fair chance of living out their lives in their own way.

2. THE RIGHT TO PRODUCE LIFE

We have still less hope of knowing whether we have a *right to breed animals* for our use. We cannot say that our health demands the breeding and killing of cattle, sheep, pigs, hens, ducks, and geese. The vegetarians have strong evidence for believing that we can get along just as well without eating meat, so long as we have milk and eggs. I think that they are wrong only in claim-ing any advantage to physical or mental health as a result of cutting out meat. But even the use of milk and eggs, which in-volves no pain, commits us to increasing the numbers of two species until they are helpless without us.

The problem of the right to kill is, therefore, complicated by the deeper question, What right have we to increase the numbers of a species with no thought but our own comfort and convenience? Most of the animals that we kill for food would never have existed at all but for us. Breeding for food is justifiable only on a tremendous assumption,—that we have a right to control the birth, life, and death of certain animal species simply for our own convenience and without any inkling of their place in the world economy; that is, of their rights. Most cattle, sheep, pigs, and poultry, with the physique that our breeding has given them, would swiftly disappear if we now gave up feeding and sheltering them. We have made them unfit to gain their living or to defend themselves. We have turned them into lumbering, helpless food supplies, ugly and ungainly beside their wild ancestors.

By what right? Simply by " right " of the stronger or rather of the more intelligent; that is, by no right at all. We can, so we do. Among men we admit no justification for such a principle. Time was when we treated savage tribes or hostile tribes as now we treat horses and cows. We killed them or used them as beasts of burden. But except in war such practices are now rarely defended. Practically all the nations of the earth are now coöperating under the League of Nations to abolish slavery and war. Even the nations that still practise both are loath to defend them.

Some of the pests which we try to extirpate or at least to decimate would otherwise eat us off the face of the earth, and would then probably perish in their turn for lack of the food we provide. No obvious benefit to them would result if we let them conquer us.

A shred of principle in our ethically senseless behavior toward other animals appears in our bird sanctuaries and national parks. There we assert in action that we intend to preserve valuable species otherwise in danger of being blotted out. If we could extend this plan further by finding a sensible way to decide how many of each species, man included, this planet ought to maintain, and how to keep them in these proportions, we should have an ethical basis for our actions. " Live and let live," in suitable numbers, would then be our theory. But, except in the cases mentioned, we have no such policy and no prospect of getting it.

I conclude that we are utterly at sea about our duties to the non-human part of creation, that is, toward all but a minute fraction of the earth's inhabitants. The right to use animals because we are their "natural" leaders and superiors is still defended on theological grounds by some Christian sects, but vehemently rejected by the Hindu and the Buddhist. It has never had, so far as I see, any foundation except in man's ability to subjugate other animals and in his inability to understand their place in nature.

Some of the more obviously heartless ways to kill animals, such as the fox-hunt, the bull-fight, and the cock-pit, are today widely condemned on the ground that they brutalize the people who take part in them, and that they are ruthlessly cruel to the foxes, bulls, horses, and cocks. I think both arguments are weak. There is no evidence, so far as I know, that the votaries of fox-hunting and bull-fighting are or are becoming any more brutal than the rest of humanity. The animals that die to furnish them sport would probably die almost as painfully without furnishing the sport, if we left them alone or merely defended ourselves and our crops against them. The brutality of a bull-fight or a fox-hunt simply brings before our dull eyes the incessant and unsolved problem of our right to subject any animals to our own uses, by breeding them, by killing them, or by hunting them. It is revolting. Why then do we not revolt? Because no reasonable alternative has yet been suggested. Gandhi gives up the problem as insoluble and so at present must we.

3. THE RIGHT TO MULTIPLY MEN

Even within the circle of our own species we know very little about our business as producers. Suppose a well-to-do and healthy married pair are fond of children. How many should they have? Ordinarily we treat the question as one of little interest. But if you happen to be the fifth child in a family, can it help seeming to you a vitally important matter that your parents did not decide to stop with the fourth? If Shakespeare's or Lincoln's parents had voluntarily ceased to have children just before these great men were born, the world would have been vastly the poorer.

So long as parents are themselves well-born, young, healthy, and well-to-do, can we deny that the chances of their bearing a remarkable child, a leader of men, are greater the more children they have? Yet very few parents, so far as I know, are guided by the recognition of this fact. In primitive farming countries where every healthy child can be expected to work on the land without wages, large families make things obviously easier for all concerned. Is this a sufficient reason for having large families? In city life economic pressure works in the opposite direction. Should its trend be followed? Should nations or international bodies concern themselves with the birth rate in any part of the earth?

Governmental efforts in this direction seem to have been rather ineffective in France. Religious influences seem more potent. Some countries in which Roman Catholicism has a strong hold on the majority have higher birth rates than most Protestant countries. Catholic influence has always been on the side of large Catholic families, the reasons given being that this is natural, that we are commanded to be fruitful and multiply, that existence is preferable to non-existence, and that the greater number born *and properly reared*, the more souls may be saved. Whatever we think of these reasons they are as good as many given for the restriction of families.

There would seem to be good sense in not allowing population to expand faster than food supply. The spectacle of Asiatic over-population and Asiatic famines is abominable. But when a people have once learned to restrict their birth rate, how is this restriction to be stopped when the deaths begin to exceed the births, as they now do in France? And will France not be worse off when her now diminishing population has been further decreased?

We feel some confidence that no racial group ought to be exterminated as a result of contact with other groups. Apparently this is happening rapidly in the Marquesan Islands. We labor to preserve the buffalo, the seal, and the aigrette when destruction threatens them. Our general notion is, I suppose, that we do not want the earth impoverished by the loss of these species. We should be sorry to lose the elephants or the giraffes as we have lost the dodos and the mastodons. But our compunction seems to be capriciously connected with size. No one would agitate for the preservation of even the harmless species of ants, or would regret it seriously if they were gone. Why not?

Should a numerous agricultural population like the Russians be encouraged by their urban rulers to stay on the land and have large families in order that they may exchange their surplus grain for the goods that Russia is supposed to need? In other words, should the production of human beings be regulated according to the contemporary conditions of world markets? Socialists have often, and I think rightly, reproached capitalistic nations for making no attempt to plan the production and distribution of goods. But what about human energies, out of whose efforts all economic goods spring? If there is anything that supremely concerns living beings it should be the quantity as well as the quality of lives produced. Yet so far as I can see, no one has yet any rationally-founded advice to give on this.

4. EUGENICS

So far as it concerns human beings the voluntary improvement of life is still in its infancy. We know something of kakogenics, the production of ill-made human creatures, feeble-minded, insane, web-fingered, haemophilic, and we do something to restrict their increase. But of the way to multiply the best sort of men and women (if we know what they are), we know almost nothing. Even the fundamental question whether increased quantity tends to higher or to lower quality is not now answerable. Of course a large number of unhealthy children brought up under unfavorable home conditions and in a country that supplies no market for their services, is not preferable to a smaller number of healthy, highly cultivated, and economically available children. But such alternatives are not often presented to us. Large families brought up in poverty are not infrequently superior in caliber to small families brought up in moderate comfort. It depends largely on the parents.

So far as I know, no one can answer satisfactorily the questions, How many children ought a family or a racial stock to have? How nearly stationary ought any nation's, province's, city's population to be? It depends on the ability of parents and children to make a life as well as a living under the conditions. No one has authoritative standards (after the few obviously hereditary traits are excluded) to decide what family or race is fitter or fittest. We do not know what combination of blacks, whites, yellows, and browns is desirable in any part of the earth or on the planet as a whole. We know almost nothing of the advantages and disadvantages of race-mixture, despite many assertions to the contrary. We do not know what percentage of the different "American" types, urban Jews, wild Westerners, unreconstructed Southerners, New England Puritans, Kentucky mountaineers, Irish Catholics, Rhodes scholars, Scandinavians, Negroes, Orientals would make a mutually educative and congenial group in a college like Harvard. Apparently the Harvard faculty thought in 1925 that twenty per cent. of Jews was about the right proportion, but why it thought so it is hard to say. Why not more or less?

We know neither what we need nor how to attain it. What we ought to do cannot even be guessed at until we know more about these fundamental facts. The idea that we should limit population in accordance with our means of subsistence seems to give us something definite and reasonable. At present, however, this principle is still at some distance from usefulness. No nation or community can apply it without a plan for national economic life, including an immigration policy and an import and export policy. Unless a nation excludes imports of foodstuffs and of the materials for clothing and building, its means of subsistence and the population which it can support will depend in part on what other nations have to export. Under free trade a nation that produces a relatively large amount of what other nations demand will be able to import (if they choose) a relatively large quantity of any surplus food supplies to be found in world markets. The food plan and the population plan of such a nation would then have to depend on corresponding plans in other nations. In the absence of such plans no single nation could work out a schedule of available living materials or an optimum rate for the increase of population. The rate would naturally shift from time to time in response to new inventions in agriculture, in transportation, or in any other branch of industry capable of increasing the food supply of a particular place.

Suppose it were possible, by international conference and agreement, to settle what supply of the means of existence is available for any nation through its own production and through exchange with other nations; there would still remain the uncertainties of weather, insect pests, labor supply, transportation, marketing, and the minor variants of taste and fashion. Moreover, it is not easy to imagine the successful workings of a program for man-production. Suppose the optimum national increment of population for the United States before 1935 has been settled at 1,000,000 babies. Who is to have the babies? How are they to be allotted among the states, the cities, and the couples? According to their population, say, in 1933? All couples without children might be allowed to plan for one baby. Half the families with one child might be allowed this year to plan for another, the other half to plan similarly next year. The families with two children might be ordered to try for a child every third year. The families with three children or more might be forbidden to have any more children unless they could arrange with some other family to give up their allotted baby.

This plan would work if there were no sterile unions, no still births, no infant mortality, and if people were satisfied to obey in the main so monotonous a law. All these conditions might conceivably be attained. Marriage or mating rates per year would still have to be settled, on a quota basis. Would anybody be satisfied? Would civilization profit? Who can say?

So far as I see, then, a population program could only be

worked out on the basis of limiting population to means of subsistence:—

(a) Provided the population concerned were willing to submit to the required regulation of marriage rates and birth rates.

(b) Provided our knowledge increased to the point required by the plan. The knowledge which we should need would include the ways to prevent or greatly to decrease sterility, still births and infant mortality; also the means to regulate crops, by irrigation, pest prevention, or otherwise.

I see no reason why mankind should not set itself to get this knowledge if it decides that such a population plan is desirable. Is it desirable? To maintain standards of living and avoid the conflicts due to overpopulation, national or international, would seem at first thought to be human needs hardly subject to debate. But any population plan must, so far as I see, decide which stocks are to be kept up and which allowed to die out. Now we have no knowledge fit to guide any such decision. At present we are attempting rather inefficiently to restrict the multiplication of the feeble-minded, of the defective delinquent; also of the syphilitic and the tuberculous during the contagious states of their disease. Some of these groups might vote to end or to limit their own subspecies of *genus homo*. We can conceive that other animal species, could we communicate with them and could they understand their plight, would wish similarly to control their numbers for the greater happiness of all concerned. Better a few horses well fed, they might say, than many half-starved.

The numbers of the feeble-minded to be permitted in any group's population-policy might depend on the need for their labor and their companionship in that community. If most of the " heavy " work were done by machines and if we all agreed in preferring it done in this way rather than by the feeble-minded, as much of it is done now, the number of feeble-minded that could make a decent life of it in contact with brighter minds would be relatively small. Could the feeble-minded be brought to agree to this? If not, can we be any surer of our right to limit their numbers, as we now try to do, than of our right to limit the number of horses?

We know well enough, I fancy, what it is for any animal to experience pain, perpetual drudgery, semi-starvation, chronic disease, continual dread of enemies, the life of the hunted. These are great evils for the non-human as for men, and ought therefore to be taken out of their lives as fast and far as we can. But non-existence on earth is, so far as we know, neither an evil nor a good for any being, human or non-human. Either it is the zero that it seems, or it is existence elsewhere, like the souls of the unborn or of the dead. In either case we have no sufficient reason either to regret it or to be glad of it, so far as I can see.

We are wholly in the dark about the rights of the various kinds of life, including man, on this planet. Till we can communicate with other animal (and vegetable?) species, we cannot possibly work out a rational plan of ethics that includes their claims to " life, liberty, and the pursuit of happiness." Our ethical relations to them will remain unsolved problems. How many children ought to be born of each race in each country, at each economic or cultural level, is a problem the rational solution of which seems also very remote. There is now a popular impression that the gross birth rate is in many, perhaps most, countries, too large. But who knows that we should not lose quality as well as quantity if we reduced our birth rate still further? Who knows that we have not already reduced quality by our present low birth rate? The problem is so complex and the unknown factors so many that we cannot, I think, be said to have reached any well-founded belief on the subject. Let us face our ignorance and think. That is our only chance to climb out of it.

DEFINITIONS

Agreement

An agreement is a declaration of an intention by the forces within a person or between two or more persons. Making, keeping, and improving agreements are necessary steps in growth. A good agreement is one in line with relevant realities in our minds and outside them. A bad one is carelessly or self-deceitfully out of line with known facts.

Need

A need is an opportunity for growth or a condition for growth. We need education and we need water. The opportunities for growth are parts of it. Its conditions, if we understood them better, would also, I suppose, be seen as parts of it. With better knowledge we might see the energies that we call food pushing out into new thoughts as the paint on an artist's brush sweeps out into new beauties.

Growth

Growth is the production of novelty within the range of a purpose and *without* dominant self-contradiction. Degeneration is the same thing *with* dominant self-contradiction. Learning, experimenting, admiring, sharing, and enjoying exemplify growth.

Right and Wrong

Right desires, agreements, or plans are those that are governed by reality as it shows itself in our needs. *Wrong* desires, agreements, or acts are those which diverge from reality and from our needs through self-deceit.

Ethical Implementation

In ethical implementation we bind ourselves by psychological, physiological, and mechanical chains, so that what we desire, agree to, and need will be carried out.

Due Care

Due care is the application of such brains and such attention as we possess to maintain the life of our needs by putting them into execution.

Supermorality

Action done for the love of some one or something, that is, from an ardent sense of need in us and for us.

FIFTY-FOUR DECLARATIONS OF WAR, 1914–1918

Of the fifty-four declarations of war made between July 28, 1914, and July 19, 1918, thirty-eight appeal to necessity in some form and sixteen do not. Most of the sixteen without mention of helplessness are those of small countries which were not in the fight at all and which put themselves on record for other reasons. This was the case, for instance, with Cuba, Siam, Hayti, and Honduras.

The only declaration in the whole fifty-four which approaches the Napoleonic *naïveté* of aggression is that of Russia against Turkey. Even this is couched as self-defense: " It is with a perfect and confident tranquillity, and invoking the aid of God, that Russia *will meet this new aggression* of the ancient persecutors of the Christian religion and of all Slav peoples. It is not for the first time that the valiant armies of Russia will have triumphed over the Turkish hordes. They will know again how to chastise the reckless enemy of our fatherland." An ardent and enjoyable self-defense!

Most of the declarations state that the nation is compelled, necessarily compelled, forced, obliged, bound, constrained much to her regret. The United States government notifies her citizens of the resolution passed by Congress (April 6, 1917) " that the state of war between the United States and the Imperial German Government which has been *thrust upon the United States* is hereby formally declared." Russia "with bleeding heart draws the sword " against Bulgaria. Japan feels " profound regret that in spite of our ardent devotion to the cause of peace " she is " compelled to declare war " against Germany.

The necessity is sometimes phrased as arising from events, aggressions, or broken promises, sometimes as a logical result of treaty obligations. I think it is fair to say that not one of the nations acknowledged that she entered the war of her own free will and for what she could get out of it. The nearest approach to this that I have seen is the statement by the Bulgarian premier, M. Radoslavoff, that "Bulgaria must fight on the victors' side . . . since only so can the important territorial extensions and further developments be secured. From the developments . . . in the various theaters of war . . . one recognizes more clearly day by day that victory is inclining on the side of Germany and Austro-Hungary."[1]

[1] Text of Manifesto issued by the Ministry of M. Radoslavoff (Oct. 8, 1915), New York Times *Current History of the War*, Vol. III, p. 465.

INDEX

(Titles in small capitals are chapter headings.)